THE NATURE OF CUSTOMARY LAW

Some legal rules are not laid down by a legislator but grow instead from informal social practices. In contract law, for example, the customs of merchants are used by courts to interpret the provisions of business contracts; in tort law, customs of best practice are used by courts to define professional responsibility. Nowhere are customary rules of law more prominent than in international law. The customs defining the obligations of each State to other States and, to some extent, to its own citizens, are often treated as legally binding. However, unlike natural law and positive law, customary law has received very little scholarly analysis. To remedy this neglect, a distinguished group of philosophers, historians and lawyers has been assembled to assess the nature and significance of customary law. The book offers fresh new insights on this neglected and misunderstood form of law.

AMANDA PERREAU-SAUSSINE is a University Lecturer in Law at the University of Cambridge and a Fellow of Newnham College.

JAMES BERNARD MURPHY is Professor of Government at Dartmouth College, Hanover, USA.

THE NATURE OF CUSTOMARY LAW

Edited by

AMANDA PERREAU-SAUSSINE

and

JAMES BERNARD MURPHY

CAMBRIDGE
UNIVERSITY PRESS

CAMBRIDGE UNIVERSITY PRESS
Cambridge, New York, Melbourne, Madrid, Cape Town, Singapore, São Paulo, Delhi

Cambridge University Press
The Edinburgh Building, Cambridge CB2 8RU, UK

Published in the United States of America by Cambridge University Press, New York

www.cambridge.org
Information on this title: www.cambridge.org/9780521115568

First published 2007
This digitally printed version 2009

A catalogue record for this publication is available from the British Library

ISBN 978-0-521-87511-0 hardback
ISBN 978-0-521-11556-8 paperback

CONTENTS

LIST OF CONTRIBUTORS

Alan Cromartie, Lecturer in Politics, Department of Politics and International Relations, University of Reading.

Ross Harrison, Quain Professor of Jurisprudence Emeritus at University College London, and Provost of King's College, University of Cambridge.

David Ibbetson, Regius Professor of Civil Law, Faculty of Law; Fellow, Corpus Christi College, University of Cambridge.

Christoph Kletzer, University Lecturer in Jurisprudence, University of Cambridge.

Randall Lesaffer, Professor of Legal History, Department of Jurisprudence and Legal History, Tilburg University.

Michael Lobban, Professor of Legal History, Queen Mary College of Law, University of London.

James Bernard Murphy, Professor of Government, Dartmouth College, Hanover, New Hampshire.

Amanda Perreau-Saussine, University Lecturer, Faculty of Law, and Fellow, Newnham College, University of Cambridge.

Jean Porter, John A. O'Brien Professor of Theology, University of Notre Dame.

Gerald Postema, Cary C. Boshamer Professor of Philosophy and Professor of Law, University of North Carolina, Chapel Hill.

Frederick Schauer, Frank Stanton Professor of the First Amendment, John F. Kennedy School of Government, Harvard University.

John Tasioulas, CUF Lecturer in Philosophy, University of Oxford, and Fellow and Tutor in Philosophy, Corpus Christi College, Oxford.

Brian Tierney, Bowmar Professor of Humanistic Studies Emeritus, Cornell University.

TABLE OF CASES

The character of customary law: an introduction

AMANDA PERREAU-SAUSSINE AND JAMES BERNARD MURPHY

A book on customary law, many modern lawyers might say, can have no relevance for them. And neither, many modern thinkers would echo, could it be of much interest. On many influential modern accounts, reliance on customary practices is a mark of inadequacy: acceptance of customs should be minimal and provisional since an unreflective attachment to customary ways of thinking is inimical both to practical thought and to political harmony. Modern societies and their legal systems depend not on enslavement to customary habits and laws but on reasoned principles and doctrines; customary laws grow up only where legislators have done a particularly poor job, leaving a need for elaborate statutory construction and legislative gap-filling. The more coherent and consistent a legal system, the less the need for such customary rules and practices: an interest in customary law reflects at worst what Jeremy Bentham called the 'sinister' interests of self-interested reactionaries, and at best the eccentric tastes of scholars, antiquarians and those purporting to be international lawyers who work in what, on such accounts, is really a lawless international world.

This brief chapter introduces the diverse views of customary law offered in this collection of essays, showing how, despite this diversity, the thirteen contributors are united in arguing that such rejections of the relevance of customary law are wrong.

Is custom all we have?

Some jurists and philosophers argue that customary practices are *all* we have to guide us in aiming to solve practical questions: moral principles, written laws, legal doctrines and philosophical writing are all articulations of pre-existing customs. Such accounts are deeply sceptical of arguments in the name of reason, arguing that those who claim a priority for rational principles said to be manifest within a set of conflicting customary practices are really claiming priority for their own preferred doctrines, doctrines which are themselves nothing but a rationalisation of a set of customary practices having no special status or claim to allegiance.

This sceptical account of practical reason is reflected in many of the contributions to this book by legal historians. As historians they are concerned to avoid allowing contemporary concerns to drive their study of earlier ideas and practices: instead they seek *first* to understand 'the specificity of a past situation', leaving readers to ask whether and how far 'the very specificity' of that earlier situation gave rise to problems analogous to those arising in the contingencies of our own age.[1] Thus David Ibbetson frames his comparative study of customary elements in the medieval laws of continental Europe and of England as a study of 'the uses of the idea of custom': his aim is to trace the different senses of custom in medieval law while prescinding from comment on the relationship between those different usages.[2] Such writers tend to treat doctrine not as leading changes in customary practice but as following and articulating the relevant changes in practice. Thus, for example, Randall Lesaffer argues that more humane customary practices and rules of siege warfare did not begin to be treated as binding rules in the early modern era as a result of doctrinal writings: 'In the final analysis, doctrine acquiesced to the fact of life that customary law in reality was not and did not have to be in accordance with rationality and morality to be accepted by states as constituting law.'

In modern societies, valid law is usually said to require democratic legitimacy, exemplified by an elected legislature. Many traditional jurists argued that custom is the only genuinely democratic mode of law-making, reflecting the actual convictions of the ordinary people who practise them, people who vote by consenting to those customs. But thinkers and writers from within the sceptical tradition represented here tend also to be sceptical about suggestions that customary practices are binding and valuable because they serve 'as a community building device for the group whose collective wisdom creates custom'.[3] Instead, these scholars argue that notions of customary law as a distillation of *popular* practices tend to be indefensible, and that the relevant customs prove to be those of an influential group of insiders. Lesaffer argues that 'the customs of war were still very much determined by the same professional elite that had dominated them for ages', and it was the notions of this elite on the requirements of honour and reciprocity that

[1] See Tierney, Chapter 5 below, pp. 101–3.
[2] Chapter 7 below, p. 151. [3] Chapter 1 below, pp. 31–3.

drove changes in the rules of siege warfare.[4] Most modern historians of the common law, including three contributors to this book, argue analogously that the common law embodies a set of *insiders'* customs, the product of lawyers' practices – among those a claim that what is done in the name of the common law reflects popular custom:[5]

> At a very basic level, no doubt, the values espoused by the common law would have been generally recognised by people in England, but the detailed working out of the rules derived from these values would certainly not have had any such populist grounding. This was all the work of lawyers, customary in the sense that the *communis opinio doctorum* might have been.[6]

Where customs conflict, hard moral, political or legal cases arise. In solving such cases, one's understanding of the nature of customary practices or laws, and in particular of the relationship between practice and legal doctrine, will become evident. Does custom provide the tacit but indispensable matrix for shared moral and legal reasoning or is it merely the dead hand of the past? Is the selection or preference of one custom over rival conflicting ones itself purely a matter of custom? And, whatever lawyers, judges and decision-makers claim, how far and in what ways (if at all) are they really constrained by past customary practices?[7]

The relation between reason and customary morality

Kant's position illustrates an extreme approach to the relationship between reason and custom. For him, customary *moral* rules and practices are only ever conditionally binding, forms of reasoning 'private' to those groups of unreflective, dependent people who accept as

[4] Chapter 8 below, pp. 201–2.

[5] Cromartie questions whether the common law 'can be indefinitely sustained on such a meagre basis' as Hale's and Blackstone's related notions of artificial reason. See Chapter 9 below, p. 227. See in particular the influential essays by A. W. B. Simpson, 'The Common Law and Legal Theory', in A. W. B. Simpson, *Legal Theory and Legal History* (London and Roncevert, WV: Hambledon Press, 1987), p. 359: and J. H. Baker, *The Law's Two Bodies* (Oxford: Oxford University Press, 2001), pp. 59–90.

[6] Chapter 7 below, p. 165.

[7] See Frederick Schauer's contribution to this volume, tracing five 'sceptical' questions, interpretative questions which 'anyone seeking to develop a theory of customary international law, or a theory of the role of custom in common law decision-making, must at least attempt to answer'. Chapter 1 below, p. 14.

authoritative the relevant practices.[8] 'Public' practical reason is of value not least because it renders moral knowledge accessible and justifiable to reflective individuals without the need for a mediating tradition: practical reason can pull itself up by its own boot-straps. So moral solutions to conflicts among customary practices are not to be found by seeking one winning principle incipient within the relevant customs. Instead, a Kantian aims to *impose* upon those practices a moral meaning conceived in line with prior rational principles, principles one imposes upon oneself because of their rationality. This means that a moral interpretation of customary practices may 'appear to us as forced – and be often forced in fact; yet, if the text can at all bear it, it must be preferred to a literal interpretation which either contains absolutely nothing for morality, or even works counter to its incentives'.[9]

Such accounts of moral principles as imposed upon custom are challenged by three contributors to this volume. Writing within the tradition of Anglo-American analytical philosophy, Ross Harrison offers an argument designed to show that morality both requires and reaches beyond convention. James Bernard Murphy traces an Aristotelian argument for why 'our choice is not between reason and prejudice or between custom and law', developing an account of custom as both conventionalising human nature and naturalising human conventions:

> Custom, Janus-like, faces toward human nature and toward stipulated law. Custom turns our natural propensities toward eating, competing, and mating into complex conventions of dining, gaming, and marrying; custom also turns our deliberate rational and legal conventions of arguing, evaluating, and judging into tacit practices as spontaneous and fluid as natural instinct.[10]

[8] See e.g. *Groundwork* 4:408: 'Nor could one give worse advice to morality than by wanting to derive it from examples. For, every example of it represented to me must itself first be appraised in accordance with principles of morality, as to whether it is also worthy to serve as an original example, that is as a model; it can by no *means* authoritatively provide the concept of morality.'

[9] Kant is writing here of the rational interpretation of scripture: *Religion within the Limits of Mere Reason* 6:110. On Kant on interpretation in this context, see Allen Wood, 'Rational Theology, Moral Faith, and Religion', in *The Cambridge Companion to Kant* (ed. Paul Guyer, Cambridge: Cambridge University Press, 1992), pp. 394–416; and Onora O'Neill's Tanner lectures, in *The Tanner Lectures on Human Values*, vol. 18 (ed. Grethe B. Peterson, Salt Lake City: Utah University Press, 1997), pp. 269–308 (also reproduced at www.tannerlectures.utah.edu/nopq.html).

[10] Chapter 3 below, pp. 78 and 58.

While some jurists like Bentham argue that custom cloaks the sinister interests of a dominant elite, Savigny and his fellow jurists of the historical school argue that custom is morality made visible, that there can be no further moral standard to erect over it. In his contribution to this volume, Christoph Kletzer defends Hegel's attempt to transcend such polar views by arguing that reason and custom evolve together towards concrete universality. Comparing the role of custom in Hegel's philosophy of right and Savigny's legal science, Kletzer develops a Hegelian argument that 'Custom and habit are not social expressions opposed to freedom, they are not expressions of the "daily grind" to be overcome by self-expressive, heroic subjectivity but they rather are conditions of this subjectivity, play-forms of freedom.'[11]

The relation between reason and customary law

Kant's approach to the relation between reason and law again illustrates an extreme position. In strong contrast to his approach on moral reasoning, Kant argues that lawyers aiming to resolve conflicts between *legal* rules and practices must *not* appeal to rational principles of justice: lawyers' reasoning must remain exclusively within the reasoning internal to legislative commands and authoritative customs. If a faculty of law 'presumes to mix with its teaching something it treats as derived from reason, it offends against the authority of the government'; a jurist 'as an authority on the text, does not look to his reason for the laws . . . but to the code of laws that has been promulgated and sanctioned by the highest authority (if, as he should, he acts as a civil servant)'.[12]

Kant's position is one that many practising lawyers would find staggering. As one Kant scholar remarks, 'it is hard to see how the practical tasks of the practising lawyer, and in particular the practical task of the judge, can be fully guided by norms set by state authority. That might be possible if legal rules were true algorithms – but it does not seem at all plausible to think that any practical rules are algorithms: they may specify what is to be done, but always under-specify what is actually done.'[13] No written law *can* give exhaustive directions on its own interpretation and application, so customary rules and practices will be needed, not just to resolve faults in codification, but to guide judicial interpretation – and these guiding

[11] Chapter 6 below, p. 138. [12] *Conflict of the Faculties* 7:22–3.

[13] Onora O'Neill, 'Kant on Reason, Authority and Interpretation' (unpublished conference presentation, Newnham College, Cambridge, September 2004), p. 12.

customary rules and practices will themselves be subject to change and development through interpretation.[14]

While for many thinkers this is enough to show that customary rules are an immanent part of any legal system, some would insist that instead custom is at best a *source* rather than a part of law and that a formal legal act such as a judicial decision is needed to convert custom into customary law. On the latter account, custom is not itself a valid part of law (akin to legislation) but at best the raw material out of which a legislature or a court might fashion genuine positive law. Thus Frederick Schauer argues that 'the important questions about customary law are questions about formal law's use of pre-legal normative practices as the basis for legal norms'.[15] And Michael Lobban offers a detailed study of the way in which nineteenth-century English common lawyers approached customary international law in very much this spirit, working on the assumption that 'international law was a source of English law without being itself part of it'.[16]

In reflecting on the nature of such customary rules and practices, while the question of how to resolve hard cases is important, it is at least as important – and as difficult – to understand 'what it is that makes the easy cases easy'.[17] This returns us to the question of what effect, if any, doctrine or reason has on customary practices, and the contributors to this volume offer diverse responses. As already seen above, the approach to the question taken by many legal historians is to offer an account of lawyers' own views

[14] Related arguments have been made against the positions of contemporary legal positivists. To argue that a particular formulation is the correct view of a rule of law, as do teachers, textbook-writers, judges and counsel, is, as Brian Simpson argues against H. L. A. Hart, 'to participate in the system, not simply to study it scientifically'. See A. W. B. Simpson, 'The Common Law and Legal Theory', in *Oxford Essays in Jurisprudence* (ed. A. W. B. Simpson, Oxford: Clarendon Press, 1973), p. 97. Gerald Postema builds a powerful critique of Bentham's position on a similar point: 'what the courts do has an important (though not necessarily decisive) impact on what the law is and what it requires.' See Gerald Postema, *Jeremy Bentham and the Common Law Tradition* (Oxford: Clarendon Press, 1986), pp. 456–7.

[15] Chapter 1 below, p. 18. Schauer follows Raz's reading of Hart in treating a rule as a 'content-independent' reason for action, and distinguishes a custom (such as waking at 6 a.m.) from a rule. Taking the example of the contemporary prohibition on slavery, he also draws a sharp distinction between the morally right and 'a series of national normative acts (not in the legal sense, and certainly not items of international law)'. Other contributors to this volume, notably Murphy (Chapter 3 below) and Harrison (Chapter 2 below), would contest such a disjunction between custom and morality.

[16] Chapter 11 below, p. 277. [17] Chapter 1 below, p. 28n34.

of the relation between practice and doctrine while aiming to avoid imposing or relying on a view of their own. In the most extreme cases, reason or legal philosophy is rejected as 'a waste of time', an enterprise 'of interest only for people too idle to engage in the intricacies of the positive law': thus Savigny writes sarcastically of how 'until today we come across people who take their own juristic concepts and opinions to be purely reasonable, only because they lack knowledge of their genealogy'.[18]

But, in his comparative study of Savigny and Hegel on customary law, Christoph Kletzer contends with Hegel that, if legal history understood as a scholarly enterprise is to be rational, then legal history understood as a series of events 'must at least be understood as making the rationality of this historical inquiry possible, as being the history of the rationality of historical inquiry. Now, historical research is not an isolated enterprise, but can be rational only in a context of freedom, i.e. in the modern rational state. Thus, rational historical enquiry is the enquiry into the development of reason as such.'[19]

And, in her study of Gratian's *Decretum*, a text which attempted to show how diverse and seemingly inconsistent canons could be interpreted and applied in a consistent way, Jean Porter concludes in Aristotelian fashion:

> Because written laws serve to formulate and correct custom, they will normally supercede and override customary law; yet, because they find their context and point within a broader framework of customary law, the customs of a people will provide the necessary context for their interpretation. What is more, written law will have no purchase on a community, unless it reflects the practices of that community in some way; even a law that sets out to correct custom will necessarily reflect other aspects of the customary practices of a community, or it will lack purchase in the community for which it is intended. Far from being a minor adjunct to the law properly so called, custom is seen from this perspective as the one essential component of any legal system, sufficient to sustain a rule of law under some circumstances, and one essential component of the rule of law under any and every circumstance.[20]

[18] Chapter 6 below, p. 128, summarising Savigny's position on legal philosophy: and quoting from Friedrich Carl von Savigny, *Vom Beruf unserer Zeit für Gesetzgebung und Rechtswissenschaft* (Hildesheim: Georg Olms, 1967), p. 115.

[19] Kletzer recognises that this line of thought makes sense only to one who believes, like Hegel, that 'reason has already actualised itself in the world . . . in the French Revolution, in the advent of the rational liberal state that guarantees mutual recognition and free citizenship to all'. Chapter 6 below, p. 145.

[20] Chapter 4 below, p. 100.

The nature of customary international law

Codify it, repeal it, abolish it; some form of customary law will inevitably reappear. But how far, if at all, does a lawyer need to rely on reasoned argument in offering an account of rules of customary law? The issue of democratic legitimacy is especially contested in the case of customary international law, which some jurists claim threatens the democratic sovereignty of national law-making. This is one of the broader questions at stake in four of the contributions to this volume on customary international law.

Two of these essays focus mainly on English approaches to international law in the nineteenth century. In chapter 10, Perreau-Saussine argues that nineteenth-century English treatises on the law of nations reflect three distinctive accounts of the relationship between reasoned argument and the practices of states. The question of the relationship between reasoned argument and customary international law also plays a key role in Michael Lobban's account of the view of the law of nations taken by English courts in the nineteenth century. Lobban suggests that the attitude of English courts to the law of nations hinged both on nineteenth-century common lawyers' own understanding of the common law (as deriving not from custom itself but from judicial decision and ultimately 'artificial reason') and on their understanding of how far the relevant rule of customary international law was understood to be rationally defensible:

> As with their use of the law of nature, it was drawn on not for the moral content of its precepts, but as a means of reasoning on the nature of the problem. In novel cases, where English law offered no clear answers, courts (particularly before the mid-nineteenth century) were content to draw on the classic natural law works of Grotius, Bynkershoek or Vattel. However, insofar as the law of nations was made up of contingent and changing state practice, it was not regarded as of itself part of the common law.

For 'sceptics' who believe that custom is all we have, to suggest that particular jurists or treatise writers could have an attributable influence on the development of international law is akin to suggesting that assisting at the delivery of a child makes one a biological parent. A history of the influence of a particular writer or jurist can and must be a history of the work of a professional tradition, of advocates' and judges' 'shared attempt at addressing and resolving the problematic of order in a diverse world'. On such accounts, 'there is a fundamental problem with assigning and measuring influence in international law, which is the ultimately collective character of so much of the work': the collective work of international lawyers is rooted in a reflective professional tradition whose customs have a long history. Central to this tradition, it is usually argued, is a style and culture traceable to Grotius and other creators of modern international law and one 'still-existing, and no longer merely European'. It is a tradition that individuals 'may influence but hardly decisively', not least since 'its outcomes at any time, though expressed definitively in terms of current international law, are at the same time part of a process, and are to that extent provisional': 'Rise and fall, rise and fall, that is its enduring significance.'[21]

In contrast, the two final contributions to this volume defend accounts of customary international law that do aim to reach beyond legal practice to fundamental principles which it is argued are in some sense prior to and constraining of that practice. Arguing that 'human institutions exist and are capable of acting intelligibly . . . only insofar as they and others recognize them as defined and governed by norms, capable of grasping and following norms *as norms* (rather than merely strategic markers of the parameters of their anomic choices)', Gerald Postema sketches a general account of custom as a 'normative practice', an account which he suggests can 'illuminate the nature and typical mode of operation of customary international law'.[22] And John Tasioulas argues that 'the account of custom we should favour is that which is best justified by a political morality that offers the most attractive specification of the values served by international law'. Tasioulas offers an interpretative understanding of customary international law in which the ethical appeal of a candidate rule of international law figures among the criteria for determining whether it is a valid rule: this account, he argues, can serve as 'a template for guiding judicial decision-making and assessing its correctness'.

While the studies in this book focus mainly on the common law and on customary international law, customary practices underpin *every*

[21] J. Crawford, 'Public International Law in Twentieth-Century England', in Jurists Uprooted: German Speaking Emigre Lawyers in Twentieth Century Britain (ed. J. Beatson and R. Zimmermann, Oxford: Oxford University Press, 2004), pp. 692, 699 and 700–1.

[22] Chapter 12 below, p. 306.

legal system. Customary rules of interpretation play a part in any legal system, however codified: no written law can give exhaustive directions on its own interpretation, so customary rules and practices inevitably guide judicial interpretation. And those customary rules and practices themselves in turn will be subject to change and development through interpretation. Ancient and modern, international, civilian and common law: every interpretation and application of a written law relies on a complicated set of shared customs. And, once given, each interpretation and application of a written law itself extends that same set of customs. As James Bernard Murphy writes, 'Like a beaver, law is both adapted to its customary environment and transforms that environment . . . Many of our customs began as laws and all successful law eventually becomes customary.'[23]

[23] Chapter 3 below, p. 77.

PART I

Custom and morality: natural law, customary law and *ius gentium*

1

Pitfalls in the interpretation of customary law

FREDERICK SCHAUER*

Much has been written on the legal status of customary law, but considerably less attention has been devoted to the question of determining the content of the customary law whose legal status (or not) is at issue. Like any other source of law, customary law presents the question of interpreting, applying, and enforcing the emanations from that source, but interpreting customary law – or interpreting the custom that is to be part of the law[1] – presents issues arguably more complex than those presented when we are considering the interpretation of constitutions, statutes, regulations, treaties, and even the common law. My goal here is to explore these interpretive questions, and to do so with perhaps somewhat of a skeptical attitude. This is not to say that such skepticism will turn out at the end of the day to be justified. It is to believe, however, that

* This paper was prepared for the Colloquium on Customary Law organized by Dartmouth College and by the Lauterpacht Research Centre for International Law at Cambridge University, and held in Cambridge on 14–16 September 2005. I am grateful for research support from the Joan Shorenstein Center on the Press, Politics and Public Policy, Harvard University, and from the University of Chicago Law School, where I served as the Daniel R. Fischel and Sylvia M. Neil Distinguished Visiting Professor of Law during the time when this paper was written and presented.

[1] There is a long-standing dispute about the status of customary law, with some (such as C. K. Allen) holding that custom is an immanent part of law in any common law system, and others (most prominently Jeremy Bentham and John Austin) insisting that a formal legal act (such as a judicial decision) is necessary to convert custom into customary law. See Rupert Cross, *Precedent in English Law* (3rd edn, Oxford: Clarendon Press, 1977), pp. 157–9; Gerald J. Postema, *Bentham and the Common Law Tradition* (Oxford: Clarendon Press, 1986), pp. 4–14 and 219–30. This is an important dispute, but nothing I say in this paper depends on its resolution. Nevertheless, both of these opposing positions should be distinguished from the sense in which a common law system just *is* itself a customary system of law, albeit not necessarily congruent with the pre-legal customs that the common law as a customary system may choose to adopt. See A. W. B. Simpson, "The Common Law and Legal Theory," in A. W. B. Simpson, ed., *Oxford Essays in Jurisprudence (Second Series)* (Oxford: Clarendon Press, 1973), pp. 77–99.

addressing such skeptical questions is an inevitable task for any satisfactory account of the role of customary law in common law adjudication, and perhaps to an even greater extent with respect to the role of customary international law as a part of international law more generally. So, although in this paper I will ask more questions than I answer, my goal is to put on the table those interpretive issues that anyone seeking to develop a theory of customary international law, or a theory of the role of custom in common law decision-making, must at least attempt to answer.

Indeed, one of my goals here is to connect questions about customary law with many of the enduring questions about legal interpretation more generally, questions whose importance seems all-too-often ignored by theorists of customary law. And so at the outset it might be worthwhile noting five of these questions. One is a question focusing on the identification of those features of some previous decision that enable subsequent decision-makers to reference that decision or to rely upon it. Thus, in a debate marked by the earlier contributions of Goodhart, Simpson, and Montrose, and furthered in more recent times by Larry Alexander, most prominently, the question was raised as to whether it was the facts of a previous decision, or the decision itself, or the words used to describe that decision, that enabled such a decision to constitute a precedent for some other decision.[2] This issue is plainly relevant to the question of customary law, for custom is itself the aggregate of a series of past acts or decisions, but in order to make sense out of these past acts or decisions we need to know which features of those acts or decisions are the ones that have the quasi-authoritative status necessary for custom itself to have such a status.

At a more extreme level, sorting out the status of customary law requires confronting the challenges of American Legal Realism, the tradition which has raised enduring questions about the extent to which, if at all, previous acts, events, or decisions actually do constrain

[2] Larry Alexander, "Constrained by Precedent," *Southern California Law Review*, vol. 63 (1989), pp. 1–64; Arthur L. Goodhart, "The Ratio Decidendi of a Case," *Modern Law Review*, vol. 22 (1959), pp. 117–24; Arthur L. Goodhart, "Determining the Ratio Decidendi of a Case," *Yale Law Journal*, vol. 40 (1930), pp. 161–83; J. L. Montrose, "The Ratio Decidendi of a Case," *Modern Law Review*, vol. 20 (1957), pp. 587–95; J. L. Montrose, "Ratio Decidendi and the House of Lords," *Modern Law Review*, vol. 20 (1957); pp. 124–30; A. W. B. Simpson, "The Ratio Decidendi of a Case," *Modern Law Review*, vol. 21 (1958), pp. 155–60; A. W. B. Simpson, "The Ratio Decidendi of a Case," *Modern Law Review*, vol. 20 (1957), pp. 413–15.

judges and other subsequent decision-makers.[3] Legal Realism, especially at its extremes, may not be plausible, but nor may it be plausible, as an empirical proposition, to believe that the canon of authoritative law is as exclusive and as constraining as pre-Realist legal theory supposed it to be. It seems strange, therefore, to consider the actual (empirical) authority of customary law without considering a long-standing debate about the empirical authority of legal norms, legal rules, and legal decisions more generally.

Closely related to these debates about the status of precedent and the status of legal authority in general are contemporary debates about legal interpretation inspired primarily by Ronald Dworkin.[4] Is there, in theory if not in practice, one right answer to any legal question? Does the interpretation of law resemble in important ways the interpretation of literature? Is legal interpretation ultimately a coherence-based and holistic practice, rather than one in which individual legal items determine particular legal results? These are the questions that Dworkin has so prominently placed on the jurisprudential agenda, and they are no less relevant when the question is the interpretation (and identification) of customary law.

In the United States, and increasingly in Canada, Australia, South Africa, and other countries with written constitutions and aggressive judicial review, many of these interpretive debates have played out as debates over the proper way to interpret a written constitution.[5] Is the

[3] See, for example, Jerome Frank, *Law and the Modern Mind* (New York: Brentano's, 1930); Laura Kalman, *Legal Realism at Yale, 1927–1960* (Chapel Hill, NC: University of North Carolina Press, 1986); Karl Nickerson Llewellyn, *The Bramble Bush: Some Lectures on Law and Its Study* (New York: Columbia University School of Law, 1930); William Twining, *Karl Llewellyn and the Realist Movement* (London: Weidenfeld & Nicolson, 1973).

[4] Especially in Ronald Dworkin, *Law's Empire* (Cambridge, MA: Harvard University Press, 1986); Ronald Dworkin, *A Matter of Principle* (Cambridge, MA: Harvard University Press, 1985); Ronald Dworkin, *Taking Rights Seriously* (Cambridge, MA: Harvard University Press, 1977).

[5] The literature, especially in the United States, is vast. A sample of the issues can be found in John Hart Ely, *Democracy and Distrust: A Theory of Judicial Review* (Cambridge, MA: Harvard University Press, 1980); Antonin Scalia, *et al.*, *A Matter of Interpretation* (Amy Guttman ed., Princeton: Princeton University Press, 1997); Akhil Reed Amar, "Intratextualism," *Harvard Law Review*, vol. 112 (1999), pp. 747–803; Richard H. Fallon, Jr., "Judicially Manageable Standards and Constitutional Meaning," *Harvard Law Review*, vol. 119 (2006), pp. 1274–332; Michael J. Perry, "The Authority of Text, Tradition, and Reason: A Theory of Constitutional 'Interpretation,'" *Southern California Law Review*, vol. 58 (1985), pp. 551–602; Frederick Schauer, "An Essay on Constitutional Language," *UCLA Law Review*, vol. 29 (1982), pp. 797–832.

process of constitutional interpretation essentially a common law process, or does it more resemble the interpretation of a statute, a regulation, a contract, or a will? Is the goal of such interpretation to interpret the words of the document as ordinary language, or instead as technical language, or as embodying the intentions of those who first wrote them, or in their best possible light in view of the demands of morality and democracy and policy? To purport to interpret customary law is to deal with many of the same issues, especially since the significant indeterminacy of customary law bears a close affinity with the linguistic indeterminacy of many of the most important and most disputed provisions in written constitutions.

Finally, but perhaps most importantly, how can the insights of disciplines other than law inform our understanding of the legal interpretive process? Are there lessons from philosophy, from psychology, from behavioral economics, and from other disciplines and sub-disciplines that can help us to make sense of the process by which customary law is created and interpreted? Implicit in this paper is an affirmative answer to this question, and thus my attempts here to relate these debates and insights outside of law is but a larger manifestation of the guiding principle of this paper – that there are many insights and challenges in the legal and non-legal literature outside of the literature on customary law and outside of the literature on international law that can valuably inform questions about the interpretation of customary law, and that have been less of a presence in the customary law and international law literatures than might be desirable.

Many of these jurisprudential and philosophical debates revolve around the respective roles of the creator of some norm and the interpreter of that norm. How much freedom do authoritative interpreters actually have? When such interpreters purport to be *describing* customary law, are they simply engaged in an act of description, or are they doing something that is more interpretive and more creative than many within the customary law tradition have been willing to admit? This question arises in each of the five debates I have just mentioned, and thus in describing this paper as having a "skeptical" cast my ultimate goal is to attempt to make the domains of customary law and customary international law less complacent than they at times have appeared to be, and to confront the same challenges that most other areas of legal analysis have been confronting for generations.

Clarifying the question

It is common ground that in some domains custom can be a source of law, and that reaching a legal conclusion based on custom can be as legitimate as reaching a legal conclusion on the basis of a statute, a legal precedent, a provision of a written constitution, or the opinion of an authoritatively recognized secondary source. With respect to such conventional sources of law, it is a trivial point that first we locate a normative rule, and then determine the extent to which, if at all, it applies to the matter at hand. All legal rules are expressed in or translatable into an if-then form, and thus the application of any of the foregoing sources typically involves, to oversimplify, determining whether the facts we have perceived fall within the scope-designating or "if" part of the rule, and, if so, then determining what the normative consequent – the "then" part of the rule – requires to be done.[6]

Seen from the perspective of this point about the basic structure of a prescriptive rule, one preliminary but key question about custom as a source of law is whether the customary source must be normative. As H. L. A. Hart so plainly stressed in his discussion of habits,[7] and others have analyzed in the context of descriptive rules,[8] not all regularities of human behavior are based on normative or rule-guided considerations. It is my *custom* – I am *accustomed* – to wake up at 6 a.m., but no rule tells me to do so, and no rule (not even my own) would be violated were I not to do so. So too with the behavior of institutions and governments. For a long time it was the practice of airlines to have names that had either geographic or weighty and serious connotations, and sometimes both, as with "British Airways" and "Air France" and "United" and "Continental." When airlines started calling themselves things like "Virgin Atlantic" and "Song" and "Ted," the practice shifted, yet no normative rule was broken. Similarly, although it is a fact that the majority of the nations of the world have names that end in "a," and thus it is a fact that nations *generally* have names ending in "a," there is no normative or prescriptive standard that is violated by Peru, New Zealand, Pakistan, and Portugal.

6 For a lengthier discussion of such structural matters about rules, see Frederick Schauer, *Playing by the Rules: A Philosophical Examination of Rule-Based Decision-Making in Law and in Life* (Oxford: Clarendon Press, 1991), pp. 23–7.

7 H. L. A. Hart, *The Concept of Law* (2nd edn., Oxford: Clarendon Press, 1994), pp. 9–12 and 55–60.

8 Schauer, *op. cit.* note 6, pp. 18–22.

Yet, although there are many pre-legal regularities that are not normative, there are many that are, and now we approach more closely the issues that surround customary law.[9] It is not mere habit that leads wholesale diamond merchants in New York, Antwerp, Johannesburg, and Jerusalem to sell to retailers (or cutters) on a "take it or leave it" basis for a package of diamonds, but rather a well-entrenched normative practice within the industry, such that departure would be the occasion for criticism or the imposition of a non-legal sanction.[10] So too with the rules of etiquette, or the rules of non-governmental organizations. One cannot call the police when a person slurps his soup or, if insufficiently senior, traverses the lawn of a Cambridge college, but there can be little doubt that these practices are imbued with all of the trappings of normativity save for the state as the source of authority.[11]

Thus, the important questions about customary law are questions about formal law's use of pre-legal normative practices as the basis for legal norms.[12] And, even more precisely, these important questions are ones about the possibility, nature, and desirability of formal law's taking as legally authoritative some pre-legal normative and authoritative practice. And the limitation to the "normative" and the pre-legally "authoritative" is crucial. It is always open for a law-maker exercising discretion to decide to follow some existing pre-legal normative or non-normative practice, but this is no different from the law-maker consulting any other non-normative or non-authoritative source of wisdom. Only when pre-legal normative customs are taken as (not-necessarily-conclusive) content-independent sources of authority do the genuine issues arise, and thus my question is about determining the content of

[9] See Deryck Beyleveld and Roger Brownsword, *Law as Moral Judgment* (London: Sweet & Maxwell, 1986), p. 125.

[10] See Deborah L. Spar, *The Cooperative Edge: The Internal Politics of International Cartels* (Ithaca, NY: Cornell University Press, 1994); Lisa Bernstein, "Opting Out of the Legal System: Extralegal Contractual Relations in the Diamond Industry," *Journal of Legal Studies*, vol. 21 (1992), pp. 115–57.

[11] On the existence of such normative customary practices, and on their predominance in less legally complex societies, see, for example, Lloyd Fallers, *Law Without Precedent: Legal Ideas in Action in the Courts of Colonial Busoga* (Chicago: University of Chicago Press, 1969), pp. 310–14; Roberto Mangabeira Unger, *Law in Modern Society* (Cambridge: Cambridge University Press, 1976), pp. 48–58.

[12] On normative custom, and on the disagreements about how to understand it and assess it, see, for example, Paul Bohannon, "The Differing Realms of Law," *American Anthropologist*, vol. 6 (1965), pp. 33–42; Stanley Diamond, "The Rule of Law versus the Order of Custom," *Social Research*, vol. 38 (1971), pp. 42–72.

those customary normative sources that have already been socially or culturally but not-yet-legally determined to be authoritative.[13]

This limitation may be slightly idiosyncratic, or at least at odds with some aspects of positive law. Consider, for example, *Mercer* v. *Dunne*,[14] in which "it was held in 1905 that the fishermen of Walmer were entitled by a local custom to dry their nets on a particular stretch of sand,"[15] despite the fact that, in the absence of the custom, the practice would have constituted an unlawful trespass. Here there is no indication that the customary practice was done under claim of right, and no indication that the practice itself became normative. A fisherman new to the Walmer area would not have been subject to criticism, we suppose, for not participating in the custom, and instead drying his nets somewhere else. Yet when, as in this example, the practice is not normative – indeed the case would strike the American property lawyer as one of adverse possession, a matter of substantive law, and not of the application of custom – the issues are different. The extent to which law does or should reflect the existing conditions of the world, an issue to which I shall return in conclusion, is important, but here, as in most of the literature on customary law, I shall limit my inquiry to the arguably narrower question of the extent to which law does or should reflect the pre-legal *normative* world – a world in which some but not all practices are authoritative – on which it is superimposed.

The questions I want to pose are largely questions existing at the contrast between statute or codified law, on the one hand, and common law and customary law, on the other. In practice, this means that these questions presuppose the (moderate) determinacy of language, various and sundry literary theorists, French philosophers, and other deconstructionists notwithstanding. Although it is obvious that the legal use of terms like "justice," "equal protection," "reasonable," "fair," "proportionate," and "necessary" provide little constraint on decision and allow much room for law-making under the rubric of "interpretation,"

[13] On understanding authority in just this content-independent way, the locus classicus is H. L. A. Hart, "Commands and Authoritative Legal Reasons," in *Essays on Bentham: Jurisprudence and Political Theory* (Oxford: Clarendon Press, 1982), pp. 243–68. See also Joseph Raz, *The Authority of Law: Essays on Law and Morality* (Oxford: Clarendon Press, 1979); Donald H. Regan, "Reasons, Authority, and the Meaning of 'Obey': Further Thoughts on Raz and Obedience to Law," *Canadian Journal of Law and Jurisprudence*, vol. 3 (1990), pp. 3–28; Frederick Schauer, "The Questions of Authority," *Georgetown Law Journal*, vol. 81 (1992), pp. 95–115.

[14] [1905] 2 Ch 538. [15] Cross, *op. cit.* note 1, p. 162.

such is not the case, or at least is not necessarily the case, when law uses terms like "two," "insect," and "parliament." It is true that most of the terms used by the law have, following Hart, a core of settled application and a fringe or penumbra of uncertainty.[16] Still, I take it as a given that common linguistic usage, whether ordinary or technical, can and often does serve satisfactorily to designate a core,[17] and that shared understandings about linguistic meaning are what typically or standardly make it possible for statutes often to generate "clear" or "easy" cases.[18] All of this may in some contexts be open to debate, but, if we are to try to focus on the special problems of customary law, and on why customary law would often seem especially problematic, we need to assume, if only for the sake of argument, that statute or codified law has the capacity to generate unique or tightly clustered interpretations, that in most advanced legal systems it often does so, and that it does so by virtue of the ability of human beings to read off from a printed page a single or tightly clustered set of meanings for particular sentences, meanings that are themselves a function of the similar capacities of individual words.

Given this background assumption, I want to proceed by offering a series of questions, each labeled with the name of a theorist who might be said to have, or at least have for me, inspired the question. Little should be made of the names, however, for my goal here is well removed from exegesis of this or that thinker. The names should, however, provide a convenient way of designating particular and skeptical questions about the practice of interpreting existing normative custom.

Hanson's question

Interpreting custom requires an interpreter. And thus we can conceive of the interpreter of custom as someone looking out over a vast sea of human behavior and identifying the particular strands, patterns, and practices that might constitute a normative custom. In doing so, perhaps she is simply looking at the law. Perhaps *all* normative customs are

[16] Hart, *op. cit.* note 7, pp. 124–54.

[17] As Lon Fuller pointed out against Hart, however, sometimes the core may be designated by purpose and not by literal meaning, Lon L. Fuller, "Positivism and Fidelity to Law – A Reply to Professor Hart," *Harvard Law Review*, vol. 71 (1958), pp. 630–72, a point which Hart ultimately conceded in H. L. A. Hart, *Essays in Jurisprudence and Philosophy* (Oxford: Clarendon Press, 1983), pp. 6–8.

[18] See Walter Sinnott-Armstrong, "Word Meaning in Legal Interpretation," *San Diego Law Review*, vol. 42 (2005), pp. 465–83.

part of the relevant body of law, such that all of the normative customs of England are immanent in the English common law, and all of the normative customs of nations – and not just those that are understood as *legally* normative under the doctrine of *opinio juris* – are part of international law. But, even if this is so, and certainly if it is not so, the normative customs of a jurisdiction that are *explicitly* incorporated within the law constitute but a subset of the totality of that jurisdiction's normative customs. And from this it follows that the task of interpretation turns out to be, in significant part, the task of selection, the selection from the universe of normative customs those normative customs that will explicitly be part of the law. The relevant custom for some decision does not simply leap out and grab the interpreter, but rather is selected by that interpreter from among the entire field of that jurisdiction's normative customs,

Once we see that the interpreter's task includes the task of selection, however, then we are forced to consider the grounds on which that selection is made. The analogy here, and the analogy that explains the name of this section, is to the idea long referred to in the philosophy of science as *theory-laden observation*. In his autobiography, Karl Popper recounts the time at the end of a lecture when he gave an assignment to the attendees, to be completed prior to the next lecture. And that assignment was simply to go out and observe. Period. Full stop. Popper's point was that simple observation, without purpose and without theory, was impossible, and he wanted his students to recognize that the task of observation required them to have, use, or develop a theory of what they were observing and why they were observing it.[19] This idea was developed more fully by Norwood Hanson,[20] and it is now more or less commonplace that the task of observing is not simply one of recording the world as it exists, but instead necessarily involves recording those parts of the world that are recorded for some reason, and then grouping those parts into categories that once again reflect a goal, a purpose, or a theory.

So too with the observation of custom. The interpreter of custom is not simply labeling all of the normative customs of the world or of England or of whatever, but is identifying some customs for some

[19] Karl R. Popper, *Unended Quest: An Intellectual Autobiography* (London: Open Court, 1976).

[20] Norwood R. Hanson, *Patterns of Discovery* (Cambridge: Cambridge University Press, 1958).

purpose, much like the practice, as has been said of determining legislative history in a non-parliamentary system with a large legislature, of looking over a crowd and picking out your friends.[21] There are many more normative customs than are explicitly incorporated into law for purposes of making a legal decision, and thus anyone who seeks to explain the incorporation of custom into law must address the question of which customs are selected, which are not selected, and what purpose, goal, theory, or whatever drives the selection of some customs while others remain disregarded. Indeed, we would not be surprised to discover that there was a custom among the non-fishermen of Walmer, especially after a few pints, to grumble about the presumptuousness of the fishermen, and the selection of the custom of the fishermen's actions rather than the custom of the non-fishermen residents' grousing about it may well reflect some unarticulated but no less real and no less causal factor that led to the selection of the particular custom that determined the outcome.

The selection of some customs but not others is not necessarily, as it may have been in my hypothetical gloss on the case of the fishermen of Walmer, driven by interpreter preferences for certain outcomes. The selection may be a function of the informational institutions that make some customs more known to interpreters than others. It may be a function of dispute-resolution mechanisms that create incentives for some customs to be pressed while others are not. And it may be a function of the behavioral aspects of human decision-making, and the way in which some facts, including some customs, are more salient for some people than they are for others. All of these factors, and undoubtedly many more, will influence the selection of some customs for attention while other customs are ignored, but the only point here is that we cannot fully understand the practice of interpreting custom until we understand that the very process of selecting the custom to be interpreted reflects background facts and norms of the interpreter and her institutional environment. The selection of what to interpret may indeed be more important to an outcome than the interpretation of what is selected, and attention to the impossibility of observation and selection that is not theory-laden helps focus our attention on this omnipresent phenomenon.

[21] *Conroy* v. *Aniskoff*, 507 US 511, 519 (1993), quoting United States federal judge Harold Laventhal. And the point is similar to that implicit in the saying that "the Devil can cite Scripture for his purpose." William Shakespeare, *The Merchant of Venice*, Act 1, Scene 3.

Wittgenstein's question

Shortly after the publication of Saul Kripke's *Wittgenstein on Rules and Private Language*,[22] a number of American legal scholars attempted to conscript Kripke's Wittgenstein into a radical indeterminacy agenda, claiming that Wittgenstein, as explained by Kripke, was challenging the very possibility of determinate linguistic meaning.[23] Once we understood Wittgenstein's message as interpreted by Kripke, so the argument went, we would understand that law's aspiration for determinate guidance removed from the ideological dimensions of particular decisions was doomed to failure. Because law's pretensions to determinacy rested on the determinacy of language, it was said, Wittgenstein and Kripke had undercut the foundations of many of law's claims to neutrality and impersonality, aspirations that often parade under the banner of the "rule of law."

Those who made this argument succeeded in little more than demonstrating that they understood neither Wittgenstein nor Kripke.[24] That language may ultimately rest on agreement, and that such agreement may in some way be contingent, says no more about the ability of contingently created language to constrain than it does about the ability of contingently created guns to cause fatal injury.[25] And the fact that the agreement can change over time once again says far less than it was alleged to say, for just as I can stand on a moving train so too can I actually *use* language and use its meanings even as language and its constituent meanings are ever so slowly shifting.

Yet, although the original claims about the relevance of Kripke's Wittgenstein to legal interpretation were somewhere between exaggerated and ridiculous, there remains an important lesson to be learned from the literature on Wittgenstein and rule-following, and it is a lesson that is especially relevant to common law and to custom. Both common

[22] Saul A. Kripke, *Wittgenstein on Rules and Private Language: An Elementary Exposition* (Cambridge, MA: Harvard University Press, 1982).

[23] A well-known example is Mark V. Tushnet, "Following the Rules Laid Down: A Critique of Interpretivism and Neutral Principles," *Harvard Law Review*, vol. 96 (1983), pp. 542–83.

[24] I will leave to others the question whether Kripke understood Wittgenstein, although I should note that I believe he did not, and that Wittgenstein's point was simply that we do not and cannot ask the very question that Kripke was asking. See G. P. Baker and P. M. S. Hacker, *Scepticism, Rules and Language* (Oxford: Basil Blackwell, 1984).

[25] Or so I have argued in Frederick Schauer, "Rules and the Rule-Following Argument," *Canadian Journal of Law and Jurisprudence*, vol. 3 (1990), pp. 187–92.

law and custom are continuously developing, and one way to understand their development is as a progression or as a series. So if we see custom as a series of social decisions and (part of) the common law as a series of judicial ones, we can then understand the act of making a particular common law decision, and less obviously the act of deciding in accordance with some custom, as being a decision involving the extension of a pre-existing series. And this is where Wittgenstein and the rule-following considerations enter the picture in a more serious way. When we have a series of decisions, and when the series up until now is *not* encrusted in a canonical linguistic definition of what that series stands for, the agent who extends the series has, in theory, a range of options about the extension of that series, in just the way in which he who seeks to extend the series 1000, 1002, 1004, 1006, . . . may have a range of options about which number is to come next, options that are less determined by the previous items in the series than is commonly supposed. So insofar as the understandings that created the previous series are more flexible than the understandings that create the rules of language, a new interpretive opportunity may turn out to be less constrained by previous members of the series than might be thought, and than might be urged by the extender of the series.

Like the lesson of theory-laden observation, this is not a lesson of radical indeterminacy, but rather a lesson about the potential for choice (although not always on the part of an individual interpreter, who may well be constrained by numerous factors external to the previous decisions[26]) built into the practices of interpretation, a potential that is often denied, especially in law, by those interpreters who wish to claim that they are doing nothing but following the dictates of the previous members of some series. The sophisticated version of this argument – the argument that constraint in fact does come from the previous decision in the series – is offered by Ronald Dworkin, especially as he uses the vivid metaphor of the chain novel to illustrate the nature of legal interpretation.[27] The author of the next chapter of the chain novel, Dworkin argues, or the next episode of a television soap opera, is constrained by notions of interpretive integrity to continue the broad themes established by the earlier chapters or episodes, even as that interpreter has a limited degree of freedom to shift the story, ever so

[26] And that is why the person who says that 1013 is the next member of the series 1000, 1002, 1004, 1006 . . . has simply given the wrong answer.

[27] Ronald Dworkin, *Law's Empire* (Cambridge, MA: Harvard University Press, 1986).

slightly, in one direction or another. This degree of interpretive freedom, argues Dworkin, is to be used to make the story "the best it can be," but there is a vast difference, he insists, between making *this* story the best *it* can be and simply writing a new story or heading off in a dramatically different direction.

There may not be that much in the distinction between Wittgenstein's rule-following lessons and Dworkin's chain novel metaphor, because both stand for the proposition that the past constrains but may not bind inexorably. And, when the past is indeed perceived as binding inexorably, the important lesson is that the bindingness comes not solely from the items of the past, but how those past items are treated by the constraints of the present. And so too with the interpretation of custom and common law. Interpreters may have good reasons for denying the degree of choice they actually have, and Dworkin may be right, as he stressed in his earlier work, to point out that interpreters may themselves not see the degree of choice they actually have,[28] but that does not mean that the choice does not exist. So when the interpreter of customary international law, for example, says that in this instance the practices of nations over some past period of years *stand for* this proposition now, it becomes permissible to ask what else those customs of the past might now be taken to stand for, and then to ask further why the selected interpretation was selected rather than some number of others that might have been equally consistent with the past decisions and the past acts, and thus, in the large, with the customs of the past.

Consider, for example, the question of slavery under international law, a question often posed independently of (or prior to) the explicit prohibition in Article 4 of the Universal Declaration of Human Rights of 1948.[29] Although there was, even prior to 1948, a series of national normative acts (not in the legal sense, and certainly not items of international law) that would constitute a progression in the direction of

[28] Ronald Dworkin, *Taking Rights Seriously* (Cambridge, MA: Harvard University Press, 1977). Understanding Dworkin's claim that there is "one right answer" to any legal question requires understanding that for Dworkin the important perspective is that of the judge making the decision. When we read Dworkin charitably, we see that his "one right answer" claim is not an ontological one, but is rather about the processes by which the judge comes to what *he* believes to be *the* right answer. And if we see the "one right answer" claim as one of judicial phenomenology and not one of legal ontology, the claim becomes far more plausible.

[29] See Anthony D'Amato, *The Concept of Custom in International Law* (Ithaca, NY: Cornell University Press, 1971), pp. 131–2. Dick W. P. Ruiter, *Legal Institutions* (Dordrecht: Kluwer Academic Publishers, 2001), pp. 119–34.

treating slavery as impermissible, the conclusion that this progression would continue, and that slavery should thus be considered violative of customary international law, presupposes a continuation of the progression in a certain way. That this was the morally right result is beyond question, but the interpretive issue is how much this result was dictated by the progression itself, and how much by the determination, independently of the progression, that slavery simply *is* morally and thus legally impermissible. And so too, in reverse, with questions of desuetude, for the practice of assuming a continuing decline in the existence or normativity of some norm from the decline that has taken place to the point of decision may again be to impose upon a trend something that may be less inherent in the trend than is commonly assumed.

None of this is to say that legal custom cannot proceed by imposing certain second-order norms on the identification of first-order norms, and it could well be that an assumption about the continuation of some past trend is one of those second-order norms. But the selection of those second-order norms will have to be based on some value or goal – the belief that customary norms tend towards efficiency, for example[30] – rather than being the product of something close to logical necessity. And thus Wittgenstein's lesson for customary law is not a lesson of legal indeterminacy, but rather a lesson about the contingency and second-order normativity of the sources of short- or intermediate-term legal determinacy.

Quine's question

Much the same question can be posed in terms of the relationship between observations (the data) and the theory that might explain them. As W. V. O. Quine – and Pierre Duhem – properly insisted, no theory or explanation or account of multiple data could ever be uniquely determined by that data. Instead, extracting a theory from the data, or imposing an explanation on a set of data, requires the use of supplementary premises in order to wind up with the one explanation among those that fit the data in preference to others which are different from

[30] See, for example, Ronald A. Cass, "Economics and International Law," *New York University Journal of International Law and Politics*, vol, 29 (1997), pp. 473–502; Jeffrey L. Dunoff and Joel P. Trachtman, "Economic Analysis of International Law," *Yale Journal of International Law*, vol. 24 (1999), pp. 1–54.

the one selected, and which have different extensions into the future, but which also fit the existing data.[31]

Any attempt to explain a past or existing custom is plagued by the same phenomenon of under-determination. Whether it be the decisions of multiple previous courts on multiple different occasions, or the multiple foreign policy or human rights decisions of multiple nations on multiple past occasions, or even just the identification of behavioral regularities of pairs of self-interested states,[32] the *statement* (the explanation) that the custom is such-and-such is a statement that could have been different but which even if different would still nonetheless have explained the same data. In science, the norms and goals of science help to make these decisions, as when we prefer simpler to more complex explanations, or when we select those explanations that appear to have the greatest future pragmatic or predictive value. So too with history, where the explanation selected by the historian to explain the past is not the only explanation that would explain the past, but may well be the explanation the fits best with the present goals and norms of the particular historian and the present goals and norms of history as a discipline and a profession. There are parallel individual and institutional norms for law, but what are these norms? Is one explanation of past custom better than another because it is morally preferable, as is perhaps the case with the conclusion that a prohibition on slavery is part of customary international law? Or is an explanation chosen over its logically equivalent competitors because it is better suited pragmatically to future application and enforcement by some court, or by some international tribunal, or by some enforcement body? Or is it grounds for selecting an explanation that the explanation selected will be more easily explainable to the non-legal actors who are expected to be bound by it?

All of these and many other background norms pervade any use of custom as a source of law, whether domestic or international. The question for law, or the question for those who would use and interpret customary law, is consequently the question of what these background norms are, how they have been chosen, how they foster the goals of the larger institutional setting in which they are employed, and how they

31 Pierre Maurice Marie Duhem, *The Aim and Structure of Physical Theory* (P. P. Wiener trans., Princeton: Princeton University Press, 1954); Willard Van Orman Quine, *Word and Object* (Cambridge, MA: MIT Press, 1960).

32 See Jack L. Goldsmith and Eric A. Posner, "A Theory of Customary International Law," *University of Chicago Law Review*, vol. 66 (1999), pp. 1113–77.

lead to the selection of some explanations for past customary acts in preference to others. Like Wittgenstein's question, and indeed to some extent like Hanson's, Quine's question is a question about unacknowledged options, and about the factors that led to the choice of one option over the typically unacknowledged but in some sense equally valid or equally available alternatives. And thus the question about some statement of a custom based on a series of events is the question of why a different statement, with different implications, but which would have been based on the same events, was not the one that in the final analysis emerged.

Llewellyn's question

Although law is not only an adversarial practice, it is significantly so. And thus it is important to see the use of customary law in its typical concrete adversarial or litigation-based context.[33] Whenever one party offers an interpretation of customary law to support its side of an adversarial proceeding, the other side, assuming it does not immediately confess error,[34] has a strong incentive to find an equally authoritative or equally persuasive source that would militate in favor of the opposite result. Sometimes this will be a statute, sometimes it will be a reported precedent decision, and sometimes it will be the published opinion of an

[33] Although much of international law arises outside of the context of formal litigation, it is nevertheless often adversarial, with nations arguing their preferred interpretations to international organizations, to human rights groups and other NGOs, and to the community of world public opinion.

[34] The statement in the text is a joke. Although the unwillingness to challenge settled law is an omnipresent legal practice all too often ignored by court-obsessed legal theorists, cases almost never get to court unless the law is less clear, and thus the likelihood that a party who has gotten as far as actual litigation will simply give up in the face of strong legal precedent is essentially non-existent. The phenomenon is generally known as the selection effect, see George Priest and William Klein, "The Selection of Disputes for Litigation," *Journal of Legal Studies*, vol. 13 (1984), pp. 1–23; Frederick Schauer, "Judging in a Corner of the Law," *Southern California Law Review*, vol. 61 (1988), pp. 1717–33, and has important implications for thinking about the interpretation of customary law. The instances of interpretation will not be a fair sample of the full scope of customary law, and so, although there are difficult and important issues involved in the interpretation of custom, the difficulty of those issues may not tell us everything about the phenomenon of customary law itself. How to resolve the hard cases is important, but equally important is to understand what it is that makes the easy cases easy.

authoritative secondary author, but often it will simply be a different item of customary law, and one that goes in the opposite direction.

One of Karl Llewellyn's most noteworthy contributions to legal theory came from identifying just this phenomenon in statutory interpretation.[35] Often in cases of contested interpretation of a statute one party will offer a venerable and unquestionably authoritative canon or maxim of statutory construction that will support the proposed interpretation. The statute is clear on its face, it might be argued, and thus there is no need to repair to the realm of the actual intentions of the legislators who enacted it. Or the purpose of the statute was to eliminate such-and-such an evil, and thus should be interpreted to encompass that evil. But, although such canons undoubtedly existed, Llewellyn argued, and although they equally undoubtedly had a strong legal pedigree in the reported cases and in the standard treatises, so too did their mirror images. If one party could argue from the canon that allowed plain meaning to trump actual legislative intent, the other party could trot out an equally venerable canon providing that actual legislative intent would prevail over inconsistent statutory words. And when one party relied on the canon of statutory purpose to urge extension of the statute to some new mischief, the other could sometimes rely on the so-called rule of lenity to argue against extension. In practice, argued Llewellyn, and in any case worth litigating,[36] for every authoritative "thrust" there was an equally authoritative "parry." As a result, all of the heavy decisional lifting was done not by the canons themselves, but by the unspoken factors that were used by the decision-maker to choose between them.

The question for customary law, then, is whether for all (or at least most) customary practice urging *x* there is a roughly equally well-entrenched customary practice urging non-*x*. This is of course much more an empirical question than it is a philosophical or jurisprudential one. But it is an empirical question about the actual array of customary norms that Llewellyn forces us to ask. Accordingly, we need to consider

[35] Karl N. Llewellyn, "Remarks on the Theory of Appellate Decision and the Rules or Canons about How Statutes Are To Be Construed," *Vanderbilt Law Review*, vol. 3 (1950), pp. 395–405.

[36] Although the term "selection effect" did not exist when Llewellyn wrote, he plainly recognized the phenomenon, and thus remained careful to restrict his claims about law's indeterminacy to the universe of cases close enough to justify litigation. See Karl N. Llewellyn, *The Bramble Bush: Some Lectures on Law and Its Study* (New York: Columbia University School of Law, 1930).

whether for any domain of customary practice the existing array of entrenched normative customs is so complex, so large, and so unsystematized[37] that mutually exclusive customs abound, such that arguments from custom can typically be met by other arguments from custom. To the extent that this is true, and again I emphasize that this is an empirical question varying from domain to domain, then Llewellyn's basic point holds, and we would then do well to examine further which views, values, factors, rules, and principles are the ones actually doing the work in choosing between the opposed customs.

Indeed, it is arguable that Llewellyn's question is even more germane to customary law than to common law generally. Although the common law does not contain the (partially successful) mechanisms of codification and systematization characteristic of civil law jurisdictions, it seeks to eliminate internal inconsistency when the opportunity arises, and treats mutually exclusive norms as at least problematic. Not so, however, with custom, and indeed in societies that value "pluralism" or "diversity" or something of that sort we should not be surprised to find plural and diverse customs. And, insofar as the practices of nations again divide into multiple groupings,[38] the practice of nations may be such that the likelihood of there being morally plausible, widely accepted, but mutually exclusive international customs is likely to increase.[39]

Another way of looking at this is through a skeptical understanding of the unspoken or tacit factors that for Llewellyn served to guide actual decisions. Llewellyn himself referred, especially in his later work,[40] to "situation sense," and in some ways this idea is akin to the "reason" that celebrants of the common law have pointed to at least since Coke. But is this reason, or situation sense, or tacit knowledge, something that is

[37] Llewellyn's point rings far more true for the unsystematized messiness of the common law than for strongly codified civil law legal systems, which often have norms, procedures, and institutions aimed at preventing just the kind of conflicts that Llewellyn found so rampant in common law systems.

[38] I suspect that when the principle of customary international law was first recognized it was widely believed that there were only two relevant groups of nations – the "civilized" (or "advanced") and the "uncivilized" (or "backwards" or "primitive").

[39] The statement in the text is not intended to express a strong moral or legal relativism, but only to recognize that international pluralism may recognize a multiplicity of morally plausible customs even as it insists that some customs are simply beyond the pale, their adoption in one or even many nations notwithstanding.

[40] Karl N. Llewellyn, *The Common Law Tradition: Deciding Appeals* (Boston: Little Brown, 1960).

widely shared, and is it something capable of breaking "ties" when two opposing parties make claims well supported by previous reasonable decisions or current reasonable arguments. In such cases, it is an empirical question as much as a jurisprudential or philosophical one whether law in general, and certainly customary law, is or can be as free of decision-maker preferences as its most vigorous proponents would suggest.

The valence of convergence (or, Kahneman's question)

The traditional picture of interpreting customary law presupposes, perhaps correctly, largely non-skeptical answers to the previous skeptical questions. It assumes that societies, including the international society of nations, have pre-legal customs, mores, rules, principles, guidelines, norms, maxims, and standards that can be identified, more or less, and that have the capacity to prefer one result to another in a significant number of actual disputes. But, even if this largely non-skeptical picture is accurate, and of course it is the picture that undergirds much of the traditional view about customary law, one more question remains.

The non-skeptical account of custom just offered acknowledges that custom is a continuously changing process. Customs change, and they generally do so in incremental response to new acts, events, decisions, and interpretations. And, although as a strictly logical matter any of these incremental changes could be for the worse as well as for the better, it is part of the account of the value of customary law, just as it is part of the account of the value of the common law, that changes will, over time, and on balance, be for the better. The common law "works itself pure," as Lord Mansfield said,[41] in a phrase made famous by Lon Fuller.[42] And so too with custom, it is said. If "custom" is the word we use to identify a group of social decisions aggregated over time and space, and which are then given normative force, then the process of aggregation, the standard picture appears to presuppose, is a largely self-correcting one. Mistakes will be identified and corrected, and, even if this is not invariably the case, it is more often the case than that the sound aspects of custom will be jettisoned only to be replaced by unsound ones. And

[41] Omychund v. Barker, 26 Eng. Rep. 15, 33 (1744).

[42] Lon L. Fuller, *The Law in Quest of Itself* (New York: Beacon Books, 1940), p. 140.

insofar as mistakes are corrected more often than sound practices are discarded, then over time custom gets better, so the conventional account continues, and the law is to be praised for drawing on and treating it as authoritative.

This picture of the self-correcting and thus largely improving nature of custom gains some support from recent work on the virtues of collective wisdom. If groups tend to make better decisions than individuals,[43] then law is well advised to come up with a mechanism to take advantage of this collective wisdom. This is what the common law does with the collectivity of common law judges, so the argument would go, and this is what both the common law and international law do when they treat as authoritative the collective wisdom of, respectively, ordinary people and the community of nations.

There is an intriguing affinity between this image of the operation of custom, on the one hand, and the epistemology embedded in the standard "marketplace of ideas" account of freedom of expression,[44] on the other. When Milton asked, rhetorically, whether anyone ever knew truth to be put to the worst in a free and open encounter,[45] when John Stuart Mill less explicitly held to the same belief in urging that seemingly wrong ideas be allowed to compete with seemingly right ones,[46] and when Karl Popper believed that the open society would be more likely to correct official error than it was to generate errors of its own,[47] all took the position that public epistemology was also self-correcting, and that sound ideas would, over time, prevail over unsound ones because of their soundness.

Much the same set of beliefs undergirds the belief in the value of custom, and indeed in the value of other and similar unregulated social epistemological processes.[48] If custom is valuable because it is informationally efficient,[49] or because it is the accumulated collective wisdom of

[43] See James Surowiecki, *The Wisdom of Crowds* (New York: Anchor Books, 2004).

[44] For an unsympathetic description, see Frederick Schauer, *Free Speech: A Philosophical Enquiry* (Cambridge: Cambridge University Press, 1982), ch. 2.

[45] John Milton, *Areopagitica* (J. C. Suffolk ed., London: University Tutorial Press, 1968), p. 126.

[46] John Stuart Mill, *On Liberty* (D. Spitz ed., New York: W. W. Norton, 1975).

[47] Karl Popper, *The Open Society and Its Enemies* (5th edn, London: Routledge & Kegan Paul, 1966).

[48] On these issues more generally, but with somewhat of a skeptical cast, see Alvin I. Goldman, *Knowledge in a Social World* (New York: Oxford University Press, 2000).

[49] See Clayton P. Gillette, "Harmony and Stasis in Trade Usages for International Sales," *Virginia Journal of International Law*, vol. 39 (1999), pp. 707–36.

people or of nations,[50] then it is premised on the belief that wisdom accumulates more smoothly than error, and that a legal process drawing on custom, and treating custom as authoritative in a content-independent way, will systematically be superior to one that ignores this important source of guidance.

Once again, however, there are skeptical questions to be asked. Is the accumulation of wisdom more likely than the accumulation of error?[51] How much explanatory force does wisdom *qua* wisdom have in explaining which social ideas will "stick" and which will be discarded, especially when compared to, for example, charisma, rhetorical power, and the antecedent needs and beliefs of the audience? Or, as Daniel Kahneman and Amos Tversky, and others, have more recently argued,[52] do various wisdom-independent social processes operate in such a way as to shake our confidence in collective social processes like custom to serve as reliable indicators of wise or valuable social policy? Insofar as this skepticism about collective wisdom is justified, and insofar as the very same processes operate in the interpretation of custom as operate in the development of custom in the first instance, then it may be the custom itself, and certainly the interpretation of it, is appropriately the target for still another skeptical question.

Conclusion: does wisdom matter?

The argument for custom is commonly put in terms of collective wisdom, collective over time and over space, but wisdom may not be the only argument for custom. Customary practice, even if it is systematically worse – or more plausibly systematically no better – than its alternatives, may still be valuable precisely because of its collectivity. That which emerges from collective practices may, to the extent that it is enforced, reinforced, and entrenched by the law, serve as a

[50] Friedrich A. Hayek, *Law, Legislation and Liberty* (Chicago: University of Chicago Press, 1978); Paul G. Mahoney and Chris W. Sanchirico, "Competing Norms and Social Evolution: Is the Fittest Norm Efficient?," *University of Pennsylvania Law Review*, vol. 149 (2001), pp. 2027–61.

[51] See Steven Hetcher, "Creating Safe Social Norms in a Dangerous World?," *Southern California Law Review*, vol. 73 (1999), pp. 1–56.

[52] A fair sampling of the literature is contained in Daniel Kahneman, Paul Slovic, and Amos Tversky, eds., *Judgments Under Uncertainty: Heuristics and Biases* (Cambridge: Cambridge University Press, 1982); Thomas Gilovich, Dale Griffin, and Daniel Kahneman, eds., *Heuristics and Biases: The Psychology of Intuitive Judgment* (Cambridge: Cambridge University Press, 2002).

community-building device for the group whose collective wisdom creates custom. To the extent that international law, for example, draws on international custom, and thus makes the collective practices of nations normative, it reinforces the collectivity of nations, independently of the wisdom of that collectivity, and that may turn out to be a good in itself.

Similarly, the enforcement of custom is the enforcement of that which has achieved a considerable degree of pre-legal compliance. *Ceteris paribus*, therefore, the enforcement and legal incorporation of custom is less costly than the adoption and enforcement of legal norms that challenge rather than further existing practices. Enforcing existing norms against outliers – consider the illegal activities in which few of us would engage even were they lawful, such as cannibalism and pedophilia – is an important function for law, whether domestic or international. But so too is the use of law to change and not to entrench custom. The legal protection of the environment, of endangered species, and of consumers, for example, is decidedly non-customary, and, although these uses of law are typically statutory, it would not be difficult to come up with common law and international law counterparts. Custom is conservative, in the (largely) non-political sense of that term, and, although it has not been my primary focus here, a full analysis of the use of custom authoritatively to inform the law must confront questions about the political valence of custom itself, as well as the political valence of the process of interpreting it.

2

The moral role of conventions

ROSS HARRISON

'Is it a custom?' the visiting Horatio asks Hamlet after hearing ordnance shot off. Hamlet replies that it is ('Ay marry is't'), but says that 'it is a custom more honoured by the breach than the observance'. This paper considers the relationship of custom to what is honourable, moral, the right thing to do. Hamlet's claim can be taken in two distinct ways. Is he making the descriptive claim that people don't actually follow the custom that much, honouring it more by breach than by observance? Or is he making the prescriptive claim that although it is the local custom it would be more honourable to breach it than observe it? The context makes the latter much more likely, not just because of Hamlet's general attitude but because of the particular way that he introduces his claim. He says, 'But to my mind, though I am a native here and to the manner born, it is a custom . . .' Although to the manner (manners; custom) born, he has his own oppositional mind. There is what people generally, the natives, find honourable, which is to fire the cannon when the king drinks. And then there is what Hamlet himself finds honourable, which is not to engage in such frippery. For Hamlet, what people conventionally find right, and consequently conventionally happens, is not what is really right. Or at least, uncertain as he is, he entertains the idea. When, earlier, Hamlet is presented with something 'common', his mother asks, 'Why seems it so particular with thee?'

In this paper I discuss the possibility of so honouring customs by their breach and also discuss, by contrast, whether observance does them honour. Does the conventional lay constraints on the moral? Or, alternatively, is it possible that anything understood to be merely conventional, and so recognised in some sense to be arbitrary, could determine what is moral? My discussion consists of three parts. The first aims to show that morality goes beyond convention. The second, with two strands, aims to show that morality nevertheless requires convention. The third describes particular examples where convention creates moral content and discusses how a consciously recognised merely conventional basis for some action need not destroy its moral force.

Morality reaches beyond convention

I commence by discussing an argument that would, if it worked, show that the content of morality consists of custom. I then claim that the argument does not work. Of course, to refute an argument for a particular conclusion will not establish its negation; it will, however, go some way towards it. So I shall be suggesting that morality must be more than the merely customary; and so, in this sense, must reach beyond convention. (I shall usually drop the rider 'in this sense' from now on. However it should be understood, as James Bernard Murphy clearly brings out in the next paper, that the customary and the conventional are not at all the same thing. In this paper, by 'conventional' I merely mean something that varies with local practice rather than deriving from an independent reality. Hence if something is customary, and custom varies with local practice, it is also, in this sense, conventional.)

First, some background assumptions that I shall not call in doubt. I assume that moral understanding is an appreciation of the normative (prescriptive, action guiding) features of particular kinds of action or states of affairs, and that moral behaviour is action guided by such appreciation. Hence, unproblematically, morals provide reasons for action. Appreciation of these moral characteristics justifies action, and hence also in a particular way explains it.

Such justification of behaviour by appreciated normative features of acts or occasions is exhibited also by behaviour not normally considered moral, such as actions in response to the claims of etiquette, prudence or positive law. How might moral action be distinguished? Etiquette, perhaps, by importance; prudence by content (that is, whose interest is in question). How law? One way (as suggested by H. L. A. Hart) is to suppose that morals cannot be consciously constructed or changed. Hence, although there may be an analogy to a Hartian rule of recognition displayed by the practice of identifying what is moral, this could not be analogous to identifying it as the product of conscious action, such as the acts of a sovereign legislature. In short, law can be consciously made and changed; morality cannot. (You can decide that you were mistaken in your moral judgments, but not decide that, although it is now moral to murder nasty people, after Tuesday it will be immoral. Compare how you can legislate for marital rape to be illegal after Tuesday.)

Now suppose we accept this. Then the following argument would seem to become available. To discover what is distinctive about moral reasons, we need to discover those elements that cannot be changed by conscious will. Since this was introduced by contrast with positive law, one way to do this is to look at sources of law and exclude those that involve such conscious decision. So we need to exclude those cases where at specific times the specific actions of individuals, or groups of individuals, make the law what it is. Such, clearly, is law created by a legislative chamber. But so also, arguably, is law resulting from the interstitial operations of a supreme adjudicative body, which by declaring the law in hard cases in effect makes it. What is left? A third source of law in addition to statute and precedent, namely custom. The argument is that we distinguish morality by excluding the made features of law. So we exclude the first two and are left with custom. Otherwise put: morality, not being consciously made by individuals, necessarily consists of common custom, on what just happens to be there independent of their framing individual wills. (There's honour for you, all the king's men might have said to Hamlet.)

By 'custom' here I mean the immemorial (or at least not specifically decided and dateable) practice of people in a particular context or place. Since other people in other places, or these people in different contexts, may act differently, such customs are in this sense conventional, although it follows from the above argument that they are not consciously set up or adopted conventions. Morality, which is at base custom, is at base merely how people happen to act (here, in this context). Now we are assuming throughout that the action is normatively guided; it is something on which agents have (as Hart would put it) an 'inner' perspective. So we reach the result that this moral action is 'merely' what people, here, happen to think right; what they happen to think properly guides their behaviour or justifies their actions; which they criticise themselves and others for not following; and so on. But at base it is 'mere' custom (or, in this sense, convention). Yet, by exclusion, and in distinction from the other sources of law, this has to be the basis of morality. Hence morality being necessarily customary, is merely conventional.

That is the apparently available argument from the uncontested assumptions to the conclusion that morality is merely conventional. But, even on its own terms, it does not work. What is wrong with it? I don't myself mind the partial overlap between law and morals it implies, as there are other ways to identify law in the overlap area.

(For law it is custom recognised by the courts; custom fitted into a single system by the courts with other sources such as precedent and statute.) And law may well include morality anyway. The interest in the argument is in the implied disanalogy between made material, as law at least partially is, and found material, as (on the hypothesis of this argument) morality is. So the question to focus on is how this disanalogy might apply to the process of adjudication. Must the way in which it is decided (for a particular people) what their morality is be intrinsically different from the way it is decided what their law is?

I think not. That is, the dateable decisions of determinate individuals might decide the morality of a people in the same way as its supreme court decides its law. This may not be the way (in our modern, Western, pluralist world) our own morality operates. But there is nothing in principle against it, and it would also seem to have been at times common practice. In his *Ethical Studies*, F. H. Bradley, like many other moral philosophers before and since, thinks that there is not normally much problem in deciding the right (moral) thing to do. However, where there is, Bradley says that it's the perceptions of the wise that will count. Both terms (perceptions; wise) he puts in Greek, signalling not only how Aristotle was the central text taught in Oxford both then and for hundreds of years before, but also the length and strength of the Aristotelian tradition. In the end, knowledge depends upon a sort of perceptive faculty. This is widely spread among a (properly educated) people. But some people (the wise) have more discriminating perceptions than others. So, although there won't be many cases of difficulty, should there be one, consult the wise.

That is a plausible, or at least long running, account of ethical knowledge. But it seems to me very closely analogous to the finding of law by supreme courts, where the specially trained legal experts see the right answer on a particular, dateable, occasion and by their perception (make? find?) the law. Experts in casuistry correspond to experts in law. However, this creates problems for the original argument. That depended upon putting adjudication beside statute as particular decisions of identifiable particular people, as contrasted with unwilled, immemorial, custom. But now the middle source, conscious adjudication by identifiable experts, looks as if it can discover (produce) morality as well as law. Yet, if so, it looks as if morality has to reach beyond conventional custom. What the experts say goes beyond what was customary before they reached their decision.

But which way does the adjudication analogy cut? That is, does it actually show that morality need not be conventional because it could be constructed and created by the perceptions of the wise? The answer depends very much on whether adjudication in the analogous legal case is taken to be interstitial legislation, a contentious matter. However, hypothetically, if it is interstitial, then morality could similarly be made by the decisions of the wise. Whereas, if the judges merely find rather than make law, then the moral experts might also be thought (contrary to appearance) to find what is moral. And, in this latter alterative, it could be said that they declare what the prevailing custom actually is even though before the hard moral case no one seemed to know. (Raised to a moral supreme court, Justice Hamlet finds that the custom is actually not to fire when the king drinks, although, of course, some people mistakenly do so.)

So far, perhaps, a stand off. But we can find other cases in which, less contentiously, individual agents engage in moral construction, and hence show that morality cannot be just custom or convention. The idea of the wise, as with supreme court justices, is that we have a body of experts who can be identified antecedent to the particular decision. However, this is not essential. People fulfilling this role may only be identified by their success and lack any prior (or independent) authority. They suggest something; it catches on; hence they have shown how things should be. Take Shelley's claim that 'poets are the unacknowledged legislators of the world'. Let us suppose here that there is no paid up, prior, guild of poets; the 'poets' are simply the people who succeed in getting listened to. Yet, if they are listened to, they may change people's perceptions. In doing so, they make the moral law; they are 'legislators'. But, without prior status or authority, they are 'unacknowledged' as such. (By wit alone, poet Hamlet suggests the future moral law, the new and superior custom; and he is listened to only because of the wit and zest of what he suggests and not at all because he is the prince.)

This, again, seems not only possible but also something that actually happens, and with plebeian poets as well as literary aristocrats. Indeed, moral philosophers sometimes suggest that people would be better off reading novels than philosophers if they wish to discover what they ought to do. Trained perception; getting people to see; making the world wise; ambitious aesthetic endeavour. Yet, if any of this is possible or actually happens, then morality must be more than custom or convention. For, in changing people's minds, the poets and novelists get them to see beyond their merely conventional ideas and behaviour. Whatever we think happens with the judgments of the wise (or the judges), we here have making rather than finding. The unacknowledged legislators make the (moral) law. Hence they cannot find what already exists in the customs of the tribe; hence morality is not restricted to the customary or conventional.

Once this idea is started, it need not be restricted to writing (to fiction, to the makings of a mind). Consider 'experiments in living', as J. S. Mill called them in *On Liberty*. Mill's idea here is that part of the value of liberty is that it permits people to experiment in how they live, and the value of that is that it enables moral discovery. That is, by experiment we can find new ways of living that are good for us. (This might be considered prudential rather than moral, but Mill's overarching utilitarian morality makes these hard to distinguish in this context: someone discovering what is good for them sets an example to others and so may promote general happiness.) The alternatives provided to common custom are not only in fictional descriptions but are also given by actual lived experience. Mill is specifically concerned to promote originality, 'genius'. He wishes throughout the essay to promote the unconventional against what people normally think, against the repressive effect of middle class public opinion. For him, and following from these premises, morality is not merely conventional. Indeed, it is necessary that it should not be so. (So Hamlet experiments . . . No, that way madness lies.)

These three examples, different from each other as they are, all show that, even if we accept the original premises that people can't consciously make morality in the way they make law, we are not forced to the conclusion that it therefore has to be constituted by prevailing custom. We may accept that mere will, or fiat, is inappropriate, but also recognise that processes phenomenologically more like perception than will may nevertheless result in morality being changed, or made, rather than it merely being declared, or found. Hence morality is more than the merely customary; morality reaches beyond convention.

That morality necessarily contains, or connects with, convention

The argument above, if it works, shows that there is more to morality than convention. In this section, I attempt to demonstrate that, even so, morality cannot dispense with it. I shall do this in two, independent, subsections, both connected with arguments in moral philosophy about moral justification. The first is based upon a claim about the way that justification should proceed; the second on the claim that it is impossible.

Reflective equilibrium

At about the time that the classically-educated Oxford philosopher F. H. Bradley published *Ethical Studies*, the classically-educated Cambridge philosopher Henry Sidgwick published *The Methods of Ethics*. In this Sidgwick describes at considerable length what he calls 'common sense morality'. The 'book' (or part of this work) in which these chapters occur has the overall title 'Intuitionism'. In it, Sidgwick describes the 'common morality which I and my reader share'. He then subjects it to a process of what he calls 'an effort of reflection' to see if it can be made consistent and determinate in the way that we expect from ethical theory. He thinks that it cannot. But before this book ends, he introduces utilitarianism and, here and in the next book, claims that utilitarianism makes the morality of common sense consistent. Therefore, he says, common sense displays 'unconscious utilitarianism'. Sidgwick is making no claim for originality of method here: in the idea of laying out the morality of his group in this way, he is consciously and explicitly following Aristotle; and the conclusion about utilitarianism and common sense is in the spirit of Hume, and also to some extent of Mill.

John Rawls has been the major influence in restarting serious philosophical argument about what we should do (as opposed to what it means to say that we should do it). He did not, of course, accept Sidgwick's utilitarianism. But he was clearly influenced by Sidgwick's method in discovering how it might be possible to do substantive normative theory. There are three elements in the brief account I have just given of Sidgwick which are important in how it influenced Rawls and so, via Rawls, how it influences us. These are common sense, reflection, and intuition. The Latin etymology of 'intuition' may mask that it is another perceptual term: to look into something. So, again, the idea is that we have a faculty of ethical knowledge, or perception, whereby we can immediately 'see' (or know) the right thing to do in many cases; unreflectively, unproblematically, and such as to give clear and unmediated reasons for action. (Sidgwick typically and carefully defines 'intuitive' as something whose 'truth is apparently known immediately, and not as the result of reasoning'; he notes that etiquette is also in this way intuitive.)

This intuition is 'common sense'. Although Sidgwick did not change the meaning of this term, I think he may have helped make one meaning more prominent. For Sidgwick it always means what is common to a people; that is, their general, shared, ethical perception. (At one point he segues from 'consensus' to 'common sense'.) Earlier, 'common sense' tended to mean instead what was common to separate senses (such as sight and touch), rather than common to separate people. It designated basic wit or intelligence, such as a resistance to affirming contradictions; whatever is held to be 'sense' or 'sensible'. (Deconstruct: 'Make her see sense'; she uses sense to see, and what she should see is sense. Why is 'sensible' not the contrary to 'insensible'?) The two uses of 'common sense' connect in that what is basic sense to each person can also be expected to be common between people. Try it for a prudential example: telling someone that touching that wire will be lethal gives a reason not to do it. This is only common sense; anyone can see that.

What we get out of this is that it is possible to describe the common moral knowledge, or beliefs, of a people. That it is common is a check on the truth of the description, but the nature of what is common is best captured by thinking of it as like perception, as an elementary sense, as an immediate apprehension of its object that people in general act on unthinkingly and confidently. That is the first two of the three elements, intuition and common sense. To these Sidgwick adds that the philosopher (if not the common people having the common sense) can engage in 'reflection' on it and make it systematic in ways that the common people are unaware of, particularly by relating it to an overarching theory of the philosopher's (such as utilitarianism).

What Rawls called the 'reflective equilibrium' is such a process of balancing theory and immediate intuitions. Theory is clarified and corrected by connecting it with particular moral judgments. (So that, for example, if utilitarianism tells us to kill Granny and give her money to Oxfam, we may intuitively feel that there is some mistake somewhere.) But that is only half the story; this would just be to take theory as an inductively based generalisation on particular judgments, refutable by a counterexample. The other half of the story is that we may also refine and correct our particular intuitions by seeing how they stand with the best theory. (So that if utilitarianism generally seems okay but does not dictate a requirement to be chaste, we may think that our intuitions about chastity are wonky.) It is in this way that Sidgwick tries to refine and improve the ethics of common sense, and it is the tacking between, and balancing of, the two perspectives that gives the promise of a justificatory method in morals which is not just banal (because it does not just reproduce what is already known), but may also be potentially convincing (since it assumes and builds on the already known).

In this account, there are two different ways in which 'particular' can be contrasted with 'general': particular people with people in general; particular perceptions with general theory. These are quite independent. However, in standard reflective equilibrium method they work together. General perceptions of particular cases or rules (called 'intuitive') are reflected on and refined by the general theory of a particular philosopher.

If it is correct that the philosopher's justificatory account depends upon presuming that there are common, shared, immediate, ethical intuitions in a particular people, then such justification is only possible if it is assumed that there is a common, customary, morality forming one base of the justification. In the first part of this paper it was suggested that not all morality has to be conventional. The reflective equilibrium more specifically suggests that conventional morality can be transcended so that justified moral advance, change, or correction, may be made. However, the presupposition of the method is that there has to be some conventional or customary morality if there is to be any such justification. So, although not all morality has to be conventional, some must be so. Some must have no other basis than being what people, here, now, happen to think or do.

Is this argument any good? It would only show that there has to be conventional morality if it may be presupposed that there has to be justification in morals and also presupposed or demonstrated that the only possible method of such justification is ultimately of such reflective equilibrium manner. ('Ultimately', because there obviously could be justification by authorities, such as doing what the book, God, or the church says; the claim would be that such justification would be intermediate because the authority itself had to be justified; and that could only be done by a reflective equilibrium method, in which the authority stands in the position of the general theory.) Needless to say, nothing like that is attempted here; these are only first suggestions. But it does seem to me that such claims are not obviously false or absurd. The short, first sketch of an argument for them would be: we do not wish to act in a manner that could not be justified; justification eventually relies either on a foundational, self-justifying, belief or on coherence between beliefs; the former is implausible; the latter implies that what we want to justify has to, on the whole, cohere with what we already believe; hence we have to start with where we are, namely our common beliefs; common sense morality is the ship with which we start even if we may rebuild it while still at sea.

Moral scepticism

The ascent to a meta position characteristic of philosophical inquiry can have corrosive effects on the truth or reality of matters taken for granted in the base, or unascended, position. Knowing the right thing to do may seem straightforward before philosophical reflection. However, once this reflection suggests that there are no independent moral values sitting there objectively in the world waiting to be discovered, then it ceases to be so straightforward. How may we assume that we know such things when there is nothing there to be known?

Notoriously (and neatly put by Hume in his playing backgammon passage), such philosophical reflection usually has zero effect on practice: the philosopher who disproves matter still eats breakfast; the philosophers who prove themselves to be alone in the universe wish to convince others that they are correct. So also here, it might be thought. We have a working practice of making moral judgments. Therefore once we get out of the study and go to play at backgammon or morality, we can pick up this practice and everything can go on as before.

There are, however, good reasons why the co-existence of an everyday practice and a philosophical belief in its basic invalidity is less stable in the moral (and religious) case than elsewhere. Other scepticisms have the form of play or hypothesis. It cannot absolutely be proved that there are tables, numbers, other people, and so on. But we assume the apples; what we seem to be eating is satisfying; and doubting the apples does not destroy the satisfaction. So such doubts seem no more than elegant intellectual play. It is otherwise with the belief that there are not (or may not be) objective values or gods. This is not play; it is real and serious. Here, to many, the philosophical sceptical arguments actually seem to work. And this, it seems, must set a problem in this area unmatched elsewhere. How can people still happily behave as if it is just true that they should do certain things once they also believe that there are no such truths to be had? Or, in terms of the previous subsection, how can morality described in terms of common sense or intuition be taken as a foundation for justification once it is discovered that there is not actually anything there to be sensed or intuited? Common sense is, of course, common; there is agreement in different people's judgments. But the fact of agreement in judgments can be explained independently of their being caused by the truth; so agreement in judgments does not entail their truth; it could, for example, arise from the interest of a ruling class in promoting an ideology.

It seems therefore that philosophical scepticism in this area should have a radical effect on our common moral beliefs and practices. Once we realise that they have no foundation in reality, we naturally get a sense of vertigo. There is nothing underneath but great depths, nothing to hold us secure where we are. I avoid here the tricky philosophical question of how good the sceptical moral argument actually is. Instead, I shall more simply assess whether it ought to have such a radical consequence for common moral belief. That is, does scepticism about the independent reality of the objects of moral judgment entail that our common or conventional beliefs cannot be also moral? I wish to argue that it does not. Rather than scepticism about moral truth destroying our common morality, it instead demonstrates that morality has nowhere but convention to go. So the conclusion, as in the previous subsection, is that morality requires convention.

I think that it is best to illustrate the possibilities by actual cases. So I shall consider what actual sceptics actually said. The sceptical claim is that all we have is a play of conflicting appearances with no underlying reality. Historically, this claim was made in the late Greek scepticism and resurfaced in Western Europe after the Renaissance. (Here, as elsewhere, rebirth went with rediscovery of ancient materials.) Its best expression, and the example I shall use, is in French thinkers from Montaigne through Charron to Bayle. Justice is seen to vary as you cross the mountains; it is one thing in France, another in Spain; so how can it be really just? As Montaigne puts it, 'if a man's justice and equity had any substance and real existence he would not let it be bound by the conditions of this country or that'. Scepticism has a destructive edge, removing the reality of justice and morality. So, or at least so it might seem, we should stop making judgments in terms of justice or morality.

Charron followed Montaigne, and his sceptical commitment is shown by the fact that he carved on the front of his house 'I know nothing', whereas Montaigne more modestly merely carved 'What do I know?' on the beam of his work room. Charron holds that 'laws and customs are maintained in credit, not because they are just and good, but because they are laws and customs: this is the mystical foundation of their authority, they have no other.' (This is from the contemporary English translation; the original, like the graffiti, was in French.) So there is nothing to rest on apart from what we do; there is no justice; there is no authority beyond custom.

This, again, seems to be merely destructive. But, in fact, these thinkers incline more to support than destruction. They turn the question round: custom may be all that we have but, on the other hand, we do happen to have it. So, with nothing beneath custom to justify it, custom itself gets ennobled, or given mystical authority. 'Now the advice which I have to give to him that would be wise', says Charron in *On Wisdom*, 'is to keep and observe both in word and deed the laws and customs he findeth established in the country where he is.' With no place else to go, you stay and endorse where you are. Hence these sceptics support what in its religious application is called 'fideism'; we should have faith in our own God precisely because this is beyond reason and, in particular, because reason cannot be used to show that there is a superior God. So also in practical life. We should keep with the customs of our country because reason cannot show anything to be wrong with them. Justice may be no more than appearance, but I accept how justice appears on my side of the mountain.

Better known than these other sixteenth- and seventeenth-century French thinkers is Descartes. He does not belong to this tradition; indeed his aim is to refute it. However, he knew it, and in *The Discourse on the Method* he assigns himself a temporary habitation in which he can rest until he has completed his task of anti-sceptical construction. Accordingly, he sets himself some rules, the first of which is to obey the laws and customs of his country as well as retaining his childhood belief in God. That is the only place to rest in a sceptical world. And in this area of enquiry even Descartes never escaped his self-assigned refugee accommodation.

So scepticism, which seems to start with such a radical spirit, may naturally end in deep-dyed conservatism. Lacking a foundation, there is no place else to go and so we conserve the customs of our country. There is an analogy here with the decline of confidence in the British utilitarian tradition, from Bentham through Mill to Sidgwick. The utilitarian principle starts with Bentham as a 'fundamental axiom'; that is, as a deliverance of moral truth by which contemporary practices can be castigated and corrected. There is no need to respect conventional custom, indeed most of it, particularly in politics and law, is held to be badly mistaken. This is radical thought. It wants to seize contemporary thought and society by the roots and, by rebuilding it from base, make it better. (The 'principle of utility' is 'the foundation of that system, the object of which is to rear the fabric of felicity by the hands of reason and of law'.)

By contrast, when we get to Mill, we are told that 'all rational creatures go out upon the sea of life with their minds made up on the common questions of right and wrong'. Nor are such made up minds to be disturbed; when we so go to sea the moral Nautical Almanack has already been calculated. We have had the 'experience' of the 'whole past duration of the human species', and this has given us what we need to know about morals. So, unlike Bentham, our own common experience, the place where we start, is basically already correct. We need no independent, radical, axiom. Even Mill's notorious 'proof' of the utility principle aims to show its correctness by citing facts about what people actually, pre-theoretically, desire. Then, as seen in the previous subsection, when we get to Sidgwick we advance by reflecting on common sense. As with scepticism, so in this Utilitarian tradition. What starts in a radical spirit ends up by being conservative. Rather than criticising and discarding common belief and custom, it accepts it. The best it hopes for is to improve common belief from within. Adrift on the sea of life it mainly relies on the pre-calculated almanac but occasionally rebuilds small parts of the ship in the only way possible while still at sea.

This brings out an assumption used but not mentioned in the argument with which the previous part of this paper began. If there were an independent moral reality, a Platonic form of the good, then people (or gods) with the right receptive faculties could apprehend its truths. That way, there could be a form of intuition, so that morality was found rather than made, and yet which was completely independent of custom. (Customs are the mere varying appearances of our lesser, lower, world and no guide at all to independent moral reality.) This Platonic picture would provide another reason, in addition to those mentioned, why the initial argument does not work. With it we could find moral (and possibly also legal) truth without resort to custom (or, in the legal case, statute or previous adjudication). However, such Platonism is currently rarely accepted, and the initial argument tacitly assumed that it was false. If true, it is another way out, and the necessary connection of morality with custom eluded. If false (as is more normally supposed), then this fits with what has just been said about scepticism. (In this brief sketch, 'Platonism', as in the philosophy of mathematics, means the doctrine that our knowledge is of entities whose existence and properties are independent of such knowledge or perception; nothing is being implied about what Plato actually thought.)

The result is that there is no place to go but custom. Or, to fit the two sections of this part together, no place to go but custom or the kind of revision of custom involved in the reflective equilibrium method. Lacking an independent place on which to stand, we cannot move the world; and so all revision or discovery has to be from the inside. We have, with Descartes, to start with the house we happen to inhabit.

Recognising behaviour as conventional does not destroy its moral force

Perhaps, as suggested in the previous section, some convention is required to give morality content. However, it may be thought that it can do so only as long as the conventional is not consciously recognised as such. Once it is recognised that an action is merely conventional, and so in that sense arbitrary, does this not destroy its moral force? For, or so at least it might be thought, once it is recognised that action varies from place to place and has no better basis than being what we happen here to do, then it cannot constitute something as important as morality. The moral 'must' is imperial and hard, not flabby and blown round by circumstance. Or so it might be thought. But, in this last section, I aim to show that this is not so. Its conclusion will be that morality happily contains recognisably merely conventional content.

In fact, I think this is easy to show and all that is needed is to assemble some reminders as to when and why morality includes recognised merely conventional elements. Let us start with a (seemingly) trivial case, language. It is purely conventional what sounds mean in a particular language. Hence, for example, it rests on nothing more than custom that 'promise' in English means promise. However, because this is in fact the local convention, I here, now, (with the standard background conditions) communicate that I am promising by saying 'I promise'. Hence the purely conventional content has moral force. Because the conventions are as they are, I become morally liable for what I, understanding these conventions, say. I use the conventions to communicate; others are entitled to rely on what I communicate; hence I am morally liable for any detrimental reliance.

That is a simple example with which to start, a reminder of how we can do things with words. However, we can also do words with things.

Non-verbal behaviour can also communicate in a conventional or customary manner, and people understanding these conventions will understand the communication. Hence, again, I may be liable for what I do because of purely conventional understandings of what this signifies. Knowing this, I may properly be taken to communicate the conventional understanding and so am responsible for making such a communication. To behave as the Romans do in Rome is to communicate something to other Romans that would not be communicated by the same kind of behaviour elsewhere.

Before considering a more specific example of this, consider the general idea of behaving properly. The root, or original, idea of the 'proper' is what is idiosyncratic or particular to something. So, in liturgy, the 'propers' are the set prayers for that particular day; to use the 'proper' application form is to use the one specifically having that function. Therefore propriety is like property: it is what particularly belongs to us. (Hobbes' word for property is in fact 'propriety'; behind all this sits the Latin 'proprius', one's own.) Hence to do the proper thing is to do our own particular thing; to behave properly is to behave in accordance with the conventions, or idiosyncratic behaviour, of our own particular tribe.

With that in mind, let us return to a particular example of saying things by flowers, or behaving in the proper way. Consider the customs and rituals connected with death, funerals and consolation of the bereaved. These obviously vary markedly in different societies and at different times and places. Yet in these situations most of us are concerned to do the proper thing, to discover the proper thing to do. That is, we want to know exactly what the local conventions are since we wish to use these conventions to communicate our feelings about the deceased. That we may think the customs silly or inappropriate may therefore be as irrelevant as thinking that 'promise' is a silly word for promise; we are caught by where we happen to be.

The key idea here is that of respect. In funerals we wish to show our respect. Respect, the recognition of the humanity and moral status of another individual, is a morally important attitude; perhaps the fundamental moral attitude. To be moral is to treat people with respect. It is morally important not just to have respect, but also to show it and act upon it. We must be able, that is, to communicate our respect. But to do this we have to use the conventional or local means of communicating. Therefore we have to respect the conventions since only by respecting the conventions can we show that we respect the people whose conventions these are. Hence consciously merely conventional behaviour has on occasion a morally significant role.

As always, there is interplay between the different normative areas here: prudence, etiquette, morality. A feeling of self-worth is important to people, so they are sensitive to disrespect. Given this, it may on occasion be prudential to avoid anything that might be construed as dissing merely to avoid the knife supplied between the ribs by someone sensitive to being dissed. Mere prudence may prevent us acting in ways that might get construed as demeaning others. Yet, in so far as being demeaned or hurt is bad in itself, it is more than prudential to avoid it. It is also moral; we shouldn't do it because it is bad for others.

And what of etiquette? An implicit problem above was that morality, if merely conventional, might collapse into etiquette. They are both no more than what this tribe happens to do. However there is a way of generalising what has just been said so that, by contrast, etiquette becomes moral. Following from the general idea of the importance of respect, it is, presumably, not just etiquette but also moral to be polite and avoid unjustified rudeness. But, so far as this is so, it involves following the conventional, local, forms; of understanding and respecting local etiquette. At least in particular contexts, such as the one I sketched above of funeral observances, bad manners may be bad morals. The proper thing to do is to do the done thing.

From this we can move to the importance, including the moral importance, of co-ordination. For, as is well known, convention co-ordinates. It enables a group of people to rely on expectations about each other's behaviour. Let us start with the simple, hackneyed, example of which side of the road to drive. This is clearly conventional; the answer changes crossing the English Channel just as justice changes crossing the Pyrenees. It just happens, here, that we drive on the left. But because this is what the local custom happens to be, this is therefore what we should also do. And do it for several different kinds of reasons, including moral ones. Although driving on the left is purely conventional, what we morally ought to do is set by this convention and depends upon it.

I said 'several reasons', because, as it happens, there is in this case also a legal reason. Driving on the left is part (here) of the positive law. But, even if this were not so, there would still be a clear moral reason to observe the convention, as well as clear prudential ones. So, to rehearse the obvious, if I drive on the left I am less likely to run into the car coming round the corner, because, the convention being what it is, I may reasonably expect it also to be driving on the left. The convention co-ordinates our activities so that we do not crash. My desire not to crash gives me a prudential reason for respecting the convention. But I also have a moral reason. I do not only want the other car not to hurt me, I also want not to hurt it. More generally, something that enables us to move freely without death and destruction is a good thing. Hence establishing and observing conventions that enable us to co-ordinate our movements is a good thing. Hence it is important that we should do what we can to observe and strengthen the convention. Hence we ought to do what is conventional. (And, given the stakes in terms of death and injury, I take it that this is a moral 'ought'.)

Consideration of the importance of co-ordination leads us to well-trodden topics in political philosophy, such as the importance of states and law. With enacted positive law, co-ordination may be achieved by explicit fiat and sanctions, making us better able to rely on each other's behaviour. And, in so far as the above moral material applies, there are moral reasons for having and obeying such positive law. The convention is good, so what upholds the convention is good. But these reasons apply also in some cases of conventions unsanctioned by law. The desirability of co-ordination and the good effects it produces are enough to make a moral reason for observing and strengthening conventions. We have, therefore, cases in which we ought to do something because it happens to be the conventional thing to do. We find out what we ought to do by discovering what, here, is conventionally done. That it rests on nothing more than mere convention and that we may be consciously aware that this is so do not prevent it being a correct source of moral behaviour.

In these cases there is mutual benefit in having an established way of doing things, even though the particular way adopted may be purely conventional (accidental; local). The mutual benefit (which may therefore also be enforced or upheld by law) requires people to act in the expected, even though merely conventional, ways. They are justified in so doing. I started with the easiest cases, such as conventions about movements when no one wants to crash. Here there is universal mutual benefit. It is harder if the benefit is general, but not universal. Then a person in the minority will not have a prudential reason to follow the convention. However, they will still have a moral one. Similarly with free rider problems, when someone wishes to benefit from others' following of the convention, but not to do so themselves. These are all familiar problems, but they do not, I think, show something particularly problematic about morals depending on conventional content. They are, rather, problems about being moral, whatever its content, and about how to combine moral requirements with individual prudential, self-interested, behaviour. We come full circle back to where we started, with promising. Just as with promising, in these cases also, it is others' justified reliance on what I am going to do that gives me my moral reason for action.

A different kind of case is where a line has to be drawn somewhere across a continuum. The line has to be drawn somewhere, but the particular point at which it is drawn is accidental or conventional. Age is an example, and in law people acquire particular abilities at particular ages. There is no suggestion that the passage of a minute makes that much difference to someone's capacity to vote or give consent to sexual relations, or that everyone's capacity develops at exactly the same rate. However, for legal purposes, it is important that there is a particular line; there is a difference in kind in the way people are legally treated on each side of the line, even though the underlying rationale only exhibits differences of degree. Here, I think, morals may be less analogous to law than in the co-ordination cases. Precision is perhaps less important, and parents are used to giving children gradually increasing responsibility. However, there is nothing preventing convention similarly drawing a precise line across a continuum; and as with the law it would enable people to know both what to expect and also whether they had been properly treated.

I conclude therefore that morality both may and should contain merely conventional elements, and that the consciousness that this is the case does not necessarily undercut its moral force.

3

Habit and convention at the foundation of custom

JAMES BERNARD MURPHY*

Introduction: a circle of concepts: nature, custom, stipulation

Philosophical jurisprudence, from Plato to Hans Kelsen, rests upon three fundamental concepts of order and three allied concepts of law: the order intrinsic to human nature grounds the natural law, the order found in informal social practices grounds the customary law, and deliberately stipulated order grounds enacted law. As with many sets of foundational concepts, these are often defined or at least described in terms of each other.[1] This set of analogies and disanalogies between nature, custom, and deliberate stipulation forms the deep structure of traditional philosophical jurisprudence: they are the conceptual lenses and tools by which philosophical analysis of law has proceeded. The history of philosophical jurisprudence reveals how rare it is to examine the lenses by which we see and the tools by which we dissect.[2]

* While revising this chapter, I have benefited greatly from the comments of Amanda Perreau-Saussine, Luke Swaine, Ferenc Horcher, Margaret Atkins, and the participants in the conference on "The Nature of Customary Law." I also want to thank my tireless research assistants and editors, Kirsten Murray and Lauren Rocco.

1 This circle of concepts lives on in Pierre Bourdieu's recent description of custom (*habitus*) both as "immanent law" and as "history turned into nature." Bourdieu, *Outline of a Theory of Practice*, trans. Richard Nice (Cambridge: Cambridge University Press, 1977), pp. 78–81.

2 Theories of positive law, for example, oscillate unstably between two implicit contrasts, with natural law and with customary law. Positive law is said to lack the intrinsic moral force of natural law: Aquinas, for example, contrasts the natural law precept ("you shall not kill") with the positive law precept ("you shall not wear garments sewn from wool and linen together"). In relation to natural law, then, the theory of positive law is an account of the relation between morality and law: does all law have some kind of moral force? Is there a moral obligation to obey the law? At the same time, however, positive law is also contrasted with customary law, in the sense that positive law is deliberately imposed or posited from above while customary law grows up from below. I analyze the structure of the discourse of positive law in Plato, Aquinas, Hobbes, and Austin in my book, *The Philosophy of Positive Law: Foundations of Jurisprudence* (New Haven: Yale University Press, 2005).

Sometimes customary habits are compared to natural instincts because they operate spontaneously, automatically, and tacitly. Custom here means a kind of second nature: our customary habits operate as unobtrusively as our breathing. In this sense, custom is like natural instinct except that it is learned in a particular social context. Yet custom is also described as a set of informal conventions, a set of practices of social coordination that arise from informal agreements without being imposed by enacted law. Custom here is an unwritten law: customary conventions differ from enacted conventions only by not being deliberately imposed.

Custom, in short, must be analyzed into two more basic notions: habit and convention. Habit and convention are logically independent. Not all habits are customary habits: many habits are purely idiosyncratic and do not serve as coordinating conventions. Similarly, many conventions are not habits. Indeed, some conventions are designed never to become habits, like the conventions defining what is fashionable or the conventions defining secret codes. Mathematicians and other special communities often adopt explicit conventions of notation, of procedure, or of protocol that, at least initially, are not habitual. Or, to use Hume's example, two rowers coordinating their strokes may do so by signal or by deliberate imitation without any element of habit. As we shall see, conventions over time often depend upon the formation of supportive habits, but not all conventions rest on habits. All customs are habitual conventions and conventional habits: custom naturalizes conventions just as it conventionalizes human nature. Clear thinking about custom will require us to distinguish the dimension of the habitual from the dimension of the conventional. I sketch such an analysis in this paper.

Both the triadic framework of nature, custom, and stipulation as well as the analysis of custom into habit and convention are to be found, at least implicitly, in the philosophy of Aristotle. Much of his most influential legal thought – the discussions of natural law, unwritten law, and equity in the *Rhetoric* – may have amounted to little more than a collection of argumentative commonplaces in his day. Nonetheless, Aristotle's legal thought has hugely influenced the development of the Western legal tradition and many contemporary legal scholars have developed the nuggets of his thought into complex theories of legal justice, legal reasoning, and legal education.[3] And I believe that clear

[3] See the collection of recent Aristotelian legal scholarship and legal theory in Richard O. Brooks and James Bernard Murphy, *Aristotle and Modern Law* (Burlington, VT: Dartmouth Publishing, 2003).

and careful thinking about custom and its relation to law requires us to follow Aristotle. This chapter develops his notions of habit and convention in relation to each other and in relation to what we mean by custom and customary law.

Transcending the nature–convention dichotomy[4]

The familiar dichotomy between nature and convention, or, as we now say, nature and nurture, displaces the unique role of custom. The ancient Greek Sophists famously framed our analysis of human social institutions in terms of a stark choice between what is natural and what is conventional.[5] Yet the greatest of the Sophists had already begun to transcend this stark dichotomy. Protagoras said: "Learning from teaching (*didaskalia*) requires both nature (*phusis*) and practice (*askēsis*)."[6] Plato also developed a version of this triad when he observed that "if you have a natural ability (*phusei*) for rhetoric, you will become a famous rhetorician, provided you supplement your ability with knowledge (*epistēmē*) and practice (*meletē*)."[7] Aristotle, in turn, agrees on the need for all three qualities: "Now some think that we become good by nature (*phusei*), others by habit (*ethei*), still others by teaching

4 My discussion here and in the next section of the kinds of social order and the logic of social order draws freely from my own work. See *The Moral Economy of Labor: Aristotelian Themes in Economic Theory* (New Haven: Yale University Press, 1993), "Nature, Custom, and Reason in Aristotelian Political Science" in *The Review of Politics* 64 (Summer 2002), 469–95, and *The Philosophy of Positive Law: Foundations of Jurisprudence* (New Haven: Yale University Press, 2005).

5 Throughout the fifth century, nomos and phusis were treated as antithetical. Some Sophists championed phusis (Antiphon, Callicles) while others championed nomos (Glaukon, Protagoras). See W. K. C. Guthrie, *History of Greek Philosophy* vol. 3 (Cambridge: Cambridge University Press, 1969), chapter 4.

6 Protagoras in *Die Fragmente der Vorsokratiker*, ed. Hermann Diels and Walter Kranz (Berlin: Weidmannsche Verlagsbuchhandlung, 1954), frag. 3. Usually *didaskalia* is rendered as "teaching" but Paul Shorey is right to argue that "learning" fits the context better, since the focus is on the conditions that promote successful learning in the student, of which teaching is only one. Shorey traces the history of Protagoras's triadic conception of education through Plato and all the way to Cicero's *ingenii, exercitatio dicendi, ratio aliqua* (*Pro Archias*). See his "*Physis, Meletē, Epistēmē*" in *Transactions and Proceedings of the American Philological Association* 40 (1909), 185–201.

7 Plato, *Phaedrus* 269D. Greek text: Oxford Classical Texts, ed. John Burnet (Oxford: Clarendon Press, 1901). All Plato translations from *Plato: Complete Works*, ed. John Cooper (Indianapolis: Hackett, 1997).

(*didakē*)."[8] Some Sophists argued that intellectual and moral excellences come from natural genius; others argued that these virtues come from deliberate teaching. But Protagoras, Plato, and Aristotle reframe the analysis. Rather than accept the choice between nature or convention, they insist on both. In this view, man is by nature a conventional animal and social conventions are how we actualize our natural potential.

The dichotomy between nature and convention obscures the crucial distinction between conventions that arise from tacit practice and conventions that are deliberately stipulated. True, we can assimilate custom to the notion of convention by distinguishing formal from informal conventions, but custom also refers to the tacit or intuitive dimension of social life. And we can assimilate customary habits to the notion of natural instincts, but then custom also refers to conventions. Therefore, it requires very Procrustean methods to force custom into the familiar dichotomy between nature and convention.

Why attempt to transcend the Sophistic dichotomy? First, a human being apart from all cultural artifice would lack his very nature. The challenge is to understand how nature and culture interact both in the development of each individual person and in the development of human social and political life. Secondly, custom tends to naturalize our conventions by making them intuitive and automatic. Individuals acquire their intellectual and moral excellence both by tacit emulation and by explicit instruction; societies acquire their conventions both by tacit practices of social custom and by the deliberate institution of legislation. When conventions become habitual they evolve from being objects of analysis to modes of analysis: habitual conventions are not what we see but the means by which we see. That is why every society depends upon foreigners to describe its customs: we cannot see our own customs because we see with them.

Aristotle used this triadic logic of explanation more than any other ancient thinker. He says, for example, "in order to become good and wise requires three things; these are nature, habit, and reason (*phusis*,

[8] Aristotle, *Nicomachean Ethics*, 1179b 20. Greek text: Oxford Classical Texts, ed. L. Bywater (Oxford: Clarendon Press, 1894). All Bekker numbers keyed to the Greek texts. To render certain technical terms consistently in English, I have sometimes altered the generally excellent translations in *The Complete Works of Aristotle*, ed. Jonathan Barnes (Princeton: Princeton University Press, 1984).

ethos, logos)."[9] Here Aristotle is speaking of the components of moral and intellectual self-realization: we must begin with the right natural capacities, we must cultivate these capacities into the right dispositions and habits of character, and we must use reason to reflectively adjust our habits in light of our ideals. In this model of self-realization, our habits presuppose our nature but cannot be reduced to it, just as our rational ideals presuppose our habits but cannot be reduced to them. Aristotle extended his triad beyond individual self-realization to the actualization of the political community. Thus, he says in many places (e.g. *Politics* 1332b 8–11), the legislator, in the deliberate stipulation of law, must take into account the natural capacities of his citizens as well as their social customs.

Although this triadic model of social explanation never achieved the ubiquity and familiarity of the Sophistic dichotomy, it appears frequently throughout the history of Western theories of language and of law. In the theory of language, we find John Poinsot (John of St. Thomas) asking "whether the division of signs into natural (*naturale*), stipulated (*ad placitum*), and customary (*ex consuetudine*) is a sound division."[10] By natural signs he means those signs that relate to their objects independently of human activity: smoke is a sign of fire. By customary signs he means those signs that arise from the tacit social practices of human communities: napkins on a table are a sign that dinner is imminent. By stipulated signs he means those signs whose meaning is deliberately appointed by an individual, as when a new word is introduced.[11] In the history of jurisprudence, our triad appears in a variety of guises. The author of the *Rhetorica Ad Herennium* (II, 19) says that law (*ius*) can arise by nature (*natura*), by statute (*lege*), and by custom (*consuetudine*) as well as in other ways. The jurist Ulpian famously distinguishes natural law, the customary law of nations, and civil law (*Digest* 1.1.1).

Recently, Friedrich Hayek has argued that the nature–convention dichotomy embodies the assumption that all social order is either natural or deliberately instituted, thereby ignoring the crucial role of

[9] Aristotle, *Politics* 1332a 38. Greek text: Oxford Classical Texts, ed. W. D. Ross (Oxford: Clarendon Press, 1957).

[10] John Poinsot, *Tractatus de Signis* [1632], ed. and trans. John Deely (Berkeley: University of California Press, 1985), p. 269.

[11] For a critique and reconstruction of Poinsot's doctrine of signs, see James Bernard Murphy, "Nature, Custom, and Stipulation in the Semiotic of John Poinsot" in *Semiotica* 83 1/2 (1991), 33–68.

spontaneous order, such as we find in language, law, and the market. "Yet much of what we call culture is just such a spontaneously grown order [e.g. custom], which arose neither altogether independently of human action [nature] nor by design [stipulation], but by a process that stands between these two possibilities, which were long considered as exclusive alternatives."[12] Hayek traces his notion of spontaneous order to Adam Ferguson: "Nations stumble upon establishments, which are indeed the result of human action, but not the execution of any human design."[13] Hayek argues that the totalitarian disasters of the twentieth century all shared the hubris of attempting to impose a deliberately stipulated order on society without regard for the existing natural and customary social orders in place. In his view, these totalitarian projects were not just crimes, they were also mistakes – the mistake of thinking that natural and customary social order could be replaced by deliberately designed order.

If we are to understand custom, we must transcend the false dichotomy between nature and convention. Custom, Janus-like, faces toward human nature and toward stipulated law. Custom turns our natural propensities toward eating, competing, and mating into complex conventions of dining, gaming, and marrying; custom also turns our deliberate rational and legal conventions of arguing, evaluating, and judging into tacit practices as spontaneous and fluid as natural instinct. Custom transforms the raw material of our generic human nature into a second, culturally specific nature: for example, we are born with the potential to learn any natural language – a propensity that custom transforms into a particular natural language. It is revealing that we call the systems of highly artificial linguistic conventions "natural" languages. Our customary languages are natural in two senses: they arise from our innate propensities, are developed into very complex and artificial systems of sound and meaning, and then, through the mechanisms of habituation, they become as tacit, spontaneous, and fluid as natural instinct. In this way our innate natural linguistic capacities are conventionalized just as our artificial linguistic conventions are naturalized.

Custom is able to effect this double transformation because of the close psychological relation of habit-formation and social convention.

[12] F. A. Hayek, "Kinds of Order in Society" [1964], in *The Politicization of Society*, ed. Kenneth Templeton, Jr. (Indianapolis: Liberty Press, 1979), p. 509.

[13] Adam Ferguson, *An Essay on the History of Civil Society* (Edinburgh: A. Millar and T. Caddel, 1767), p. 187.

If our habits were not shaped by social convention and if our social conventions were not generally habituated, there would be a deep chasm between our natural propensities and our social conventions. Our spoken languages would feel as forced and artificial as Esperanto or Fortran; our social life as challenging and strange as Kabuki theater. We would have to choose between the easy but crude natural propensities to grunt or to feed and the very demanding but refined conventions of speaking and eating. To some extent, no doubt, each of us does feel torn between the attractions of simpler, more natural modes of expression and the elaborate refinements of social conventions. But custom greatly reduces the chasm between easy spontaneity and challenging social choreography. Through custom, a great deal of artifice in our manners and mores, the labor of centuries, has become easy, spontaneous, reflexive, and even pleasurable.

Ethos and habit: the first face of custom

In Aristotle the words ethos and nomos both refer to custom, but each has a different semantic field. Ethos, as customary habit, faces toward nature and the subrational passions while nomos, as customary convention, faces toward law and reason. Ethos naturalizes our conventions into our second nature, while nomos conventionalizes our natural propensities into an unwritten law. Aristotle often uses the term ethos to describe, not just the customs of men, but also the habits of animals. In a passage describing the *scala naturae* quoted above, he says that some animals are influenced by ethos, while man alone has reason (*Politics* 1332b 4). As we shall see, Aristotle closely links reason with nomos; he never says that animals are guided by nomos. In his treatise *History of Animals* (HA), Aristotle uses the word ethos to describe the behavior of animals: he says that sheep gather together "within the sheepfold because of their ethos" (HA 611a2).[14] More often he uses *ēthos*[15] to describe the distinctive character of animals: "Their activities and modes of living vary according to their characters (*ēthē*) and their food" (HA 588a 18). Just as animals are closer to nature and farther from

[14] Greek text: *Aristotle: Historia Animalium Vol. I: Books I–X: Text*, ed. D. M. Balme (Cambridge: Cambridge University Press, 2002).

[15] Aristotle tells us that *ēthos* comes from ethos at *Eudemian Ethics* 1220a 39. Greek text: Oxford Classical Texts, ed. R. R. Walzer and J. M. Mingay (Oxford: Clarendon Press, 1991).

reason, so are children and barbarians. Thus Aristotle says that the young are guided more by character (*ēthos*) than by reason (*logos*), whereas the old are more guided by reason than by character (*Rhetoric* 1389a 33 and 1390a 16).[16] And he claims that "many barbarians have a custom (*ethos*) of plunging their children at birth into a cold stream . . . For human nature should early be habituated (*ethizein*) to endure all which by habit (*ethizein*) it can be made to endure" (*Politics* 1336a 15ff).

The reason why the conduct of animals, children, and barbarians is regulated by ethos rather than by nomos, is that they are all dominated by the non-rational soul. Aristotle famously says that moral virtue comes from habit, as evidenced by the fact that the word moral (*ēthikē*) comes from *ethos* (*Nicomachean Ethics* (NE) 1103a 16; *Eudemian Ethics* 1220a 40). The moral virtues, he says, are perfections of the nonrational part of the soul while the intellectual virtues are perfections of the rational part of the soul (NE 1103a 4). For this reason, he says, the intellectual virtues stem from teaching while the moral virtues stem from habit (NE 1103a 16). By ethos, we educate our passions, appetites, and pleasures so that they harmonize with the demands of practical reason. Animals, children, and barbarians also have passions, appetites, and pleasure that should be habituated in accordance with practical reason, but in their cases the reason which regulates their habits must come from an adult Greek. Similarly, Aristotle strongly contrasts the mere handicraftsman (*cheirotechnēs*) who works by habit (*ethos*) from the master-craftsman (*architektōn*) who works by reason (*logos*). He even says that handicraftsman makes things without knowing what he is making, just as fire burns (*Metaphysics* 981b 3). So ethos is more like nature than reason.

That ethos looks to nature more than to reason is evident in Aristotle's doctrine that ethos becomes a second nature. Aristotle frequently emphasizes the continuity between our natural propensities and our acquired habits. Ethos is like nature because it is spontaneous, voluntary, and pleasant: "it must be pleasant to move toward a natural state of being . . . Habits (*ethē*) also are pleasant; for as soon as a thing has become habitual (*ethos*) it is virtually natural (*physei*)." By contrast, what is painful is what is forced on us "for force is contrary to nature (*para physin*)." In order to acquire a new skill, we must force ourselves to concentrate, strain, and apply effort, all of which, says Aristotle, is

[16] Greek text of *Rhetoric*: Oxford Classical Texts, ed. W. D. Ross (Oxford: Oxford University Press, 1959).

necessarily painful: "they all involve compulsion and force, unless we are accustomed (*ethisthōsin*) to them, in which case it is ethos that makes them pleasant" (*Rhetoric* 1369b 34ff). Once we have mastered a skill, however, it becomes both habitual and pleasant. Ethos is like nature because it creates a predictable pattern of events: "what happens often is akin to what happens always, natural events happen always and habitual events often" (*Rhetoric* 1370a 7). Ethos is like nature because it is difficult to change: "it is easier to change a habit (*ethos*) than to change one's nature; even habit is hard to change just because it is like nature" (NE 1152a 30). Ethos is like nature because it is automatic, reflexive, and rapid: "If, then, the mind has not moved in an old path, it tends to move to the more customary (*synētheia*); for custom (*ethos*) now assumes the role of nature. Hence the rapidity with which we recollect what we frequently think about. For as one thing follows another by nature (*physei*), so too that happens by custom (*synētheia*), and frequency creates nature" (*Memory* 452a 28).[17] Ethos is like nature, finally, because it plays such a large role in our lives: "in every one ethos is a matter of importance, since it soon becomes nature" (*Problems* 949a 28).[18] In short, Aristotle makes it clear that habit naturalizes our conventions to such an extent that our second nature becomes almost indistinguishable from our original nature; indeed, he even says that our second nature largely replaces our first.

The shortcoming of Aristotle's use of ethos to refer to both habit and custom is that he has no easy way to distinguish habit from custom. Not all habits are customary habits; many are purely idiosyncratic.[19] So Aristotle does not distinguish individual habits from social customs. Similarly, by using the word ethos to describe both the instincts of animals as well as the customs of men, Aristotle does not always distinguish the natural behavior of animals from the acculturation of men. He refers to an animal's or plant's species-specific behavior as its character (*ēthos*, HA 488b 12, 588a 18), whereas we think of habits as what

[17] Greek text: G. R. T. Ross, *Aristotle: De Sensu and De Memoria* (Cambridge: Cambridge University Press, 1906).

[18] Greek text: *Aristotle: Problems II*, ed. W. S. Hett (Cambridge, MA: Harvard University Press, 1937).

[19] Aristotle's term for a stable disposition, *hexis*, is sometimes translated as "habit" but a *hexis* is an objective and unchanging disposition, not a subjective psychological habit that waxes and wanes. Aristotle calls science, art, wisdom, and the moral virtues "*hexeis*"; but a virtue is much more than a habit.

individuate us and of customs as what distinguish one society from another within the same species.

Nomos and convention: the second face of custom

If ethos looks toward our passionate nature then nomos looks toward our rational law. Aristotle frequently associates nomos with mind (*nous*) and with reason (*logos*). Although nomos refers broadly to conventions both legal and customary, the etymology of nomos implies that the convention stemmed from an act of deliberate stipulation.[20] This etymology helps us to understand Aristotle's strong identification of law with reason: "nomos has compulsive power, while it is at the same time a reason (*logos*) proceeding from a sort of practical wisdom (*phronēsis*) and mind (*nous*)" (NE 1180a 21). Aristotle says that for nomos to rule is for "God and mind alone to rule," because "nomos is mind without desire" (*Politics* 1287a 29–32).[21] In short, ethos we share with other animals while nomos we share with God.

Aristotle develops not only a rationalist account of law but also a legalist conception of reason. Virtue, he says, means not only to act in accordance with reason (*kata logon*) but to act by means of reason (*meta logou*): "It implies that the agent is conscious of the rule he follows, that he acts not merely 'by rule' but 'with a rule'."[22] To act according to reason is thus to act according to an external standard, such as law (*kata nomon*). Accordding to Aristotle, logos is like a lawgiver, since logos

[20] According to Ostwald: "There is universal agreement, as far as I know, that this noun (*nomos*) is derived from the same root as *nemō*, whose basic concept involves a 'distribution' or 'assigning' of some kind." To which W. K. C. Guthrie adds: "That is to say, it presupposes an acting subject – believer, practitioner or apportioner – a mind from which the nomos emanates." Ostwald, *Nomos and the Beginnings of the Athenian Democracy* (Oxford: Clarendon Press, 1969), p. 9; Guthrie, *History of Greek Philosophy*, vol. 3, p. 55.

[21] Since Aristotle says that law proceeds from practical wisdom *phronēsis*, he cannot literally mean that law is reason without desire. Practical wisdom is rational desire and a desiring reason. "For Aristotle moral action was reason penetrated by desire, and law was the handmaid of morality: it existed to habituate men to virtue. Law must therefore share the appetitive and purposive element which is found in virtue itself." Francis Wormuth, "Aristotle on Law," in his *Essays in Law and Politics*, ed. Dalmas H. Nelson and Richard L. Sklar (Port Washington, NY: Kennikat Press, 1978), pp. 14–26, at p. 17.

[22] John Burnet's gloss on NE 1144b 25 in his *The Ethics of Aristotle* (London: Methuen, 1900), p. 37.

commands, orders, and defends.[23] So closely linked are nomos and logos that in some places the Aristotelian manuscripts vary and scholars cannot agree about which is correct: for example, "this is why we do not allow a man to rule, but nomos (or logos)."[24] Since Aristotle often treats these words as synonyms, either makes perfect sense.

Applied to custom, Aristotle's close identification of nomos and logos seems odd. We can see how statutes might embody deliberate stipulation, but what about customary conventions? Such customs seem to arise from human conduct but not from any deliberate design. Yet there are a number of passages in which nomos refers broadly to convention, both customary and legal. Whenever Aristotle adopts the Sophistic contrast of nature and convention (nomos), he uses nomos broadly to include customs and laws. First, contrasting natural justice to conventional justice (*dikaion nomikon*), he uses nomos to refer broadly to conventions, including weights and measures, which are often informal. He says that these kinds of conventional justice, which include both customs and statutes, are just by agreement (*kata synthēkēn*: NE 1134b 18 and 35). Secondly, contrasting slavery according to nature with slavery according to convention, he uses nomos to include custom, illustrating conventional slavery by reference to the custom that "whatever is taken in war belongs to the victors" – a convention that clearly was not statutory (*Politics* 1255a 5). Thirdly, Aristotle says that money (*nomisma*) "exists not by nature but by nomos" (NE 1133a 29) because money rests upon an agreement (*kata synthēkēn*) – yet money can arise from customary agreements about a medium of exchange.

In such contrasts between nature and nomos, Aristotle clearly uses nomos to include both customary conventions and legal enactments. When Aristotle wishes to emphasize the customary and informal character of conventions, he uses variants of nomos, such as *nomima* and forms of the verb *nomizō*. By contrast, when Aristotle wishes to emphasize the statutory character of conventions, he modifies nomos with variants of the verb *tithēmi*, to lay down: a statute, then, is a convention that is imposed or "laid down."

Aristotle also compares statutes to customary conventions when he contrasts written to unwritten law (*nomos agraphos*), saying that a legislator

[23] NE 1114b 29; 1115b 19; 1117a 8; 1119a 20; 1125b 35; 1138b 20. On logos as nomos, see René Gauthier and Jean Jolif, *L'Ethique à Nicomaque* (Louvain: Publications Universitaires, 1970), vol. 2, p. 149.

[24] NE 1134a 35. Gauthier and Jolif favor nomos but Bywater favors logos.

"should provide enacted laws (*nomoi*) both written and unwritten" (*Politics* 1319b 40). It is not clear how a legislator can enact customs, but Aristotle wants legislators to be concerned with both fostering customs and laying down laws. And he makes it quite clear that not only is the unwritten law custom but also that "customs (*ethē*) have more authority and concern more important matters than do written laws" (*Politics* 1287b 5). Aristotle does not explain here why custom is more authoritative and concerns more important matters than statutes. Perhaps custom is more authoritative because it rests upon ancient and widely shared norms while written laws often rest merely upon transient partisan regimes or because the very weighty matters of family life and divine worship are largely regulated by custom. In the *Rhetoric* (1375a 16), Aristotle points to another advantage of custom: "written laws depend on force while unwritten laws (*dikaia agrapha*) do not." Here Aristotle is referring to the habitual dimension of custom: because habits create a second nature, we do what custom demands spontaneously, without coercion.

Sometimes Aristotle contrasts written and unwritten law, not as statute and custom, but as local law and universal law. "Law (*nomos*) is either special (*idios*) or universal (*koinos*). By special law I mean that written law which regulates the life of a particular community; by universal law, all those unwritten things which are supposed to be acknowledged everywhere" (*Rhetoric* 1368b 7). Aristotle illustrates some of the principles of the universal unwritten law: "gratitude to, or requital of, our benefactors, readiness to help our friends, and the like" (*Rhetoric* 1374a 24). Some customs, in other words, are purely local conventions while others are universal norms: "Universal law is the law of nature (*kata physin*). For there really is, as everyone to some extent divines, a natural justice and injustice that is common to all, even to those who have no association or agreement with each other" (*Rhetoric* 1373b 6). Commentators vary in their assessments of the transformation of unwritten law from local custom into the law of nature.[25] Aristotle

[25] Rudolf Hirzel sees only a nominal change: "Die Sache bleibt, die Namen wechseln." But Francis Wormuth sees "an astonishing evolution." Hirzel, *Agraphos Nomos*, Abhandlungen der Philologisch-historischen Classe der Königlich Sächsischen Gesellschaft der Wissenschaften, XX.1 (1900), p. 3. Wormuth, "Aristotle on Law," p. 21. But Wormuth goes on to say (p. 23) that we ought not to build an Aristotelian jurisprudence on the basis of a few sentences in the *Rhetoric*: "We are not obliged to believe that the *Rhetoric* is doing anything more than reporting the stock phrases of current oratory; and indeed the huddling together of unwritten law, universal law, natural justice, and equity is unlike the careful analysis Aristotle bestows on ideas he takes seriously."

moves rapidly around his circle of interdefinability: custom is both second nature and unwritten law – and universal unwritten law is the law of nature!

If ethos created ambiguities by sometimes blurring the important distinction between idiosyncratic and social habits, nomos creates some ambiguities between customary and legal conventions. We saw that Aristotle says that money (*nomisma*) exists, not by nature, but by nomos. Does he mean that money arises from customary usage or from legal enactment? According to Eric Roll, the medieval scholastics translated Aristotle's nomos as *lex*, leading them to confuse legal tender money with money as a medium of exchange created by usage.[26]

In some places, it is genuinely difficult to decide whether Aristotle is referring to custom or to law. He says that "nomos does not command a man to kill himself, and what it does not command, it forbids" (NE 1138a 6).[27] Some commentators claim that Aristotle here means that "law does not expressly permit suicide, and whatever killing is not expressly permitted must be assumed to be forbidden."[28] Although this might be a plausible interpretation of the law of killing, Aristotle's claim is much broader. J. A. Stewart argues that Aristotle's claim is much more plausible if we think of him as referring to custom rather than to law: "Custom or fashion does not tell Oxford undergraduates to go down to the River in academic dress; it therefore forbids them to do it. Nor do the Statutes of the University tell them; but the Statutes do not therefore forbid them. The Statutes are neutral in this matter, as in many others in which fashion takes a side."[29] Unfortunately, even Stewart's gloss lacks precision: he should say that custom requires that one wear non-academic dress when going down to the River and by requiring non-academic dress, custom implicitly forbids academic dress. But Stewart's general point is right, namely that custom is silent less often than is law.

[26] Eric Roll, *A History of Economic Thought* (Englewood Cliffs, NJ: Prentice-Hall, 1956), p. 34.

[27] Gauthier and Jolif comment: "Cette assertion surprenante a reçu un assez bon nombre d'explications." *L'Ethique à Nicomaque*, vol. 2, p. 423.

[28] See Burnet, *The Ethics of Aristotle*, p. 244. Max Hamburger follows Burnet and claims that Aristotle's text here "seems to be somewhat corrupt." *Morals and the Law* (New Haven: Yale University Press, 1951), p. 80.

[29] J. A. Stewart, *Notes on the Nicomachean Ethics of Aristotle*, vol. 1 (Oxford: Clarendon Press, 1982), p. 390.

Custom and law, or custom v. law?

Aristotle, then, uses two very different words for custom. Ethos focuses upon the habitual or tacit dimension of custom while nomos focuses on the conventional dimension of custom. What is the relation between habit and convention in custom? Conventions serve to coordinate complex arenas of human activity; they usually coordinate much more effectively when they become habitual. If the conventional meanings of words were not grasped automatically by habit, then communication would grind to a halt, like the millipede trying to move each foot by explicit decision. Conversely, if habits were not conventional, we would be reduced to very diverse and idiosyncratic grunts, gestures, and actions, without any means of harmonizing mutual expectations of conduct. Either way, human social life as we know it would be impossible.

Habit gives convention psychological force and performative skill: habitual conventions have spontaneity, speed, and efficiency; they are usually pleasant, familiar, and easy. Conventions give habits cultural sophistication and a social life: conventional habits are often refined, elegant, meaningful, and shared; they enable us to know what to expect in the behavior of others, enable us to conform to others' expectations, and provide common criteria for evaluating our own and others' conduct. Of course, the marriage of habit and convention is not always a happy one: habitual conventions are often rigid, mechanical, blind, and stupid – think of the customary habits defining honor, insult, and duels. We often fail to reflect upon or critically challenge our habits and, even were we to decide to change them, our old habits would interfere with learning new ones, as we Americans discover in trying to speak a foreign language, or to drive in England. Similarly, conventionalized habits are often fussy, extravagant, superfluous, and silly – think of the customary conventions governing early modern court life. Conventions can become so artificial and elaborate that they smother the activities they are meant to foster, like overly burdensome legal procedures. Nonetheless, as a broad generalization, we might say that conventions without habits are a burden while habits without conventions are a bore.

Custom will relate to law in very different ways depending upon whether we focus upon the dimension of habit or of convention. Many disputes about the relation of custom to law stem from a failure to distinguish habit from convention. For example, most jurists list custom as one among several independent sources of law, but the jurists of the historical school often assert that all law is custom.[30] How could all law be custom if custom is but one source of law? If we are focused on conventions, then custom is but one source of our legal conventions; but if we are focused on habits of tacit knowledge and skill, then all law rests upon custom, in the sense that the interpretation and application of law rest upon deep reservoirs of tacit know-how.

Similarly, it is often asserted that the growth of law means the decline of custom. But this could refer to two distinct processes: one whereby what is tacit and habitual becomes explicit and stipulated, another whereby informal conventions give way to legally imposed agreements. What we know about human cognition, however, shows that cognitive complexity requires ever greater capacities for habitual routines in information processing and skillful performance: the growing complexity of the interpretation and application of law means a greater role for customary habits in the lives of lawyers.

As for conventions, by focusing merely on their sources, we might well conclude that custom and law are mutually exclusive sources of our conventions, since every convention begins either as informal practice or as stipulated law. On this view, the growth of legal conventions inevitably shrinks the field of customary conventions. But custom is not best thought of merely as a *source* of law: custom is just as often a *consequence* of law. Customary conventions do not cease being customs when they become enforced by law. And Robert Ellickson shows that the growth of law often stimulates the growth of customary conventions as alternatives to increasingly burdensome legal procedures.[31] Rather, law in many jurisdictions ceases to be law when it loses the support of custom and falls into desuetude. In short, because legal conventions survive only by becoming customary, the growth of law means the growth of custom. Some contemporary scholars of international law argue that there are several ways in which the growth of deliberately stipulated law of treaties and conventions has fostered the profusion of new customary international law. For example, Theodor Meron argues when a large number of states convene to promulgate new rules protecting human rights, a custom of human rights norms emerges which binds

[30] See, for example, James C. Carter *Law: Its Origin, Growth, and Function* (New York: De Capo Press, 1974), p. 173.

[31] Ellickson, *Order without Law* (Cambridge, MA: Harvard University Press, 1991), chapters 3–6.

even the states not party to the original conventions.[32] In his much controverted view, treaties and conventions can give rise to parallel norms of customary international law, with a wider range of jurisdiction. Indeed, H. W. A. Thirlway argues that custom operates not only in support of written law, but also to supplement written law and even to alter or abolish it.[33] "We have endeavored to show that so far from supplanting customary law, and reducing its field of operation to a minimum, the codifying of great tracts of international law will, on account of the practical and political difficulties of amending multilateral treaties, whether codifying or otherwise, give over the development of international law almost entirely into the hands of custom, operating upon and beyond the codifying treaties."[34] According to these scholars, at least, the growth of law in no way competes with the growth of customary habits or customary conventions.

Those who want to stress the continuity between custom and law will say that both are systems of conventions, that is, agreements to coordinate expectations and conduct. Lon Fuller, for example, argues that customary law does not arise merely from repeated or uniform habits, but from the need for social coordination: "Customary law arises, then, out of situations of human interaction where each participant guides himself by an anticipation of what the other will do and will expect him to do." Customary law, he says, is like contract law: "its underlying principle is a reciprocity of expectations."[35] They will argue that law is best understood, not as a command from sovereign to citizen, but as a framework of rules coordinating the legitimate expectations among citizens. On this view, legal conventions do not arise *ex nihilo*, but reinforce, supplement, or abrogate existing customary conventions. The rules of law rarely create new forms of human activity; instead,

[32] "In the highly codified humanitarian law context, the primary and most obvious significance of a norm's customary character is that the norm binds states that are not parties to the instrument in which that norm is restated. It is, of course, not the treaty norm, but the customary norm with identical content, that binds such states." Theodor Meron, *Human Rights and Humanitarian Norms as Customary Law* (Oxford: Clarendon Press, 1989), p. 3.

[33] Thirlway compares custom to equity, whose relation to written law has been categorized as "equity *secundum legem*, equity *praeter legem*, and equity *contra legem*"; in the same way, he says, custom operates by virtue of the law itself, custom supplements the deficiencies of law, and custom alters or abolishes law. *International Customary Law and Codification* (Leiden: A. W. Sijthoff, 1972), p. 95.

[34] *Ibid.*, p. 146. [35] Fuller, *Anatomy of the Law* (New York: Mentor, 1969), p. 116.

they tend to regulate and modify on-going customary human enterprises. The rules of law, then, are more like the rules of etiquette or grammar than like the rules of games or sports.

Those who emphasize the continuity will also insist that custom and law regulate conduct most effectively when they rest upon habits. Indeed, Aristotle says that "nomos has no power to command obedience except that of ethos, which can only be given by time, so that readiness to change from old law to new weakens the power of law" (*Politics* 1269a 20). Aristotle overstates his case here because both custom and law have other ways of encouraging conformity besides the force of habit, namely, social ostracism and legal sanction. Too much change in either custom or law weakens their effectiveness as conventions because it unsettles the expectations upon which we rely in coordinating our plans.

Any particular act of interpretation or application of law must rest largely on tacit customary habits. The cognitive habits by which we interpret and apply law cannot themselves all be reflectively stipulated because they are the means by which we interpret and stipulate. You can't drive nails if you are focused on how to hold the hammer and you can't interpret laws unless you can rely upon a habitual grasp of the meaning of virtually all the terms. For example, it is often asserted that many provisions of business contracts can only be interpreted in relation to the habitual expectations of that business. Lon Fuller famously offered as an example an ordinance prohibiting "vehicles in the park" which will be interpreted one way where parks are places of repose and quite another way where parks are places of merriment.[36] Apart from the shared customary understandings of human institutions, like parks, interpretation of law would always be indeterminate or arbitrary.

Much of these shared understandings must remain tacit: at any particular occasion, we can bring some of our tacit understandings to explicit critical reflection, but not all of them at once. Like Neurath's ship at sea, we can focus on this or that problem and make selective repairs, but only by relying implicitly on the soundness of the rest. Or, as Wittgenstein argued, the application of rules to cases cannot be wholly determined by rules without generating an infinite regress. In this view, the habits of courts are as much a part of our law as are the decisions of courts: *cursus curiae est lex curiae*.

Those who emphasize the contrast between custom and law will also develop two independent lines of argument. First, they will draw

[36] *Ibid.*, p. 93.

attention to the difference between legal conventions as positive law, in the sense of deliberately laid down by the sovereign legislator, and customary conventions arising informally from human social practices. But it turns out to be quite difficult to distinguish sharply formal legal conventions from informal customary ones. Voluntarist positivists, like Hobbes and Austin, argued that, since law is a command of the sovereign will, the only organ for directly articulating that will is legislation; the decisions of courts and the customs of merchants could be interpreted as the indirect will of the sovereign with the fiction that "whatever the sovereign permits, he commands." H. L. A. Hart effectively demolished the voluntarist theory of law by showing that laws need not be commands and that persons in authority have reasons for permitting customs even when they disapprove them. Hart famously attempted to distinguish legal from other kinds of conventions on the basis that law involves a union of primary and secondary rules, where the secondary rules are rules about the primary rules, namely, how to identify, apply, and change them.[37]

Whether this adequately distinguishes legal from other conventions is disputed on the basis that the conventions governing private associations, such as sporting clubs, are also unions of primary and secondary rules. For this reason, Joseph Raz distinguishes legal systems from other systems of conventions, not on the basis of differences between types of conventions, but on the basis of the authority claimed by various systems of conventions. What makes legal systems unique, he says, are the claims to be comprehensive, supreme, and open to absorbing other systems of norms.[38]

Some argue that customary conventions arise spontaneously while legal conventions are deliberately made. John Finnis says that customs, unlike laws, are not "made" because "no one sets himself (themselves) to make a custom."[39] But powerful states often precisely set themselves to make customary international law, as the United States did successfully in the Truman Proclamation and as the United States hopes to do by its recent invasions of Afganistan and Iraq.[40] Now it could be said that even the United States cannot make customary international law unilaterally, unless its conduct is in some sense accepted or taken up by other

[37] Hart, *The Concept of Law* (2nd edn, Oxford: Clarendon Press, 1994), chapter 5.

[38] Raz, *The Authority of Law* (Oxford: Clarendon Press, 1979), pp. 116–21.

[39] Finnis, *Natural Law and Natural Rights* (Oxford: Clarendon Press, 1980), p. 277.

[40] On the Truman Proclamation, see Byers, *Custom, Power, and the Power of Rules* (Cambridge: Cambridge University Press, 1999), pp. 90–2.

nations. The invasion of Iraq might well not create a new customary law of preventive war; it might instead provoke clear rejection of the whole doctrine. Precedents similarly do not make new law unless they are taken up in practice; even statutes, in some jurisdictions, can fail through desuetude. So neither custom nor law is made wholly unilaterally: they both require some degree of social uptake.

The effort to distinguish legal from other kinds of conventions has been especially difficult in the case of the common law. Every legal theorist who makes a strong distinction between custom and law must decide whether common law is custom or law. When Thomas Hobbes thinks of common law as custom, he denies it is law: "Custom of itself maketh no law . . . [I]f custom were sufficient to introduce a law, then it would be in the power of every one that is deputed to hear a cause, to make his errors law." Yet Hobbes also offers arguments for why common law might be understood as an indirect command of the sovereign, if the judges are ministers of the sovereign: "in *England* it is the King that makes the Laws, whosoever Pens them."[41] Jeremy Bentham similarly oscillates between arguing that common law is not law and that common law is judge-made law, that is, judicial legislation. Austin thought that common law represented the tacit will of the sovereign because whatever the sovereign permits, he commands. "Now when customs are turned into legal rules by decisions of subject judges, the legal rules which emerge from the customs are *tacit* commands of the sovereign legislature."[42] Austin did, however, reject Bentham's expression "judge-made" law, arguing that the law arising from judicial decisions is different in character from the law made by legislators.

Thus, champions of statute make common law into an indirect mode of legislation, while champions of custom make common law into a kind of custom. St. German said that those customs of the realm neither against the law of God nor against the law of reason are properly called the common law.[43] Blackstone also defined common law in relation to the "unwritten law" of custom, saying that common law included

[41] Hobbes, *Elements of Law*, ed. Ferdinand Tönnies (2nd edn by M. M. Goldsmith, New York: Barnes and Noble, 1969), Part 2, section 10, para. 10, p. 190. Hobbes, *A Dialogue Between a Philosopher and a Student of the Common Laws of England*, ed. Joseph Cropsey (Chicago: University of Chicago Press, 1971), (11), p. 59.

[42] Austin, *The Province of Jurisprudence Determined*, ed. H. L. A. Hart (London: Weidenfeld and Nicolson, 1954), p. 32.

[43] St. German, *Doctor and Student*, ed. T. F. T. Plunckenett and J. L. Barton (London: Selden Society, 1974), chapter 7.

general customs, particular customs, and certain particular laws. But Blackstone goes on to say that only general customs are "the common law, properly so called."[44] Similarly, James Carter argues that Austin's definition of law is actually a definition of legislation: "It properly defines *legislation* – that is, law consciously enacted by men."[45] Carter himself strongly contrasts law with legislation and asserts that all law is custom. Friedrich Hayek sharply distinguishes the spontaneous order of markets from the deliberately designed order of organizations; he then argues that common law and custom are examples of spontaneous order while legislation is an example of designed order.[46]

Law remedies the deficiencies of custom

We have seen that among jurists there is very little agreement about the relation of custom to law. Some jurists focus on the habitual, tacit, and spontaneous dimension of custom which they contrast with the explicit, stipulated, and deliberate nature of enacted law while other jurists focus on the conventional dimension of custom which they compare to legal conventions. Custom is thus bafflingly like and unlike law. To clarify the relation of custom both to nature and to law, I will sketch an Aristotelian theory of the kinds of order we find in society.

Aristotle has only specific and no generic words for "order." We can see the different species of social order in his terms for describing "good social order": *eukosmia*, *eunomia*, and *eutaxia*: here *kosmos* connotes natural social order, *nomos* connotes customary order, and *taxis* connotes deliberately stipulated order, as in the order of battle.[47] Knowing the kinds of order in society gives us the basis for forming reliable expectations about human conduct: order is the basis for inference.[48]

[44] *Blackstone's Commentaries*, vol. 1, Introduction section 3.

[45] Carter, *Law: Its Origin, Growth, and Function* (New York: G. P. Putnam, 1907), p. 182.

[46] Hayek, *Law, Legislation, and Liberty*, vol. 1 (Chicago: University of Chicago Press, 1973), pp. 72–94.

[47] See *Politics* 1299b 16, *Nicomachean Ethics* 1112b 14, and *Politics*, 1326a 30.

[48] Order, says Hayek, is "a state of affairs in which a multiplicity of elements of various kinds are so related to each other that we may learn from our acquaintance with some spatial or temporal part of the whole to form correct expectations concerning the rest, or at least expectations which have a good chance of proving correct." Hayek, *Law, Legislation, and Liberty*, vol. 1 (Chicago: University of Chicago Press, 1973), p. 36. Hayek here draws on Stebbing: "When we know how a set of elements is ordered we have a basis for inference." L. S. Stebbing, *A Modern Introduction to Logic* (London: Methuen, 1950), p. 228.

Scholars are not sure whether the Greek word *kosmos* was first used about social order and then applied to nature or was first used about natural order and then applied to society.[49] In the first document in the history of Western philosophy, Anaximander develops an elaborate analogy between the natural cycle of the seasons and the legal cycles of transgression and retribution. This fragment (DK 12 A9) is the first expression of natural law because Anaximander describes the uniformities of nature as just (*dikē*).[50] Indeed, the Greek word for natural cause (*aitia*) is a legal term for guilt – the cause is guilty of the effect.[51] So law is natural and nature is lawful. What about custom? Here we move within the same circle of analogies, since custom is both "second nature" and "unwritten law."

But Aristotle also offers us another way to understand the relations between nature, custom, and stipulation. In his classification of the kinds of souls, Aristotle does not define a genus of soul and the species of plant, animal, and human souls. Instead, Aristotle says that the plant soul is living (that is, nutritive and reproductive), the animal soul is living plus sensitive, and the human soul is living and sensitive plus rational.[52] This kind of classification by progressive or nested hierarchy is often much more informative than a simple genus/species classification and Aristotle uses it in several contexts.[53] I believe Aristotle thought

49 "It may be that, from the beginning, *kosmos* was applied to the world of nature by conscious analogy with the good order of society." Charles Kahn, *Anaximander and the Origins of Greek Cosmology* (New York: Columbia University Press, 1960), p. 223.

50 In Kahn's translation: "And the source of coming-to-be for existing things is that into which destruction, too, happens, according to necessity; for they pay penalty and retribution to each other for their injustice according to the ordinance of time." According to Kahn's interpretation of this fragment, "the elements feed one another by their own destruction, since what is life to one is death for its reciprocal. The first law of nature is a *lex talionis*: life for life." *Anaximander and the Origins of Greek Cosmology*, p. 183.

51 Hans Kelsen sees the word *aitia* as central to early Greek conceptions of natural law: "It is significant that the Greek word for cause, *aitia*, originally meant guilt: the cause is guilty of the effect, is responsible for the effect . . . One of the earliest formulations of the law of causality is the famous fragment of Heraclitus: 'If the Sun will overstep his prescribed path, then the Erinyes, the handmaids of justice, will find him out.' Here the law of nature still appears as a rule of law: if the Sun does not follow his prescribed path he will be punished." Kelsen, *Pure Theory of Law*, ed. Max Knight (Berkeley: University of California Press, 1970), p. 84.

52 *De Anima* 414a 29–415a 13.

53 For the classification of integers, see *Metaphysics* 999a 6; for categories of being, see *Nicomachean Ethics* 1096a 17; for constitutions, see *Politics* 1275a 35. D.W. Hamlyn describes the advantages of classification by progressive hierarchy: "An account of figure

that nature, custom, and deliberate stipulation also formed such a nested hierarchy: "In every case the lower faculty can exist apart from the higher, but the higher presupposes those below it."[54] Nature represents the physical, chemical, and biological processes of the cosmos; nature can and did exist apart from human custom and deliberate stipulation. Human custom is rooted in the physiology of habit but transcends habit by becoming a social system of conventions. Custom presupposes nature, but custom can exist without being the object of rational reflection and stipulation: language existed before grammarians.

Custom arises from nature and stipulation from custom. But doesn't custom also shape nature just as stipulation shapes custom? Stipulated conventions in language and law do shape customary practice. In what sense is nature, custom, and law a hierarchy if causality can work both upwards and downwards? Custom can shape nature only by enlisting the powers of nature, as when we use energy to defy gravity or breed new species of plants and animals. Similarly, enacted law can shape custom but only to the extent that it enlists the power of custom, such as customary habits of obedience. Deliberately stipulated law, whether enacted or judicial, shapes custom mainly by fostering new customs to replace older ones. But whether law reinforces, supplements, or revokes custom, it always presupposes custom.

This nested hierarchy of nature, custom, and rational stipulation is pervasive in Aristotle's thought. First, for Aristotle, nature, custom, and rational stipulation articulate the hierarchy of the *scala naturae*: "The other animals for the most part live by nature, though in some respects by habit as well, while man lives also by reason, for he alone has reason."[55] Secondly, nature, custom, and rational stipulation form the same nested hierarchy in individual development as they do in the ladder of nature. Aristotle says that there are three kinds of human

in general or soul in general . . . will be uninformative about figures and souls, not just in the way any generic definition is uninformative about the details of the things to which it is applied, but also because it will omit the crucial point that figures and souls form a progression." *Aristotle's De Anima II and III* (Oxford: Clarendon Press, 1968), p. 94.

54 R. D. Hicks, *Aristotle: De Anima* (Cambridge: Cambridge University Press, 1907), p. 335. The student of Thomas Aquinas who completed his commentary on the *Politics* had already observed about Aristotle's triad: "Quare hoc oportet consonare inter se, scilicet naturam, consuetudinem, et rationem: semper enim posterius praesupponit prius." *In Libros Politicorum Aristotelis Expositio*, ed. Raymundi Spiazzi (Turin: Marietti, 1951), p. 386.

55 *Politics* 1332b 2.

faculties (*dynameis*): those that are innate (*suggenēs*), those that come by practice (*ethos*), and those that come from teaching (*mathēsis*). These three faculties form a hierarchy: "The contribution of nature clearly does not depend on us ... while argument (*logos*) and teaching (*didakē*) surely do not influence everyone, but the soul of the student must have been prepared by habit (*ethos*)."[56] So habit presupposes nature while rational argument presupposes habits. Thirdly, this hierarchy is found in Aristotle's discussions of legal order: "We have already determined what natures are likely to be most easily moulded by the hands of the legislator. All else is the work of education; we learn some things by habit and some by instruction."[57] Just as the legislator is responsible for attempting to shape the natural potential and the tacit customs of his city, so every person is responsible for making the best he can of his natural potential and his habits of character.

Deliberate rational instruction will be effective only if young people have first acquired the proper habits, just as deliberate legislation will be effective only where the citizens have acquired the proper customs: "Now, in men reason and mind are the end towards which nature strives, so that the birth and training in custom (*ethos*) of the citizens ought to be ordered with a view to them" (*Politics* 1334b 15). And Cicero deploys this triadic scheme in his famous description of the evolution of law from the principles of nature, through custom, to the deliberate stipulation of statutes: "Law (*ius*) initially proceeds from nature, then certain rules of conduct become customary by reason of their advantage; later still both the principles that proceeded from nature and those that had been approved by custom received the support of religion and the fear of legislation (*lex*)."[58] Here Cicero sees that the deliberate imposition of law does not create social or legal order, but reinforces, revises, or supplements the existing natural and customary order. Both Thomas Aquinas and John Austin cite this passage from Cicero with approval.[59]

What does it mean to say that law proceeds from custom? Let's begin with law stipulated by legislators and by judges. This law is generally intended not to create a new social order de novo but to reinforce,

[56] Aristotle, *Metaphysics*, 1047b 31. Greek text: Oxford Classical Texts, ed. Werner Jaeger (Oxford: Clarendon Press, 1957). *Nicomachean Ethics* 1179b 21.

[57] *Politics* 1332b 8. "Now, in men reason and mind are the goal of nature, so that the birth and training in custom of the citizens ought to be ordered with a view to them." *Politics* 1334b 15. I have here adopted Jowett's translation.

[58] Cicero, *De Inventione* 2.53.160.

[59] Aquinas, ST, I-II, 95.2c and Austin, *Lectures on Jurisprudence*, lecture 30.

supplement, or suppress existing customs. The attempt to create a new social order by means of deliberate stipulation is called totalitarianism. The power of custom is nowhere more evident than in the failure of the twentieth-century totalitarian projects despite the application of immense energy and violence. Law arises because of the profound shortcomings of customary social order: groups with incompatible customs come into conflict, interpretations of shared customs come into conflict, and rapid social change creates urgent demands for new customs. Law is not the foundation of social order but a remedy for the deficiencies of custom.

But how can we clearly distinguish the stipulated order of law from the spontaneous order of custom if some law is customary? Indeed, some law is not made but found already existing in the practices of a people. Nonetheless, even this customary law has a stipulated dimension, in that courts must set forth general criteria defining which customs will likely be enforced by law. No society can undertake to provide legal enforcement of all customs, so every society must decide which customs will be doubly enforced, both by customary sanctions and by legal sanctions. Customary law therefore refers to that subset of customs deliberately chosen for special enforcement. In this sense, customary law reflects not just the habitual and spontaneous order of custom but also the deliberately stipulated order of law. Moreover, although anyone can stipulate the customs of language into a grammar or the customs of courtesy into a code of manners, not anyone can stipulate which kinds of customs shall be enforced by law. Only someone in a position of authority can stipulate what kind of customs will be treated as lawful. But that authority need not be political authority: an eminent legal scholar, whether Gratian or Savigny, may stipulate principles for the enforcement of custom that are widely accepted among judges.

What kinds of customs tend to be enforced by law? The principles governing the enforcement of custom vary widely across societies. Is there any common core of principles? I think there are a few observations about the legal enforcement of custom that hold generally across societies. To begin with, customs are not enforced piecemeal; instead, every society defines broad domains of conduct in which customs will be legally enforced and domains in which customs are largely shielded from law. Some societies enforce customs of religious observance, others exempt religious customs; some societies enforce customs defining marital responsibilities while others largely shield intimate relations from legal processes. What basis is there for this distinction of domains?

Probably, customs will be legally enforced in domains of conduct that occasion the most violent social conflict: often, but not always, customs defining property rights, fair exchange, marriage and kinship, personal injury and homicide. In these domains, common lawyers have developed three basic criteria for evaluating customs by means of the doctrines of expectation, reliance, and harm. These three tests of custom are applied in a serial order of stringency. Virtually all customs, as conventions, create mutual expectations of conduct. Yet we rely on only some of these expectations in making commitments, and, when those expectations upon which we have relied are frustrated, we may be materially harmed. So, even though virtually all customs give rise to expectations about others' conduct, we rely upon only a small subset of those expectations and our reliance leads us to be harmed in still fewer instances.

Each of these doctrines of expectations, reliance, and harm is subject to normative qualifications that they be reasonable, legitimate, and consistent with public policy or with sound morals. All societies refrain from enforcing customs they regard as unreasonable or immoral. We have no legal right to expect that we can turn back the odometer on a car we are selling, even if that is custom; we have no right to rely upon the promises of a minor, an incompetent, or someone known to be dishonest; we cannot claim to be lawfully harmed if we are cheated by a prostitute. But, where we can show legitimate expectation, substantial reliance, and material harm in a particular domain of social life, then courts may well enforce customary rules of exchange or other promises. It is not the case, as John Austin argued, that particular customs are not lawful until a court enforces them; rather, a court enforces them because, as a class of customs meeting established legal criteria, they are regarded as already lawful.

Law can only be understood in its natural and customary habitat. An ecological approach to law would study it in relation to its customary niche. Like a beaver, law is both adapted to its customary environment and transforms that environment. If we were to wax Hegelian, we would say that law is custom coming to self-understanding and that law is the vehicle by which custom regulates its own evolution. Just as grammarians bring our tacit knowledge of language into explicit focus, so lawyers bring our implicit knowledge of custom into explicit focus. And just as good grammarians strive to both describe and improve our linguistic customs, so do good lawyers. Many of our customs began as laws and all successful law eventually becomes customary. Law is only, to offer a blizzard of metaphors, the focal point, the cutting edge, the tip of the iceberg, of custom. Unfortunately, custom is widely neglected in legal theory and legal philosophy, in part as a reaction against the extravagant claims about custom made by the historical school. To some extent, the ecological approach to law pioneered by Savigny, Maine, and Carter lives on in legal anthropology and legal sociology. But many heirs of the Enlightenment today think that law and custom are incompatible, that social progress means the replacement of irrational custom by rational law. In this view, rational reflection in general ought to replace subrational prejudice. But our choice is not between reason and prejudice or between custom and law. Prejudice and custom are psychologically and socially necessary parts of human life: most of our knowledge and skill must remain tacit because of our severe cognitive limitations. Instead of hoping to replace prejudice with reason or custom with law, we should instead aim to make both our prejudices and our customs more rational and decent.

4

Custom, ordinance and natural right in Gratian's *Decretum*

JEAN PORTER*

As historians of law have long recognized, Gratian's *Harmony of Discordant Canons*, commonly known as the *Decretum*, is a foundational text for modern Western jurisprudence.[1] Even though this text presents many interpretative difficulties, in part because it has almost certainly been altered and expanded in a variety of ways, its main purpose is clear enough. That is, as the title indicates, it represents an attempt to show how the diverse and seemingly inconsistent canons of the church can be interpreted and applied in a consistent way – in a word, harmonized. In the first twenty distinctions of the *Decretum* Gratian sets forth the general principles governing the interpretation of laws. (Thus, modern commentators often refer to these distinctions as the "treatise on laws," a

* This paper was originally delivered at a conference, "The Nature of Customary Law," at Newnham College, Cambridge University, September 14–16, 2005. I would like to thank my respondent, Professor Annabel Brett, the editors of this volume, and the other participants, for many stimulating and helpful comments.

[1] Gratian's *Decretum* is available in a number of editions; for reasons of convenience, I relied on the Rome edition of 1582. All translations of Gratian are my own. However, I checked my translations against Augustine Thompson's; see *Gratian: The Treatise on Laws (Decretum DD. 1–20), with the Ordinary Gloss*, Augustine Thompson, translator of Gratian, and James Gordley, translator of the Gloss, with an introduction by Katherine Christensen (Washington, DC: Catholic University of America Press, 1993). I also draw on Christensen's comprehensive introduction for general information on the background, overall purpose and structure of the *Decretum*.

All references to the *Decretum* are taken from the first part of the book, which consists of *distinctiones* comprising a series of texts (*capitula*) interspersed with Gratian's own comments (*dicta*). The citations follow the standard form for this part: *distinctiones* and *capitula* are cited by number, as for example, D.1, C.2, and Gratian's own *dicta* are cited by reference to the *capitulum* before or after which they appear, by *ante* or *post capitulum* (a.c. or p.c.). The *dicta* in the opening remarks of a *distinctio*, that is, *in principio*, are cited simply by pr., as in D.1, pr.

usage I follow.) While these distinctions do not comprise a fully worked out theory of law, they do set forth a coherent conception of law developed in what was to become the preferred scholastic way – that is to say, through the selection and interpretation of authoritative texts, here including copious citations from patristic sources and Isidore's *Etymologies* as well as legal texts properly so called.

The *Decretum* begins as follows:

> The human race is ruled by a twofold rule, namely, natural right and practices. Natural right is that which is contained in the law and the Gospel, by which each person is commanded to do to others what he would wish to be done to himself, and forbidden to render to others that which he would not have done to himself. Hence, Christ says in the Gospel, "All things whatever that you would wish other people to do to you, do the same also to them. For this is the law and the prophets."
>
> (*Decretum* D.1, pr.)

These remarks are clearly relevant to the topic of customary law, and their relevance would be still more apparent if I were to translate the word rendered by "practices," *moribus*, with the more usual "customs." At the same time, it is hardly surprising that Gratian's challenging remarks on natural right (more commonly rendered "natural law") have received far more scholarly attention than his treatment of customary law.[2] In contrast to his challenging remarks about natural right and its relation to revelation, Gratian's treatment of custom seems on a first reading to be straightforward, albeit not fully consistent. On closer examination, however, this treatment turns out to be more central to his overall project, and more interesting, than we might have suspected. In fact, Gratian devotes considerable attention to custom, seen in relation both to written law, which is its corollary, and natural and divine right,

[2] Gratian says that we are ruled by "natura . . . jure," usually translated as "natural law" on the assumption that the English terms "law" and "right" can be used interchangeably as translations for *jus* unless the context clearly indicates one or the other. Until recently, I shared this view, but I have become persuaded that the distinction between *jus* and *lex* ("law") as used by the scholastics should be reflected in translation. For one thing, the scholastics themselves consistently distinguish between the two, although the exact terms in which they do so vary – a fact which, in itself, suggests that the distinction was widely acknowledged and not dependent on the specifics of any one author's approach. Secondly, it seems to me that, whatever the specifics of their views, the scholastics consistently regard *jus* as a basis for a juridical (or quasi-juridical) judgment; this idea is better captured by "right" than by "law."

to which, together with written law, it is contrasted and subordinated. Certainly, this attention is in part a reflection of his sources, particularly the patristic and classical sources mediated to him through earlier collections of canons. Yet Gratian was not simply a compiler of texts; the extensive remarks on custom that he takes from his sources have been chosen advisedly, and his own analysis indicates a distinctive position on the issues that emerge there.[3]

Admittedly, Gratian's work is not generally known, and, apart from specialists in medieval law, those historians who read him have been inclined to focus on the inconsistencies and (from our perspective) the odd gaps in his work. More recently, scholars have begun to offer a more positive – and, I believe, a more accurate – appraisal of Gratian's abilities as an analytic jurist and of the lasting significance of his work. Thanks to Anders Winroth's recent *The Making of Gratian's Decretum*, we are in a better position to appreciate the extent to which inconsistencies within the *Decretum* reflect the complicated history of the text.[4] Even before Winroth's work, however, scholars had begun to reassess the *Decretum*, placing it within the context of Gratian's own situation and his aims and methods of working, rather than evaluating it in terms of our very different expectations. Seen from this perspective, the *Decretum* is a remarkably bold and innovative text. As its proper title indicates, it attempts to set forth the laws, or canons, of the Roman church in a systematic way, in the process indicating the principles in terms of which they can be consistently interpreted and applied. While the secular jurists of the late eleventh century are generally regarded as the "fathers"

[3] To a considerable extent, Gratian's sources are mediated to him through earlier collections of (broadly) legal material; these earlier sources include, besides Isidore of Seville, Augustine, Gregory the Great, numerous other patristic authors as well as the decrees of councils and papal letters and decrees. I rely here especially on André Gouron, "Non dixit: Ego sum consuetudo," 133–40 in *Zeitschrift der Savigny-Stiftund für Rechtsgeschichte*: *Kanonistiche Abteilung* 105:74 (1988), and Peter Leisching, "Consuetudo und ratio im Dekret und der Panormia des Buschofs Ivo von Chartres," *ibid.*, 535–41. In addition, for a general overview of Gratian's sources, see Jean Gaudemet, "La Doctrine des sources du droit dans le Décret de Gratien," *Revue de droit canonique*, 1 (1950), 5–31. For a more recent treatment, emphasizing Gratian's analytic skill and intellectual creativity, see Martin Brett, "Canon Law and Litigation: The Century before Gratian," 21–40 in *Medieval Ecclesiastical Studies in Honour of Dorothy M. Owen*, M. J. Franklin and Christopher Harper-Bill, eds. (Woodbridge: Boydell Press, 1995).

[4] Anders Winroth, *The Making of Gratian's Decretum* (Cambridge: Cambridge University Press, 2000).

of modern jurisprudence, Gratian's *Decretum* may well be regarded as the first free-standing treatise of jurisprudence – by which I mean, the first attempt to set forth principles of jurisprudence independently of commentary on an established text.

What is more, Gratian's work on custom holds special interest for us, because it reflects the situation of a society in transition from a legal system based largely on custom to a system of written, codified laws. In this context, the meaning and legal force of custom and its relation to written law were pressing issues, not only within specialized contexts, but in the ordinary practices of almost every community and jurisdiction. Admittedly, there are tensions within his treatment of custom, but, as we will see in more detail below, these reflect tensions within his sources, and even more importantly within his own society.[5] If we dismiss Gratian's work, we risk missing (what he is almost uniquely positioned to teach) the ways in which custom and written law stem from common principles and function together as two complementary and mutually correcting approximations of these principles. That, at any rate, is what I will try to show in what follows.

The *Decretum*: context and purposes

Gratian's identity, and the history and purposes of the work that bears his name, raise notoriously difficult questions.[6] This might seem surprising, since as we have just noted the full title of the *Decretum* indicates the aim of the work – that is, to show how to bring harmony out of discordant canons. As such, it reflects the same felt need for coherence and systematization that we find in other classics of early scholasticism, including Abelard's *Sic et non* and Peter Lombard's *Sententiae*. But this

[5] In "Non dixit: Ego sum consuetudo," Gouron argues that, while Gratian's sources reflect a strikingly negative view of custom, they also reflect a sense that custom should be subject to rational appraisal and confirmed when it is in conformity to reason. As for the relation between local communities and centralized authorities in Gratian's own time, and the effect of this relation on the formation of law, see Brett, "Canon Law and Litigation" and R. M. Helmholz, "The Universal and the Particular in Medieval Canon Law," 641–59 in *Proceedings of the Ninth International Congress of Medieval Canon Law*, P. Landau and J. Mueller, eds. (Vatican City: Biblioteca Apostolica Vaticana, 1997).

[6] We know nothing about Gratian, beyond the fact that his name has consistently been attached to the *Decretum*, and the date, history of composition, and overall purposes of that work have all been disputed. For a good recent survey of these debates, see Winroth, *The Making of Gratian's Decretum*, 1–18.

being said, much about the purpose of this work remains unclear.[7] Is the *Decretum* simply an academic exercise, or is it a textbook, a manual of actual cases, or a compendium of laws? On a more substantive level, what is the focus of the account of law developed here – on the application of laws through adjudication, or the creation of laws by means of legislation? In addressing these questions, our task is more difficult because we know virtually nothing about Gratian himself, and the text that bears his name has almost certainly been expanded and altered in some ways. Nonetheless, if we are to draw anything of substance from the Decretum, it will be necessary to approach it with at least a general sense of the assumptions and purposes underlying its composition.

In order to do so, it will be helpful to begin by reminding ourselves of the immediate context of this work. Whatever its exact dating, the *Decretum* is a work of the first half of the twelfth century. As such, it stems from the processes of social and institutional reform and expansion which reshaped western European society over a period extending from the late eleventh century through the early fourteenth century.[8] Most importantly for our purposes, these processes both fostered and were then sustained through a rapid development of legal structures and jurisprudence in the early scholastic period. After an extended period of reliance on customary law and localized procedures for the resolution of disputes, the rapid expansion and centralization of society meant that

[7] There are probably few scholars today who would regard the *Decretum* as a "pure" academic treatise, but, as Stanley Chodorow points out, this view was widely held among an earlier generation of scholars; see *Christian Political Theory and Church Politics in the Mid-Twelfth Century: The Eccesiology of the Gratian's Decretum* (Berkeley: University of California Press, 1972), 5–6. As the title of his book indicates, Chodorow himself locates the *Decretum* firmly in twelfth-century church politics (see *ibid.*, 47–64 for a summary of the argument), and, while the specifics of his argument would be challenged, the general claim that the *Decretum* reflects the institutional concerns of its time seems to be widely accepted. For an important alternative construal of the institutional and social significance of the *Decretum*, see R. W. Southern, *Scholastic Humanism and the Unification of Europe* (Oxford: Blackwell, 1995), vol. I, 283–318.

[8] With respect to the development of law in this period, the relevant articles in *The Cambridge History of Medieval Political Thought, c.350–c.1450*, J. H. Burns, ed. (Cambridge: Cambridge University Press, 1988) offer a most valuable overview; see especially R. Van Caenegem, "Government, Law and Society," *ibid.*, 174–210, and K. Pennington, "Law, Legislative Authority and Theories of Government, 1150–1300," *ibid.*, 424–53. Brett locates Gratian's work specifically within the context of the development of law, as (in a different way) does Peter Landau; see Brett, "Canon Law and Litigation," and Peter Landau, "Wandel und Kontinuität im kanonischen Recht bei Gratian," 215–33 in *Sozialer Wandel im Mittelalter: Wahrnehmungsformen, Erklärungsmuster Regelungsmechanismem*, Jürgen Miethke and Klaus Schreiner, eds. (Sigmaringen: Jan Thorbecke Verlag, 1994).

more formal legal processes were both possible, and increasingly necessary.[9] At the end of the eleventh century, the civilians began to develop a system of jurisprudence through commentary and reflection on Justinian's *Digest* and other Roman legal texts, through which they could review and regularize laws and develop generally recognized standards for legal procedure. The situation within the church was somewhat different, since there was by now a fairly extensive body of church law whose authority was, at least broadly and in principle, accepted by all. However, the relevant canons were difficult to locate and establish, and scarcely any attempts had been made to present them in a comprehensive and systematic way.[10] Nonetheless, civil and canonical jurists were confronted with similar practical challenges, and they responded to these challenges in broadly similar ways.

The practical challenges confronting both civil and canonical jurists first emerged out of the rapid expansion of litigation during this period, the growing pressure on higher-level and more centralized courts and the correlative need for common standards of legal practice.[11] These challenges arose, moreover, in the context of societies that had long relied on processes of adjudication and determinations of the state of the law in order to establish legal criteria in particular cases. For both these reasons, the jurisprudence emerging out of this context focused, initially at least, on questions of interpretation and application of existing laws, rather than on the creation of new laws. What resulted was – at least initially – a jurisprudence for the judge, who had a long-standing and active role to play in the society of the time, rather than for the legislator, who was just now emerging as a major force in European society. It is

[9] Van Caenegem claims that, after the close of the great period of Carolingian legislation near the end of the ninth century, the European continent lived without positive legislation for over two centuries, during which such legal development as there was took the form of developments in customary law; see Van Caenegem, "Government, Law and Society," 181–2.

[10] There were earlier collections of church canons, but Gratian seems to have been the first to offer an analytic treatment of the relevant texts. For two good assessments of the significance of Gratian's achievement *vis-à-vis* his predecessors, see Brett, "Canon Law and Litigation" and Landau, "Wandel und Kontinuität im kanonischen Recht bei Gratian."

[11] This is also of course the era of the great reforming popes and the emergence of strongly centralized forms of government in both church and civil society. However, I agree with Brett that, at least within the church, the emergence of a centralized system for adjudication was driven more by the demands of litigants themselves, together with the sheer volume of cases reaching the curia, than by papal efforts to impose their authority from above; see Brett, "Canon Law and Litigation," 31–2.

hardly surprising in this context that the processes of legal reform were initially carried out through processes of adjudication, informed by legal scholars who had no scruples about reforming existing laws in the light of rational criteria. Of course, the complex, centralized communities of western Europe could not long function with such a high level of judicial activism, and both civil and canon lawyers increasingly turned their attention to lawmaking, seen as distinct from adjudication. Nonetheless, the emerging discipline of jurisprudence continued to focus on the courtroom rather than the legislator's chamber, at least through the early scholastic period.

When we examine the *Decretum* in this context, we begin to get some sense of the kind of work with which we are dealing. In the first place, it is apparent that the *Decretum* is not a systematic compilation of laws, organized after the fashion of a code of civil or canon law. After setting forth the general principles governing the application of laws, Gratian proceeds to the examination of cases, setting forth the issues and the relevant canons raised by each one, and showing how conflicting law can be resolved in each case. Richard Southern has suggested that Gratian was himself a practicing lawyer, and the *causae*, or cases, around which the second part of the *Decretum* is structured, are imaginary lawsuits of a kind that might actually be adjudicated.[12] But, as Anders Winroth has pointed out, it strains credulity to regard the convoluted narratives presented in the *causae* as realistic depictions of actual lawsuits, albeit imaginary ones. They seem much more likely to be classroom examples, contrived to bring out specific sets of issues in a perspicuous way.[13]

At the same time, however, if the *Decretum* is a textbook, it is clearly intended for a classroom oriented immediately to practical activities of legal advocacy and adjudication – a book for law students, as it were, rather than for legal theorists on the one hand, or for legislators on the other. This brings us to an important point. Seen from the perspective of our own expectations, Gratian has surprisingly little to say about the ways in which specific precepts – practices or written ordinances – come to have the force of law. But a theory of legislation would not be germane to his immediate purpose. Rather, he aims to set forth principles by which existing laws can be brought into a coherent order, with the

12 Southern, *Scholastic Humanism* 303–5.

13 Winroth, *The Making of Gratian's Decretum*, 7–8; similarly, Brett argues that, while the *Decretum* is hardly usable as a manual of laws, it is an "outstanding text-book for the teaching of the law." Brett, "Canon Law and Litigation," 24.

ultimate aim of interpreting and applying them in a consistent and equitable way – aims which are clearly relevant to the principles governing legislation, but which are nonetheless distinct. That is why he does not address the kinds of questions that have come to dominate modern theories of law, which reflect the concerns of the legislator and assume that the first questions to be addressed have to do with the legitimacy of enactments. From this standpoint, the very idea of customary law is likely to appear to be oxymoronic, since it is one of the hallmarks of custom that no one enacts it. For Gratian, in contrast, the pressing questions have to do with the norms properly governing the application of existing laws, norms which for him derive more or less directly from natural right and reason. It is only when customs – or written laws, for that matter – come into conflict with other aspects of the law, or reveal themselves to be irrational or pointless, that questions about their fundamental status as laws come into play.

Seen in this light, the distinctions with which Gratian begins the *Decretum* appear as an analytic account of the proper principles of adjudication, built up through the judicious selection and placement of the relevant authorities and through Gratian's interpretative *dicta*. Thus, he begins by reflecting on the most general principles of judgment and the distinctions among diverse kinds of rights and laws; he then proceeds to consider specific kinds of civil and canon law in more detail. In the process, he does consider the sources and proper exercise of legislative authority, but his treatment of the relevant issues is not extensive. Rather, his remarks reflect the concern of a jurist who is attempting to determine just what should count as law, or as legally defensible right, in a context in which written law is still incomplete, in flux and partially implicit.

In what follows, I will examine Gratian's account of custom seen in relation to natural right on the one hand and written law on the other. Before doing so, one other point is in order. I am persuaded by Winroth's recent argument that the *Decretum* as we now have it represents a later expansion of a shorter and more tightly focused work, which he regards as Gratian's original text.[14] At any rate, since on his showing the bulk of the first twenty distinctions, including all those cited below, are part of the original work, nothing in what follows will stand or fall on the adequacy of his theory. When I refer to "Gratian," I simply mean the

[14] Winroth, *The Making of Gratian's Decretum*, passim; for a complete list of the texts that Winroth regards as part of the first recension of the book, see *ibid.*, 197–227.

author of these first distinctions in their original form (that is, apart from a few interpolations), whom I identify, following Winroth, with the author of the original form of the *Decretum*.

Natural right and practices

Throughout the treatise on law, Gratian consistently distinguishes between custom (*consuetudo*) and the more general term, *mos*, which I render as "practice." Practices (*mores*) comprise positive human laws, including both customs and written law (*constituto*); as such, they stand on one side of a line dividing particular, local, and changeable human law from universal and immutable natural right.[15] Thus, while the distinction between custom and written law is important, it is less significant than the division between these two kinds of human convention and natural right. By the same token, we cannot understand Gratian's treatment of either custom or written law without at least some sense of what he means by natural right.

As we have already observed, Gratian's opening remarks, that natural right is that which is contained in the Law and the Gospel, have puzzled – not to say, exasperated – generations of scholars. We are accustomed to think of natural right or natural law as a universally accessible rational standard of morality, and for that reason Gratian's remarks are likely to strike us as obscure or confused – particularly since Gratian also seems to regard natural right as a universally valid principle of laws (D.6, p.c.3). But, as I have argued elsewhere, his point becomes clearer when we place his remarks within the context of the contemporaneous revival of Roman law.[16] Seen in this context, the opening words of the *Decretum* stand in pointed contrast to Justinian's *Digest*, which also begins (or very nearly so) with a definition of natural law, drawn in this instance from the second-century jurist Ulpian, according to which the natural law is "that which nature teaches all animals" (*Dig.* I, 1, 1.3). By setting a

[15] I use "positive law" as a term of convenience for whatever counts as conventional law, in contrast to natural right – in this context, customs and written, statutory law.

[16] See Jean Porter, *Natural and Divine Law: Reclaiming the Tradition for Christian Ethics* (Ottawa: Novalis, 1999), 29–131. I am still persuaded by this reading, even granting Winroth's argument, set out in 146–74 of *The Making of Gratian's Decretum*, that the reception of Roman law and the emergence of the *jus commune* occurred almost simultaneously with the first recension of the *Decretum*, and not (as is more commonly believed) during the end of the tenth and the beginning of the eleventh centuries. As Winroth notes, the Gratian of the first recension quotes the *Digest* four times, and very likely used the Justinianic *corpus* as first hand; *ibid.*, 151.

theological definition, clearly indebted to Hugh of St. Victor, at the beginning of his *Decretum*, Gratian endorses Hugh's position that natural right, at least as seen from the perspective of canon law, can only adequately be understood through scripture.[17] By implication, the civilians' understanding of natural right derived from Ulpian does not provide a suitable starting point for a properly theological understanding of law.

Yet this approach need not imply that the civilians' conception of natural right is wrong, or has no place within ecclesiastical jurisprudence. On the contrary, Gratian goes on to incorporate the key elements of a Roman conception of natural right as mediated through Isidore, whose own sources clearly overlap with those of the *Digest*.[18] He also endorses other conceptions of natural right, including the basic equation between natural right and reason. At least, this would seem to be implied when he follows statements that customs and ordinances are subordinate to natural right with texts asserting that these forms of law are subordinate to reason, or even to considerations of intelligibility and appropriateness. Thus, in the distinction devoted to the relation between natural right and customs, Gratian begins by stating that no one is permitted to act contrary to natural right (D.8, a.c.2), and he then goes on to cite texts saying that no one may act against God's command (D.8, C.2) or against reason and truth (D.8, C.4–9). Similarly, in D.9 he develops the same point with respect to written laws, defending the claim that written laws yield to natural right (D.9, pr.) by citing texts

[17] See Hugh of St. Victor, *De sacramentis* I 11.7, for the relevant text. Peter Landau argues that one of the distinctive features of the *Decretum* is the way in which it brings together the sacramental and the juridical aspects of church life: see Landau, "Wandel und Kontinuität im kanonischen Recht bei Gratian," 229–30. This line of interpretation lends further support to the view that Gratian's appeal to Hugh's influential treatise on the sacraments represents an attempt to establish a theologically sound alternative conception of natural right.

[18] Gratian's attitude to Roman law has long been disputed. Chodorow claims that Gratian deliberately excludes Roman law from consideration: see *Christian Political Theory*, 60–4. In my view, however, the prominence that Gratian gives to Isidore's treatment of Roman law makes this line of interpretation unlikely (see D.1, C.7–12 and D.2 in particular). What is more, as Brett remarks, "Directly, Gratian makes a good deal less use of the civil law he found in his sources, but it is striking how much they influenced his *dicta*, expositions of points of detail prefacing a number of his texts, and the clearest indication of his own thinking" (Brett, "Canon Law and Litigation," 30). And, if Winroth is correct, Gratian's limited use of Roman legal materials may also reflect a later reception of the latter than we have assumed (see note 13 above).

that assert the priority of Scripture (D.9, C.3), sound judgement (D.9, C.4) or sound reasoning (D.9, C.11).

The implication is clear: scripture, reason, truth and sound judgment can all be considered as pre-conventional principles setting the criteria for evaluating human practices. This line of analysis does not imply that every scriptural norm can be taken as an expression of natural right (D.6, p.c.3). Gratian's point is, rather, that any principle that can be regarded as a pre-conventional natural right reflects divine wisdom and will, and thus stands in the same authoritative relation to human law as does Scripture itself. This is a critical move, especially given the fact that Gratian is dealing with canon law, which could well be given a quasi-divine status. Gratian will have none of this; not only are the canons of the church to be evaluated in light of Scripture and rejected if they are contrary to its precepts, but by the same token they are also to be interpreted, and if necessary rejected, in light of their congruity or otherwise with natural right. This becomes clear in the *dictum* with which he concludes D.9:

> Since, therefore, nothing is commanded by natural right except that which God wishes to be done, and nothing is forbidden except that which God forbids to be done, and finally since there is nothing in the canonical scriptures apart from what is found in divine laws; and the divine laws are consonant with nature; it is plain, that whatever can be shown to be contrary to the divine will or the canonical scriptures, the same is also found to be contrary to natural right. Hence, whatever is regarded as yielding to the divine will, or to canonical scripture, or to divine laws, natural right is also to be given precedence over it. Therefore, ordinances, whether ecclesiastical or civil, if they are shown to be contrary to natural right, are to be altogether excluded.
>
> (D.9, p.c.11)

The relative and provisional status of human practices is also expressed in terms of a distinction of origins, drawn from Isidore: "Divine laws are established by nature, human laws are established by practices" (D.1, C.1.1). As the text goes on to explain, this accounts for the variability of the latter, since "different things seem good to different people" (*ibid.*). The same distinction can likewise be expressed in terms of a division between what is naturally permissible or legitimate, and the restrictions introduced by positive law: "What is permissible is divine law; the right is human law" (D.1, C.1.2). This observation leads on to a *dictum* further qualifying the distinction between divine and human laws: "For everything that is permissible is included in the term, divine or natural law; by the term human laws, is understood practices put in writing and handed down as right" (D.1, p.c.1).

These remarks clearly imply what Gratian goes on to say, namely, that both custom and written law are subordinate to natural right, in such a way that the former cannot contradict the standards set by the latter. Here, however, he is making a more basic point. That is, natural right is a basis for legitimation, permissive in force, in addition to providing criteria for limitation and restriction. Indeed, if placement is our guide, the permissive force of natural right is more fundamental than its restrictive force, which is discussed later (specifically, in Dd.8, 9). Certainly, the universally applicable scriptural norms, considered as revealed formulations of natural right, place stringent restrictions on human activity (D.13, pr.). Outside the sphere set by these norms, however, it would seem to be human conventions, rather than natural right as such, which limit and restrain the sphere of permissible human activity. That is why Gratian endorses Isidore's remark that "the right is human law" – because outside the sphere set by revealed laws, it is human laws rather than natural right which determine rights in a juridical sense, that is to say, claims that can be asserted and defended in a court of law. Gratian makes this same point further on, at the beginning of his exposition of the priority of natural right to human practices, observing that, while all things are common by natural right, ownership has been established by natural right (D.8, pr.). This might seem to contradict his claim that natural right is immutable, unless we realize that, as Brian Tierney points out, the institution of property is not regarded as contrary to natural right – rather, it is regarded as a conventional practice limiting and qualifying what can be claimed on the basis of natural right.[19]

This brings us to a critical point. It is certainly the case that natural right, comprehensively understood, serves as a supreme criterion for interpreting human law, whether customary or written. Gratian repeatedly underscores the relative status of all human laws, written as well as

[19] Brian Tierney, *Medieval Poor Law: A Sketch of Canonical Theory and Its Application in England* (Berkeley: University of California Press, 1959), 30–1; Chodorow cites and develops Tierney's point in *Christian Political Theory*, 106. However, I do not agree with Tierney and Chodorow that the natural right referred to at D.8, pr. is simply equivalent to a primitive state of human existence; rather, Gratian is once again making the point that pre-conventional natural right is fundamentally permissive, only becoming restrictive through a formulation qualifying it in the requisite ways.

customary, ecclesiastical as well as secular, and, by the same token, the distinctions among these different kinds of laws are less important than their shared characteristics as provisional laws, meant to be evaluated in light of an absolute standard. At the same time, however, natural right as such has no direct juridical force. The basic principles of reason, truth and justice must be formulated – and therefore restricted in scope, made determinate – in order to serve as a basis for adjudication.[20] Of course, revealed law itself offers one such set of formulations, but even these precepts leave much undetermined. Within this latter sphere of the *fas*, the permissible, human practices, including both custom and written law, provide the specific determinations necessary to give practical meaning and force to natural right. The subordination of practices to natural right is thus qualified and balanced by the indeterminacy of natural right apart from the specifics of human practices, and custom and written law can be considered together as two alternative and (ideally) complementary ways of giving expression and force to natural right. This fundamental parity is clearly expressed early on: " 'Right' is a general name, whereas 'law' is a kind of right. Furthermore, 'right' [*jus*] is so called because it is just [*justum*]. Now right is determined by laws and practices" (D.1, C.2).

Custom and ordinance

When he turns his attention to the distinction between custom and ordinance (that is to say, written law), Gratian reminds us that this distinction presupposes a more basic parity between these kinds of law, considered as two ways of expressing the principles of natural right. He does so by way of a citation from Isidore, who says that "Law is written ordinance," whereas

> Custom is a kind of right instituted by practices, which is taken for law when law falls short. Nor does it make a difference whether it relies on what is written, or on reason, since law is also approved by reason. Furthermore, if law relies on reason, law will be anything that may now

[20] For both Gratian and his commentators, as well as most theologians writing on natural right or natural law in the next century, natural right or law in its primary sense is identified with a general principle or a capacity for practical discernment, rather than with specific precepts *per se*; see *Porter, Natural and Divine Law*, 88–91. As Brian Tierney shows in some detail, the conception of natural right as an individual capacity or power led in the thirteenth century to the emergence of an idea of subjective individual rights: see Tierney, *The Idea of Natural Rights* (Atlanta: Scholars Press, 1997), 43–75.

> rely on reason, or at least that which is consistent with religion, that which is congruent with discipline, that which leads to salvation. Moreover, it is called custom because it is in common use.
>
> (D.1, C.5)

These remarks suggest that the boundary between custom and written law cannot be drawn too sharply; both kinds of law rely on reason, and, what is more, any customs confirmed by reason can take on force of law. This implies that custom is not merely a supplement to written law but exercises independent legal force. At the very least, custom is a source for written law. As Gratian goes on to explain, "When therefore it is said that it does not matter whether custom relies on writing or reason, it is apparent that custom is in part put into writing, and in part is preserved only by the practices of its followers. That which is put into writing is called ordinance or right. That which is not rendered in writing is simply called by the general name of custom" D.1, C.5. In contrast to law (*lex*), which is by definition a written ordinance (D.1, C.3), "Practice (*mos*) is longstanding custom handed down only through practices" (D.1, C.4).

Reading further, we find that custom is more or less equivalent to common practice – more or less, because long-standing practices apparently have a greater claim to be regarded as customary law (D.12, C.6, 7; cf. D.12, p.c.11). The gloss helpfully adds that not every commonly accepted practice constitutes custom in the relative sense; some practices are merely tolerated, or else they go on in spite of a society's contrary commitments (gloss on D.1, C.5).[21] In order to count as customary law, a practice must not only be congruent with natural right; it must also reflect social approbation and a collective intent to establish or endorse norms for behavior. Just as written law must be promulgated in order to have legal force (D.4, p.c.3), and legally authoritative judgments presuppose power or authority as well as rational discernment (D.20, pr.), so the practices of a community must in some way reflect the will of the people in order to count as customary law.

This being so, we are not surprised to read further that "Laws are instituted with promulgation and are more firmly established when they are approved by the practices of those who observe them," and, correlatively,

[21] This refers to the gloss, or line-by-line commentary, on the *Decretum* composed (probably) by Johannes Teutonicus around 1215 and subsequently accepted as the standard, or "ordinary," gloss. As such, it was traditionally published together with the *Decretum*. For further details, see Christensen's introduction to *Gratian: The Treatise on Laws*, xvii–xviii.

a law can be invalidated simply by being ignored (D.4, p.c.3). The observance of the people confirms that an ordinance meets with its approval, or at least that it is in congruity with its settled way of life, whereas a failure to observe the law may indicate that it is an imposition, foreign to the practices of the people for which it is intended. This line of interpretation gains credibility when we read further that no one should promulgate laws that are at odds with the customs of the people for whom the laws are intended (D.8, C.2). This need not imply that such a law would be invalid. The text from Augustine cited here goes on to say that, even though long-established custom ought to be respected, nonetheless it yields to divine authority, and, given the context, this would seem to be the point Gratian wants to underscore. Nonetheless, this text offers one more indication that Gratian (and his sources) place a high value on the normative force of custom, suggesting at the very least that legislators should maintain a conservative attitude *vis-á-vis* the customs of their community, respecting and preserving them as far as possible and departing from them only when necessary.

This is just the kind of attitude that we would expect, given the kind of society inhabited by Gratian's immediate forbears – that is to say, given the predominantly rural and decentralized character of European society through the end of the eleventh century. In this kind of society, local custom was in fact central to legal practices, and it would generally not be necessary or wise to challenge these customs. But this conservative stance was harder to maintain in the expansive and increasingly centralized European society taking shape in Gratian's own day. In this context, legislators and judges had to enjoy some flexibility and freedom to innovate if they were to respond to changing conditions. What is more, for better or for worse – arguably, for both – the late eleventh and twelfth centuries see the emergence of a strong, centralized church governance centered on the Pope and the bureaucracies of the Roman See. Gratian clearly supports this development, and yet it is not apparent how support for a centralized church government can be reconciled with enthusiasm for local custom.

Given this context of social and political tensions, we should not be surprised to find that Gratian's very positive view of custom is balanced – perhaps, even undercut – elsewhere in the treatise on laws. Most fundamentally, custom apparently only has legal force with respect to matters not covered by written law: "Custom is a kind of right instituted by practices, which is taken for law when the law is deficient" (D.1, C.5.1). Further on, we read that custom yields to written law (D.11, a.c.1). What is more, respect for custom should not be taken so far as to undermine the authority of the legitimate leaders of a community; when custom conflicts with the decrees of such an authority, it must give way (D.11, C.4). Nor can we appeal to custom to justify practices that are unreasonable, depraved or even pointless; Gratian quotes Gregory the Great citing the patristic remark that Jesus did not say, "I am the custom," but "I am the truth" (D.8, C.5). At the very least, these comments would seem to reflect a different spirit from the distinctions cited above, one that prizes reasonableness, innovation and change in contrast to tradition, conservation and stability. What is more, at least some of these distinctions seem to come into direct conflict with those cited above, considered precisely as matters of law. How is it possible to say both that a decree must be confirmed by custom in order to be firmly established, and that written law overrides contrary custom – which by definition would not confirm the law in question?

Gratian is aware of these tensions and sets out to resolve them; that conclusion is at least suggested by the amount of sustained attention that he gives to custom throughout the first twenty distinctions, and by the ways in which he qualifies and balances restrictions on custom. Most fundamentally, his treatment reflects his desire to maintain a proper balance between the claims inherent in customary law with the claims of centralized authority, which are typically expressed through written law. Gratian is commonly, and rightly, regarded as one of the most influential early supporters of a strongly centralized form of church governance, and, more specifically, in the newly emergent monarchial papacy.[22] Whatever we may think of this development today, it is not hard to see why Gratian and so many of his contemporaries would have welcomed it. Some kind of centralized government was necessary if the church was to function effectively in a rapidly expanding society, and, what is more, the papacy had been a force for reform since the time of Gregory VII. At the same time, however, a close examination of the treatise on laws suggests that Gratian was also sympathetic to the countervailing demands of the local churches. This sympathy is expressed through his generally positive treatment of customary law, which, we should recall, is typically the law of relatively small, internally

[22] Gratian's strong support for papal authority has often been noted. For a clear and persuasive argument, grounded in a comprehensive review of relevant texts, see Jean Gaudemet, "La primauté pontificale dans le Décret de Gratien," 137–54 in *Studia in Honorem Eminentissimi Cardinalis alphonsi M. Stickler*, R. J. Card. Castillo Lara, ed. (Rome: Libreria Ateneo Salesiano, 1992).

cohesive and isolated communities. This comes through very clearly in D.12, in which Gratian approvingly cites a whole series of authorities defending the legitimacy of *local* customs over against those who would disregard or extirpate them without good reason (D.12, C.3–10) – significantly, placing these within the context of the general principle that no one is permitted to act without regard for justice (D.12, pr.). In reading these texts, the emphasis should be placed on "local" – Gratian is here expressing a concern to protect the autonomy and integrity of local communities as far as possible, given the conditions of the time. To be sure, he also insists that written law can depart from custom, or even override it – but, at the very least, these texts drive home the point that written law should not undercut local custom without good reasons for doing so. Uniformity as such is not a value, even in the centralized church that Gratian defends.

Gratian has a further reason for giving a central role to custom that stems more specifically from the ecclesiastical and theological nature of his project. That is, that there are many church practices that cannot be justified on the basis of scripture, and do not reflect rational exigencies in any obvious way, either. If these are to be retained as part of the common and accepted practices of the church, it is necessary to grant some authority to them simply on the grounds that they are long-established practices of the Christian people – and, by implication, this means that the customs of the Christian people must be acknowledged as having some legal force, independently of the written laws of church authorities (D.12, C.11). At the same time, Gratian immediately adds a *dictum* stating that, while we should defer to the customs of the universal church or long-standing (presumably local) custom, newer practices should be abrogated if changing circumstances suggest it (D.12, p.c.11). As the next text indicates, this restriction is motivated, at least in part, by a desire to preserve the freedom of the individual Christian (D.12, C.12).

The tensions in Gratian's remarks on custom thus stem both from his sources and more importantly from social conditions and legal practice in his own day. At the same time, however, he indicates how these tensions can be harmonized – not perfectly, perhaps, but adequately, given the practical aims of litigation. In order to see how he does so, we must keep in mind that, throughout the *Decretum*, Gratian is attempting to reconcile diverse elements of a complex and sometimes inconsistent textual tradition, in the process eliciting a coherent conception of law from the manifold perspectives incorporated in his sources. The placement of diverse approaches relative to one another carries much of the interpretative weight here. Gratian indicates which elements of the field he takes to be central or paradigmatic by identifying them as the general categories; these, in turn, provide a framework for interpreting the specific claims and approaches found in what follows.

With respect to customary law, the immediately relevant general category is that of *mores*, practices, which are comprised of customs and ordinances, that is, written laws. As we noted above, practices are mutable and provisional, in contrast to the unchanging and universal natural right. Both custom and ordinance are valid only insofar as they are in congruity with the standards of natural right, and yet natural right cannot serve as a basis for actual legal practice unless it is specified in some way. Custom and written law represent two centrally important forms of this specification, and, by the same token, these are legitimate only insofar as they can be construed as expressions of natural right in some way or other. In order to identify the proper boundaries between them, we must begin by placing them as two kinds of expression of the rational standards that are alone normative in the proper sense – that is to say, standards that ought to be obeyed because they reflect demands of natural right, reason and equity. Given this starting point, these criteria themselves go a long way towards determining the relative force and authority of customary and written law.

Seen from this perspective, the priority of written law to custom is not so prejudicial to custom as we might assume. Recall that both custom and ordinance are initially presented as expressions of reason (D.1, C.5). Seen from this perspective, it does not much matter whether a given practice is expressed through written law or handed down through custom, since whatever reason confirms will have the force of law (D.1, p.c.5). I do not think Gratian means here to deny the necessity for legally authoritative promulgation (in the case of written law), or confirmation that a custom reflects the approbation of the people, normally by way of long-standing usage – both claims that he affirms elsewhere. His point, rather, is that custom and ordinance represent two distinct but interrelated ways of expressing the demands of natural right in a particular time and place. Certainly, written law will normally represent a more perspicuous and clearly authoritative expression of natural right than does custom – if only because written laws are intentionally and (we hope) clearly formulated to serve just that purpose. Yet there seems to be a presumption here that written laws will often be formulations of what has hitherto been customary practice, at least on the assumption that the custom in question is well established and genuinely rational.

By the same token, Gratian introduces the negative appraisals of custom collected in D.8 with a *dictum* asserting that neither customs nor written laws should be received as law if they conflict with natural right (D.8, a.c.2). In such a case, the practices in question would not deserve to be regarded as customary usages or rights, claims having force of law, but would count, rather, as depraved or (at best) as mere usages. In cases such as these, the (so-called) customs of a community can and should be set aside by written law. Yet, by the same token, written law also yields to natural right, and any ordinance of civil or canon law is to be rejected if it is contrary to natural right (D.9, passim; see especially C.11). Seen from this perspective, Gratian's claim that an ordinance is confirmed by the practice of the people, and his further observation that such an ordinance may be abrogated by non-observance, appear as counterweights to the claim that written law supercedes custom. That is, when an ordinance is irrational or unjust, or in some other way at odds with natural right, the non-reception by the people offers one way of rejecting and correcting the putative ordinance in question. Thus, there is no necessary inconsistency in saying that written law abrogates (some specific) custom, while at the same time custom (broadly considered as an ensemble of practices) can abrogate written law.

If we grant Gratian's claim that any kind of law is only valid if it is in accord with natural right, then the seeming inconsistencies in his treatment of custom and ordinance can indeed be harmonized, at least to a considerable extent. A customary practice contrary to an unjust ordinance would not be an example of a custom that is contrary to a genuine law – since an unjust ordinance is by definition not law in the full, normative sense. And, by the same token, an ordinance issued contrary to depraved usage would not represent a real instance of genuine customary law being overridden by written law, since the depraved usage would not have the force of law. Genuine customs and written laws will thus normally confirm and reinforce one another, laws formulating and expressing customs, customs confirming laws by embedding them in the lived practices and ongoing experiences of the community.

Of course, formal rational consistency is one thing, legal practice is another. The theoretical congruence between good customs and good written laws will not guarantee that customs and laws will never come into conflict – not least because we cannot always expect clarity or consensus on what counts as good customs or good laws. At any rate, whatever the merits of the case may be, local custom will always have the potential to exercise a practical veto over written law. A law that is not accepted by the community is practically unenforceable, whether we want to regard it as legally valid or not.[23] It would be asking a good deal from Gratian, or any other legal theorist, to develop a legal theory that could anticipate, or much less resolve, all such inconsistencies and contingencies. Arguably, one of the strengths of Gratian's treatise on laws is precisely that it does not impose an overly simplistic analysis onto the complexities of law as it is practiced and lived.

I turn now to my final point. There is at least one sense in which custom can be said to be prior to written law – admittedly, not in a way that Gratian himself pursues, but one suggested by and consistent with his overall account. Recall that on his view any legitimate judgment or ordinance will be an expression of natural right (not necessarily the only one possible), at least in the sense of being congruent with reason and equity. Thus, all such judgments and laws can be regarded as expressions of natural right, and therefore as themselves comprising natural right in an extended sense. Hence, natural right properly so called cannot be exhaustively equated with positive laws, and yet well-ordered positive laws may legitimately be understood as comprising a kind of natural right. Once we appreciate this point, we can more readily appreciate why the division between natural right and convention cannot simply be equated with a division between two sets of explicit laws. Natural right as such can have no legal (or, I would add, broadly practical) force, unless it is expressed through specific formulations; and yet these formulations have legal force only insofar as they manifest natural right in some way. The division between natural right and convention must be located first of all within specific judgments and laws; thus understood, it tracks the distinction between the particular formulation of the rule, and the considerations in virtue of which the rule is regarded as reasonable and just. On this basis, we can then go on to develop a substantive account of natural right, seen as the normative ground and criterion for

[23] Helmholz offers a good example of this in the English non-reception of *privilegium fori*, the principle that clerics cannot be tried in secular courts. Even though the contrary British custom of trying clerics in civil court was expressly condemned by the Rota in the 1370s, it persisted without noteworthy modification. Here is a clear example of a written law being abrogated, in effect if not in legal theory, by a contrary custom – in the teeth of a formal declaration that the custom in question was illegal. See Helmholz, "The Universal and the Particular," 651–2, for details.

social conventions, by reference to those general features in terms of which a range of positive judgments and laws are regarded as just.

We noted above that Gratian claims that an unreasonable custom or ordinance does not count as a genuine law. This line of analysis complicates that claim, but not in a way that is fatal to his best insights. On the contrary, it offers a way of preserving what is valid in that claim, while casting it in a more realistic fashion. That is to say, understood in this way, both custom and written law can be placed on a kind of sliding scale between the ideal and the actual, and evaluated accordingly. Our grasp of a given conventional norm, whether custom or written law, will always be grounded in the actualities of practice – if only because we cannot grasp a practical norm without some sense of the kinds of actions that would count as obeying or transgressing it. By the same token, we cannot even begin to formulate the rational purposes behind the norm, and the ideals it embodies, without some reference to the specific ways in which those purposes and ideals are to be carried out. Yet, in the very process of formulating these ideals, we will inevitably become aware of the ways in which the norm falls short of, or contravenes, these ideals – and, to that extent, falls short of the more comprehensive ideal of a genuine law. This need not imply a global rejection of the custom or ordinance in question, but it should at least prompt efforts towards revision.[24]

Seen within this context, custom would seem to stand in a mediating role between natural right in the most basic sense, and written law. The customary practices of a community reflect a historically informed and socially located expression of natural principles of action. As such, they reflect the particularity and mutability proper to human, as opposed to divine and natural law. Yet the contingency of customary practices is not sheerly arbitrary or unbounded. To the extent that these practices stem from natural and rational principles, they reflect something of the universality and stability of these principles, and can be understood and applied accordingly. At the same time, custom is of course not written law, and in this respect too it resembles natural right properly so called. Considered relative to natural right, customs are particular formulations – albeit, not verbal formulations – which are under-determined by the rational principles from which they stem. Yet, considered relative

[24] Compare Lon Fuller's defense of the claim that "both rules of law and legal systems can and do half exist": Fuller, *The Morality of Law* (2nd edn, New Haven: Yale University Press, 1964), 122.

to written law, the customs of a community, to the extent that they reflect rational and equitable standards, function much as natural right itself does. That is to say, they provide the unarticulated starting points and the necessary contexts for interpretation and application that must be in place, in order for a system of written laws to get off the ground in the first place. To put it another way, the customs of a people mediate between natural right and written law, and, while they are not by themselves sufficient law, written law could not function apart from this context.

Precisely because they stem from rational principles, at least in some ways and up to a point, the customs of a people can be subject to self-reflective, rational scrutiny, developed, made explicit, and where necessary reformed or abandoned. This is the process that will normally lead to the articulation of written laws. Because written laws serve to formulate and correct custom, they will normally supercede and override customary law; yet, because they find their context and point within a broader framework of customary law, the customs of a people will provide the necessary context for their interpretation. What is more, written law will have no purchase on a community, unless it reflects the practices of that community in some way; even a law that sets out to correct custom will necessarily reflect other aspects of the customary practices of a community, or it will lack purchase in the community for which it is intended. Far from being a minor adjunct to the law properly so called, custom is seen from this perspective as the one essential component of any legal system, sufficient to sustain a rule of law under some circumstances, and one essential component of the rule of law under any and every circumstance.

5

Vitoria and Suarez on *ius gentium*, natural law, and custom

BRIAN TIERNEY

Although the worlds of Vitoria and Suarez were remote from our own, some of the problems these authors faced resemble ones that still concern modern jurists and political philosophers; and these problems involve not only the content of international law but also its grounding in custom or natural law or positive enactments. In this paper I want to suggest that Vitoria displayed considerable versatility in deploying various norms of international law – or even in inventing such norms on occasion – but without any serious concern for the grounding of these norms, whether in custom or in some other source. Suarez, on the other hand, coming two generations later, presented a detailed account of the sources of *ius gentium* within a massive synthesis that included full-scale treatments of natural law and customary law.

Past and present

Anthony Pagden has warned us against studying earlier ideas on international law with present-day concerns in mind:

> [B]y re-describing the battles of the early modern world in modern terms, by making Francisco de Vitoria the remote ancestor of the Charter of the United Nations or the Bill of Rights, the specificity of the conflict is lost, and with it the possibility of its significance as a process over time.[1]

Such statements are of course platitudinous among historians. It is precisely the specificity of a past situation that we need first to understand. Evidently we cannot study the works of the past profitably by imposing modern ideas on them; but, in the case of such Spanish

[1] Anthony Pagden, *The Uncertainties of Empire: Essays in Iberian and Ibero-American History* (Aldershot: Variorum, 1944), p. x.

authors as Francisco de Vitoria, it is the very specificity of their historical situation that gave rise to problems analogous to those that international lawyers face nowadays. This is especially true in the field of human rights. Much of the modern thinking about rights in international law arose out of an appalled reaction to the atrocities of the Nazis in World War II. In an earlier age the Spanish conquests in the New World and the savageries inflicted on the indigenous American peoples by the conquistadors – luridly chronicled by Las Casas and others – gave rise to similar concerns among Spanish jurists and theologians. They too had to consider human rights within the framework of an emerging international law.

In the aftermath of the two World Wars many international lawyers became dissatisfied with the Eurocentric positivist paradigm that had prevailed during the preceding century. Territories inhabited by "backward" peoples were no longer regarded as *res nullius*, to be rightfully occupied by "civilized" Western powers. At the same time the widespread acceptance of codes and conventions regarding universal human rights gave a new urgency to problems of humanitarian intervention. Questions like these arose. When can one sovereign state rightfully intervene in the affairs of another? (To remove a tyrant? To prevent a massacre?) What practices (if any) freely accepted by one people are so abhorrent to the rest of the international community as to justify their suppression by external powers? Are practices that have become customary in the international community binding on all its members and if so why?

Underlying all such issues in the development of modern international law is the problem of how the various rights and obligations that are asserted can be legitimately grounded. For many jurists a simple reliance on legal positivism does not provide an adequate response to the evils of the Nazi regime. Hence there has been a considerable revival of natural law thinking, or an emphasis on *ius cogens* understood as "imperative norms," or an appeal to "the principles accepted by all civilized nations." But no general agreement has resulted. Jacques Maritain, who helped to shape the United Nations Universal Declaration on Human Rights, once observed a little ruefully that his group all agreed so long as no one asked them why they agreed.

I have mentioned these modern issues because all of them were also considered *mutatis mutandis* by the Spanish authors of the sixteenth century. But the Spanish neoscholastics approached their problems from within a different world order; they had no United Nations or

International Court of Justice to appeal to. Still more importantly, the sixteenth-century authors addressed their problems from within a world of thought different from ours, a *mentalité* shaped by Roman and canon law and by Aristotelian–Thomist philosophy. A consequence of this was that the Spanish scholars were not only struggling to comprehend the new situation created by the discovery of a New World; they were also struggling within a network of old texts that were often difficult to harmonize with one another. We in turn can only address their thought meaningfully if we first familiarize ourselves with some aspects of this material.

From the twelfth century onward medieval jurists and theologians wrote extensively about the different varieties of law, but no coherent synthesis emerged concerning the relationship between natural law, customary law, and the law of nations. The classical sources of Roman law referring to the *ius gentium* did not provide any clear guidance; they offered only a tangle of apparently conflicting texts. An influential passage of Ulpian included in the *Digest* gave a threefold classification of law as natural law, the law of nations (*ius gentium*), and civil law. Natural law was a law common to all animate creatures – it included such things as procreation and the rearing of offspring; *ius gentium* was a law common to all humankind; and civil law was the law peculiar to a particular society or *civitas*.[2] This seems straightforward enough, but other texts of Roman law made no reference to a distinction between natural law and the *ius gentium*. They distinguished only between natural law and civil law or between the law of nations and civil law.[3] One text referred to the common use of the open sea as pertaining both to the law of nations and to natural law without any distinction of meaning.[4] As Peter Stein noted, Roman jurists often used the two terms interchangeably.[5] In the *Institutes*, for instance, we can read of "natural law . . . which is called the law of nations."[6] And yet sometimes the two kinds of law were sharply distinguished from one another. Another text of the *Institutes* observed that: "By natural law all men were born free . . . But afterward slavery came in by the law of nations."[7]

[2] T. Mommsen and P. Krueger (eds.), *Digesta*, in *Corpus Iuris Civilis* (3 vols., Berlin: Weidmann, 1868), vol. 1, *Dig.* 1.1.1.
[3] *Dig.* 1.1.11, 1.1.9.
[4] P. Krueger (ed.), *Institutiones*, in *Corpus Iuris Civilis*, vol. 1, *Inst.* 2.1.1.
[5] Peter Stein, "Roman Law," in *The Cambridge History of Medieval Political Thought* (Cambridge: Cambridge University Press, 1988), p. 44.
[6] *Inst.* 2.1.11. [7] *Inst.* 1.5pr.

According to this last argument, servitude was introduced by the law of nations pertaining to the conduct of war when the custom arose of enslaving captives rather than killing them.[8] This explanation of the origin of slavery was very commonly cited in medieval and early modern writings and it eventually gave rise to problems concerning the authority of customary international law.

Medieval canonists and theologians introduced further complications. For the classical jurists natural law was a philosophical concept without real legal force; they never asserted that natural law would override positive human law if the two conflicted. But Gratian's *Decretum*, the great twelfth-century compendium of canon law, declared that any custom or statute contrary to natural law was "vain and void."[9] And in the next century Thomas Aquinas maintained that all human laws must conform to natural law, either as logical inferences from the basic principles of natural law or as supplements intended to provide a common rule where natural law left some issue undecided.[10]

These doctrines left medieval thinkers and their early modern successors with a problem that never seems to have concerned the classical jurists – how to explain and justify the existence of human institutions introduced by the *ius gentium* that were contrary to natural law. For instance, according to one text of the *Decretum*, universal freedom and common ownership of property pertained to the natural law; but servitude and private property evidently existed in the real world. One solution maintained that the term *ius naturale* could have a merely permissive sense. Natural law did not only command and forbid certain ways of behaving but also indicated kinds of conduct that were good in themselves – like community of property – but not actually commanded.[11] This argument became important in some later discussions of the *ius gentium*.[12]

[8] *Inst.* 1.3.2.

[9] E. Friedberg (ed.), *Decretum Magister Gratiani*, in *Corpus Iuris Canonici* (2 vols., Leipzig: Tauchnitz, 1879), vol. 1, *Dist.* 8 *dictum post* c.1.

[10] *Summa theologiae*, in R. Busa (ed.), *S. Thomae Aquinatis opera omnia* (7 vols., Stuttgart: Frommen-Holzboog, 1980), vol. 1, 1.2ae.95.2.

[11] *Decretum Gratiani*, *Dist.*1 c.7. The concept of permissive natural law was introduced by the canonist Rufinus, c.1160. It subsequently had a long history in Western law and political thought. For an outline of this development see B. Tierney, "Permissive Natural Law and Property: Gratian to Kant," *Journal of the History of Ideas* 63 (2001), 381–99.

[12] See above, p. 90.

An underlying assumption of canonists and theologians alike was that human sinfulness had made necessary the establishment of laws and institutions that would not have been needed if humankind had remained in a state of innocence. Already in the mid-twelfth century the canonist Rufinus described how humans, after the Fall of Adam, lived in a brutish and savage way; but, he explained, they retained enough sense of justice to come together and enter into compacts with one another and so establish the first principles of the *ius gentium*.[13]

Before turning to the texts of Vitoria we need finally to consider a little further the term *ius gentium* itself. In the *Digest*, *ius gentium* was defined as "the law that natural reason has established among all human beings"; it was not a law regulating relations between sovereign states but rather a set of legal principles that were commonly accepted by all peoples.[14] Accordingly, modern writers often observe that, in the classical sources, *ius gentium* did not mean international law as the term is used nowadays. This is true of course, but it is not quite the whole truth. For our inquiry it is also relevant that the *ius gentium* of classical and medieval lawyers did include much that we should now regard as principles of customary international law – the inviolability of ambassadors for instance, and the freedom of the open sea, and the right to wage war in self-defense. Suarez was the first to distinguish within the *ius gentium* between a law *inter gentes* and a law *intra gentes*, between international law as we should say and commonly observed municipal laws. But earlier, when Vitoria discussed the Spanish conquests in the Indies and the rights of American Indians, he too was necessarily concerned with aspects of the *ius gentium* as a law "between peoples."

Vitoria and the Indies

For a system of international law to grow up there has to exist both a variety of independent states and also a sense of community among them sufficient to make possible the acceptance of some common rules of law. In Vitoria's world the medieval dream of a universal empire still lingered on among some thinkers, but Vitoria himself denied that either

13 H. Singer (ed.), *Die Summa Decretorum des Magister Rufinus* (Paderborn: Ferdinand Shöningh, 1902), p. 4.

14 *Dig.* 1.1.9. I have conventionally translated *ius gentium* as "law of nations," but it will be understood that the words do not always, or usually, have the same sense as the modern term "international law."

pope or emperor possessed a universal temporal jurisdiction.[15] Vitoria also wrote, however, that every Christian country was part of one Christian commonwealth and that, indeed, every commonwealth was a part of the whole world.[16] When he addressed the problems of the Indies, therefore, his thought reflected both the reality of a world of independent peoples and the ideal of a cosmopolitan world order.

In his *Relectio de Indis* Vitoria presented all the arguments he could muster concerning the justice or injustice of the Spanish claims in the Indies. Specifically, he discussed three themes that still interest modern international lawyers – the idea of universal human rights, the idea of humanitarian intervention, and the idea of free intercourse among nations.

Vitoria introduced the first theme by asking whether the Indians possessed a rightful *dominium* – understood as both ownership and jurisdiction – in their own lands before the arrival of the Spaniards. He was asking, that is, whether the Indians could rightfully hold property and form their own legitimate governments. In his earlier commentary on Aquinas Vitoria had written that in the beginning God had given "right and dominion" over the whole world to the whole human race, and in the *Relectio de Indis* he added that dominion was "nothing but a right."[17] It would seem then that the Indians shared in this God-given right unless there was some reason that excluded them.

Much earlier, in the mid-thirteenth century, Pope Innocent IV had acknowledged that "dominion, possession, and jurisdiction" could rightfully belong to infidels.[18] But the infidels that Innocent had in mind were Muslims, people at least as advanced in civilization as the Christians themselves. In extending the argument to include an alien people, considered barbarous in their way of life, Vitoria was really asking whether universal human rights existed, rights that inhered in all people, however different they were from civilized Christians. He could think of several reasons why the Indians might be incapable of

[15] Francisco de Vitoria, *Relectio de Indis*, ed. L. Pereña and J. M. Peres Prendes (Madrid: Consejo Superior de Investigaciones Cientificas, 1967), 1.2.2, p. 36, 1.2.5, p. 46.

[16] *De potestate civili*, ed. T. Urdanoz, in *Obras de Francisco de Vitoria* (Madrid: Biblioteca de Autores Cristianos, 1960), §13, p. 168, §21, p. 191.

[17] *De justitia*, ed. V. Beltran de Heredia, in *Francisco de Vitoria: Commentarios a la Secunda Secundae de Santo Tomas* (6 vols., Salamanca: Biblioteca de Teologos Españoles, 1932–52), vol. 3, 2.2ae.62.1, p. 71; *De Indis* 1.1.13, p. 28.

[18] *Commentaria Innocentii Quarti . . . super libros quinque Decretalium* (reprint, Frankfurt: Minerva, 1968), 3.34.8.

holding such rights. It might be because, as barbarians, they were natural slaves according to the teaching of Aristotle, and so incapable of possessing anything as their own, or because they were sinners and pagans and so lacked rightful dominion, or because they were witless or irrational. But Vitoria dismissed all these arguments. The slavery that took away the right of ownership was a penal institution of human law, he argued; no one was such a slave by nature.[19] Sin and infidelity did not in themselves take away rightful dominion.[20] It was true that irrational creatures, brute animals, could not be subjects of rights, but the Indians were not irrational; they had their own ordered way of life that required the use of reason. And besides, the existence of a whole race of irrational humans was intrinsically impossible; it would imply a failure of God and nature.[21] The implication of the argument was that all humans (but no non-human creatures) were endowed with some basic rights. Vitoria concluded therefore that the Indians were rightful rulers and owners of their own lands. It followed from this that the Spaniards could not claim dominion over the Indies by "right of discovery." Vitoria noted that by natural law and the law of nations a *res nullius* belonged to the first occupant; but the lands in question were not *res nullius*; they were already occupied by a people who held rightful possession of them.[22]

Having established that the Indians did indeed have rights, Vitoria next put forward a series of arguments in favor of the Spanish claims; and here he introduced the second theme mentioned above, the idea that the law of nations might permit one people to intervene in the affairs of another on humanitarian grounds. Vitoria acknowledged that the sinful practices of the Indians in general could not justify a Spanish invasion, not even their alleged sins "against nature" that were regarded as particularly abhorrent such as incest and sodomy and intercourse with animals.[23] But Vitoria thought that the particular practices of cannibalism and human sacrifice did call for foreign intervention. The reason for this was that these practices involved the taking of innocent

19 *De Indis*, 1.1.16, p. 31.

20 *Ibid.*, 1.1.10, p. 25. Vitoria held that the Spaniards had a right to send Christian missionaries to the Indies and to make war in defense of them if they were attacked. But this was an argument based on Christian faith not on the *ius gentium*. There was no reciprocity about it. Vitoria certainly would not have welcomed pagan missionaries in Christian lands. See *De Indis*, 1.3.8, p. 87, 1.3.11, p. 89.

21 *Ibid.*, 1.1.12, p. 26, 1.1.15, p. 30, 22 *Ibid.*, 1.2.10, p. 54.

23 *Ibid.*, 1.2.22, p. 70, *De temperantia*, in Urdanoz, *Obras de Francisco de Vitoria*, pp. 1040 and 1050.

human life, and, Vitoria argued, any person could and should intervene to protect the victims in such cases. The innocent victims had a right to defend themselves and so others, especially princes, also had a right to defend them even, if no other means were effective, by instituting a change of regime. In such a case, Vitoria held, "their rulers may be changed and other princes set up." It did not matter if the innocent victims did not request this help or even refused it for they could not renounce their right to life. "No one can give another the right to kill him," Vitoria wrote. The laws authorizing such practices were oppressive and tyrannical, and the Spaniards could rightfully defend the Indians against such tyranny even if they did not welcome the foreign intervention.[24]

Another of Vitoria's arguments concerning humanitarian intervention has a ring of later imperialist rhetoric. Even if the Indians were not irrational, Vitoria suggested, they might be so weak-minded as to be incapable of managing their own affairs like children, and then perhaps the Spaniards could establish a sort of guardianship over them for their own good. One is reminded of Kipling's "white man's burden" and his natives who were "half devil and half child." Vitoria himself, however, did not endorse the argument he presented. He said it could be "mentioned for the sake of argument but certainly not asserted with confidence."[25]

Vitoria's idea of invading a people to save them from tyranny even when the invaders were not welcomed as liberators may seem questionable nowadays. But a modern reader might still find much of his argument about the right of humanitarian intervention to be acceptable. The only such right that Vitoria recognized unreservedly was a right to protect innocent human life.

In considering humanitarian intervention, then, Vitoria was on the whole cautious and moderate. But when he turned to the third theme mentioned above, the *ius gentium* concerning free intercourse among nations, he seems to have abandoned caution and instead displayed a rather bold creative imagination in discovering or inventing new rights for the Spaniards within the law of nations. Vitoria began like this:

> The first proof comes from the law of nations which either is natural law or derives from natural law . . . Among all nations it is considered inhumane to treat guests and travelers badly without some special cause.[26]

[24] *De Indis*, 1.3.14, p. 94, *De temperantia*, p. 1051.
[25] *De Indis*, 1.3.17, p. 97. [26] *Ibid.*, 1.3.1, p. 78.

Vitoria went on to argue that this provision of the *ius gentium* conferred specific rights on the Spaniards in relation to the Indians whose lands they entered, and that the Spaniards could justly make war on the Indians if these rights were violated.

Starting out from "a natural communion and partnership among men," Vitoria proceeded to claim that the *ius gentium* conceded to foreigners a right to trade freely with the Indians, along with rights to land on their coasts, to travel through their lands and to settle there – and all this without the consent of the Indians themselves.[27] Vitoria also claimed for the Spaniards a right to search for gold and to export it – the law of *res nullius* applied as much to gold in the ground as to fish in the sea, he asserted.[28] As the argument goes on it becomes more and more unpersuasive, and not only to a modern reader. Vitoria's immediate successors at Salamanca also criticized his more extreme claims. Melchior Cano observed that the Spaniards did not enter the Indian lands merely as travelers "unless we call Alexander a traveler." And Domingo de Soto pointed out that the Roman law of *res nullius* did not permit one people to plunder the resources of another; the French could not enter Spain to seek out treasure, nor could the Spaniards enter France for that purpose.[29]

One has the impression that Vitoria himself was not convinced by all the arguments that he put forward in favor of the Spaniards. He introduced them as grounds that "might" justify the Spanish conquests and he several times added the qualifying clause "provided that no harm comes to the Indians." (But Vitoria knew that in fact grievous harm had come to them.) Certainly some of his arguments were out of touch with the realities of international relations in the sixteenth century. Vitoria was living in an age of dawning mercantilism. Kings took for granted the right to control imports and exports, especially the export of precious metals, and to exclude foreign ships from trading with their possessions. And of course the Spanish kings did not concede to other European nations the rights in the Indies that Vitoria claimed for the Spaniards as universal rights, grounded in natural law and the law of nations.

[27] *Ibid.*, 1.3.1, pp. 78–81. [28] *Ibid.*, 1.3.3, p. 82.

[29] Melchor Cano, *De dominio Indorum*, in Juan de la Peña, *De bello contra insulanos*, ed. L. Pereña *et al.* (Madrid: Consuejo Superior de Investigaciones Cientificas, 1982), p. 579; Domingo de Soto, *De iustitia et iure*, ed. V. Diego Carro and M. Gonzáles Ordóñez (5 vols., reprint, Madrid: Instituto de Estudios Politicas, 1968), vol. 3, 5.3.3, p. 423. For a recent modern criticism of Vitoria's argument see Georg Cavallar, *The Rights of Strangers* (Aldershot: Ashgate, 2002), pp. 110–12.

The grounding of *ius gentium*

However we judge Vitoria's treatment of the *ius gentium* in his arguments about the rights of the Spaniards in America, there can be no doubt of his passionate concern for the issues of justice and morality that were involved in the Indies debates. But when we turn to Vitoria's treatment of the grounding of the *ius gentium* the situation is quite different. A major task for early modern jurists was to determine whether the law of nations was derived from natural law or positive human law and, if the latter, what kind of human law was involved. Vitoria referred to these issues at various points in his works but without producing any coherent doctrine or, apparently, even attempting to do so. When his scattered comments are brought together they do not provide a consistent teaching but only a mish-mash of discordant texts. In various contexts Vitoria wrote that the *ius gentium* derived its authority from natural law, from custom, from an initial consent at the beginning of the human race, or from a continuing virtual consent of all nations or a majority of them. Perhaps Vitoria regarded the problem as a juridical one, not of primary importance for a theologian.

Vitoria seems often to have equated *ius gentium* with *ius naturale*. In introducing his argument about free intercourse among nations he wrote, as we saw, that the *ius gentium* "either is natural law or derives from natural law."[30] Vitoria also associated the rules of the law of nations with those of the law of nature in a variety of other contexts. For instance, cannibalism and human sacrifice were prohibited by both laws, and the doctrine of *res nullius* was approved by both of them.[31] Vitoria also wrote that a person born in a given land acquired citizenship there by virtue of "the law of nature and of nations."[32] And again, in arguing that a ruler held jurisdiction over resident aliens in his land, Vitoria wrote that "He has this by the law of nations . . . Indeed it seems that he has the right by natural law."[33] Vitoria also suggested that it was this grounding in the law of nature that gave to the *ius gentium* its binding force.

[30] Above, n. 26. [31] *De temperantia*, p. 1051; *De Indis*, 1.3.3, p. 82.
[32] *De Indis*, 1.3.4, p. 83.
[33] *De iure belli*, in Urdanoz, *Obras de Francisco de Vitoria*, §19, p. 828.

> Since many things issue from the law of nations, note that, insofar as the *ius gentium* is derived from natural law, it has a manifest power of creating rights and obligations.[34]

So far Vitoria's teaching seems plain enough. But immediately after the passage just quoted he wrote that the *ius gentium* might not be founded on natural law but on human consent.

> Given that the law of nations is not always derived from natural law, still the consent of the greater part of the whole world seems sufficient, especially when it is for the common good of all.[35]

Vitoria went on here to envisage a primeval institution of the *ius gentium* by majority consent at the beginning of the human race. If, he argued, after the Flood the greater part of mankind had agreed that envoys should be inviolate, the sea common, prisoners of war enslaved, and strangers welcomed and not driven away, then these things would have the force of law even if a minority had dissented.[36] Elsewhere Vitoria had argued that when a people instituted a government for itself unanimous consent was not necessary; the vote of a majority would suffice.[37] Here he applied the same principle to the origin of the law of nations.

Another argument asserting that the authority of the law of nations was derived from human institution did not mention a specific historical origin. Vitoria began here by arguing that a king was bound by his own laws; then he added as a corollary that all kingdoms were likewise obliged by the law of nations.

> From all this we infer a corollary, that the law of nations does not have its force from a pact or agreement among men but rather it has the force of legislation (*legis*). For the whole world, which is in a sense one community, has the power of enacting laws that are just and fitting for all, such as we find in the law of nations. So it is evident that those who violate the law of nations sin mortally.[38]

According to this passage the law of nations was not derived from natural law or from customary usage but from some presumed enactment of positive law.

In other contexts, though, especially when discussing the laws of war, Vitoria did treat custom as a source of the *ius gentium*. He wrote that the

34 *De Indis*, 1.3.3, p. 82. 35 *Ibid.* 36 *Ibid.*
37 *De potestate civili*, in Urdanoz, *Obras de Francisco de Vitoria*, §14, p. 178.
38 *Ibid.*, §21, p. 191.

provisions of the law of war were largely determined by the law of nations and that, accordingly, custom could give authority to wage war.[39] Similarly the law of nations concerning treatment of captives was shaped by the custom that prisoners of war were not to be killed but rather treated as slaves.[40] Vitoria observed here that when Christians waged war against Saracens it was licit for them to enslave even innocent women and children of the enemy; but he added that this provision of the *ius gentium* did not apply to wars among Christian peoples.[41] Here there seems to be a different *ius gentium* for Christians and for infidels.

Vitoria addressed the question of the grounding of the *ius gentium* most systematically in his commentary on the *Summa theologiae* of Thomas Aquinas. Here, following Aquinas, he asked "whether the law of nations is the same as natural law."[42] Aquinas maintained that *ius gentium* and *ius naturale* should be distinguished from one another, and Vitoria here accepted this view; but he did not agree with all the arguments that Aquinas advanced in support of it. Aquinas had simply accepted Ulpian's definition of natural law as a law that pertained to all animals. He also held that, although the *ius gentium* could be distinguished from natural law, its content was derived from natural law as conclusions from premises. Vitoria questioned both these assertions.

As to the first, Vitoria always rejected the view that there could be a natural law that applied to irrational creatures. Accordingly, he held that the Roman law doctrine did not provide a proper way of distinguishing between *ius naturale* and *ius gentium*. According to the juristic definition, natural law was a law that pertained to all animals; but Vitoria pointed out that there were various rules of natural law that clearly applied only to humans. For instance, he noted, "To return a deposit is of natural law and to worship God is of natural law." Since these rules were common to humans but not to all animals they would belong to *ius gentium* rather than *ius naturale* in the juristic classification; but Vitoria argued that this was to extend too far the range of the *ius gentium* into the realm of *ius naturale*.[43]

The real distinction, Vitoria held, was that the law of nature was good in and of itself, but the *ius gentium* was not good by its very nature; it

[39] *De iure belli*, §9, p. 823. Vitoria discussed the binding force of customary law in his commentary on *Summa theologiae* 1.2ae.97.3 (Heredia, *De justitia*, p. 440), but he did not mention the *ius gentium* in that context.

[40] *De iure belli*, §49, p. 850. [41] *Ibid.*, §42, p. 846.

[42] *De justitia*, 2.2ae.57.3, p. 12. [43] *Ibid.*, p. 14.

derived its just quality from human consent. Accordingly, theologians did not include rules of natural law within the *ius gentium*, but rather such things as manumissions and private ownership of property. And so, Vitoria concluded, the *ius gentium* ought to be classified as positive law rather than as natural law.[44]

Vitoria also considered another question raised by Aquinas – whether the rules of the *ius gentium* were derived necessarily from natural law. He concluded that they were not. If the *ius gentium* followed as a necessary consequence from natural law it would *be* natural law, Vitoria argued. He held that the institutions of the *ius gentium* were not absolutely necessary for the preservation of natural law even though they were very fitting and "almost necessary."[45]

A further question raised by Vitoria was probably the one that interested him most as a moral theologian. If the *ius gentium* consisted of positive law rather than natural law, then would it be sinful to violate the *ius gentium*? If the Spanish were at war with the French and they killed a French ambassador how could one know whether the Spanish accepted the *ius gentium* or whether they sinned in violating it? Vitoria gave the same answer as in the *De Indis*, but with a more detailed argument. Some parts of the *ius gentium* were derived from private pacts, but other parts were based on the common consent of all nations and peoples.

> In this way ambassadors are admitted by the law of nations and are inviolable among all nations ... In the same way prisoners taken in a just war are made slaves according to the law of nations; hence it is always illicit to violate the law of nations contrary to the common consensus.[46]

Vitoria argued that, since the law of nations was established by a virtual consensus of the whole world, it could be abrogated only if the whole world came together for that purpose, and this he held to be impossible. Still, he conceded that the law could be abrogated in part and here, as in the *De Indis*, he noted that the *ius gentium* concerning enslavement of captives was not observed among Christian nations.[47]

This last argument may remind us of the various tensions and apparent contradictions inherent in Vitoria's work. If a contrary custom of the Christian people could abrogate a provision of the law of nations, then it would seem that the customs of other peoples could also abrogate it in part. But Vitoria's whole argument about the rights of Spaniards in America assumed that the same *ius gentium* was binding on all peoples.

[44] *Ibid.* [45] *Ibid.*, p. 16. [46] *Ibid.*, p. 15. [47] *Ibid.*, pp. 16–17.

Again, in the commentary on Aquinas, Vitoria declared clearly and emphatically that the *ius gentium* was positive human law, that it was not natural law and not necessarily derived from natural law. But in the *Relectio de Indis* he stated with equal clarity that the *ius gentium* "either is natural law or derives from natural law." In the Aquinas commentary Vitoria wrote that theologians, unlike jurists, did not include principles of natural law in the *ius gentium*, but in other contexts, for instance when discussing cannibalism and the law of *res nullius*, he mentioned rules that were common to both laws. In some contexts Vitoria treated custom and usage as the ground of *ius gentium* but he also found its origin in a primeval agreement at the beginning of the human race. Sometimes the *ius gentium* expressed the consent of the whole world, sometimes the agreement of a majority that was binding on the rest. One is left to conclude that Vitoria was simply not very interested in the grounding of the law of nations. Indeed he acknowledged as much himself. At the outset of his discussion on the *ius gentium* in the commentary on Aquinas he observed:

> First of all, I will say this, that the argument concerns the name, not the thing; it does not matter much whether you say this or that . . .[48]

James Brown Scott, an enthusiastic admirer of Vitoria, maintained that the Spanish scholar was the real founder of the modern law of nations.[49] But Vitoria had no such ambition or achievement. He was concerned only to respond to the contingencies of his own age, not to create a new system of international law, and this is especially evident in his treatment of the grounding of the *ius gentium*. Vitoria argued in different ways in different contexts according to the particular position he wanted to sustain at some point in his argument. In view of the widespread concern among modern theorists to find a secure ground for the law of nations, his insouciance about the whole question may seem surprising. But Vitoria was interested in his own problems, not in ours.

Suarez on customary law

Francisco Suarez presented a treatment of the *ius gentium* significantly different from that of Vitoria. Unlike Vitoria, Suarez was not interested

48 *Ibid*., p. 13.

49 See C. Rossi, *Broken Chain of Being: James Brown Scott and the Origins of International Law* (The Hague: Kluwer Law International, 1998).

in exploring every possible provision of the law of nations that might establish the justice or injustice of the Spanish conquests in America – by the time he wrote Spanish rule there was a well-established fait accompli and the urgency had gone out of the older controversies. On the other hand, and again unlike Vitoria, Suarez was very interested in defining unambiguously the source and ground of the law of nations – now understood both as the classical *ius gentium* and as international law in the modern sense of the term – and to locate this law within the framework of an all-embracing system of jurisprudence.

This undertaking required Suarez to explore carefully the characteristics of the *ius gentium* that distinguished it from civil law and from the law of nature. The difference between civil law and the *ius gentium* was easy to explain: the former was the law of particular societies, the latter a law common to the whole world. The relationship between *ius gentium* and natural law was more subtle. After all, a well-known text of Roman law declared that the *ius gentium* was "a law that natural reason has established among all men."[50] And the text might equally well have served as a definition of natural law. Suarez himself wrote that the *ius gentium* had a close affinity with natural law and that Roman law sometimes confused the two kinds of law. But, Suarez insisted, the issue was not one of mere words; rather it was important to emphasize the difference between the two concepts.[51] His own position was clear. The *ius gentium* was not natural law and it did not form a part of natural law; it belonged to the sphere of positive human law, and within the realm of human law it was a form of customary law. Accordingly, Suarez wrote that "*ius gentium* differs from natural law because it is based on custom rather than nature."[52] In the same passage he explained that the *ius gentium* differed from civil law in that it was established through the custom of all or nearly all nations.

Suarez wrote very extensively about customary law and, since he classified the *ius gentium* as a kind of custom, we can best approach his way of understanding the law of nations by first considering his treatment of custom in general. The announcement of our conference

[50] *Dig.* 1.1.9.

[51] *Tractatus de lege et legislatore Deo*, ed. M. André and C. Berton, in *R. P. Francisco Suarez . . . opera omnia* (26 vols., Paris: Vivès, 1856–61), vol. 5, 2.17.2, p. 162, 2.19.1, p. 166.

[52] *Ibid.*, 2.19.6, p. 168.

listed several topics for discussion, e.g. What good justification is there, if any, for treating custom as a source of law? How do customary practices become law? What moral standards must custom conform to? There were further questions about desuetude of custom, interpretation of codified law through custom, the relationship between municipal customary law and customary international law and between customary international law and national sovereignty. Suarez discussed all these questions, usually at great length.

Suarez began with a definition of custom that was taken from Isidore of Seville and included in Gratian's *Decretum*. "Custom is a kind of law (*ius*) introduced by usages and accepted as law when enacted law (*lex*) is lacking."[53] But Suarez at once perceived a difficulty. It was in fact the one inherent in the first question just listed. Usage, understood as a repetition of particular acts, was a matter of fact. How could such fact give rise to law?[54] Suarez would give a detailed answer to this question later, but first he went on to describe three kinds of custom. The first was universal custom and this was the *ius gentium*, "truly a kind of custom."[55] Common or public custom was the custom of some province or place, and private custom was the custom of particular individuals. Only the first two kinds of custom, according to Suarez, could give rise to binding laws. And such customs could be established only by communities having the inherent power of making laws for themselves, cities or peoples with "the power of being bound by their own laws." In cases where such a people had established a prince with legislative authority his consent was also required, but tacit acquiescence would usually suffice.[56]

How, then, could a people introduce a new customary law for itself? Suarez's first reply, reiterated at various stages of his subsequent argument, was that custom was formed by "a frequent repetition of similar actions" by a community or the greater part of it.[57] A minority could not institute a law binding on the whole but in any corporate body the consent of a majority was held to be that of the whole group, Suarez

[53] *De legibus*, vol. 6, 7.1.1, p. 135. [54] *Ibid.* [55] *Ibid.*, 7.3.7, p. 143.

[56] *Ibid.*, 7.3.10, p. 145. Suarez subsequently offered detailed arguments about the kind of princely consent that was required in different circumstances, but these particular arguments are not relevant to the *ius gentium* since there was no prince standing over all the nations.

[57] *Ibid.*, 7.1.4, p. 137, 7.9.12, p. 173.

held.[58] He noted that some authorities would exclude women in reckoning the majority, but he rejected this view.[59]

There had been a substantial body of earlier argument about the number of acts required to institute a custom and about the length of time through which the acts had to be repeated. Suarez adopted a flexible stance in considering these issues. It was true "absolutely and without qualification," he wrote, that frequency of actions was necessary to establish a custom, but Suarez thought that there was no criterion for fixing a definite number of acts. The only general rule was that there should be a sufficient number to manifest the consent of the people and the tacit approval of the prince.[59] The actual number could vary according to the exigencies of the subject matter. In considering the length of time necessary to establish a custom Suarez introduced a comparison with the law of prescription. Just as a private right could be established by prescription of long duration, in the same way a custom could acquire "prescriptive force." But the "long duration" required for prescription in the private sphere was defined as "at least ten years"; so Suarez argued that the same time would suffice for the introduction of a "prescriptive custom" establishing a new law.[60] However, Suarez further noted that, although the laws held that long duration was sufficient to establish a custom, they did not deny that a shorter period might suffice. He held, therefore, that a "non-prescriptive custom" could be established in a shorter period than ten years with the consent of prince and people. But he thought that a definite period for the establishment of such a custom could not be fixed. The decision could be left to "the judgment of prudent minds."[61] A judicial decision of a magistrate could also confirm the existence of such a custom; but Suarez rejected the idea that a judicial ruling was necessary to establish the validity of a customary law. "A judge has no power to make law," he wrote.[62] When a magistrate gave a judgment in accordance with a customary law, he did not establish the law but merely acknowledged that it already existed.[63]

We are still left with a fundamental question. How could a mere repetition of acts by a people or its greater part establish a binding law?

[58] *Ibid.*, 7.9.13–14, p. 174. Suarez also rejected here the view of some jurists who held that a two-thirds majority was needed.

[59] *Ibid.*, 7.10.3–4, pp. 175–6.

[60] *Ibid.*, 7.8.8–9, pp. 166–7, 7.15.5, p. 191.

[61] *Ibid.*, 7.15.8–9, pp. 192–3.

[62] *Ibid.*, 7.11.14, p. 180.

[63] *Ibid.*, 7.11.4, p. 177, 7.15.9, p. 193.

The answer was implicit in a text of Roman law that influenced all future discussions on the authority of custom.

> Since statutes are binding on us only because they have been accepted by the judgment of the people . . . What does it matter if the people declares its will by voting or by the very nature of its actions?[64]

Here it was not the mere repetition of actions that established a custom, but the fact that the actions expressed the will of the people. In developing this argument Suarez wrote that the acts introducing a custom must be voluntary because they must manifest consent.[65] He especially emphasized the role of will and intention. A repetition of acts in itself could only establish a custom of fact; it was of the essence of customary *law*, as of law in general, that its establishment be intended;[66] and an intention to establish only a custom of fact would not suffice. Suarez mentioned here several devotional practices common among Christians, for example to receive ashes on Ash Wednesday, to receive a palm on Palm Sunday, to take holy water at the church door. These were customs observed by the majority of the people, but they did not establish an obligation in law because they were not practiced with that intention.[67] To establish a customary law it was essential that the custom be instituted "with the will and intention that it become a law for posterity." A repetition of acts for a thousand years would not establish a law without this intention.[68]

In other contexts Suarez considered how custom could abrogate or interpret law and how it could fall into desuetude. He also undertook to explain "the moral nature and effects of custom."[69] Here he wrote that a custom could be good or bad and reasonable or unreasonable. A bad custom could only be a custom of fact since "an evil law is no law"; a bad custom should not be called true law but rather an abuse or corruption. The definition of an unreasonable custom was more complicated. Certainly a custom contrary to divine or natural law would be unreasonable and so invalid, but Suarez held that this was not the only kind of unreasonable custom. A customary practice might be wholly good in itself but still be considered unreasonable as a source of law. For instance, a community might observe the practice of attending Mass every day; this would certainly be good in itself; but it would be unfitting

[64] *Dig.* 1.3.32. [65] *De legibus*, 7.12.1, p. 181. [66] *Ibid.*, 7.14.5, p. 189.
[67] *Ibid.*, 7.14.6, p. 189. [68] *Ibid.*, 7.14.7, p. 190, 7.15.10, p. 193.
[69] *Ibid.*, 7.6.1, p. 155.

that the custom be intended to introduce a binding obligation.[70] From another point of view, a custom that was not intrinsically evil could be considered unreasonable if it tended to encourage sinful behavior – for instance a custom that imposed only a light pecuniary penalty for homicide. On the positive side, a reasonable custom was one that was introduced for the common good and that was not unduly burdensome.[71]

If we return now to our initial question – "What good justification is there for treating custom as a source of law?" – we can finally note that Suarez's lengthy arguments led to a clear and simple answer. Custom could institute law because

> in a legitimate custom all the elements necessary for the establishment of a precept or law can exist together . . . suitable subject matter, power, and will sufficiently manifested externally.[72]

Suarez also observed that the definition of custom originally given by Isidore applied "rigorously" to the *ius gentium*.[73]

Ius gentium, natural law, and international law

In his detailed exposition of customary law, Suarez was primarily concerned with municipal law, but he pointed out that the law of nations had developed in an analogous way.

> Just as in one city or province custom introduces law, so too in the whole human race laws could be introduced by the usages of peoples.[74]

Suarez's teaching that the *ius gentium* was indeed a form of positive human law, and specifically of customary law, was first developed in order to refute a widespread contrary opinion of his time which maintained that the *ius gentium* was really natural law or a part of natural law. (Grotius, writing a few years later, observed that writers everywhere confused the law of nature with the law of nations.) Suarez accordingly embarked on a detailed treatment of the relationship between *ius gentium* and *ius naturale*.

He approached the problem in a rather circuitous way by first considering several ways of distinguishing between the two laws that he considered invalid or inadequate. The first argument he presented was rooted in Roman law and was still widely held by jurists of the sixteenth

70 *Ibid.*, 7.6.2, p. 155. 71 *Ibid.*, 7.6.7, p. 157, 7.6.10, p. 158. 72 *Ibid.*, 7.14.3, p. 188.
73 *Ibid.*, 7.3.7, p. 143. 74 *De legibus*, vol. 5, 2.19.9, p. 169.

century. It maintained that the difference between natural law and the law of nations was simply that the former applied to all animate creatures, the latter only to humankind. In this argument the *ius gentium* was that part of the natural law that pertained especially to humans.[75] Suarez rejected the argument mainly because, like Vitoria, he could not accept the view that natural law applied to irrationals. Earlier he had quoted Aquinas's definition of natural law as "the participation of the rational creature in the eternal law." Now he pointed out that the natural law that directed human behavior was quite different from the natural instinct of animals. As regards procreation, for instance, that was mentioned as an example of natural law in the relevant text of the *Digest*, animals mated promiscuously but natural law prohibited such behavior among humans.[76]

This argument explained why the *ius gentium* could not be regarded as one part of a natural law that inhered in both humans and irrational animals; there was no such natural law according to Suarez. But the problem remained of distinguishing between a *ius gentium* that was introduced by human reason and a natural law that was also inherent in man's rational nature. Suarez suggested several ways of distinguishing between the two laws but dismissed each one as unsatisfactory. In each case, he argued, the characteristic that was supposed to distinguish between the laws was in fact common to both of them.

The most interesting argument and the one that Suarez discussed in most detail suggested that natural law laid down binding rules of conduct while the *ius gentium* merely permitted or conceded various courses of action. Suarez began his response by distinguishing two senses of the word *ius* as meaning either a right (a "moral faculty") or a binding law.[77] To understand his further argument we must recall a teaching that Suarez discussed in other parts of his work, the idea, rooted in twelfth-century jurisprudence, that permissive law was a ground of rights. If, then, the *ius gentium* consisted only of permissions or concessions it would be a structure of rights without any binding laws. Suarez argued, however, that the *ius naturale* and the *ius gentium* each contained both precepts and permissions. The *ius gentium* regarding treatment of ambassadors, for instance, was "clearly expressed in the form of a command." Other rules of the *ius gentium* were permissive in nature and Suarez gave a number of examples; but he argued that a

[75] *Ibid.*, 2.17.3, p. 160, citing *Dig.* 1.1.1 and *Inst.* 1.2.1. [76] *Ibid.*, 2.17.6, p. 161.

[77] *Ibid.*, 2.18.2, p. 163. Suarez first introduced this distinction at 1.2.5–6, p. 5.

permissive law itself could not be entirely separated from preceptive law. If the law conceded a right to someone it implied an obligation on others not to interfere with the exercise of the right; the *ius gentium* that permitted the occupancy of vacant places, for instance, required that others not interfere with the first occupant.[78] Suarez concluded therefore that the argument about permissive law did not differentiate adequately between the law of nature and the law of nations.

Then at last Suarez moved on to explain the real difference between the two laws. The essential difference was that the rules of the *ius gentium* – unlike those of natural law – were not derived by reasoning from basic moral principles to necessary conclusions. Natural law defined conduct that was wrong intrinsically and *per se*; the *ius gentium* rendered certain acts wrong because it prohibited them.[79] So the *ius gentium* was "in an absolute sense human and positive." All law could be divided into natural and positive and into divine and human; the *ius gentium* was not natural or divine law; therefore it must be positive and human law.[80]

Suarez next distinguished between the law of nations and civil law, and here again he emphasized the customary basis of the *ius gentium*. This law was established, he wrote, not by the custom of one particular people but "through the customs . . . of all or nearly all nations."[81] However, Suarez discerned a difficulty here. Earlier he had written that the precepts of the *ius gentium* were introduced "through the free will and consent of mankind."[82] Now he observed that it seemed impossible for a universal law to originate in human will and opinion since opinions varied so much among different peoples. Suarez responded with a text already cited – just as rules of law could be introduced by the custom of one people or province so too laws could be established by usage among the human race as a whole; and this was especially true of the *ius gentium* because its rules were mutually advantageous and in close agreement with natural law.[83]

Suarez's endeavor to place the law of nations accurately between natural law and civil law led him to an important new step in the development of the idea of international law. Suarez made a crucial distinction between two meanings that had always been implicit in the old term *ius gentium*, but never disentangled from one another.

[78] *Ibid.*, 2.18.5, p. 164. For Suarez's earlier treatments of permissive law see 2.14.6, p. 137, 2.14.16, p. 140.
[79] *Ibid.*, 2.19.2, p. 166, 2.20.6, p. 171. [80] *Ibid.*, 2.19.4, p. 167. [81] *Ibid.*, 2.19.6, p. 168.
[82] *Ibid.*, 2.17.8, p. 162. [83] *Ibid.*, 2.19.9, p. 169 (above, n. 74).

> A matter can be said to pertain to the *ius gentium* in two ways; in one way because it is a law that all the various nations and peoples should observe toward one another (*inter se*); in another way because it is a body of law that particular cities and kingdoms observe within their own borders (*intra se*), which is called the law of nations because of the similarity and agreement of these laws.[84]

The first meaning of *ius gentium* was what we should nowadays call international law. This was *ius gentium* properly understood according to Suarez, the kind of *ius gentium* that clearly distinguished the law of nations from civil law. But in its second sense *ius gentium* really was a form of civil law, called a law of nations merely by analogy.[85] The *ius gentium* "properly so called" was a body of international law introduced little by little by usage and tradition without any special meeting or consent of all peoples at any particular time.[86]

This international law included such things as the immunity of ambassadors, the law of war, the enslavement of captives in war, and the making of truces and treaties. The law was rooted in the fact that every state, although a perfect community in itself, was also a member of a universal society within which each required association and intercourse with the others for their mutual advantage.[87]

Suarez next asked whether the universal law of nations could be changed or abrogated by the individual nations that had established it – in modern language he was discussing the problem of the relation between international law and national sovereignty. In other contexts Suarez discussed the abrogation of natural law and of civil law; he concluded that a rule of natural law could never be abrogated but that civil law could be changed by the authority competent to establish it. Against this background the law of nations, carefully placed by Suarez in an intermediate position between natural law and civil law, offered its own distinctive problems.

Suarez first argued that the law of nations was in principle subject to change since it was instituted by human consent. Then his two-fold division of the *ius gentium* came into play. The *ius gentium* considered as a body of law common to many countries posed no real problem for Suarez; such laws were essentially civil laws, instituted by the power of each state for its own people and so changeable by each state within its own borders without the consent of other peoples.[88]

[84] *Ibid.*, 2.19.8, p. 168. [85] *Ibid.*, 2.20.3, p. 171, 2.20.7, p. 171. [86] *Ibid.*, 2.20.1, p. 170.
[87] *Ibid.*, 2.19.8–9, p. 169. [88] *Ibid.*, 2.20.7, p. 172.

The *ius gentium* understood as international law raised a more difficult issue since this law was established by the mutual consent of all peoples. Suarez argued that even this law could be altered if all the nations agreed to the change, but he thought that this would be impossible in practice. There remained the possibility that an individual nation might ordain that some rule of international law not be observed among its own people. Suarez accepted this as "morally possible" and mentioned the inevitable example, the non-observance among Christian peoples of the rule concerning enslavement of prisoners of war.[89] He did not pursue the issue in detail at this point but returned to it when he considered the *ius gentium* again within his treatment of customary law in general.

There Suarez noted that the *ius gentium* could not be abolished as a whole since this would require all the nations to concur in establishing a contrary custom, and again Suarez held this to be practically impossible. The real problem concerned the status of a local custom in relation to some rule of the universal international law. Suarez explained that the problem did not concern a custom in accordance with the law of nations or one outside (in addition to) the law of nations but only one directly opposed to the law. Some authorities, he noted, maintained that the *ius gentium* actually was natural law and held therefore that any custom opposed to the *ius gentium* was necessarily invalid.[90] But Suarez had already ruled out that line of argument. His own view was that it was not impossible for a part of the *ius gentium* to be abrogated by a local custom. This was not "absolutely repugnant," he wrote. The point was that the rules of the *ius gentium* did not refer to acts that were intrinsically evil in themselves as the natural law did.

> The reason is that what is contrary only to the law of nations is not intrinsically evil, since its opposite is not a matter of intrinsic obligation according to the law of nature.[91]

Suarez went on to mention again the non-observance by Christian peoples of the rule of the *ius gentium* concerning enslavement of captives, and concluded that a custom of one people contrary to the *ius gentium* could be approved and tolerated provided that it did not seriously injure another people.[92] Finally Suarez argued that not only a prince and people together could abrogate a rule of the *ius gentium* by

[89] *Ibid.*, 2.20.8, p. 172. [90] *De legibus*, vol. 6, 7.4.5, p. 146.
[91] *Ibid.*, 7.4.6, p. 146. [92] *Ibid.*, 7.4.7, p. 147.

instituting a contrary custom, but that a prince alone could do so by enacting a law that was expedient for his own subjects. For instance, a prince might decree that within his realm there should be no slavery.[93]

There is a certain uneasiness in the argument that Suarez presented. He wrote that "the *ius gentium* is truly law and binds as true law,"[94] but also that individual nations were not always obliged by the law. As we saw, the reason was that acts contrary to the *ius gentium* were not necessarily intrinsically evil or violations of the law of nature. But the binding force of the *ius gentium* did not derive from the fact that its precepts were intrinsically good. (That was just what Suarez denied.) The authority of the law of nations – like that of customary law in general – came from the fact that it was instituted by the will and consent of all or the greater part of a community, in this case a community of nations. It did not follow that a particular member of the community could choose to depart from the law because its chosen course of action would not violate the natural law.

The fact that enslavement of captives was indubitably a principle of the *ius gentium*, included in the relevant texts of Roman law, and that, none the less, this practice was not observed among Christian nations, posed a persistent problem for early modern jurists. A fairly simple solution might have been found in some of Suarez's scattered comments. He wrote that the *ius gentium* included permissions as well as precepts and that the word *ius* in the term *ius gentium* could mean either a right or a body of law. And, in making this point, he mentioned in passing the enslavement of captives as a *ius* in the first sense of the term.[95] Moreover Suarez also held that a right derived from the *ius gentium* could be voluntarily renounced.[96] If in his subsequent arguments he had clearly defined the enslavement of captives as a right conceded by international law there would have been no problem in a particular prince or people rejecting this part of the *ius gentium*. But Suarez did not pursue this line of argument.

Suarez presented a much more systematic account of the *ius gentium* than Vitoria, but in the work of both authors there remained a tension, not fully resolved, between the idea of international law and the idea of national sovereignty.

[93] *Ibid.*, 7.4.8, p. 147. [94] *Ibid.*, 7.3.7, p. 143. [95] *De legibus*, vol. 5, 2.17.2, p. 160.
[96] *Ibid.*, 2.20.6, p. 171.

6

Custom and positivity: an examination of the philosophic ground of the Hegel–Savigny controversy

CHRISTOPH KLETZER

Introduction

In December 1812 things seemed to get out of hand in the legal faculty of Berlin University. Its most celebrated jurist, the aristocrat and leading light of self-confident metropolitan Prussian culture, Friedrich Carl von Savigny, threatened to resign from the faculty. It is hard to overestimate the weight of this threat.[1] Since his early masterpiece, *Das Recht des Besitzes* (*On the Rights of Possession*), Savigny had been hailed the new pontiff of Roman Law. His students admired him endlessly, some even likened him to Christ.[2] And, if ever this Olympian was to throw his high-born contempt at someone, the object of Savigny's anger would surely have had to play possum – or so it seemed. Not so Eduard Gans:[3] this

[1] Hermann Kantorowicz once noted that the name of Savigny was 'unique in the sense that in his country it has become sacrosanct. By sacrosanct I mean it is protected by public opinion to the extent that an attack on it no matter how justified is condemned as positively wicked, even as the act of a traitor.' Hermann Kantorowicz, 1937, 'Savigny and the Historical School of Law' in *Law Quarterly Review* Vol. 53, 326–43, at 326; see also Hermann Kantorowicz, 1912, *Was ist uns Savigny?* in *Recht und Wirtschaft* No. 2 (1911–12), 47–54 and No. 3, 76–9. Even Savigny's later opponent in the codification controversy, Anton Friedrich Justus Thibaut (1772–1840), threw him flowers and assured the twenty-four-year-old Savigny on the occasion of commenting on his treatise on possession, 'that the study of your work has filled me with infinite joy, and that among all civilists you are the one, to whom I feel drawn in the most irresistible way'. See Mathias Freiherr von Rosenberg, 2000, *Friedrich Carl von Savigny (1779–1861) im Urteil seiner Zeit* (Frankfurt am Main: Lang), 29; Anton Friedrich Justus Thibaut, 1997, *Über die Notwendigkeit eines allgemeinen bürgerlichen Rechts für Deutschland. Nachdruck der Ausgabe von 1814* (Goldbach: Keip).

[2] Rosenberg, *Savigny*, 137.

[3] For a more detailed narrative of the Gans–Savigny controversy see Terry Pinkard, 2000, *Hegel: A Biography* (Cambridge: Cambridge University Press), 530–4.

offspring of a Jewish banking family had originally attempted to join the faculty of law in Berlin, but at Savigny's instigation he was denied the possibility, arguably because of his Jewish background. Gans had originally been confident that he could rely on the Prussian emancipation edict of 1812, but Savigny had written his reports to the Prussian ministry of culture arguing for the impossibility of appointing a Jew to the law faculty, and, at some point, the relevant passage of the emancipation edict was rescinded by royal cabinet order, on request, of course, of the influential faculty of law.[4] Because of these events, it was not hard to guess what kind of enemy Gans would become.[5] What is more, Gans could count on a close personal and academic friendship with the influential Hegel, who, in turn, had a mutually beneficial relationship with the Prussian minister of culture, Altenstein.[6] Three years after Gans had converted to Christianity he became *Extraordinarius* in Berlin, and, half a year later, Altenstein used a short absence of the crown prince, Friedrich Wilhelm – who, too, was a fierce opponent of Gans[7] – to prompt the king to promote Gans to professor.

Savigny's threat to resign was therefore a gamble – one which he lost. Gans arrived, and Savigny absented himself from the administration of

[4] This order has become known as 'lex Gans'. See Hanns Günther Reissner, 1965, *Eduard Gans: ein Leben im Vormärz* (Tübingen: Mohr Siebeck), 91f; and Hans-Joachim Schoeps, 1968, *Preussen. Geschichte eines Staates* (Berlin: Propyläen), 124.

[5] In his *System des römischen Zivilrechts*, for instance, Gans calls the *Historische Rechtsschule* a 'cooperative of careerists with the aim of mutual promotion.' Eduard Gans, 1827, *System des römischen Civilrechts* (Goldbach: Keip), 160. For further polemical engagement of Gans with the *Historische Rechtsschule* see Eduard Gans, 1981, *Naturrecht und Universalrechtsgeschichte*, edited by Manfred Riedel (Stuttgart: Klett-Cotta), 156–237. But it was not only Gans who thought so little of Savigny. In a conversation recorded by Jhering, Bismarck (who, just as Jhering, had been a student of Savigny) called the latter a 'vain fop, a quite paltry man'. Rosenberg, *Savigny*, 140.

[6] 'Altenstein had used him [Hegel], to rid himself of the arguably very cliquish scholarly aristocracy of Berlin (v. Savigny, Schleiermacher etc.), i.e. to find a scientific counterpoise on which he could rely.' That at least is how Hegel's contemporary, Heinrich Leo, saw it. See Günther Nicolin, 1970, *Hegel in Berichten seiner Zeitgenossen* (Hamburg: Meiner), 454.

[7] After the resignation of Savigny from the faculty the crown prince wrote to him: 'I cordially lament our juridical faculty in relation to its accession and departure and I understand only too well why swan and goose [a pun on the name *Gans*] cannot swim in the same pond. God forbid, that the pond becomes a puddle. The first step is done!' Crown Prince Friedrich Wilhelm to Savigny on 31 December 1828. See Adolf Stoll, 1939, *Friedrich Carl von Savigny. Ein Bild seines Lebens mit einer Sammlung seiner Briefe*, Vol. 3 (Berlin: Heyman), 281.

the faculty. The Hegel camp had won at least one battle in a fierce conflict that was fought by proxy wars and surrogate polemics.

We have started this paper with a digression on Gans not for Gans' sake but for Hegel's. We have done this because the 'Gans incident' described above was the only occasion on which Hegel and Savigny came into public, though still indirect, polemical contact. This fact is rather curious, given that both were luminaries in their field, emphatically public figures and heads of powerful intellectual groupings at the University of Berlin and both scorned the other feverishly.

But, apart from this lack of direct *public* conflict, the two men's works also exhibit a curious mutual indifference. In Savigny's published works there is, to my knowledge, not one mention of Hegel's name;[8] and, conversely, in Hegel's opus including the extensive manuscripts of the lectures he gave, we can find only one passing mention of Savigny's name.[9]

What could account for that? Well, it is the slight difference in discipline – Hegel's *philosophy of right* as against Savigny's *legal science* – that must have made an engagement with the other seem futile from the very beginning.[10] Savigny was convinced that legal philosophy, and thus also Hegel's attempts in this field, were a waste of time, that such an enterprise could be of interest only for people too idle to engage in the intricacies of the positive law *in concreto*. For him, natural law – and

[8] Kuno Fischer reports a letter of Savigny to Creuzer dated 6 April 1822: 'What I reprehend in Hegel is by no means only his haughty and shallow verdict about some other sciences, but that one and the same conceit spreads over the whole world, in order that his zealous students secede from all religious relations, and that even Fiche is surpassed by Hegel in this respect; equally, his awry, inverted, obscure behaviour and language in all matters not scientific.' Fisher also cites the following oral comment by Savigny: 'At the University the collegial relations have never been good, but in the Academy there was peace. Well, we have never allowed Hegel to enter it.' Kuno Fischer, 1963, *Hegels Leben, Werke und Lehre* (Darmstadt: Wissenschaftliche Buchgesellschaft), 1251.

[9] In his Heidelberg lectures of 1818/19, Hegel expressly mentions Savigny while criticising his views in relation to the loss of property. G. W. F. Hegel, 1983, *Die Philosophie des Rechts. Die Mitschriften Wannenmann (Heidelberg 1817/18) und Homeyer (Berlin 1818/19)*, edited by Karl-Heinz Ilting (Stuttgart: Klett-Cotta), §27, 54.

[10] Wolfgang Schild, 1978, 'Savigny und Hegel. Systematische Überlegungen zur Begründung einer Rehtswissenschaft zwischen Jurisprudenz und Philosophie' in *Anales de la Catedra Francisco Suarez* Nos. 18–19 (1978–9), 271–320, who tries to analyse the whole relation of Hegel and Savigny in light of this mutual disrespect for the other's discipline. Ultimately this attempt had to fail, because both Hegel and Savigny did – if only covertly – engage in his opponent's discipline. Thus, even though the mutual scorn may explain the lack of engagement on the surface of their work, it becomes irrelevant as soon as we reach more fundamental strata.

Savigny seemed to have taken the whole enterprise of legal philosophy to be a subspecies of natural law, and very likely he took Hegel to be a natural lawyer – was not a highly complex and eternally valid emanation of reason, but a mere abbreviation or simplification of positive law. In a spirit anticipating Nietzschean themes he wrote: 'Once, by simply omitting some obvious peculiarities, the Justinian Institutions were turned into natural law, which was then thought to be an immediate demand of reason: nowadays nobody lacks pity for such an operation – however, until today we come across people who take their own juristic concepts and opinions to be purely reasonable, only because they lack knowledge of their genealogy.'[11] Thus there was nothing of value that Savigny could have told legal philosophers on their terms, or have learned from them. Little did Savigny know that Hegel himself viewed the relationship between natural and positive law in strict parallel to the relationship 'between Institutes and Pandects'.[12]

Hegel, on the other hand, was little impressed by Roman law,[13] the ultimate source of complexity for the scientific wit of the historical school. Hegel shared this disinclination towards Roman law with many of his contemporaries. In any case, the historical school's focus on Roman law must have been highly surprising for outsiders, especially since, at the end of the eighteenth and the beginning of the nineteenth centuries, Roman law seemed to approach the end of its validity.[14] It was

[11] Friedrich Carl von Savigny, 1967, *Vom Beruf unserer Zeit für Gesetzgebung und Rechtswissenschaft* (Hildesheim: Georg Olms), 115.

[12] G. W. F. Hegel, 1998, *Elements of the Philosophy of Right*, edited by Allen W. Wood, translated by H. B. Nisbet (Cambridge: Cambridge University Press), §3, 29.

[13] 'Thus in Roman law, for example, no definition of a *human being* would be possible, for the slave could not be subsumed under it; indeed, the status of the slave does violence to that concept.' Hegel, *Elements*, §2. 'Apart from this, the very *inconsistency* of the Roman jurists and praetors should be regarded as one of their greatest virtues, for it enabled them to dissociate themselves from unjust and abominable institutions, although they were at the same time compelled to invent verbal distinctions on the *callide* (as when they called *bonorum posessio* what nevertheless amounted to an inheritance) and even silly excuses (and silliness is equally an inconsistency) in order to preserve the letter of the Twelve Tables, for example by the *fictio* or *hypokrisis* that a *filia* was a *filius*.' Hegel, *Elements*, §3, 34.

[14] Since its reception in the German lands Roman law had been valid law. The *Historische Rechtsschule* soon divided into Romanists and Germanists. Because Savigny led the Romanists and because he obsessively sought to return to 'purest origins' and what is 'native in the sources', it appeared that *only* Roman law was of relevance in Germany. In the introduction to his opus magnum, *Das System des heutigen Römischen Rechts* ('The System of Today's Roman Law'), Savigny could therefore write: 'Accordingly the exposition of today's Roman law, at which the present work is aimed, will need only

becoming evident that Roman law was responsible for the uncertainty of the law, the length of the legal proceedings and the sophistry of the legal profession.[15] Given these strong anti-Romanist currents in academic circles, and the fact that the German *Bürgerliches Gesetzbuch* had been delayed until 1900, the fact that Roman law continued to be applied in Germany as valid law until modern days gives vivid proof of the historical school's influence. Be that as it may, Romanists like Savigny were not the audience to which Hegel would have directed his legal philosophy.

But, beside this curious biographical and bibliographical lack of intersection, does their work on legal matters share any common features? Both Works represent a turn to *history*, both attribute a significant role to what they call *Volksgeist*, both reverse the negative valuation of custom and habit that resulted from Kantian moral philosophy of autonomous subjectivity, and both have a negative attitude towards natural law even though ultimately their own stance cannot shake off some kind of natural law semblance. This closeness has tempted some commentators and historians of ideas even to put the same label on both thinkers, something like *conservative, apologetic historicism*. But, yet again, the similarities are spurious, and, if one scratches the surface of the similarities, an unbridgeable opposition is found lurking beneath.

This paper tries to elaborate this intellectual opposition that lies hidden beneath a spurious intellectual affinity which in turn lies hidden beneath a lack of public intersection. In order to do so, it focuses on the one theme that simultaneously links and separates the two thinkers: custom and customary law. What will thereby become apparent is that their different assessments of the role that customary law should

few additions to become an exposition of the *common law* of Germany.' Friedrich Carl von Savigny, 1840, *System des heutigen Römischen Rechts* (Berlin: Veit), vol. 1, §2, 5. Savigny's system clearly laid claim to presenting valid law and thus a law that was directly applicable by the German courts.

15 Reimund Scheuermann, 1972, *Einflüsse der historischen Rechtsschule auf die oberstrichterliche gemeinrechtliche Zivilrechtspraxis bis zum Jahre 1861* (Berlin: DeGruyter); Hans Thieme, 1936, 'Die Zeit des späteren Naturrechts. Eine privatrechtsgeschichtliche Studie' in SavZGA vol. 56 (1936), 202–63 at 241ff; Peter Bender, 'Die Rezeption des römischen Rechts im Urteil der deutschen Rechstwissenschaft' . . . schaft (Diss. Iur. Freiburg im Breisgau, 1955). See also Thibaut, *Notwendigkeit*: 'The last and chief source of law for us, consequently, is the Roman statute books; that is, the work of a nation which was very unlike us, and from the period of the lowest decline of the same, bearing the traces of decline upon every page. One must be completely caught in passionate one-sidedness if one seriously rates the Germans as fortunate on account of the adoption of this ill-devised work, and recommends further retention of the same.'

play, especially in relation to codification, bring to light a much more fundamental intellectual opposition on positivity, reason and the role of philosophy in general. What makes Hegel disagree with Savigny's evaluation of the relationship of customary law to codification, is not any immediate difference in the theory of customary law as such, but the intellectual basis on which this theory stands.

The *Volk* and customary law

Savigny's theory of customary law follows analytically from his *Rechtsquellenlehre* (doctrine of legal sources), and in order to understand the former we have to have a look at the latter. According to this analytic derivation, the doctrine of legal sources first defines all law as positive law, it then teaches that the common consciousness of the *Volk* (the people) can be the only true source and substance of this positive law and then comes to the conclusion that it is primarily via *customary law* – to be precise, via *custom* – that we can have access to the positive law hidden in the consciousness of the people. This chapter will follow this line of argument in some detail.

The curious fact that in Savigny's mature work legal philosophy expresses itself solely by means of such a doctrine of legal sources should become less peculiar when we briefly reflect on the implications that the enterprise of a doctrine of legal sources as such has. What distinguishes such a doctrine from legal philosophy in the most general meaning of the latter term is that it does not attempt to find any conceptual definition, criterion or critique of the law, but that it aims only at the precise exposition of the law's sources. As such it takes a decisively anti-philosophical stance. In this meta-doctrinal decision to focus on a doctrine of legal sources, however, Savigny has already implicitly defined his own jurisprudential stance as legal positivism: if the truly interesting theoretical question is not the question as to the nature of the law but as to the sources of the legal rules, then the *existence* of those rules is already presupposed as unproblematic. 'Everywhere where a legal relation becomes problematic and where we become aware of it, a rule regulating this relation is always already existing and it would thus be unnecessary and actually impossible to invent such a rule in retrospect.'[16] This presupposition of the existence of the rule as always already existent, a presupposition which marks an intellectual place

[16] Savigny, *System*, 14.

for which Kelsen will later coin the phrase *basic norm*, fixes all law as positive law: 'In relation to this quality of the law, according to which it already has actual existence as given in every situation, we call it *positive law*.'[17]

The positivity of the law is a function of its temporality, more precisely, of the temporal relationship of the law to the scholarly engagement with it: the law is an intellectual entity which precedes its scholarly reflection, it is not subjective spirit, but positive, or, in Hegelian terms, *objective* spirit. The positivity of the positive law thus finds its expression not in its being *voluntarily* created by a formal legal authority, but simply in its being there, its being *given*. Whatever we may think of the law or want it to be, the concrete historical existence of the positive law in its very specific determination always precedes our reflections and renders them belated.

Savigny's focus on the legal sources thus rules out every conceptual, abstract, 'philosophic' approach to the law as misguided, misdirected, as ultimately missing the concrete object – it did for legal epistemology in the early nineteenth century what *naturalism* did for general epistemology in the late twentieth century.[18]

This conception of the law as always already existing both rules out an abstract philosophical approach to the law as being either superfluous or erroneous and also prefigures Savigny's whole legal philosophy. It is a striking peculiarity of Savigny's position that he generates nearly all of his fundamental legal-philosophical determinations of the positive law by means of an original and arguably sincere rebuff of legal philosophy *in toto*. This is an apt illustration of the old elenctic insight that the rejection of philosophy is itself a strong philosophic position, not only in the abstract colloquial sense, but in the very concrete sense of a philosophic position which is able to generate concrete philosophic content from the rejection of philosophy. However, all philosophical self-rejection has its limits. It will be precisely the limitations and conceptual poverty of Savigny's further philosophical framework, a framework which does not allow us to understand *givenness* as *reason*,[19] that will ultimately make his position indefensible.

17 *Ibid.*

18 According to this line of thought, we should not get carried away in our theoretical questions about the nature of law (or science) when we always have before us the concrete incarnation of this law (and science). Those philosophical questions are not only redundant but positively harmful. Savigny thinks that legal science can be based solely on its own presupposition, i.e. on history, and does not need to be given a leg up by philosophy. See Alexander Rosenberg, 2000, *Philosophy of Science: A Contemporary Introduction* (London: Routledge), 153–5.

19 Savigny, *System*, 4.

So, Savigny's presupposition of the law as always already existing only seemingly abrogates all the pressing problems that 'abstract' philosophy of law and natural law theory dealt with over the millennia. If Savigny is claiming that legal philosophy obfuscates our view of the actual law by conjuring up an artificial, invented law, then he leaves open a whole series of questions that were usually answered by this abstract philosophical inquiry: even if one concedes that positive law always already exists, one must nevertheless wonder how, in what form, this positive law exists. Clearly, Savigny does not want to claim that the positive law exists either as a collection of written texts or as a prefigured eternal order in the heavens. Savigny's famous answer, mediating between those options, is that it is the *Volksgeist*, the spirit of the people, in which the positive law has its 'invisible' existence.

In order to better understand what Savigny means with *Volk*, we have to distinguish it from two other groups of people: from the *State*, on the one hand, and from the *mob*, on the other. The *Volk* differs from the State insofar as the latter is the external embodiment of the former. So, whereas the *Volk* has fuzzy and overlapping limits, the State has clear boundaries. In the State the *Volk* gains true personality, i.e. the capacity to act. On the other hand, the *Volk* differs from the unorganised accumulation of people by its 'spiritual unity'[20] and by a common language. The *Volk* is a *trans-historic, natural whole.*[21]

It is striking that Savigny does not reflect on the dialectic tension that lies hidden in this 'whole' which should at the same time be 'natural'; he lacks the insight that only spirit can provide for unity. It is therefore no wonder that, on the same page, Savigny determines this 'natural whole' also as a 'spiritual unity', which is its straight opposite. The *Volk* is this middle concept: it appears as 'natural' when compared with the artificiality of the State and as 'spiritual' when compared with the unordered arbitrariness of the mob.

Now, the positive law lives in the consciousness of this *Volk*, just as language does. Accordingly, it does not live there as a sum of abstract rules but in the form of an organic whole, as a body of interrelated legal institutes. Those *legal institutes* (*Rechtsinstitute*) are the deepened ground, the essence of the legal rules; they constitute objective right, just as the *legal relations* (*Rechtsverhältnisse*) are the deepened ground, the essence of the rights and entitlements of people and constitute

[20] *Ibid.*, 19. [21] *Ibid.*

subjective right. And, just as every court judgment determining the subjective rights of the parties has to be subsumed under a certain abstract objective legal rule, so every legal relationship stands as a token under a type of legal institute. Now, the *true* form and representation of the positive law is the organic whole of the legal institutes, from which the legal rules have to be drawn by way of abstraction.

Given this invisible, yet stratified, existence of the positive law in the *Volk*, the question that arises is how this positive law expresses itself so that we can ever know it with any degree of certainty. Puchta's answer to this question, in which he is followed by Savigny, is *customary law*. But from the very beginning Savigny expresses concerns about this term and its history. It could easily mislead us:

> The name could too easily tempt one to the following analogy. Whenever in a legal relation something had to happen, it was in the beginning utterly irrelevant what would happen; chance and arbitrariness determined a decision. Now, when the same case occurred again it was simply more convenient to repeat the same decision rather than to come up with a new one and with every new repetition this procedure had to seem more convenient and natural. In this way over time the status of being law was acquired by a rule which originally did not lay any more claim to validity than its opposite would have and the ground of choosing this rule rather than the other was custom alone.[22]

The real relationship of law and custom, according to Savigny, is the reverse: the positive law is not created by custom but custom is created by the positive law which has its invisible existence in the consciousness of the *Volk* as natural agreement of opinion. Custom is the expression of this natural agreement of opinion. Accordingly, customs are not the basis of validity of the positive law but only its *Kennzeichen* (indicator), referring to a hidden, deeper legal existence. No law, Savigny agrees with Puchta, can ever be created by external actions, customary or not, but only by the internal, spiritual event of a natural agreement of opinion in a people.[23] Put briefly, custom is the *ratio cogniscendi* of positive law, not its *ratio essendi*.

[22] *Ibid.*, 34–5.

[23] Georg Friedrich Puchta, 1928, *Das Gewohnheitsrecht* (Erlangen: Palm). Apart from Savigny, the 'Romanists' Göschen, Böcking and Arndts also explicitly adopted Puchta's spiritualistic doctrine. The 'Germanists' denied the need for an explicit doctrine of customary law and required that all those questions should be decided according to Roman law. See Scheuermann, *Einflüsse*.

> This basis [of the positive law] has its existence, its actuality in the common consciousness of the people. This existence, however, is invisible – how can we know it? We can only know it if it reveals itself in external action, if it steps out into *Übung* (practice), *Sitte* (conventions), *Gewohnheit* (custom): it is from the uniformity of continued and thus lasting conduct that we can see its common root which is opposed to mere coincidence, the *Volksglaube* (belief of the people). Custom thus is the indicator of positive law and not the basis of its creation.[24]

We have to be very cautious here: it is not customary law which is the indicator of positive law but custom. What we have before us are only two levels: the spiritual level of positive law and the factual level of custom. So where should 'customary law' fit? Well, nowhere really. Custom itself is not law and the positive law owes nothing to custom. No law is ontologically determined as being 'customary'. All law is created only by the '*innere, stillwirkende Kräfte*'[25] (inner, silently working forces) of the consciousness of the people. The only option left is to reserve the title 'customary law' to that part of the positive law which was *discovered* via custom. As such it is not an ontological determination of the law but only an epistemic or heuristic determination. Ultimately, Savigny has to find out, 'customary law' is an unlucky word formation that arose out of confusion over the real relationship of law and custom. Savigny himself therefore once referred to it as the 'so-called customary law'.[26]

What is surprising in this relationship is that Savigny on other occasions still talks about customary law in terms of a legal ontology. But, even though customary law for Savigny undoubtedly marks out the oldest, strongest and most fundamental source of law, it nevertheless only gives us *indirect* knowledge of the positive law, necessary only for those who view the law from the outside without themselves being part of the legal community. Whoever is part of the legal community could do without this appeal to customary law. 'For those [who are members of the legal community] such a conclusion from the single cases of the custom is superfluous, because their cognition is an *immediate* one, based only on direct intuition.'[27]

What is 'law' in customary law thus stays hidden behind the custom. The positive law may be concrete, but it is still invisible; it may be 'out there', but it is strictly speaking imperceptible. As such, the true but

[24] Savigny, *System*, 35. [25] Savigny, *Beruf*, 13. [26] *Ibid.*, 14. [27] Savigny, *System*, 38.

'invisible' law bears strong resemblance to Kant's thing-in-itself and will ultimately face the same polemic: why first refer to an ultimate source of concreteness and immediacy against metaphysics, if this ground is then relegated to an eternal beyond, a *Hinterwelt* of invisibility? Savigny's solution to the problem by means of a putatively immediate, but nevertheless intellectual *intuition* of the positive law by the members of the *Volk* corresponds to Jacobi's unsuccessful solution of the Kantian problems by retreating to feeling and intuition.

In any case, even though Savigny's theory stood in stark contrast to the traditional theories of customary law, it still had a strong influence on the court practice in relation to the application of customary law. Whatever the differences in the details there may have been within the traditional understanding, the prevalent opinion on the nature of customary law has uniformly been that legislation enjoyed primacy. In the *usus modernus pandectarum*, for instance, it was taken for granted that the ground of validity of customary law can only be found in the explicit or tacit acceptance by the legislator.[28] Customary law was something akin to a mere fact that received its legal status only through tacit or explicit acceptance by legislation.

Now, the historical school's *spiritualistic* conception of customary law, the elimination of the factual element in favour of the invisible concord of the people, led to a quite different view on the role that customary law should play in court proceedings. The traditional doctrine had seen customary law as being only slightly elevated from the level of fact, not clearly enough, however, to fall under the general rule of *iura novit curia*. Accordingly, the party relying on a rule of customary law had to bear the burden of proof of its existence just as they would have if they claimed a simple fact.[29] The historical school's concept of customary law led to a change in this doctrine. Lacking factual admixtures customary law is now seen to be law proper, the most fundamental law, and it was therefore for the court to establish its existence and extent. In order for the court to establish that a certain custom can be taken to rest on a common conviction of the people, three elements had to be fulfilled: (i) the practice establishing a custom had to be accompanied by an *opinio necessitatis*; (ii) the practice had to be rational, i.e. not contrary to higher principles or *boni mores*; and (iii) it had to be

[28] See for instance Christian Friedrich Glück, 1797, *Ausführliche Erläuterung der Pandecten nach Hellfeld. Ein Commentar*, Part 1 (Erlangen: Palm), 447. See Scheuermann, *Einflüsse*, 81.

[29] Glück, *Pandecten*, 476.

conducted free from error.[30] If a practice which conformed with those three requirements had been conducted consuetudinarily, the court was authorised to infer from this practice the common conviction of the people, i.e. the existence of customary law.[31]

The fact that the German courts accepted a doctrine of customary law which on its own admission allowed one to speak only of 'so-called' customary law might initially sound paradoxical. But it was mainly the requirement of the courts to be given a theoretically founded but still easily applicable doctrine that can account for the fact that the historical school's doctrine of customary law soon took complete sway over the German courts. No court ever criticised Puchta's spiritualistic doctrine and only in connection to the issue of derogation from statute by customary law did the courts not follow the historical school.

One final issue deserves discussion: from very early on it has been claimed that the historical school's doctrine of customary law was itself *a-historic* insofar as it was not in accordance with the Roman sources.[32] Contemporary Romanists tend to agree with this criticism and to confirm that the classical jurists have not had a similar doctrine of customary law.[33] The spiritualistic twist in particular, it is said, cannot be foisted onto the Romans, as for them customary law required not only the *consensus omnium* but also, constitutively, the purely factual element of *consuetudo*.[34] Thus, it is said, Puchta's and Savigny's doctrine is not in line with *pure* Roman law and therefore not in line with their own criterion of validity.

This criticism is misguided. Both the doctrine of customary law and the veneration of pure Roman law are lateral results of the school's *Rechtsquellenlehre*. Thus, the doctrine of customary law, itself being a direct result of the doctrine of legal sources, does not need confirmation by those sources which are relevant only due to the same doctrine of legal sources. Neither Savigny nor Puchta ever claimed that *everything* they would ever write had to be in line with pure Roman law.

[30] Puchta, *Gewohnheitsrecht*, vol. II, 29ff. [31] *Ibid.*, 81.

[32] Siegfried Brie, 1899, *Die Lehre vom Gewohnheitsrecht. Eine historisch-dogmatische Untersuchung* (Breslau: Marcus), p. III/IV; and Alfred Pernice, 1901, 'Parerga X. Nachtrag über Gewohnheitsrecht und ungeschriebenes Recht' in SavZGA, vol. 22 (1901), 55–95, at p. 69: 'Puchta and Savigny have not shown that their doctrine is based in Roman sources.'

[33] Burkhard Schmiedel, 1966, *Consuetudo im klassischen und nachklassischen römischen Recht* (Wien: Böhlau), 6–7.

[34] D.1.3.32 and D.1.3.35.

In particular, that part of their doctrine which bestowed significance on Roman law in the first place cannot itself be dependent on a confirmation by Roman law. Now, this part is their *Rechtsquellenlehre*. And as the doctrine of customary law follows analytically from this doctrine of legal sources it equally does not need confirmation by Roman law. The problem of the historical school's doctrine of customary law is not its divergence from Roman law but rather the fact that the entire justificatory work has to be done by a *Rechtsquellenlehre* which understands itself as being ultimately unanswerable to philosophic discourse.

Custom and *Sittlichkeit*

To be sure, Hegel did not write extensively on *customary law*, and neither did his helpmate in legal theory, Eduard Gans. So, as concerns the details of a doctrine of customary law, it is unclear to what extent Hegel would have agreed with Savigny. In any case, it is unlikely that Hegel would have been especially fond of Savigny's notion of the *invisible* existence of the law within the people, as Hegel's criticism of Kant's concept of the thing-in-itself can be easily transformed into a criticism of this doctrine: if we know what we cannot perceive, then why call it absolutely unknowable? The representation of it as unknowable must have other motives than the ones put forward in the theory itself. If the hidden, invisible law that lives in the people was open to intuition, as Savigny himself claims, if it is thus directly discernible, highly visible, then why call it invisible in the first place? If customary law is a mediation of the true, hidden positive law, superfluous for those initiated in a society, as Savigny himself claims, then why call it the most direct legal source? Why not be frank and call *direct intuition* of the legal scientist, that is, of Savigny, the main source of the law? Savigny has no answers to those questions and it is doubtful if he would have deemed those questions worth answering.

What is beyond doubt, however, is that Hegel shared with Savigny a strong veneration of custom. Hegel's revaluation of custom involves not the negation but the overcoming of Kant's philosophy of autonomy, of free, self-reflective agency, of *subjective spirit* in favour of custom and habit, of *objective spirit*, i.e. of an intellectuality which not only is subjective, 'in our heads', but has the character of actuality, objectivity. Custom, Hegel would say, is not the opposite of autonomy, it is its *truth*.

In his positive evaluation of habit Hegel sets himself against his rationalistic contemporaries and takes up a thread that has been spun throughout Western history and that occasionally surfaced, say, in the works of Aristotle, Plutarch, Aquinas or Montaigne. In this tradition habit is seen as a central conceptual node in the discourse of moral philosophy: single actions are not relevant for the assessment of the morality of conduct but only habit is. Only habitual actions come into question for moral appraisal or condemnation. Even in Kant's philosophy we can find echoes of this insight: in the various formulae of the categorical imperative it is not *single intentions* for actions that are tested for universality, but *maxims*, i.e. possible rules of habits.

But Hegel not only takes up this tradition, he also *transforms* it by short-circuiting the Aristotelian focus on habit with the Kantian reciprocity of morality and freedom: if according to Aristotle habitual action is the true object of morality and if according to Kant only action within the spectre of morality is truly *free* action, then custom and habit are an expression of *freedom*. Custom and habit are not social expressions opposed to freedom, they are not expressions of the 'daily grind' to be overcome by self-expressive, heroic subjectivity, but rather they are conditions of this subjectivity, play-forms of freedom.

How does Hegel link up custom and freedom, those two concepts that intuitively conflict? If we have a look at Hegel's system in its entirety we can see that custom and habit first appear at a very surprising stage: straight after the discussion of madness. Accordingly, for Hegel the first and most prominent role for custom to play is being a remedy against what he calls madness.[35] Habit is the only cure for the exaggerated sense of the self, a self-feeling, that has posited itself as absolute and hallucinates its own determinations into a delusional world. Against this complete immersion of the self in its feeling, against this lack of being able to distinguish between oneself and the world, habit is the first step of objective consciousness out of its mere subjectivity. Now, we can only understand the role custom plays here when we understand that this 'madness' against which habit is the only remedy is not a rare aberration to be found only in some human exemplars, but a fundamental and necessary determination of *Geist* as such, of spirit in the stage of its coming to actuality. *Geist*, or, in our case, *Wissen* (knowledge), is this intricate combination and reflection, positing and presupposition of its own determinations and the world's givenness, and it has to go through a whole series of incomplete stages in which either the world

[35] G. W. F. Hegel, 1995, *Enzyklopädie der philosophischen Wissenschaften im Grundrisse. 1830. Dritter Teil. Die Philosophie des Geistes* (Frankfurt am Main), §§409–10.

is consumed by the subject or the subject is consumed by the world. Habit is one of the ways to remedy the imbalance and ultimately to reconcile both. In habit the soul is *liberated* from its self-feeling, thus making space for the world:

> The soul's making itself an abstract universal being, and reducing the particulars of feelings (and of consciousness) to a mere feature of its being is Habit. In this manner the soul has the contents in possession, and contains them in such manner that in these features it is not as sentient, nor does it stand in relationship with them as distinguishing itself from them, nor is absorbed in them, but has them and moves in them, without feeling or consciousness of the fact. The soul is freed from them, so far as it is not interested in or occupied with them: and whilst existing in these forms as its possession, it is at the same time open to be otherwise occupied and engaged – say with feeling and with mental consciousness in general.
>
> Habit is rightly called a *second nature*; nature, because it is an immediate being of the soul; a second nature, because it is an immediacy created by the soul, impressing and moulding the corporeality which enters into the modes of feeling as such and into the representations and volitions so far as they have taken corporeal form.[36]

According to this 'Aristotelisation of Kantianism' – this elevation of the Kantian discourse of duty and inclination, freedom and natural causation, onto the spiritual level – habit is the first *idealisation* of the naturally given, for example the transformation of the body into a canvas of abstract rules and regularities. This, in turn, allows an abstraction of the body and its sentient nature, thus freeing up intellectual resources to encounter the world.

Understood in this way, habit is an apt first illustration of what Hegel at later stages of his system will call *Sittlichkeit.*

> But if it is simply *identical* with the actuality of the individuals, the ethical [*das Sittliche*], as their general mode of behaviour, appears as *custom* [*Sitte*]; and the *habit* of the ethical appears as a *second nature* which takes the place of the original and purely natural will and is the all-pervading soul, significance, and actuality of individual existence. It is *spirit* living and present as a world, and only thus does the substance of spirit begin to exist as spirit.

[36] *Ibid.*, §410 Addition.

> Custom is what right and morality have not yet reached, namely spirit. For in right, particularity is not yet that of the concept, but only of the natural will. Similarly, from the point of view of morality, self-consciousness is not yet spiritual consciousness ... Education is the art of making human beings ethical: it considers them as natural beings and shows them how they can be reborn, and how their original nature can be transformed into a second, spiritual nature so that this spirituality becomes *habitual* to them. In habit, the opposition between the natural and the subjective will disappears, and the resistance of the subject is broken; to this extent habit is part of ethics.[37]

Sittlichkeit has its first appearance as custom. This implies both that custom is a token of *Sittlichkeit* and that *Sittlichkeit* is not exhausted by custom.

But what is *Sittlichkeit*? Well, it is the *concrete actuality* of freedom. All Right, according to Hegel, is *freedom existing as Idea*. And by 'existing as Idea' Hegel does not mean existing as an 'ideal', or having existence as a mere representation in our heads, but the straight opposite: existing as Idea means having rational actuality. All Right is the *existence* of freedom, existence not in our heads, but in the world. In Right, what moral philosophy only *demands* already *exists*. In abstract Right, freedom exists as property and contract; in positive morality, it may exist as good intention and welfare; but all this existence of freedom is *abstract*, i.e. is detached from the fullness of concrete social life. In abstract Right we are *persons*, and in morality we are *subjects*. It is only in *Sittlichkeit*, in custom, that freedom will have *concrete* existence in the world, that we cease to be mere persons or subjects and determine ourselves as free *humans*.

So, whereas in Kant's philosophic system various *concepts* of freedom may be philosophically tested, transcendentally deduced, deemed practically actual and theoretically problematic, in the Hegelian system custom *is* freedom, custom *is* the Kantian concept of freedom that has found *actuality* in the world.

As *concrete* actuality of freedom, *Sittlichkeit*, accordingly, is not something that pertains to humanity as such, but to a specific *Volk*. Again, Hegel and Savigny seem to converge. But again the convergence is misleading: whereas for Savigny the *Volk* has the determination of being *natural*, something grown, given, the Hegelian *Volk* as the ethical substance *is* freedom and as such is opposed to nature. Hegel's *Volk* is

[37] Hegel, *Elements*, §151 Addition.

not determined, it determines itself, it has made itself *freely*.[38] Accordingly, it would be absurd to deny it the capacity to freely and consciously give itself a legal code.

Positivity, reason and history

But ultimately it is not Hegel's attitude towards custom as such that set him in conflict with the historical school's approach to law. With a lot of good will both theories up to this stage could be seen as different, but maybe complementary, facets of the same enterprise, with Hegel focusing more on the broader social and intellectual formations and Savigny on the concrete historical sources of German law.

What really set them apart is not their valuation of custom but their concept of *positivity*, a difference which has had strong repercussions on both schools' assessments of the role that customary law should play in relation to legislation.

There are two main senses in which Hegel's concept of positivity differs from that of the historical school. First, (i) Hegel's notion of positivity is broader and conceptually sharper. Secondly, and more importantly, (ii) whereas Savigny's conception of positivity mainly helps him to mark out the limits of reflection, Hegel's is a philosophically potent relational concept that mediates between reason and history.

So, (i) whereas for Savigny the positivity of the law is grounded only in its historicity, Hegel takes positivity in a much broader sense, of which historicity is but one element:

> Right is in general *positive* (a) through its *form* of having validity within a state; and this legal authority is the principle which underlies knowledge of right, i.e. the *positive legal science*. (b) In terms of *content*, this right acquires a positive element (α) through the particular *national character* of the people, its stage of *historical* development, and the whole context of relations governed by *natural necessity*; (β) through the necessity whereby a system of legal right must contain the *application* of the universal concept to the particular and *externally* given characteristics of objects and instances – an application which is no longer a matter of speculative thought and the development of the concept, but subsumption by the

[38] See also Armin von Bogdandy, 1986, *Hegels Theorie des Gesetzes*, (Freiburg: Alber), 206–17.

> understanding; (γ) through the *final* determinations required for *making decisions* in actuality.[39]

This section is at least *en passant* a comment on the method of the historical school.[40] In it, Hegel agrees with Savigny that the specific history of a people is one determining factor of the particularity, the determinate character of the law. But so are the climate, the nature of the landscape, the religion and extra-legal customs. It must have seemed to Hegel and other authors that all that Savigny had done was to take *one* element of Montesquieu's *De l'Esprit des Loix*, i.e. the historicity of the positive law, and raised it to absoluteness. And, apart from this 'stage of *historical development*, and the whole context of relations governed by *natural necessity*', Savigny also did not take into consideration the positive *determination* of the law owing to the need for *application*, and, most importantly, coming from its *form* of having validity within a particular state.

But it may even be possible to reconcile those differences by coming up with a concept of history rich enough to incorporate all those positive elements. So, turning to the second difference (ii) we can see that what marks out the fundamentality of their difference has to do with the precise *role* that the concept of positivity should play in their theories, with the strategic work this concept was supposed to do. Savigny took positivity to be a result of temporality *simpliciter*, i.e. of the fact that we encounter the law as always already existent. Determining the law as positive in this sense made a reference to the possible content of the positive law superfluous because positivity is an epistemically necessary option and not an ontological determination of the law. As such an epistemic determination, the positivity of the law is mainly a determination of the limits of reflection. But, in determining the limits of reflection, positivity simultaneously determines the beginning of the world: it marks the point where science should stop and where the world begins,

[39] Hegel, *Elements*, § 3. See also Eduard Gans, 1971, 'Naturrecht von Gans. Im Wintersemester 1828 bis Ostern 1829' in *Philosophische Schriften*, edited by Horst Schröder, (Glashütten im Taunus: Detlev Auvermann), 37–154.

[40] This is confirmed by the remarks following it: 'To consider the emergence and development of determinations of right *as they appear in time* is a *purely historical* task. This task . . . is meritorious and praiseworthy within its own sphere, and bears no relation to the philosophical approach – unless, that is to say, development from historical grounds is confused with development from the concept, and the significance of historical explanation and justification is extended to include a justification which is *valid in and for itself*.' Hegel, *Elements*, §3 Remark.

it demarcates word and object, reason and world. As such, *positivity* is constituent not only of the positive law but, more importantly, of *legal science*. But Savigny does not reflect on the fact that in setting the boundaries of reason positivity has already overreached these boundaries and rationalised the beyond.

In Savigny's work positivity thus plays the role of generating a proper object of his science. Keeping this in mind we can better understand why Savigny was so keen to portray the law as not being made, but as just being there. What lies at the heart of the problem is a *contest of faculties*: if the law is just *there*, then the only competent discipline to deal with it is legal science and the supreme faculty in relation to law is the legal faculty owing no intellectual deference whatsoever to the faculty of philosophy. The lawyer would be a master in his own house. If, on the other hand, the positive law is not only out there but *made*, if it is itself a product of philosophic intellect, of reason, then its academic treatment is a *reflective* enterprise and should have its principal seat at the faculties of philosophy, even if the detailed dogmatic treatment of it – which in a Hegelian context would be characterised as merely *verständig* (understanding-like) as opposed to *vernünftig* (rational) – would be delegated to the faculties of law.

So, ultimately, Hegel agreed with Savigny on the temporality of the law, on the fact that the law is always already there. What he was contesting, however, were the theoretical implications this is supposed to have and the philosophical options it is supposed to leave open: the fact that the positive law is always already existent renders a reflection on the rationality of its content superfluous only if one (i) has an a-historic metaphysical concept of reason as a pool of standards somehow eternally hovering above and outside history, and (ii) denies the possibility and necessity of a rational theory of history.

(i) Reason according to Hegel is not a detached world of independent standards but *absolute mediation*. It is in this sense that Hegel identifies reason and freedom. Both are this absolute power to be able to bear *the other*, to be able to remain with oneself while being with the other. Now, why this should be a definition of *reason* may become clearer when we reflect on the fact that *cognition* and *knowledge* are such forms in which we have to be with the other (the world) without losing ourselves to the other, where we have to combine a given, arbitrary content with necessity without thereby destroying the givenness of the content or breaking the necessity of the form. Kant's *synthetic a priori* is nothing but an expression of this structure, and all epistemology before Hegel up till today, including controversies between coherence-theories of truth and correspondence-theories of truth, has struggled with the dialectic of being with oneself while being with the other. Equally, the question why this self-sustaining in the other should be a definition of *freedom* should become clearer when we reflect on the fact that the Kantian attempt to find a transcendental deduction of freedom was precisely this attempt to find the possibility of an action that has the determination *absolutely* in itself and yet leaves mere thought and engages with a world.

Reason thus is always above mere opposition of itself and its other, and the relation of reason and positivity cannot be that of simple opposition as Savigny wanted to have it. Positivity rather is *one* moment of reason:

> The general mode by which experience first makes us aware of the reasonable order of things is by accepted and unreasoned belief. Similarly, the consciousness a citizen has of his country and its laws is a perception of reason-world, so long as he looks up to them as unconditioned and likewise universal powers, to which he must subject his individual will. And in the same sense, the knowledge and will of the child is rational, when he knows his parents' will, and wills it. Now, to turn these rational (of course positively rational) realities into speculative principles, the only thing needed is that they be thought.[41]

In Hegel's system positivity does not mark the limit of knowledge but constitutes the self-introduction of reason. Every time Hegel tries to introduce the reader to what reason actually is, he in one way or another refers to positivity, be it in his double-thesis of the identity of actuality and rationality, in his reflections on the relation of understanding, dialectics and speculation or in his methodological reflections in the preface to the *Phenomenology*.

(ii) On a similar note, the positivity of the law would render a reflection on the rationality of its content superfluous only if one denies the possibility and necessity of a rational theory of history.

But, Hegel claims, it is impossible to deny this possibility and at the same time engage in historical studies that claim to be rational, as the only rational conception of history is that history itself is the history of rationality.

[41] Hegel, *Enzyklopädie*, §§81–2.

Now, why should this be so? We are certainly used to thinking that the rationality of history as a scholarly enterprise (*historia rerum gestarum*) is to be distinguished from the rationality of history as a series of events (*res gestae*). But Hegel's philosophy of history is an attempt to show precisely the opposite:

> The only Thought which Philosophy brings with it to the contemplation of History, is the simple conception *of Reason*; that Reason is the Sovereign of the World; that the history of the world therefore, presents us with a rational process. This conviction and intuition is a hypothesis in the domain of history as such. In that of Philosophy it is no hypothesis.[42]

Whoever finds the idea that 'Reason is the Sovereign of the World' ridiculous, if not appalling, may be calmed with the following line of thought: history (*res gestae*) is not only a collection of happenings divorced from our own existence, but it is also the sum of our own *preconditions* as cultural beings. As such, history is also the sum of the preconditions of a properly rational historical enquiry, which, too, is a cultural expression. If, now, this historical enquiry (*historia rerum gestarum*) is to be rational, then history (*res gestae*) must at least be understood as making the rationality of this historical inquiry possible, as being the history of the rationality of historical inquiry. Now, historical research is not an isolated enterprise, but can be rational only in a context of freedom, i.e. in the modern rational state.[43] Thus, rational historical enquiry is the enquiry into the development of reason as such.

This line of thought, of course, only makes sense if we are convinced that reason has already actualised itself in the world. And this is precisely what Hegel thought had happened in the French Revolution, in the advent of the rational liberal state that guarantees mutual recognition and free citizenship to all. In the post-Revolutionary state precisely this Reason that throughout history has expressed itself solely in *demands* made by philosophers has become actual. And it is only in this context that Hegel's *dictum* in relation to the codification controversy can be fully appreciated: 'To deny a civilised nation, or the legal profession

[42] G. W. F. Hegel, 1995, *Vorlesungen über die Philosophie der Geschichte* (Frankfurt am Main: Suhrkamp), 20.

[43] Hegel in some passages even equates *res gestae* and the state: 'Only in a State cognisant of Laws, can distinct transactions take place, accompanied by such a clear consciousness of them as supplies the ability and suggests the necessity of an enduring record.' Hegel, *Philosophie der Geschichte*, 84.

within it, the ability to draw up a legal code would be among the greatest insults one could offer to either.'[44]

The crucial term here is *civilised*. It means *post-Revolutionary*, or, in modern terms, *post-historical*. In times in which reason's demands have been actualised in a people, it can be neither for the philosophers to *demand* a new law nor for legal historians to claim that the true law was made a thousand years ago by jurists who 'calculated with concepts' – it can only be for the people themselves to consciously and freely make themselves through the law.

In this ultimate turn from custom to legislation, Hegel introduces a surprising re-Kantianisation of his previous standpoint on custom. According to Kant's moral philosophy, the universal moral law is not limitation but an expression of our freedom, because it was not somebody else that gave us this law but it was we as rational beings who have given us this law. If, conversely, we follow our whims we may think ourselves to be free, but actually we are following the laws of our inclination, i.e. the causal laws of our dark biological nature. Both the moral law and the law of inclination may be *ours*, but only the former is *ours* in the emphatic sense that it is thought and thus completely self-transparent. True freedom is not satisfied with contingent, arbitrary accordance to 'one's' law; but only accordance with a law of which we can at the same time know *how* it came about and *why* we are following it can constitute freedom. To be free, moral action needs to be accompanied by *self-consciousness*, by thoughtful insight into this relationship of oneself to the moral law.

Hegel assesses the relation of legislation and customary law along similar lines, without, however, falling back behind his previous Aristotelian turn, without slipping back into a Kantian dualism that included a devaluation not only of inclination but also of customs. So, if we act according to customary laws, we may follow *our* laws. However the element of self-consciousness is lacking: 'Customary laws contain the moment of being *thoughts* and of being *known*. The difference between these and statutory laws consists simply in the fact that the former are known in a subjective and contingent manner, so that they are less determinate for themselves and the universality of thought is more obscure.'[45] The problem with custom thus is that we lack precise knowledge of its origin and we do not really know *why* we are following it. What is more, the lack of knowledge about the reasons for following it

[44] Hegel, *Elements*, §§211 and 241. [45] *Ibid.*, §211 Remark.

are an integral part of the logic of custom: we act in accordance with certain rules, because it is custom, because 'that's the way things are done here'. This tautology – 'things are done this way because things are done this way' – is but an expression of this lack of self-transparency.

With the positive statutory laws of a rational state, however, this defect is remedied. In following them we *are free* in a Kantian sense, not only because we follow rules which are *ours*, but also because it is completely transparent to us *how* they have been made and *why* we are following them. Living under positive statutory norms, nothing remains hidden and man becomes absolutely self-conscious.

Conclusion

It can therefore be said that both thinkers' stance towards customary law was inextricably linked to their attitude towards the French Revolution. Both were clearly conservatives, but the object of conservation could not have been more different: whereas Hegel sought to defend the status reached by the French Revolution, substantially expressed in Napoleonic codifications of private law, Savigny wanted to defend the old Roman law (the validity of which was founded on customary law) against revolutionary innovations like Napoleonic codes. Whereas Hegel wanted a conservation of the revolution, Savigny wanted a conservative revolution, a *restoration* of the pre-revolutionary order.

In customary law Savigny found the *paradigm* and object lesson of his doctrine of legal sources: law is not a social technique of human improvement, not a tool completely at our avail, but, like language, it lives a life of its own in the consciousness of the people, it has its intrinsic rules of generation and development. Furthermore, as all law is firmly based on the broad common consciousness of a people, all law is fundamentally democratic. However, this had two surprising results. First, Savigny's focus on customary law made it nearly disappear between custom and positive law in general. This need not be a weakness but may be proof of the doctrine's intellectual strength and liveliness, capable of overcoming old conceptual formations in favour of true substantive relations. Secondly, the democratic foundation of all law does not lead to an empowering of the people but ultimately to an empowering of the juristic experts.

Hegel's reflections on custom and customary law partially took the same origin but led him to completely different results. Hegel introduces *two* Copernican folds: he first uses an Aristotelian lever to turn Kant's individualistic moral philosophy around, to understand Kantian freedom in terms of *Sittlichkeit*. But then he uses a Kantian lever to turn this Aristotelian ethical life around to show that in the modern rational state Kantian autonomy is reached. Whether or not this double-move has been successful is still a matter of learned debate.

Be that as it may, Hegel still emerges from the intellectual struggle as victor. He has to: on a conflict between philosophy and its rejection only philosophy can sit in judgment. And, as declaring the rejection of philosophy victorious would mean revoking its own authority, philosophy can do nothing else but affirm itself in every instance.

PART II

Custom and law: custom, common law and customary international law

7

Custom in medieval law

DAVID IBBETSON

In 1982, in his monograph on custom in the Middle Ages, the Belgian scholar John Gilissen remarked on the lack of studies in English concentrating on the subject.[1] The situation has not improved significantly. Apart from two articles by Albert Kiralfy and one by Paul Brand, such attention as has been given to the topic has been concerned with particular customs, especially manorial customs, borough customs, and the custom of merchants.[2] The present paper will not fill this gap, but will try to set the uses of the idea of custom in England against the better-studied continental background.

Custom in Roman law

Although the part played by custom, *consuetudo*, in Roman law is outwith the scope of the present paper, many of the ideas found in the Middle Ages were rooted in Roman soil. It cannot therefore be wholly ignored. Two texts in particular were influential, one in the Digest attributed to Julian,[3] but generally regarded as having suffered some

[1] J. Gilissen, *La Coutume* (Turnhout: Brepols, 1982), 17.

[2] A. K. R. Kiralfy, 'Custom in Mediaeval English Law' (1988) 9 *Journal of Legal History* 26; A. K. R. Kiralfy, 'Custom in Mediaeval English Law', in *La Coutume* (Brussels, Recueils de la Société Jean Bodin, 1990), vol. 2, 379; Paul Brand, 'Local Custom in the Early Common Law', in P. Stafford, J. Nelson and J. Martindale (eds.), *Law, Laity and Solidarities: Essays in Honour of Susan Reynolds* (Manchester: Manchester University Press, 2001), 150. For earlier work, see F. A. Greer, 'Custom in the Common Law' (1893) 9 LQR 153; E. K. Braybrooke, 'Custom as a Source of English Law' (1951) 50 *Michigan Law Review* 71; C. K. Allen, *Law in the Making* (7th edn, Oxford: Oxford University Press, 1964), 67–111, at 152–6; W. S. Holdsworth, *History of English Law* (London: Methuen, 1903–66), 2.375–91, 3.256–75.

[3] D.1.3.32: De quibus causis scriptis legibus non utimur, id custodiri oportet quod moribus et consuetudine inductum est; et si qua in re hoc deficeret, tunc ius, quo urbs Roma utitur, servari oportet. Inveterata consuetudo pro lege non immerito custoditur, et

post-classical or compilatorial alteration, and one in the Code ascribed to Constantine.[4] Out of these texts, together with some others of less central importance, we may distil a number of points. First, stress is laid on the long-standingness of a practice: it is referred to, for example, as *inveterata*, *longa*, or *diuturna*.[5] Secondly, it is described as flowing from the (tacit) agreement of the people.[6] Thirdly, it is unwritten, contrasted with written *lex*.[7] Fourthly, it may or may not prevail over a contrary *lex*.[8] And, fifthly, it must not be contrary to reason, *ratio*.[9] It must be emphasised that these features were not characteristics of some putative Roman theory of custom; they were simply ideas found in the Roman texts which could be drawn on by medieval jurists, ideas which made up the conceptual vocabulary utilised in the Middle Ages.

In addition, we might point to two further features. First is that, alongside the foundation of custom in long-standing practice, a relationship was also seen between custom and judicial practice. According to Ulpian, when a specifically local custom was relied upon the first question was whether it had been judicially recognised;[10] and Callistratus allowed for a stream of similar decisions to be treated on a par with custom in the interpretation of an ambiguous *lex*.[11] Secondly, we might tentatively draw a link between custom and juristic opinion. Pomponius, dealing with the sources of Roman law, says that it flows either from written *lex*, or from the unwritten *ius civile* found only in the interpretation of jurists.[12] Both of these lines, although not in themselves dealing with custom, were to re-arise in the Middle Ages.

hoc est ius quod dicitur moribus constitutum. Nam cum ipsae leges nulla alia ex causa nos teneant quam quod iudicio populi receptae sunt, merito et ea quae sine ullo scripto populus probavit tenebunt omnes: nam quid interest suffragio populus voluntatem suam declaret an rebus ipsis et factis? Quare rectissime etiam illud receptum est ut leges non solum suffragio legis latoris sed etiam tacito consensus omnium per desuetudinem abrogentur.

[4] C.8.52.2: Consuetudinis ususque longaevi non vilis auctoritas est, veterum non usque adeo sui valitura momento ut aut rationem vincat aut legem.

[5] D.1.3.32; C.8.52.2; Inst. 1.2.9.

[6] D.1.3.32; D.1.3.35; Inst.1.2.9. Also G.3.82 (not known in the Middle Ages).

[7] D.1.3.33; Inst. 1.2.9. [8] D.1.3.32 (may); C.8.52.2 (may not).

[9] C.8.52.2. CF also the Interpretation to C.Th.5.20.1, that it must not be contrary to *utilitas*.

[10] D.1.3.34. [11] D.1.3.38.

[12] D.1.2.2.12. Note also that in Gaius' treatment of the sources of Roman law in G.1.2–7 there is no reference to custom; the only unwritten source is juristic opinion.

Custom in the Middle Ages: continental Europe[13]

The senses of custom

In broad terms, it is possible to identify three senses in which the idea of custom, *consuetudo*, surfaces in medieval law: custom as normative practice, custom as unwritten law, and custom in opposition to law.[14] In the first sense, and the least technical 'custom' refers to the way in which a particular group orders its affairs. Looked at from the group's own standpoint, it is 'the way we do things'. When referring to custom in this way, the ideas of *consuetudo* and *lex* run very close together. '*Lex et consuetudo*', as a composite term, means simply the law of some particular place or group. Byzantine charters might refer to agreements made *secundum legem et consuetudinem Romanorum*;[15] such a usage is found by the twelfth century in a variety of contexts, for example in notarial documents or in grants of urban privileges.[16] Moreover, within the ethical world of the Middle Ages both law and custom formed part of the same system, not self-standing but subordinate in authority to the law of God.[17] In its second usage, custom occupies a position in direct opposition to law. *Lex* is defined as written law, *ius scriptum*, whereas *consuetudo* is unwritten, *ius non scriptum*. This distinction is firmly

[13] See in particular the following: S. Brie, *Die Lehre vom Gewohnheitsrecht* (Breslau: Marcus, 1899); H. Pissard, *Essai sur la Connaissance et la Preuve des Coutumes* (Paris: Rousseau, 1910); F. Calasso, *Medio Evo del Diritto* (Milan: Giuffrè, 1954), 181–214; E. Cortese, *La Norma Giuridica* (Milan: Giuffrè, 1962–4), 2.101–67; J. Gilissen, *Introduction Historique au Droit* (Brussels: Bruyant, 1979), 231–76; J. Gilissen, *La Coutume* (Turnhout: Brepols, 1982) (Typologie des Sources du Moyen Âge Occidental, fasc. 41); the collection of essays in *La Coutume* (Brussels: De Boeck-Wesmáel, 1990) (Recueils de la Société Jean Bodin, vols. 51 and 52) (the 'Rapport de Synthèse' by Jean-François Poudret, at 511–45, provides a good comparative introduction); R. Garré, *Consuetudo: Das Gewohnheitsrecht in der Rechtsquellen- und Methodenlehre des Späten Ius Commune in Italien (16.–18. Jahrhundert)* (Studien zur Europäischen Rechtsgeschichte, vol. 183) (Vittorio Klostermann: Frankfurt, 2005), 53–86.

[14] Gilissen, *Coutume*, 22–4, adopts a rather different tripartite division: custom as one of the sources of formal law, custom as the totality of law applicable to a particular socio-political group, and customs as particular rules of law.

[15] Calasso, *Medio Evo del Diritto*, 184.

[16] F. Calasso, *Il Negozio Giuridico* (Milan: Giuffrè, 1959), 90–1; J. Gilissen, 'Loi et Coutume: Esquisse de l'Évolution des Sources du Droit en Belgique du XIIe au XXe Siécle', VIe Congrés International de Droit Comparé (1962) 39 *Revue de Droit International et Droit Comparé* 1, at 7; E.-J. Tardif, *Coutumiers de Normandie* (Rouen/Paris: A. Lestringant/A. Picard, 1896), vol. 2, 6. Note too the title of the Latin version of the *Très Ancien Coutumier*, the *Statuta et Consuetudines Normannie*.

[17] Calasso, *Medio Evo di Diritto*, 199–204.

drawn in Isidore of Seville's *Etymologia*,[18] and it was probably from this that it passed into Gratian's *Decretum* in the middle of the twelfth century:

> That [custom] which is reduced to writing is called *constitutio* or *ius*; that which is not reduced to writing is called by the general name *consuetudo*.[19]

The early thirteenth-century civilian Azo similarly defined *consuetudo* as *ius non scriptum*,[20] but by the middle of the century this aspect of his definition was being denied.[21] By this time the practice was developing of putting customs into written form, a response to learned laws, both as a form of competition with them and as a means of marking the validity of customs within the terms of the learned laws themselves;[22] the contrast between written laws and unwritten customs, therefore, began to break down. None the less, the definition continued to be found in less scholarly works of the later Middle Ages.[23] In its third sense, like the second, custom is contrasted with law, but the contrast is rather different. Whereas in the former *lex* and *consuetudo* were complementary, a legal system being made up of written and unwritten rules, in the latter there was a strong opposition between them. Law was the given, custom something which either added to it or took away from it. Moreover, eventually if not at first, the law determined the sphere of application of a custom and the conditions of its validity. What we might call 'customary law', in this sense, exists in contrast to 'common law', as a local

[18] Etym. V.3.2: Lex est constitutio scripta. Mos est vetustate probata consuetudo, sive lex non scripta.

[19] D.1, C.5: Quae in scriptis redacta est, constitutio sive ius vocatur; quae vero in scriptis redacta non est, generali nomine, consuetudo videlicet, appellatur. For Gratian's treatment of custom, see R. Wehrlé, *De la Coutume dans le Droit Canonique* (Paris: Sirey, 1928), 87–93; for its derivation from Isidore, see C. G. Fürst, 'Zur Rechtslehre Gratians' (1971) 88 *Zeitschrift der Savigny-Stiftung für Rechtsgeschichte (Kanonistische Abteilung)* 276, at 280–1.

[20] Azo, *Summa Codicis*, ad C.8.52 No. 1: Ius non scriptum moribus populi diuturnis introductum.

[21] See for example the *Repetitio* of the Orléans professor Jacques de Révigny on Inst. 1.2.9, printed by L. Waelkens, *La Théorie de la Coutume chez Jacques de Révigny* (Leiden: Brill, 1984), 421–2. More generally, L. Mayali, 'La Coutume dans la Société Romaniste', in *La Coutume*, vol. 2, 11, 18–19; Gilissen, *Coutume*, 25–7.

[22] Gilissen, *Coutume*, 86–92; A. Gouron, 'La Coutume en France au Moyen Âge', in *La Coutume*, vol. 2, 193, at 203–4; cf. below, p. 161, for English law.

[23] J. Boutillier, *Somme Rural* (Paris 1603), 3: 'Droit non escrit est la coustume en païs coustumier'; P. Wielant, *Praktijke Civile*, Inleiding, cap. 29: 'Costume is recht niet gescreven . . .' (Antwerp 1573, reprint ed. I. Strubbe, *Fontes Iuris Batavi Rariores*, No. 3 (Amsterdam: Graphic, 1968), 27). Gilissen, *Coutume*, 21.

or particular rule different in some way from the general rule; each of these terms presupposes the other.[24]

Although each of these senses has its own distinct focus, there are considerable conceptual overlaps between them, repeatedly playing on ideas found in the Roman texts. Loosely, it can be said that the first two senses predominated in the early Middle Ages, reflecting on the way in which law was rooted in custom; from the middle of the twelfth century the third sense begins to come through more strongly as the contrasts came to be drawn between the civil and canon law and the (predominantly unwritten) rules of particular places, or between the general law of some region and the special law of some particular place.[25] As German scholars have described it, alongside customary law (*Gewohnheitsrecht*) there grew up a body of doctrine relating to legal customs (*Rechtsgewohnheiten*),[26] reflecting the self-conscious juridification of society in the twelfth and thirteenth centuries.

Characteristics of custom in the Middle Ages

From whatever standpoint we look at it, a primary characteristic of custom as it was seen in the Middle Ages was that it was discovered by looking backwards. Roman texts had touched on its antiquity;[27] the idea was borrowed by the earliest of the medieval glosses which stressed that its origins should go back before the limit of man's memory, though by contrast John Bassianus fixed it at ten years.[28] Building upon this, Azo equated the long use which grounded a custom with the Romans' periods of prescription (ten, twenty, thirty or forty years, depending on the circumstances).[29] Such an equivalence was rapidly rejected,[30] but it is revealing: just as prescription was both a source of rights and a means of destroying pre-existent rights, so too for Azo the enforcement of customs simultaneously

[24] H. P. Glenn, *On Common Laws* (Oxford: Oxford University Press, 2005), 16–20.

[25] Hence, too, the contrast between general customs and special customs: Cortese, *La Norma Giuridica*, 2.122–6.

[26] See G. Dilcher *et al.*, *Gewohnheitsrecht und Rechtsgewohnheiten im Mittelalter* (Berlin: Duncker & Humblot, 1992).

[27] Above, p. 152.

[28] Mayali, 'La Coutume dans la Société Romaniste', in *La Coutume*, vol. 2, 11, 24, with references at notes 56–8. See in particular gloss *inveterata* ad D.1.3.32.

[29] Mayali, *ibid.*, with note 59; Cortese, *La Norma Giuridica*, 2.143–5, especially note 102. Azo, *Summa Aurea*, ad C.8.52.

[30] Though it was not completely grubbed out: A. LeBrun, *La Coutume* (Librairie Générale: Paris, 1932), 45, n. 5.

involved a departure from the ordinary course of the law. In the fourteenth century Bartolus recrystallised the approach of Bassianus, fixing the appropriate period for the establishment of custom as ten years.[31]

More importantly, Bartolus related the period of usage to a second characteristic of custom in medieval law, its foundation in the consent of the people, an idea which was also found in Roman law.[32] For him, long use was the *causa remota* of enforceable customs, with the tacit consent of the people as their *causa proxima*.[33] Medieval lawyers had picked up the Justinianic notion of tacit consent without relating it to long use; rather they were concerned with the question of whose consent counted.[34] More commonly, though, it was used as an unexplored notion which could be used to describe how it was that certain practices should be given normative force, what one recent writer has described as a '*fantasma dialettico*'.[35] None the less, despite the plasticity of the idea, it reveals the way in which customary law was recognised as growing from within society rather than being imposed from above by legislation; in the terminology of Walter Ullmann, it reflects ascending rather than descending power.[36]

Custom, *consuetudo*, had two principal antitheses. First was *mos*, which we should translate as habit; second was *lex*, which here means legislation. Both of these pairings were highly complex, and it is only possible here to touch on them; and although they can cast light on the medieval understanding of custom we must not suppose that the relationships were satisfactorily worked out.

It is easy, when dealing with the relationship between habit and custom, to say that habit represented a factual regularity while custom was normative. This is true, but it does not explain how habit became custom, nor does it explain why custom is normative. To begin with the second question, it has been seen that the justification was found in the (tacit) consent of the people; in modern terminology, it can be said

31 Ad C.8.52.2 No. 16. W. Ullmann, 'Bartolus on Customary Law' (1940) 52 *Juridical Review* 265, at 275; cf. Mayali, 'La Coutume', 25, n. 63. Note also *ibid.*, 22, n. 47, pointing out that Bartolus' ideas were largely drawn from his predecessors, so that his importance was more as a synthesiser than as an original theorist.

32 Above, p. 152. 33 Ad D.1.3.30 No.17. Mayali, 'La Coutume', 21.

34 Cortese, *La Normal Giuridica*, 2.101–67, especially at 103.

35 G. Garancini, 'Consuetudo et Statutum Ambulant Pari Passu: La Consuetudine nei Diritti Italiani del Basso Medio Evo' (1985) 58 *Rivista di Storia del Diritto Italiano* 19, at 42. See further below, p. 174.

36 W. Ullmann, *Principles of Government and Politics in the Middle Ages* (London: Methuen, 1966), 20–1 and 280–7.

therefore that it was based on a conventionalist understanding of the nature of custom.[37] Just as the basis of legislation was the will of the prince, so the basis of custom was the will of the people.[38] Equally potent was the analogy with contract, where the parties were treated as having a sovereign power to create their own world of rights and duties;[39] here, as with custom, it was not simply a unilateral act of will that was required, but an agreement, *consensus*. We must not, of course, read back into the Middle Ages our own theories as to why contracts or legislation generate obligations; for the medieval lawyers *voluntas* and *consensus* were sufficient in themselves. This understanding leaves two unresolved problems. First is that the notion of tacit consent, unless it is genuinely no more than an unspoken agreement, operates only as a rhetorical device justifying some conclusion *as if* there had been consent, hence begging the whole question.[40] Secondly, the focus on the conventional nature of custom disengages it from the habitual dimension: habit may be evidence of *consensus*, but no more than that.[41]

The second antithesis is that between custom and *lex*.[42] The Roman texts were ambivalent on the question whether contrary custom prevailed over legislation, *Digest* D.1.3.32 saying that it could, *Codex* C.8.52.2 saying that it could not. This ambivalence was closed down by the medieval jurists: a gloss on D.1.3.32 attributed to Irnerius was unequivocal in its placing *lex* above custom, on the basis that by his time the people had transferred their power to the ruler. This was consolidated by Placentinus, arguing that D.1.3.32 should be interpreted as saying that a later custom could displace an earlier custom but not a written *lex*, and it became the dominant line throughout the Middle Ages. In so far as there was any residual law-making power in the people, it was said by Johannes Bassianus, this depended on the acquiescence, *patientia*, of the ruler. This hierarchy of *lex–consuetudo* strongly reflected the contemporary political theory according to which law-making power was vested in the prince; and for all that the lawyers were grounding their arguments on the Roman texts they were wholly conscious of the political realities of their own time.

[37] See, for example, Professor Murphy's paper in the present volume.

[38] Cortese, *La Normal Giuridica*, 2.1–167. [39] *Ibid.*, 2.115–20.

[40] Above, p. 152. [41] See further below, p. 173.

[42] Cortese, *La Normal Giuridica*, 2.126–38; P. Stein, *The Teaching of Roman Law in England around 1200* (London: Selden Society, 1990), lviii–lxi.

At least from the point of view of the medieval jurists, this hierarchisation meant that the validity of any custom was to be determined by the law. Bartolus emphasised the importance of proving the fact of the custom, unless it was so notorious that the judges could take notice of it without further proof: *in hoc multum pendet vis istius materiae.*[43] For him, the custom must have been evidenced either by writing or by two witnesses.[44] But, even if it was proved, it did not follow that it would necessarily be recognised. In addition, once again picking up on a reference from C.8.52.2, found also in the writings of the Church fathers,[45] it had to accord with *ratio*.[46] As a matter of theory, it marked the subordination of custom to natural law – the decretals referred explicitly to *ius naturale* in this context[47] – and as a matter of practice it enabled judges to refuse to give effect to customs of which they disapproved.[48]

As Bartolus recognised, one of the most important aspects of custom was the way in which it was to be proved; and, since custom existed on the interface between formal law and popular practice, it would be a mistake to concentrate solely on juristic writings and to ignore what was actually going on. In the early Middle Ages, when law and custom were not substantially distinct, judges might sit with assistants whose duty it was to articulate what the customs were (or, we might say, what the law was), and whose statements might have had binding force on the judges.[49] Customs might be formulated orally and locked in place by frequent repetition, like the German *Weistümer* and their analogues in Switzerland and the Netherlands.[50] Above all, from the eleventh century onwards, and right across Europe, there are found written redactions of

[43] *Repetitio* ad D.1.3.32, No. 21.

[44] Ad C.8.52.2, Nos. 29–33; *Repetitio* ad D.1.3.32, Nos. 21–4.

[45] E.g. Tertullian, *De Corona*, cap. 4 (Migne, *Patrologia Latina*, vol. 2, cols. 81B–82A); Cyprian, *Epistolae de Baptismate Haereticorum, ad Quintum* (Migne, *Patrologia Latina*, vol. 3, cols. 1106A–1106B); Augustine, *De Musica*, lib. 2, cap. 8, s. 15 (Migne, *Patrologia Latina*, vol. 32, col. 1108); Augustine, *De Baptismo contra Donatistas*, lib. 4, cap. 5 (Migne, *Patrologia Latina*, vol. 43, col. 157).

[46] Brie, *Gewonheitsrecht*, 67–78; Calasso, *Medio Evo del Diritto*, 202–4; Gilissen, *Coutume*, 30–1.

[47] X.1.4.11.

[48] Cf. Hostiensis, *Summa Aurea*, De Consuetudine, rubric: Utrum autem sit rationabilis vel non relinquo iudici cum nec certa regula possit tradi.

[49] Pissard, *Coutumes*, 52–9.

[50] D. Werkmüller, 'Gewohnheitsrecht in Deutschen Weistümern', in *La Coutume*, vol. 2, 311.

the customs of particular places, ranging in size from large territories to small villages.[51] But not all customs would have been put in writing or locked in memory, and even those that had been might still require interpretation or analogical extension, so there remained a function for customary courts after this model: best known are the *Schöffen* of Germany and elsewhere, whose function was to 'speak' the law.[52] More importantly, as law and custom began to separate out around the twelfth century, as higher courts exercised appellate functions over lower tribunals, and as local laws began to be fitted together into larger systems of common law, some mechanism had to be invented to inform the judges what the customs of a particular place were. The developed Franco-Flemish practice of the later Middle Ages provides a good illustration.[53] In 1270, Louis IX formalised the pre-existing practice of discovery by inquisition, introducing the *enquête par turbe*.[54] This was a judicial process whereby a group of respectable citizens, typically numbering ten, from the place whose custom was in issue would be required to inform the court what the custom was. They would do this in the first place with a single voice, but then each would be required individually to give their reasons, saying when and where they had witnessed acts in accordance with the custom. There should be some continuity in time, though the period of continuity was not fixed in the manner pointed to by the learned lawyers. The *enquête par turbe*, clearly, was a way of proving custom which could be applied at a local level just as much as in the Parlement, and juristic texts such as Philippe de Beaumanoir's *Coutume des Beauvaisis* seem to suggest that by the end of the thirteenth century some form of proof would always be required. Practice, however, was more nuanced. If a custom was notorious, the judges might take notice of it; it was only if it was not so well known that it was necessary to

[51] Gilissen, *Coutume*, 56–7. A very early example is the *Usatges de Barcelona*, whose roots may go back as far as the 1060s, but in general there is very little evidence of this practice before the middle of the twelfth century: A. Gouron, 'La Coutume en France au Moyen Âge', in *La Coutume*, vol. 2, 193, at 198–207.

[52] J. P. Dawson, *A History of Lay Judges* (Cambridge, MA.: Harvard University Press, 1960), 94–102; Gilissen, *Coutume*, 74–7.

[53] Gilissen, *Coutume*, 65–8; Gilissen, 'La Preuve de la Coutume dans l'Ancien Droit Belge', in *Hommage au Professeur Paul Bonenfant* (Limal, G. Despy, chemin de Messe: Brussels, 1965), 563; Pissard, *Coutumes*; R. Filhol, 'La Preuve de la Coutume dans l'Ancien Droit Français', in *La Preuve* (Brussels: Recueils de la Société Jean Bodin, 1965), vol. 2, 357.

[54] Pissard, *Coutumes*, 98–159. L. Waelkens, 'L'Origine de l'Enquête par Turbe' (1985) 53 *Tijdschrift voor Rechtsgeschiedenis* 337.

prove it.[55] That said, careful lawyers intending to rely on a custom would allege it and offer proof of it so as to cover themselves against the possibility that the judges would not be sufficiently sure of it to apply it without the need for proof;[56] the one custom which never needed to be proved was the custom of the Parlement itself, the *stilus curiae*, for here the judges were sovereign. In this way, local customs were integrated into the law applied in France and Flanders, subject to the control of the Parlements. Despite this control, the customs retained their integrity and individuality; at the time of the formal homologation of customs in the sixteenth century it has been estimated that there were still many dozens of different sets of customs in Flanders and in France.[57]

Normally the events relied on by the *turbe* to evidence a custom would have been acts of positive observance, but they might also have been judicial decisions.[58] Such a form of proof had been envisaged in the Roman law texts[59] and it is discussed by the learned lawyers in the Middle Ages.[60] Some texts, such as the Norman *Assises de Jerusalem*, point to judicial decisions as the only possible source of proof of custom,[61] and the Castilian *Siete Partidas* similarly provided that long practice gives rise to a customary rule only when fortified by two judgments to that effect rendered by competent judges.[62] Though the argument that judicial decisions were everywhere the only form of proof of custom has been roundly rejected,[63] it remains the case that they were one possible form of proof. As a result we can observe both a judicialisation of custom, separated out from the behaviour of individuals, and also the growth of a form of case-law reasoning.[64] A second form of appropriation of custom away from popular practice is touched on by

[55] Though, even in the case of notorious custom, recourse might be had (or required) to the *enquête par turbe*: J.-F. Poudret, 'Réflexions sur la Preuve de la Coutume devant les Jurisdictions Royales Françaises aux XIIIe et XIVe Siècles, notamment le Rôle de l'Enquête par Turbe' (1987) 65 *Revue Historique de Droit Français et Étranger* (4th series) 71.

[56] Pissard, *Coutumes*, 88, 129, n. 1. [57] Gilissen, *Coutume*, 33–40.

[58] Pissard, *Coutumes*, 88–9; LeBrun, *La Coutume*, 38–9. [59] Above, p. 152.

[60] Cortese, *La Norma Giuridica*, 2.146–50.

[61] John of Ibelin, *Le Livre des Assises* (ed. P. W. Edbury; Leiden: Brill, 2003), 69, 110, 624–5.

[62] P.1.2.5; but note the gloss *fueren dados* of Gregory Lopez (*ad loc*), that such a rule would be impracticable.

[63] É. Lambert, *Études de Droit Commun Législatif* (V. Giard and E. Briáere: Paris, 1903), 208–804; LeBrun, *Coutume*, 33–42; P.-C. Timbal, 'Coutume et Jurisprudence en France au Moyen Âge', in *La Coutume*, vol. 2, 227.

[64] P. Stein, 'The Civil Law Doctrine of Custom and the Growth of Case Law', in *Scintillae Iuris: Studi in Memoria di Gino Gorla* (Milan: Giuffrè, 1994), 1.371.

Baldus. For him the *communis opinio doctorum* – rules and interpretations on which all or most of the learned lawyers agreed – should be enforced as if they were custom.[65]

Custom in medieval English law

As on the European continent, English law recognised a plurality of aspects of the word *consuetudo*, shifting in emphasis from general custom-as-law towards special customs-in-law. There are many parallels at a detailed level, too, for English law's approach to custom owed a good deal to Roman law and the medieval commentators. The thirteenth-century *Tractatus de Legibus et Consuetudinibus Angliae* known as Bracton makes frequent reference to the term, and it provides a good basis to begin to analyse the various senses of the word in English usage.[66] Bracton, too, provides us with our only substantial discursive legal text before the sixteenth century, and we may suspect that it was the principal channel through which the continental learning about custom came into English law.

After Bracton we lack any clear guide to thinking about custom; there is nothing in England, except perhaps a few words of Sir John Fortescue, to parallel the continental outpourings of juristic writers. This lack has to be remedied by recourse to legal records and to forensic discussions contained in the Year Books, though because of the nature of the sources the framework into which these have to be fitted has to be provided by the historian himself. The primary distinction that has to be drawn is that between general and special customs. On the one hand is custom more or less equivalent to law, on the other custom as something standing in opposition to law or in derogation from it. In practical terms, this distinction maps effectively onto statements internal to a particular system and statements external to it. The former is typified most obviously by statements of common lawyers that the common law is custom, but we can find it all the way down the hierarchy of courts in England. The clearest example of the latter are statements by common lawyers relating to the rules of other courts: if those rules are different

[65] Ad X.1.2.5 No. 8: opinio communis habet vim consuetudinis; *Syntagma Communium Opinionum* (Lyons, 1608), Praefatio, No. 33. Cf. above, p. 152, for a similar argument in Roman law.

[66] G. E. Woodbine, ed., S. E. Thorne, trans , *Bracton on the Laws and Customs of England* (Cambridge, MA: Belknap Press, 1968) (hereafter *Bracton*).

from the common law, then they can be justified as the customary law of those courts. The mapping is not perfect, since all courts (except those which applied the civil law[67]) belonged to the overarching common law, so that there was a clear consciousness in subordinate courts that their rules might be called customs in the narrow sense in so far as they differed from the predominant rules of the common law. None the less, provided this is borne in mind, the distinction between internal and external treatments of custom is a useful one.

Custom in Bracton

In so far as Bracton purports to contain any reflective treatment of the nature of custom, it is to be found in the introductory material at the start of the treatise.[68] This is very substantially derivative; Azo's *Summa Codicis* is its primary legal source, though there is a certain amount of biblical reference too, and it is possible that the author had looked directly at relevant texts in the Corpus Iuris of Justinian and the Decretals. Unsurprisingly, therefore, it largely reproduces the standard approach of the medieval civilians and canonists, though without any of the more sophisticated thought of Azo and his successors. Bracton's core sense of custom, *consuetudo*, is little different from law, *lex*, as might have been expected from the use of the pair of terms in the title of the work.[69] At a greater level of specificity it is equated with *ius non scriptum*, when making the point that English law can properly be called *lex* despite its unwritten form;[70] custom is something approved by the practice of those who use it;[71] the authority of custom and long use is not slight.[72]

As well as this idea of general custom, the term *consuetudo* is also used to refer to special customs, particular practices which have become – or, perhaps more properly, which are – binding: where something is approved by practice it sometimes takes the place of *lex*.[73] The hinterland

[67] E.g. the ecclesiastical courts, the Admiralty, and the courts of the Universities of Oxford and Cambridge.

[68] *Bracton*, 2.19–28. See also F. W. Maitland, *Select Passages from the Works of Bracton and Azo* (Selden Society, vol. 8, London, 1895), 18–42. See too Dr Cromartie's paper in this volume.

[69] Above, p. 161.

[70] *Bracton*, 2.19. The text goes on to repeat the point earlier made in the preface to Glanvill that it is not absurd to call English laws *leges*.

[71] *Bracton*, 2.22; Inst. 1.2.9. [72] *Bracton*, 2.22; C.8.52.2. [73] *Bracton*, 2.22.

between the two senses is brought out in one passage where Bracton twists Azo:

> Civil law <which may be called customary law> has several meanings. It may be taken to mean the statute law of a particular city.
>
> Ius autem civile <quod dici poterit ius consuetudinarium> pluribus modis ponitur. Uno modo pro statuto cuiuslibet civitatis.[74]

Azo's text provides a definition of civil law, what we would call the positive law of some place, falling between his discussion of the law of nature and his discussion of the law of nations. It is apparently mutated, perhaps perverted,[75] by the author of Bracton into a definition of the law of some particular city, implicitly contrasting it with the wider common law; and it is only in making this contrast that the city law falls to be described as 'customary'. This is the sense given to Bracton's passage by Maitland and Thorne, and it may well be right; yet it requires only a slightly different meaning to be given to *civitas* – something like 'community' – for the text to be a simple adaptation of Azo's passage to the particular circumstance of the English common law, a law described as customary in the opening words of the treatise.[76]

There are many references to custom outside this opening section; and, although there is nothing there approaching a theoretical discussion, a good deal more can be gleaned from the un-self-conscious uses of the terminology than can be picked up from the sections lifted from Azo and the learned laws. Inevitably, sometimes *consuetudo* has its general meaning very close to *lex*, both standing alone and explicitly paired with *lex*, but it is far more common for it to refer to local customs contrary to the normal rules of the common law.[77] There are examples of general statements of the law being qualified by 'unless there is a custom to the contrary', be it the custom of a manor, a town, a county, or just simply a custom without any further designation,[78] and many more examples of statements in passing making reference to particular customs.[79] Sometimes

[74] *Bracton*, 2.27. In the Bractonian text the section in angled brackets is interpolated into Azo.

[75] Maitland, *Bracton and Azo*, 39. [76] Above, p. 162.

[77] I omit the uses of *consuetudo* in the sense of feudal liabilities (most obvious in the name of the writ whereby feudal dues could be demanded, the Writ of Customs and Services), and also in the sense of tolls (the root of the modern customs duty).

[78] *Bracton*, 2.42, 2.43, 2.180, 2.221, 2.255, 2.268, 2.350, 2.362, 2.380, 3.109, 3.152, 4.54.

[79] *Bracton*, 2.178, 2.222, 2.229, 2.250, 2.255, 2.263, 2.268, 2.271, 2.272, 2.321, 2.380, 2.381, 2.382, 3.39, 3.181, 3.295, 3.388, 3.399, 4.49, 4.50, 4.52, 4.53.

a specific custom is referred to: the custom of London allowing land to be sold,[80] the custom of London and Oxford allowing land to be left by will,[81] a custom of Hereford and Gloucester allowing the otherwise unlawful killing of an outlaw,[82] a custom of Kent, London and Lincoln about dower,[83] a custom of Ipswich allowing a sixteen-year-old to transfer land,[84] a custom of Cornwall relating to villein marriage,[85] customs of the Bishop of Winchester relating to socage wardship.[86]

More awkward are statements justified by reference to a custom of the realm, *consuetudo regni*. It is impossible to be sure whether anything more is meant than that something is the law, using *consuetudo* in its more general sense, but sometimes there seems an implicit recognition that the English rule is in some way different, although it might not always be clear what it was different from. The phrase is several times used, for example, in dealing with bastardy, where the common law had consciously adopted (or retained) a different rule from that recognised by the Church.[87] Occasionally there is an explicit contrast with the custom of some other place,[88] or a parallel with the 'ancient custom of the fees' lifted directly from Magna Carta;[89] and once it is said that *lex* agrees with the custom of England, the *lex* concerned being precisely located in the Digest of Justinian.[90]

Custom is rhetorically rooted in the past, and it is not surprising that there are in Bracton some references in passing to old customs.[91] But it is striking how few such references there are, and it is only in dealing with the acquisition of private rights (rather than the establishment of norms of behaviour) that there is any sense that custom might have any relationship to prescription.[92] In this respect the thirteenth-century English common law seems to have remained truer to classical Roman law than had the learned laws of the time.[93] Customary norms, clearly, did not depend on any precise long usage: sometimes, reflecting the idea found in continental Europe,[94] the existence of the custom is supported by express reference to a single judicial decision in the recent past,[95] and, whether or not the decision had itself been based on an investigation of

80 *Bracton*, 3.295. 81 *Ibid.* 82 *Bracton*, 2.362. 83 *Bracton*, 2.267.
84 *Bracton*, 2.51. 85 *Bracton*, 3.293. 86 *Bracton*, 2.249, 255.
87 *Bracton*, 2.186, 4.258, 4.259, 4.260, 4.261, 4.294, 4.295, 4.297, 4.298. See J. H. Baker, *Introduction to English Legal History* (4th edn, London: Butterworths, 2002), 489–90.
88 *Bracton*, 2.229 (Normandy), 4.298 (France).
89 *Bracton*, 2.245, from Magna Carta (1215), c.2. 90 *Bracton*, 2.101, citing D.39.5.15.
91 *Bracton*, 2.245, 2.306, 2.351, 4.54. 92 *Bracton*, 2.171, 3.182, 3.191.
93 Cf. above, p. 152. 94 Above, p. 160. 95 *Bracton*, 2.350, 3.389, 4.53.

the length of some usage, it is clear that for the author of Bracton it was the judicial pronouncement that mattered rather than any practice that might have lain behind it.

Post-Bractonian law: the common law as custom

Modern legal historians would readily accept that the medieval common law was essentially customary, though they would stress that the custom from which they stemmed was not that of the English people as a whole but of the lawyers.[96] At a very basic level, no doubt, the values espoused by the common law would have been generally recognised by people in England, but the detailed working out of the rules derived from these values would certainly not have had any such populist grounding. This was all the work of lawyers, customary in the sense that the *communis opinio doctorum* might have been.[97] This is not to say that it was just judge-made: it was the product of the whole legal culture focused first on Westminster Hall and later on the Inns of Court, where lawyers lived, discussed, taught and learned together, though its most important and most enduring emanation were the pronouncements of judges collected together in the Year Books. It is easy for a legal historian to say this, rather harder for a medieval lawyer to do so: for him to have asserted that something was the law simply because the lawyers said it was would not have been obviously attractive.

Hence, when a medieval common lawyer looked to the customary nature of English law, it was to attribute it to the custom of the people. Its clearest statement is to be found in Sir John Fortescue's polemic, *De Laudibus Legum Anglie*, dating from the middle of the fifteenth century. For Fortescue all positive law was derived from natural law, from custom, or from statute. Few of the technical rules of English law could plausibly be equated with natural law, and relatively few of them were statutory; so it follows that for Fortescue most must have been outcrops of custom.[98] They were, for him, genuinely the custom of the people, and he rather implausibly suggested that they had remained

[96] A. W. B. Simpson, 'The Common Law and Legal Theory', in *Legal Theory and Legal History* (Hambledon Press: London and Ronceverte, WV, 1987), 359: J. H. Baker, *The Law's Two Bodies* (Oxford: Oxford University Press, 2001), 59–90.

[97] Above, p. 161.

[98] S. E. Chrimes, ed. and trans., *Sir John Fortescue, De Laudibus Legum Anglie* (Cambridge: Cambridge University Press, 1949), 36–41.

unchanged through the various governances of Britons, Romans, Danes, Saxons and Normans.[99] But this is nothing but a rhetorical flourish whose purpose is to show that English law is of great antiquity and – hence – worthy of the greatest respect.[100] Coke was to do the same in the more politically charged atmosphere of the early seventeenth century, only just holding back from saying, with even greater implausibility than Fortescue, that the common law had been given to these islands – we can only think of it in geographical terms – by Brutus after he had fled Troy.[101] Rhetorically speaking, it was the equivalent of the trope in the royal coronation oath, the promise that the King would uphold his subjects' good customs.

There is, perhaps, a hint in Fortescue's passage that law-as-custom depended upon long, perhaps immemorial, usage; and a Year Book case of his time goes so far as to apply the language of prescription to general customs, saying that it was through this that they had become common law:

> There are two manners of prescriptions: one which extends throughout the whole realm, which is properly law; and another which some county, or some town, city or borough has had since time [immemorial] . . .[102]

Although there is good manuscript authority for 'prescriptions',[103] it is nonsensical and has to be emended to 'customs' in order to make sense.[104] But that this use of the language is found shows just how easy was the terminological slippage between custom and prescription, and how easy the prescriptive dimension of custom appropriate to external statements about the practice of subordinate courts could seep upwards into internal statements about the common law itself.

[99] *Ibid.*, 38–41. [100] Cf. the remarks of Professor Chrimes: *ibid.*, 160, n. 4.

[101] E. Coke, *Third Reports*, viii.

[102] YB P. 7 Hen. VI f.31 pl.27, at f.33: Et sont ii maners de prescriptions; sc. un qe va per my le Royaum, et c'est proprement Ley: un autre qu tiel Pais, ou tiel Ville, Cite, ou Burgh ad eu de temps, etc.

[103] Cambridge University Library, MS Gg 5.8(14) f.viii^{v}; Harvard Law School, MS 171(b) (unfol.).

[104] Neither of these can be described as a manner of prescription; the second limb is describing something which has been prescribed, not the prescription itself; and it would have been inappropriate to speak of prescription in the first limb, since prescription involves both the creation and destruction of rights and here there would have been nothing to destroy.

Post-Bractonian law: custom in inferior courts

Common lawyers' statements equating common law with custom are almost inevitably internal. The same is not true of subordinate courts, for by the middle of the thirteenth century they formed very much a part of the common law system.[105] That said, though, especially at the lower reaches of English society, courts might retain a sufficient degree of autonomy that we can sensibly draw parallels with the Westminster courts at the apex of the system. Manorial courts, the lowest level of all, are especially instructive.[106] There are two principal reasons for this. First is that they provide the greatest contrast with the professionalised legal culture of the royal courts; in the absence of such a cohesive body of people functioning as repositories of the law (or the custom), questions would more easily arise as to what the custom (or the law) was, and these questions could not be answered by using the sort of sophisticated analogical reasoning which came to characterise the common law. Secondly, much of the work of manorial courts was concerned with unfree villein tenants, for whom the use of any other court was a practical, and in many cases a legal, impossibility. Hence in these courts, despite their lowliness, we still find a strong degree of effective autonomy.

Within this context, *consuetudo* is frequently used in the general sense meaning little more than law. Villein tenants would hold their land 'according to the custom of the manor', connoting no more than that they held it on the usual rules. Equally, though, *consuetudo* might refer to some particular customary rule. A manorial tenant claiming some right according to a particular custom in a manorial court might explicitly state what the custom was, and in such cases we can be assured that *consuetudo* meant something more specific than simply the rules applicable in the place. In this sense, customs could be controversial. The defendant in the action might deny the custom which the plaintiff had alleged, and in such a case there had to be some means of deciding between these two positions. The principal means of resolving disputes in manorial courts by the beginning of the fourteenth century was the jury,[107] and the determination of what the custom was fell to them in

105 It is a matter of controversy how far and how fast common law norms spread downwards and outwards, but it is not relevant to the present discussion.

106 See in particular L. Poos and L. Bonfield, *Select Cases in Manorial Courts* (Selden Society, vol. 114, London, 1998).

107 J. S. Beckerman, 'Procedural Innovation and Institutional Change in Medieval English Manorial Courts' (1992) 10 *Law and History Review* 197.

exactly the same way as the finding of the facts. Commonly, indeed, the manorial court roll would not distinguish between the custom and the facts, and it is likely that this reflects a similar ambiguity in the jury's verdict; all it might record was that the decision was in favour of the plaintiff or the defendant, and if it was the latter there would be no way of knowing whether the decision had been reached because the plaintiff's claim was factually flawed or because there was no custom as had been alleged.[108] Sometimes, though, the jury would say explicitly what the custom was and the court roll would reflect this. In the manor of Tooting in 1281, for example, the roll records:

> It is presented by unanimous verdict of the whole court that if anyone marries a woman who has right in any land according to the custom of the manor and is seised thereof by the will of the lord, and the said woman surrenders her right and seisin into the hands of the lord and her husband receives that right and seisin from the hands of the lord, in such case the heirs of the woman are for ever barred from the said land and the said right remains to the husband and his heirs. Therefore let William Wood, whose case falls under this rule (*qui in hoc casu est*), hold his land in manner aforesaid.[109]

No reasons are given for this, and we cannot look behind the verdict to see what led the jury to take this view. It may be that they had better memories than whichever of the litigants they found to be wrong. In some cases we see that recourse was had to previous rolls of the court, particularly where there was a dispute between the lord of the manor and the tenants, though such cases are far rarer than would be expected if this sort of written evidence was routinely relied upon.[110] But court rolls were only evidence for the jury, not a substitute for their decision. What we do not find is any sense that the existence of a custom was dependent upon any sort of prescription, though that something could be described as an ancient use was as powerful a rhetorical justification as it was in the common law.

Cases inevitably arose where the jury did not know what the custom was. If we take knowledge in a strong sense, this must have been a

[108] 114 SS xxxiii.

[109] F. W. Maitland, *Select Pleas in Manorial Courts* (Selden Society, vol. 2, London, 1888), 29. Other examples are 114 SS 2 pl.2 (Barnet, 1306), 12 pl.10f (Hatfield Chase, 1325), 19 pl.18 (Methley, 1340).

[110] 114 SS lxii, lxvi, lxviii–lxix; 130 pl.167 (Cranfield, c.1312); 154 pl.204a (Burnham Thorpe, 1481).

common occurrence in cases where there was a dispute about a custom's existence; we would not normally be able to see this, though, for the jury would normally reach a decision that the custom did or did not exist, and any doubts that they may have had will be hidden behind the certainty of the decision. Behind the guise of their finding of the custom they would, perhaps unwittingly, have been creating it, in exactly the same way as a common law judge finding and applying a rule would be engaged in an incremental exercise of law-creation. We cannot rule out the possibility that the custom was being created as a justification for reaching some desired decision, and not as a disinterested exercise in formulating a general rule which could then be applied to the facts of the case;[111] this is no less a possibility in a sophisticated legal system, though the fact that the jury was part of the same small community as the litigants would no doubt have made it more likely to occur in a manorial court than in Westminster Hall.[112]

Sometimes the jury openly stated that they did not know the custom, as in a Yorkshire case raising the question of the rights of succession to a man who had been found after his death to have been a bastard.[113] Never before had the situation occurred among the jurors' community that a man had been bastardised after his death. In such a case any statement of what the custom was would have been wholly new: the rule would have been created, not discovered. No doubt any decision of a jury as to what a custom was might have involved a departure, conscious or unconscious, from what had gone before, but on occasion they admitted openly that they were departing from past practice in saying that something was the custom.[114] However much the investigation of a custom generally involved looking back into the past, it need not be so. Customs could be changed. Tenants could negotiate for a change in their inheritance customs;[115] a lord's council could take it upon itself to decide what a custom was, despite the fact that the villeins of the manor had a clear memory of it.[116] The customary law of manors, like the common law

[111] L. Bonfield, 'The Nature of Customary Law in the Manorial Courts of Medieval England' (1989) 31 *Comparative Studies in Society and History* 514, nuanced in 'What Did English Villagers Mean by "Customary Law"?', in Z. Razi and R. Smith, eds., *Medieval Society and the Manor Court* (Oxford: Clarendon Press, 1996), 103.

[112] P. Hyams, 'What Did Edwardian Villagers Understand by "Law"?', in Razi and Smith, eds., *Medieval Society and the Manor Court*, 69, at 101–2.

[113] 114 SS lxiii, 132 pl.173 (Methley, 1331).

[114] 114 SS case 18 (lxiv).

[115] 114 SS lxv, citing G. Homans, *English Villagers of the Thirteenth Century*, 126–7.

[116] 114 SS lxxi, 133 pl.174 (Burnham Thorpe, 1334).

itself, was in a state of tension between fidelity to the past and the desire to reach the right result for the present and the future.

Between the manorial courts and the courts at Westminster there was a great range of courts of greater or lesser jurisdiction.[117] Some were highly professionalised. The London courts, for example, might almost have appeared to be an offshoot of the courts at Westminster dealing specifically with London claims, with advocates who were equally at home before the King's Bench.[118] Outside London too there is clear evidence of the existence of some sort of legal profession in borough courts and county courts by the beginning of the fourteenth century.[119] Courts such as these would have been well integrated into the common law system, though they would still have recognised and preserved their own set of customs. Those of London were sufficiently well developed that Sir Robert Brooke, compiling his Abridgement in the middle of the sixteenth century, treated the title *London* separately from his general title on *Customes*. The Kentish inheritance custom of gavelkind was equally well known, so much so that common law judges would take judicial notice of it and not require it to be proved.[120] Far lowlier courts might have been consciously integrated into the common law system, though less firmly. The Devon and Cornwall stannary courts, for example, were created by royal charter, adopted common law forms of action, and were under the formal control of a lord warden; but in reality this control was relatively weak, and greater force was given to the customary practices of the tinners themselves, the foundation charter of 1305 providing for juries consisting exclusively of tinners in cases concerning the stannaries.[121] Similarly, the forest courts, governed by royal statutes, were under the jurisdiction of the justices of forest sitting in eyre; but sittings of these justices were infrequent, and day-to-day jurisdiction was exercised by the non-professional verderers who were more familiar with the customary rules relating to the expeditation of dogs than with

117 E. Coke, *Fourth Institute*, provides an excellent view of these.

118 P. Tucker, 'London's Courts of Law in the Fifteenth Century: The Litigants' Perspective', in C. Brooks and M. Lobban, eds., *Communities and Courts in Britain, 1150–1900* (London and Rio Grande: Hambledon Press, 1997), 25.

119 P. Brand, *The Origins of the English Legal Profession* (Oxford: Blackwell, 1992), 114–15.

120 YB 5 Edw. IV f.8; T. Robinson, *The Common Law of Kent: Or the Customs of Gavelkind* (1731), 38–9. For Kentish customs generally, see N. Neilson, 'Custom and the Common Law in Kent' (1924–5) 38 *Harvard Law Review* 482.

121 R. Pennington, *Stannary Law* (Newton Abbot: David & Charles, 1973), 13–21.

the niceties of the common law.[122] Those appointed as verderers were supposed to be familiar with the law, though before the printing of John Manwood's *Forest Laws* in 1598 (subsequently incorporating a set of norms known as the *Assisa et Consuetudines Forestae*[123]) this can have meant no more than that they should know the formal rules of the courts and have a good sense of the working of the customs. Merchants' courts would, no doubt, have had exactly the same character. Although the substantive law they applied was (at least largely) the same as the common law and their prime differentiation from the common law lay in their procedural rules,[124] the merchants themselves played a larger part in them than did Westminster-trained common lawyers, and the law that they applied was refracted through the eyes of the merchant community.[125]

As in manorial courts, in these courts what was custom and what was law tended to merge together. A jury of tinners in the stannaries would have acted in the same way as a manorial court jury, the verderers in a forest swanimote would apply their own understanding of the practices in reaching their decisions. Higher up the system, the identification of custom might have been more formal. A London case of 1454 serves as an excellent illustration. A man brought a plaint of debt against a widow, who claimed the right to wage her law. The plaintiff claimed it was a custom that the defendant should be barred from waging her law if two or three reputable citizens testified that the claim was well grounded. The defendant denied that there was any such custom. The point was therefore referred to the Mayor and Alderman, who, 'having examined the ancient books of the City and many records and old processes and judgments and held diligent discussion and mature deliberation', determined that the custom stated by the plaintiff had existed from time out of mind.[126]

122 J. Manwood, *Treatise and Discourse of the Lawes of the Forrest* (1598); C. Hart, *The Verderers and Forest Law of the Dean* (Newton Abbot: David & Charles, 1971), ch. 1.

123 1615 ed., f.8.

124 J.H. Baker, 'The Law Merchant and the Common Law before 1700', in *The Legal Profession and the Common Law* (London and Ronceverte: Hambledon Press, 1986), 341, 345–52; C. Donahue, 'Medieval and Early Modern Lex Mercatoria: An Attempt at the Probatio Diabolica' (2004) 5 *Chicago Journal of International Law* 21, at 26–31.

125 M. Basile, J. Bestor, D. Coquillette and C. Donahue, *Lex Mercatoria and Legal Pluralism: A Late Thirteenth-Century Treatise and Its Afterlife* (Cambridge, MA: Ames Foundation, 1998), especially at 23–34.

126 P.E. Jones, ed., *Calendar of Plea and Memoranda Rolls, 1437–1457* (Cambridge: Cambridge University Press, 1954), 149.

Post-Bractonian law: the common law and local custom

These inferior jurisdictions were not in themselves sovereign. Customs applied in them as law might also be relevant in actions brought at common law, and the common law courts had a supervisory power over such local courts. Here there was no question of the judges simply relying on their own knowledge and treating the customs as law. The responsibility of the judges was to apply the common law, and if local custom was to be applied it was as something contrary to the common law which had to be properly proved and approved.

From this standpoint, custom was different from law and if it was to be kept in check some effort had to be made to define what was meant when it was said that something was a custom. So far as definition was concerned, the central feature of a custom was that it should be old. There are frequent references in the Year Books to customs being prescribed,[127] though it was recognised that this might not be a technical prescription as of a private right, for it was open to those who could not prescribe (such as tenants at will) to ground a custom in long usage.[128] Exactly what was meant by prescription might once have been controversial. The issue arose in the specific context of jurisdictional franchises in Edward I's *Quo Warranto* campaign of 1279–94, where there was a good deal of confused debate about what length of usage had to be shown in order to ground a claim to such a right; although the claims here were to private rights the issues that arose were the same as arose in other contexts, and the language of custom was used in pleas relating to them.[129] It was finally settled by statute that exercise of the right since 1189 (already by then established as the limit of legal memory) had to be proved.[130] This became the standard form for alleging customs of whatever sort. This approach to custom is of more value to the legal historian interested in the perceived nature of custom than it would

[127] E.g. YB 45 Lib. Ass. 8; YB P. 7 Hen. VI f.31 pl.27, at f.33; YB M. 5 Edw. IV f.8 pl.23; YB P. 18 Edw. IV f.3 pl.15.

[128] YB P. 18 Edw. IV f.3 pl.15.

[129] E.g. *R.* v. *Robert of Ferete* (Cumberland, 1292–3, *P[lacita] Q[uo] W[arranto]* 125); *R.* v. *Geoffrey of Mowbray* (Cumberland, 1292–3, *PQW* 127); *R.* v. *John Baliol* (Northumberland, 1293, *PQW* 594); *R.* v. *Gerard of Salvin* (Yorkshire, 1293–4, *PQW* 219–20); Sutherland, *Quo Warranto*, 109, n. 2 (with further, less explicit, references).

[130] D. W. Sutherland, *Quo Warranto Proceedings in the Reign of Edward I* (Oxford: Clarendon Press, 1963), 70–110. Statute of Quo Warranto 1290 (*Statutes of the Realm*, 1.107).

have been to the medieval lawyer; proof that something had existed as a custom time out of mind was practically impossible, and since individuals might act contrary to customs just as easily as they could break the law there was not even a negative inference that could be drawn from a demonstration that the alleged custom had not in fact been observed. Its only effect in legal reality was that it might be impossible to rely on a local custom when the place concerned had not existed in 1189.

The real question, as a matter of practice, was how a particular custom could be proved. Except perhaps in the case of the tenures of Borough English or the Kentish gavelkind, which were sufficiently well known that the judges might take notice of them of their own motion,[131] the common law courts relied on local knowledge to establish this. Although there was nothing formally equivalent to the Franco-Flemish *enquête par turbe*,[132] the methods of discovering what an English county custom was would not have been very different. There are references in the thirteenth- and fourteenth-century eyre rolls to the whole county (*totus comitatus*) recording that something was their custom and reporting accordingly to the common law judges,[133] and the same practice is still referred to in Kent and London centuries later.[134] Although matters of law were not normally tried by the country, and the custom took effect as a particular law applicable to the parties, there was no difficulty in allowing this mode of discovery of custom in counties and other places whose courts were not courts of record.[135] It was different with chartered boroughs, which were of record. Here the alleged custom had to be proved by the foundation charter or some other written record, in the same way as was commonly found in continental Europe.[136] Such customs would be recognised, provided only that they were properly proved.

Once proved, it was for the common law court to determine its application to the facts in dispute. Repeatedly it was said that the custom would be interpreted strictly, thereby minimising the disturbance to the common law (and, it might be noted, consolidating and strengthening the

131 YB M. 5 Edw. IV f.8 pl.23; YB M. 21 Edw. IV f.55 pl.28 at f.56; Robinson, *Gavelkind*, 38–9.

132 Above, p. 159.

133 R. C. Palmer, *The County Courts of Medieval England* (Princeton: Princeton University Press, 1982), 293, n. 112.

134 Robinson, *Gavelkind*, 260; Greer, 'Custom in the Common Law' (1893) 9 LQR 153, at 154.

135 YB H. 21 Edw. III f.46 pl.65. 136 YB H. 21 Edw. III f.46 pl.65; cf. above, p. 158.

application of the common law within the community).[137] Moreover, the custom must be the custom of a place or of a group to which the parties belonged; if it was the custom of a particular court which might have had jurisdiction over the parties it would not be applied in litigation between them at common law.[138] But the common law courts did more than simply hold the custom in its bounds and apply it: they assessed it. Sometimes, no doubt in most cases, it was held to be good;[139] but the courts were not shy of overturning a custom if they believed it to be bad. A leet custom, for example, was held unacceptable as being tantamount to extortion;[140] and in the later fifteenth century it was said more generally – with strong overtones of the learned laws[141] – that a custom contrary to reason would be rejected.[142]

Every sophisticated legal system, we may suspect, has to find mechanisms to reconcile the expectations of those subject to the law with the authority inherent in the very idea of law. Seen in this light, within the medieval legal tradition custom can be seen as a form of safety valve enabling courts to derogate from the common law when there was sufficient pressure to do so. The Roman law texts provided a range of rhetorical justifications for departing from the normal rules, and these were picked up by medieval lawyers both in England and on the European continent. It is important for the historian not to put too much weight on these justifications. They expressed, to be sure, factors which would have made it seem appropriate to depart from the normal rule, though the fact that the various reasons given were found in the Roman texts may lead us to question even this. Moreover, the requirement that a custom accord with *ratio*, a requirement again found in the Roman texts, provided a way to reject practices which as a matter of fact did otherwise satisfy the conditions of a valid custom.

We should not, in any specific case, take the justification provided as truth. That something was customary was a backward-looking reason for a forward-looking conclusion, and the more the conclusion was desired the flimsier might be the reason provide for treating it as law. This is not to say that effort would not be taken to prove the custom, and the occasional foray into legal records to find judgments in which

[137] YB M. 11 Hen. IV f.29 pl.55, at f.30; YB M. 11 Hen. IV f.33 pl.61; YB P. 21 Edw. IV f.24 pl.10.
[138] YB M. 1 Edw. IV f.5 pl.13. [139] E.g. YB M. 14 Hen. IV f.2 pl.5.
[140] YB M. 9 Hen. VI f.44 pl.27; cf. YB H. 2 Hen. IV f.15 pl.19, at f.16.
[141] Above, p. 152. [142] YB P. 21 Edw. IV f.28 pl.23.

the alleged custom was applied should put us on our guard against too cynical a treatment of the allegation of custom as a source of some particular rule. But, as is generally the case with law, the aim in practically every dispute was to achieve consistency with the past at the same time as getting the result which was thought to be right, the reconciliation of the authority of law with the perceived ideal of justice. The legal recognition of customs was, perhaps, just one more way to try to find this balance.

8

Siege warfare in the Early Modern Age: a study on the customary laws of war

RANDALL LESAFFER

The sack of Tienen

On 8 June 1635, a Franco-Dutch army, under Stadtholder Frederick Henry (1625–1647), arrived before the town of Tienen. Three weeks earlier, the French had entered the Spanish Netherlands and had joined up with the Dutch troops of Frederick Henry. Now, the joined forces had begun their march towards Brussels.

The purpose of the invasion was to drive the Spanish from the Netherlands. Pamphlets were circulated to exhort the people of the Spanish Netherlands to rebellion.[1] The small town of Tienen was part of the first line of defence of Brussels. A Spanish force of 1,200 men under Captain Martino de los Arcos, well supplied with arms and ammunition, was there to defend the town.

Upon his arrival, Frederick Henry sent a trumpeter to summon surrender. He promised the burghers of Tienen their liberties and the practice of their religion. Without consulting the town magistrate, Captain De los Arcos refused. He stated that 'the arms of his Majesty were in town and that it was not customary in such circumstances to surrender a place or town without having seen and heard one another, as both had powder and ammunition'.[2] The next day, the trumpeter made two more appeals; twice he was turned down. Meanwhile, De los Arcos promised the town magistrate to surrender after the first skirmishes.[3]

[1] Letter of the Cardinal-Infante, 6 June 1635, Brussels, General National Archives, Council of State 1599.

[2] Tienen, City Archives, J. L. de Wouters d'Oplinter, *Extract uyt sekere oude schriften, berustende ten comptoire, opden stadhuyse der stad Thienen* ... (s.d.) (my translation).

[3] A. Van Gramberen, 'Over de verwoesting van Tienen in 1635', *Hageland Gedenkschriften*, 6 (1912) pp. 158–63.

Surprisingly, there were no skirmishes before the main assault. Around 1.30 p.m. the enemy artillery opened fire and 6,000 men started the attack. After four hours of fighting, the Spanish captain agreed to request terms of surrender. The town magistrate had convinced him, arguing that his honour was safe.[4] An agreement to cease hostilities was reached with a French officer. Frederick Henry refused to commence negotiations before the Spanish commander came out to meet him. De los Arcos delayed for half an hour, which proved fatal. During that interval, the Dutch and the French forced an entrance into the now undefended town and started to plunder and sack it brutally.

The French and the Dutch leaders were embarrassed by the events at Tienen. The sack dealt the deathblow to the coalition's hopes to win over the population of the Spanish Netherlands. It did not take the allies long to lay the blame at each other's doorstep.[5] Frederick Henry attempted to deflect part of the blame by taking some disciplinary measures.[6] The Spanish government in Brussels made the most of the dreadful event to discredit its enemies and secure itself against an uprising. Its counter-declaration of war against France referred to the cruelties committed against 'the town of Tienen, God, the Sacraments and churches, priests, religious men and women, elderly, women and children'.[7]

Siege warfare before Westphalia

Under the laws of war, a besieged town had the right to a negotiated surrender. When it asked for terms in time, it would be spared plunder or massacre. If it was taken by assault, it could be sacked and pillaged and quarter could be refused to all inside. Moreover, if a town had not surrendered before the batteries of the artillery of the enemy had been

4 P. V. Bets, *Campagne des Français et des Hollandais dans les provinces belges en 1635 et Notre-Dame consolatrice de Tirlemont* (Brussels, 1859); Jean-Antoine Vincart, *Les Relations militaires des années 1634 et 1635, rédigées par Jean-Antoine Vincart* (Brussels, 1958); Lutgart Vrancken, 'Tienen in de eindfase van de 80-jarige oorlog 1621–1648', in *Tienen 1635. Geschiedenis van een Brabantse stad in de zeventiende eeuw* (Tienen, 1985), pp. 13–54; Jan Wauters, *Bijdragen tot de geschiedenis van Tienen* (Tienen, 1962).

5 See, e.g,. J. A. De Worp (ed.), *De briefwisseling van Constantijn Huygens (1608–1687)* (The Hague, 1914), vol. 3, p. 317; François de la Rochefoucauld, *Oeuvres* (Paris, 1964), p. 417.

6 Letter of Constantijn Huygens to Amalia of Orange of 10 June 1635, in De Worp, *Briefwisseling* (The Hague, 1913), vol. 2, p. 73.

7 *Declaration de son Alteze touchant la guerre contre la Couronne de France*, 24 June 1635 (my translation).

raised and fire had been opened, it lost its right to negotiated surrender. This meant that the garrison and citizens could only throw themselves at the mercy of the enemy in surrendering unconditionally later on.

The sack of Tienen reads like a textbook example for a discussion on these rules. The Spanish felt they had the law on their side in strongly making their case. For his part, Frederick Henry was undoubtedly aware of the rules when he reprimanded De los Arcos for having stalled too long and for having brought disaster over Tienen himself.[8] Whether the coalition army broke the laws of war turns on the question whether its soldiers took Tienen before negotiations had begun and before a truce had been agreed or not. According to one French commander, a cease-fire was agreed – at least on his section of the parapet – when the Spanish first asked for parley.[9] But it is not clear whether this truce applied to the entire front. Also, it may have been countermanded by the Stadtholder's demand to see De los Arcos in person before negotiations could start. Frederick Henry was indeed clever, if not sincere, in reprimanding De los Arcos. Under the laws of war, he could not reproach De los Arcos for not answering the first summons, but he upbraided him for having waited so long to ask for terms and for stalling on coming out. In doing so, he did not deny outright that parley had begun, but laid the responsibility for the confusion that led to the sack with the Spanish commander.

The basic rules concerning siege warfare were established in the Late Middle Ages. Beneath them lurked a double logic that made for a self-defeating combination. On the one hand, the besieging army wanted the siege to be brief. Raising the cost of resistance was a potent argument to persuade a town to surrender or to stir up dissent within the walls.[10] Honour was also involved. It was considered an insult for citizens to refuse a summons from a prince. This insult caused the forfeiture of life and goods. On the other hand, the sovereign of the defending garrison had an interest in the defenders holding out as long as possible. Again, honour – of the defending commander – was at stake. The practice of the Late Middle Ages shows both these concerns. According to late-medieval custom, a military commander who surrendered before the first gunshot

[8] Vrancken, 'Tienen', p. 34.

[9] Letter of General Espanin to Cardinal De la Valette, 25 July 1635, in Erycius Puteanus, *De obsidioni Lovaniensi* (Leuven, 1636).

[10] Raymond de Fourquevaux, *The Instructions sur le Faict de la Guerre of Raymond de Beccarie de Pavie, sieur de Fourquevaux* (1548, G. Dickinson, ed., London, 1954), chapter 3, pp. 82–3.

was fired was presumed to have acted treasonably. The dual logic behind the rules of siege warfare left him in a quandary. The Hundred Years' War abounds with examples of harsh reprisals against towns that, and commanders who, defended themselves obstinately. Also, examples can be quoted about commanders brought to trial for having failed to hold on long enough.[11] In this sense, the behaviour of Captain de los Arcos at Tienen becomes understandable.

The Military Revolution (1560–1660) changed the face of warfare. Sieges superseded pitched battles at the apex of war. The Eighty Years' War (1568–1648) between Spain and the United Provinces is a prime example of this new kind of warfare. The war offers insight into the application of the laws of war in relation to sieges. In a letter to King Philip II (1555–1598), the Spanish general Fadrique Alvarez de Toledo (1537–1583) proposed to treat, upon recapture, towns that had surrendered to the Dutch before the batteries were raised while having the means of defence, on the same footing with towns that had acted treasonably and defected to the Dutch. But towns which had been taken by storm or after the batteries of the artillery had been raised, had to be pardoned. Don Fadrique's statement reflected the two concerns underlying the law. Towns that surrendered too readily would be punished, but obstinate defence was not required.[12]

In the first years of the Eighty Years' War, dozens of towns were taken and retaken. Some towns were sacked after they had been taken by storm and some received lenient conditions after an obstinate defence. In 1572, the Spanish sacked Mechelen after it had been taken by storm. Some months earlier, the town had refused entrance to a Spanish garrison and allowed the Dutch rebels in. Many towns, such as Zutphen (1572) and Naarden (1572), were sacked in subsequent years. The Spanish command singled out these towns because of their rebellious obstinacy and hoped to turn them into examples. In all, these massacres remained more exception than rule. Haarlem, which had held out against its besiegers for months and had forfeited its rights to

[11] Maurice H. Keen, *The Laws of War in the Late Middle Ages* (London, 1965), pp. 119–29; Theodor Meron, *Henry's War and Shakespeare's Laws: Perspectives on the Law of War in the Later Middle Ages* (Oxford, 1993), pp. 75–130; Geoffrey Parker, 'Early Modern Europe', in Michael Howard, George J. Andreopoulos and Mark R. Shulman (eds.), *The Laws of War: Constraints on Warfare in the Western World* (New Haven and London, 1994), pp. 40–58, at p. 48.

[12] Letter of 30 December 1573, in M. Gachard (ed.), *Correspondance de Philippe II sur les affaires des Pays-Bas* (Brussels, 1851), 1st series, vol. 2, pp. 446–51.

a negotiated surrender, was granted conditions anyway (1573). The citizens were allowed to buy off plunder – not an uncommon feat – and the soldiers were given the choice between departing without their weapons and throwing themselves at the mercy of the victor. Unwisely so, they chose the latter and most were put to death. The leaders of the town archers were killed as rebels, but most other citizens saw their lives saved. The treatment of Haarlem was uncommonly harsh and, being considered treacherous by the Dutch, it did certainly stiffen the resistance. But it did not constitute a clear break with the customs of war.[13] In the subsequent years and decades, other towns received more lenient conditions, although many of them had refused to surrender before the batteries were raised.[14]

The following trends can be discerned from the practices of the Eighty Years' War. First, as a rule terms became harsher the longer the besieged delayed surrender. This was a matter of expediency and deterrence. Secondly, the rule that towns which did not surrender before the raising of the batteries forfeited their right to parley was not disputed but often waived by the besieger. In the context of a rebellion, where royal honour and obedience to royal authority were at stake, this is remarkable. However, conditions were often harsh. In some cases, the town had to buy off pillage and some were killed. In other cases, conditions were more lenient.

The 'classics of international law' from around 1600, such as Pierino Belli (1502–1575), Albericus Gentilis (1552–1608), Balthasar de Ayala (1548–1584) and Hugo Grotius (1583–1645), all addressed the problem of siege warfare in their treatises on the laws of war, albeit briefly. Their expositions were fragmentary and instrumental to more elaborate discussions on enemy personnel and property.

Pierino Belli (1563), who had practical experience in military justice, commented most extensively on siege warfare. A town should only be plundered as a punishment for some 'great wrong and crime in which the whole population ... had shared'. The resistance of civilians against

[13] Letter of the Duke of Alva to King Philip II of 28 July 1573, in Gachard, *Correspondance de Philippe II*, vol. 2, pp. 391–2.

[14] Jean-Léon Charles, 'Le sac des villes dans les Pays-Bas au XVIe siècle. Etude critique sur des règles de guerre', *Revue internationale d'histoire militaire* 24 (1965) pp. 288–301; Léon van der Essen, 'Kritisch onderzoek betreffende de oorlogvoering van het Spaans leger in de Nederlanden in de XVIe eeuw, nl. de bestraffing van opstandige steden', *Mededelingen van de Koninklijke Vlaamse Academie voor Wetenschappen, Letteren en Schone Kunsten van België*, 12 (1950) issue 1.

a prince was not a crime in itself. For this, Belli invoked Bartolus (1314–1357).[15] But Belli's main concern was the risk of commanders surrendering their fortresses too soon, which he considered treasonable. Belli quoted examples from Roman history to deliver a moral lesson to the commanders of his day and age. Only under extreme duress – 'all the people perishing of hunger and privation' – could surrender be condoned.[16] He referred to *Digest* 48.4.3, which made the commander who 'surrenders in war or recklessly yields a citadel or camp' liable for *maiestas*.[17] However, this rule only applied if the commander had evil intent – treason? – or was manifestly negligent.[18] For this mitigation Belli found support in the Gospel.[19] At the end of his treatise, Belli repeated that a commander must not yield his fortress unless it became impossible to hold it.[20]

Balthasar de Ayala, military auditor in the Spanish army in the Netherlands, wrote an extensive treatise on the laws of war and military discipline. Ayala referred to the basic rule of siege warfare – only conquered, not surrendered towns could be pillaged – in the context of a general discussion on enemy property. He traced the rule back to Roman history, quoting Livy. Ayala went on to argue, on the basis of *exempla* from classical history, that the division of the spoils fell to the army commanders. Sometimes, generals allowed their soldiers to plunder for themselves. But, even then, the prince must be allowed his share. Ayala also emphasised the many instances of classical history, which showed looting only to be allowed after the commanders had expressly said so. More than once the greed of soldiers had spoiled an uncompleted victory and turned it into defeat. Ayala referred to a recent ordinance of the Spanish King.[21]

In his *De Iure Belli libri tres* (1588–1589), the Oxford law professor Albericus Gentilis, announced, as a principle of the 'rights of humanity and the laws of war, that the life of anybody who surrendered to the enemy ought, on principle, to be spared'.[22] The rules of siege warfare

[15] Pierino Belli, *De re militari et bello tractatus* 4.8.23 (Herbert C. Nutting, trans., Classics of International Law, Oxford and London, 1936).

[16] 8.1.38–42. [17] Trans. Alan Watson *et al.* (Philadelphia, 1985), vol. II.

[18] 8.1.66. [19] Belli 10.2.93. With reference to Mark 13.34.

[20] 10.2.109–10, also 10.2.97–8, 102 and 105–6. With reference to the canon lawyer Martinus Garatus Laudensis.

[21] Balthasar de Ayala, *De Jure et Officiis Bellicis et Disciplina Militari libri III* 1.5.4–11 (John P. Bate, trans., Classics of International Law, Washington, 1912).

[22] Albericus Gentilis, *De Iure Belli libri tres* 2.17.351 (text of 1612, John C. Rolfe, trans., Classics of International Law, Oxford and London, 1933).

were discussed in the context of this general rule. First, the soldiers and citizens found in towns, which had been taken by assault, had not surrendered and thus did not benefit from this *lex generalis*. Secondly, any surrender, even at the latest possible moment, counted as surrender and triggered the application of the general rule of mercy. Gentilis supported his argument with several examples from Antiquity. He then turned to contemporary practice – like that of Alva – of refusing pardon to towns that had surrendered after the batteries of the artillery had been raised. For this practice, he also found support in Roman history – there the right to surrender was lost once the battering ram had touched the walls – and in *Deuteronomy*.[23] Gentilis did not think that this rule should be applied at all times. There was room for the belligerents to make agreements. But he acknowledged that surrender at the last moment might be refused, as a deterrent.[24] In relation to conditional surrender, Gentilis elaborated on the agreements whereby the besieged town promised to surrender on a given date, unless it was relieved in time.[25] His concern for humanity, which permeates the entire treatise, is clear from his statements about unconditional surrender. Gentilis argued that surrender at the mercy of the enemy meant that at least the lives of the defeated had to be spared. The claim that slavery was out of the question because it constituted a kind of death he called 'a quibble of the civil law'.[26] Unconditional surrender meant surrender to the 'will, control, consent, power, discretion, judgment, wisdom, grace, piety, equity, conscience, [and] declaration of the enemy'. But all these did not supersede the 'bounds of law and custom'. Divine and human law commanded men to act according to justice and, in case of doubt, custom 'furnishe[d] the best rule of conduct'. Custom, so it appeared, dictated moderation.[27]

Grotius was the least explicit about siege warfare. He enumerated the sacking of a town taken by storm among the cases in which commanders according to custom allowed their soldiers to pillage, quoting examples from Roman history.[28] It was Roman custom that commanders could decide upon the division of the spoils, even if they were accountable to the Roman people. Grotius, however, ascertained that the municipal law could deviate from these general rules. In other words, being granted

[23] 20.12–3. [24] 2.17.351–5. [25] 2.17.361–2. [26] 2.17.363. [27] 2.17.365.

[28] Grotius, *De Jure Belli ac Pacis libri tres* 3.6.18 (text of 1646, Francis W. Kelsey, trans., Classics of International Law, Washington, 1913).

parts of the spoils constituted a favour to the army, not a right.[29] Grotius stated that a surrender upon the condition of life should not be rejected during battle or siege. This was a rule from the law of nature and the 'usage of more civilized peoples'.[30] He referred to the Roman custom that the right to surrender was lost once the battering ram had shaken the wall. The custom was now applied to unfortified towns that had awaited the opening of cannon fire. But Cicero, so Grotius went on, had counselled mercy even if surrender came after the battering of the walls had begun.[31]

All authors acknowledged the right to pillage a town taken by storm. Gentilis and Grotius had qualms about the old rule that surrender upon terms could be refused once the batteries had been raised, but they did not outlaw the custom outright. They emphasised that the victor could always grant conditions and stated that natural law, justice or honour, or even the 'usage of civilized peoples' dictated a lenient treatment of the vanquished. And, if the rule was applied, the lives of those who surrendered at the mercy of the victor should be spared. While Gentilis and Grotius were concerned with questions of morality and humanity, Belli and Ayala were more interested in military discipline and the authority of the prince over his armed forces. Dissuading commanders from yielding too readily was Belli's foremost concern. Overall, doctrine and practice rather matched.

Siege warfare after Westphalia: practice

During the century after Westphalia (1648), the military, institutional and intellectual context of European warfare changed. There was a substantial increase in the size and cost of armies. A further step was taken in the professionalisation of warfare. The century after Westphalia saw a growing control of public authority over war and the armed forces. After 1660, the old elites lost much of their political and military autonomy, in exchange for which they gained a stake in central government as its officials or officers. Whereas the Thirty Years' War (1618–1648) was the period of the military entrepreneur who rented out his services and those of his mercenaries to princes and republics, after Westphalia state control over the armies grew. The high command of the European states' armies and the corps of regimental officers might still hail from the same international, noble elites from which the great

[29] 3.6.19–25. [30] 3.11.13. [31] *De officiis* 1.11.35; Grotius 3.11.14.

condotierri of the early seventeenth century sprang, but now they became officers appointed and paid by the governments. In the process of state-building, the emergence of a fiscal and logistic apparatus that served to field and sustain large armies was an important factor. War was gradually monopolised by the sovereigns of Europe.[32]

The eighteenth century was the era of the so-called cabinet wars. In historiography, the idea looms large that wars became limited, in both goals and scale. Though many of the eighteenth-century wars were devastating, the thought that war under the late *ancien régime* was the domain of a professional, international elite that went about its business in a civilised way and according to strict rules, is a resilient one. The humanising ideals of the Enlightenment are often quoted in this respect. The famous episode of the battle of Fontenoy (1745), where the English commander invited the 'gentlemen of the French Guard' to fire first – which they gracefully declined – is an image too powerful not to overshadow our views of the period.[33]

As a consequence of the gradual monopolisation of war by central government, the 'international' laws of war and the 'internal' rules of military discipline, imposed by public authority or military command upon the armed forces and soldiers of a single state, became two separate bodies of law.[34] This development was part and parcel of the more general articulation of the law of nations as an autonomous body of law, separate from private law and from municipal law. This in itself was a consequence of the emergence of the internally sovereign state and its attempt to monopolise international relations, including warfare. Central governments, in their desire to monopolise warfare, tried to usurp the field of military discipline and everything related to the inner control over the army and to isolate it from the body of law dealing with the interaction with foreign body politics and foreign armies. The change can be discerned in practice as well as in doctrine. For practice we refer to the emergence of municipal legislation on military law and jurisdiction in the form of general ordinances issued by the prince, and

[32] David Parrott, *Richelieu's Army: War, Government and Society in France, 1624–1642* (Cambridge, 2001); and Guy Rowlands, *The Dynastic Sate and the Army under Louis XIV: Royal Service and Private Interest, 1661–1701* (Cambridge, 2002).

[33] Armstrong Starkey, 'War and Culture, a Case Study: The Enlightenment and the Conduct of the British Army in America, 1755–1781', *War & Society*, 8 (1990) pp. 1–28.

[34] Barbara Donagan, 'Codes of Conduct in the English Civil War', *Past and Present*, 118 (1988) pp. 65–95, at pp. 75–6 and 82–4.

codes of conduct issued by military high command.[35] These came, at least partly, to replace the customs of war and military discipline that had been developed by the professional international elites since the Middle Ages. Doctrine offers another example. While Ayala and Belli's treatises, as their titles indicate, covered both the laws of war and the rules of military discipline, later treatises did not. The authors of the seventeenth and eighteenth centuries who dealt with the laws of war restricted their discourses by and large to the 'international' laws of war. References to military law became instrumental to the discourse on the laws of war, for example when the author discussed the application of an 'international' rule at the municipal level.

Let us first turn to the 'international' laws of war. Although many towns were sacked during the late seventeenth and early eighteenth centuries, the large majority of successful sieges ended in negotiated settlements. As the customs and rituals of siege warfare became more elaborate, so did the agreements or treaties of surrender – the capitulations. By the beginning of the eighteenth century, however, some stipulations had become so customary that they were briefly referred to without them being expounded. During the seventeenth century, if a capitulation granted a garrison the right to leave with all honours of war, it was stated in detail what that meant. In some eighteenth-century capitulations, there was only a brief reference to the customary marks of honour.[36]

If a garrison or city magistrate, or both, asked for parley, a truce was agreed. During the truce, all siege or fortification works had to be stopped. Hostages were exchanged. The surrendering town then proposed terms, which were accepted, amended or rejected by the besieging commander. Besieger and besieged often agreed on a period after which the defenders, if the siege was not broken or lifted, would surrender.

Though it was almost never applied, not all traces of the old rule that a town which had not surrendered before the batteries of the artillery had been raised lost its right to conditional surrender had disappeared from

[35] For the Spanish Netherlands, the ordinances of 23 May 1587, 7 November 1601, 13 May 1613, 28 February 1628, 18 December 1701 and 10 April 1702.

[36] [C]on todos los honores militares': Capitulation of Barcelona of 10 August 1697, Art. 1, in Clive Parry (ed.), *The Consolidated Treaty Series* (Dobbs Ferry, 1969), vol. 21, pp. 343–5, at p. 345 (CTS); 'toute marques d'honneur qu'on peut donner en pareil cas': Capitulation of Guelders of 12 December 1703, Art. 5, CTS, vol. 21, pp. 15–23, at p. 18; 'avec les marques d'honneur accoûtumées' Capitulation of Ulm of 11 September 1704, Art. 1, CTS, vol. 25, pp. 157–61, at p. 159.

memory. In its stead came the rule that a town which surrendered too late was open to pillage and the commander forfeited his life. Surrendering too late now meant that a breach had been made and the artillery of the enemy had come within a hundred yards of it. But the rule rather served as a threat than that it was actually observed.[37] To the contrary, the courageous defence by a military commander – not by a civilian – was often referred to as honourable.[38] The balance between deterrence and honour shifted to the latter. The honour of the professional officers was considered of great value and was reciprocally respected. However, obstinacy was not endlessly condoned.[39] Also, it came to be expected[40] that a town or fortress surrendered as soon as its rations and ammunition were down to two days, so that the town would not have to be supplied by the victor.[41] Rationality and honourable behaviour were expected from both sides.

Towns that did not have a royal garrison within their walls were to surrender upon first summons from a royal army. This was an army of a sovereign prince or republic that had artillery. It was also considered dishonourable for the commander of a 'royal' garrison to surrender before the first shots were fired. In view of the evolving rule about belated surrender, this did not leave him with an insurmountable dilemma like before, although municipal rules still could cause this.

In most cases, a capitulation granted the defeated garrison the right to depart with all honours of war. A time was settled at which the garrison would start the evacuation. Often, one of the gates would be surrendered to the besieger in advance, as a surety. The capitulation stipulated through which gate or breach the garrison was to leave. The treaties were most elaborate on the matter of 'honours' granted the besieged. In many cases, these implied that the soldiers would leave with their weapons and luggage, drums beating, trumpets sounding, flags flying,

[37] See the fall of Verrua in 1704 to the troops of the Duke of Vendôme (Louis Joseph, 1654–1712). The Duke threatened the commander of the garrison, who had held out to the last moment, with death after he had surrendered to the mercy of the Duke, but the threat was not carried out; John Wright, 'Sieges and Customs of War at the Opening of the Eighteenth Century', *American Historical Review*, 39 (1934) pp. 629–44, at pp. 631–3.

[38] Capitulations of Lille of 23 October 1708, CTS, vol. 26, pp. 229–50.

[39] Note 37 above.

[40] When Rheinberg surrendered after all supplies were exhausted, the defending commander received marks of honour: Capitulation of 7 February 1703, in Wright, 'Sieges and Customs of War', p. 640.

[41] Wright, 'Sieges and Customs of War', pp. 631–3.

arms at the ready, match lighted on both ends and bullets in their mouths – as they would have in battle. But in some cases, conditions were not so lenient and the departing garrison had to march in a more subdued way. Leaving without arms was the harshest treatment, short of being made prisoners of war.[42] The commanders in most cases agreed that the victors would not try to persuade the soldiers of the departing garrison to change sides. The defeated garrison was allowed to take some cannons and ammunition. The capitulation normally stipulated to which place the garrison would retreat, in how many days and by what route. It also included provisions about the escort that would accompany it and about passports. Food and supplies for a number of days – usually four – were to be provided by the victor, as well as transport. The capitulations almost always stipulated the exchange or release – usually without ransom – of prisoners of war. They provided for the payment of all debts the soldiers of the garrison had to the civilian population. But in most cases it was agreed that no soldier could be detained on account of those debts. The departing soldiers – and, eventually, the citizens – were granted a fixed period – often three months – during which they could sell their assets in the fallen town. The terms of capitulations greatly varied in regard to the treatment of deserters. Under some treaties, the defeated army was forced to surrender them; in other treaties, it was stated that the defeated army was allowed to use covered wagons which would not be searched. In still other treaties, it was expressly stated that deserters were allowed to leave with their new comrades.

As the seventeenth century turned into the eighteenth century, the treatment of the garrison and of civilians became formally distinguished in the capitulations. The agreements now fell into two distinct parts and often conditions were negotiated separately. This was a consequence of the professionalisation of war and its monopoly by the state. In the century after Westphalia, war became not only the business of professional soldiers, but also of the princes of Europe, not of their subjects. Though, of course, civilians largely remained the victims of war, they came to be treated to an ever greater extent as its innocent victims, who upon conquest transferred some of their obligations to their new – often temporary – masters.[43] On the other hand, rebellious towns as a rule

[42] Capitulation of Diest of 25 October 1705, CTS, vol. 25, pp. 339–42.

[43] Irénée Lameire, *Théorie et pratique de la conquête dans l'ancien droit: Etude de droit international ancien* (5 vols., Paris, 1902–11).

were refused conditions and were expected to throw themselves at the mercy of their sovereign.[44] Apart from this, the large majority of sieges ended with liberal terms for the civilian population. Their liberties were safeguarded, as were their lives and property.[45] Some capitulations allowed citizens who chose so to leave with the garrison. Capitulations also laid down the conditions under which the victor could occupy the town.[46]

Let us turn to the municipal laws of military conduct. The municipal ordinances of the seventeenth and eighteenth centuries were by and large concerned with matters of jurisdiction and procedure. The substantive laws applied were either customs and codes of conduct issued by military commanders or rules taken from the *ius commune*, Roman law.[47] Later on, royal ordinances, such as the famous Ordinance of Philip V of Spain (1700–1746) of 18 December 1701, included substantive military law, defining misdemeanours and punishments.[48]

As regards siege warfare, two things stand out. First, governments aspired to bring plunder under their control. In the Spanish Netherlands, the rule was introduced that soldiers could only gain ownership over booty through a decision of the auditor of the army.[49] Secondly, concern about early surrender remained. King Louis XIII of France (1610–1643) instructed his commanders only to surrender after the enemy had made a wide breach in the walls and several assaults had been pushed back.[50] In 1705, Louis XIV (1643–1715) ruled that commanders were only to surrender after the first assault had been repulsed once the breach was

[44] Wright, 'Sieges and Customs of War', p. 639.

[45] At Cartagena in Colombia, the French privateers who took the town were less lenient towards the civilians. The latter were allowed to leave the town, but had to leave behind all their money, gold, silver and jewellery. That these conditions were imposed upon them by privateers underscores that this was no longer common behaviour in public warfare; Capitulation of Cartagena of 2 May 1697, Art. 4, CTS, vol. 21, pp. 297–300, at p. 299.

[46] These generalisations are based on some thirty capitulations from between 1650 and 1710, all to be found in CTS, vols. 2–26.

[47] 'En jugeant, il se conforment aux Loix, & droit commun, & aux ordonnances, bans, & coutumes, privileges, & constitutions de Guerre . . .': Ordinance of the Duke of Parma of 23 May 1587 for the Spanish army in the Netherlands, Art. 24, in Pierre-Winand Clerin, *Code militaire des Pays-Bas, contenant les edits, ordonnances etc. ensemble un commentaire sur le placard du prince de Parme de 1587* (Maastricht, 1721), p. 136. See also Clerin's commentary on p. 137.

[48] Published in Clerin, *Code militaire*, pp. 275–313.

[49] Ordinance of 1587, Art. 22, pp. 127–9.

[50] Wright, 'Sieges and Customs of War', p. 630.

made.[51] In combination with the rules under the law of nations, this still left the commanders with a problem. That commanders were at risk of prosecution is shown by the case of the Spanish officer Juan de Lipouby, who in 1652 had unsuccessfully defended the town of Rethel. The charges brought against him – no fewer than thirty-six – read like a catalogue of all things a defending commander could do wrong. It was, among others, alleged that he had wanted to surrender after the first assault while the enemy had only made a small breach, through which no immediate attack was to be feared; that he had refused to defend the castle though it was fortified; that he had not asked for a fixed time for surrender to allow the Spanish army to come to his rescue; and that he had forwarded the terms of surrender to the enemy instead of leaving the initiative with them. While the unlucky officer rejected most charges as being untrue, to the last charge he could answer that he had behaved as was customary under the laws of war.[52] Though the prosecutor refrained from stating it, he implied that Lipouby had acted treasonably. An even worse fate befell the Dutch commander of a citadel in Julich in 1621. He was put to death for surrendering.[53]

The separation of the laws of war from the municipal laws of military conduct had a salutary effect on the former. Within the limits of military law, the concern with treason and early surrender continued to loom large, but it was ostracised from the laws of war. This left them free to lord over what now became a game of deterrence and seduction, of stick and carrot, a ritual dance of threats and promises between besieger and besieged. They served as a tool to induce the besieged to surrender quickly, while still allowing leeway for even a late surrender to be worth their while. With time, the focus shifted from the deterrent capacity of the rules of siege warfare to the humanisation of warfare. The professional and international elites that officered the armies of Europe developed an elaborate etiquette, the impact of which was felt in the laws of war and the ways these were applied. The laws of war now allowed a garrison commander to hold out until the fall of his fortress was as good as certain. As long as he remained within the broad limits set by the laws of war, he was assured of honourable surrender

[51] Ordinance of 16 April 1705.

[52] '[T]oca al sitiador el proponer las condiciones por que toca notoriamente al sitiado, como tambien el cauteralas, y esto es cosa averiguado segun la costumbre de la milicia.' Brussels, General National Archives, Military Tribunals 413, charge 27.

[53] Cornelius van Bynkershoek, *Quaestionum Juris Publici libri duo* 1.25.4 (Tenney Frank, trans., Classics of International Law, London and Oxford, 1930).

and retreat. The kings and governments did nothing to stop this development, as they were keen to save their expensive armies from destruction. Professional warfare brought some breathing space for civilians. Though they remained targets, particularly during sieges, they were increasingly treated as non-combatants who should not be held accountable for the war or for what had happened during the siege.

Siege warfare after Westphalia: doctrine

Now we'll turn to some authors of the late seventeenth century and early eighteenth century who covered the customary laws of war of their age: Samuel Rachel (1628–1691), Johann Wolfgang Textor (1638–1701), Cornelius van Bynkershoek (1673–1743) and Emer de Vattel (1714–1767). Of these, only Textor and Vattel made more than a few remarks on siege warfare, and very concise ones at that. They were, just as Rachel and Bynkershoek, more concerned with describing the general rules about enemy personnel and property in a somewhat systematic way. The rules of siege warfare were considered either a particular application thereof or *lex specialis*.

Rachel, writing in 1676 when professor at Kiel, recognised that the law of nations – that is, the enforceable, positive law of nations – allowed the killing of all enemies, including women, children and prisoners of war, and the destruction and plundering of all enemy property.[54] This extended to private property owned by the enemy sovereign and by his subjects. For this he found support in Justinian.[55] Rachel also referred to the *Digest* to sustain his claim that enemies who had surrendered became slaves.[56] But, with Grotius,[57] he ascertained that this rule had fallen into disuse among Christians, so that it was hardly applied under the law of nations.[58] Rachel distinguished between rules of positive law of nations that were in accordance with the law of nature (*ius gentium verum*) and those that were not (*ius gentium putativum*). Whereas they were both enforceable *in foro externo*, only the former were just and enforceable *in foro interno*, in conscience. This may be seen as an implicit appeal not to apply the harsh and unjust laws of war. Rachel did not elaborate.[59]

[54] Samuel Rachel, *De jure naturae et gentium dissertationes* 2.47–8 (John P. Bate, trans., Classics of International Law, Washington, 1916).

[55] 2.49. With reference to D. 41.1.5.7 and Inst. 2.1.17.

[56] D. 49.15.5.1 and 49.15.12 pr., with power over life and death, D. 1.6.1.1 and Inst. 1.6.1.

[57] 3.7.8. [58] 2.50. [59] 2.42 and 2.56. Some brief remarks in 2.99–100.

Johann Wolfgang Textor, professor of law at Altdorf and Heidelberg, authored *Synopsis iuris gentium* (1680). Textor accepted that, according to the positive law of nations, one was allowed to harm his enemy, his subjects and their property during war.[60] Women and children, however, often fell within the protection of the law of nations; Grotius had made a provision to that extent.[61] Textor acknowledged that the killing of people should be tempered for some categories of persons – elderly, children and women – referring to a decree by Pope Alexander III (1159–1181).[62] Whereas killing was allowed during battle, it was not when an enemy had surrendered or laid down his arms. Among those who had surrendered, the instigators of the war were allowed to be singled out for punishment, even to be killed.[63] Textor agreed on principle with Grotius that one should spare the lives of those who offered surrender during a battle or a siege.[64] There were, however, two exceptions. First, a besieger might refuse surrender if the town had almost been taken, as Gustav Adolph (1611–1632) had done before Frankfurt-an-der-Oder (1631). Secondly, those who had committed grave offences could be refused the right to surrender upon condition of their life.[65] Textor clung to the old rule from Roman law that prisoners of war were to be enslaved,[66] but he acknowledged that this rule had fallen into disuse among Christians. Some three hundred years earlier the custom had been introduced to ransom prisoners of war instead. Turks and other 'barbarians' did turn their prisoners into slaves. Though they certainly had the right to retaliate in kind,[67] Christians did not do so.[68] Whereas the law of nations allowed a victor to kill the enemies who had thrown themselves at his mercy, it befitted the captor to show clemency. Textor, however, condoned setting examples in order to secure the future safety of the state.[69]

As far as captured property was concerned, immovable goods fell to him 'under whose auspices the war [was] being waged'.[70] The same went, as indeed was customary in reality, for valuable goods such as artillery and important prisoners.[71] All other booty belonged to the soldiers who took it. On this point, Textor disagreed with Grotius and other writers.[72] Textor argued that states did not wage wars to enrich

[60] Johann Wolfgang Textor, *Synopsis iuris gentium* 18.15 (John B. Bate, trans., Classics of International Law, Washington, 1916).
[61] 3.4.6–9. [62] X. 1.34.2; Textor 18.16. [63] 18.17–9. [64] 3.11.13. [65] 18.22–4.
[66] With reference to Inst. 1.2.2 and 1.3.2 and to the Old Testament, Joshua 9.23–7.
[67] With reference to Alciatus (c.1490–1550) on D. 50.16.118. [68] 18.38–42.
[69] 28.15–22. [70] 18.63. [71] 18.63–4. [72] Grotius 3.6.8; Textor 18.65–6.

themselves, whereas soldiers often took considerable risk to plunder. The German professor claimed to have contemporary practice on his side.[73] The many examples quoted by Grotius and others to show that the spoils of war did fall to the state or were divided among the troops by the military commanders did not serve to contradict him. These were all examples whereby the enemy had surrendered or had been completely conquered. In these circumstances, of course, the spoils – all the enemy has owned – fell to the conquering state to which the former enemy now belonged.[74]

The Dutch Cornelius van Bynkershoek, President of the Court of Appeal of Holland and Zeeland (since 1724), was a practitioner of law. In his *Questionum Juris Public libri duo* (1737), he stated that in war one had the power of life and death over one's enemies. If this right was seldom exercised and wars rarely escalated into wars of extermination, this was the consequence of voluntary clemency. Bynkershoek claimed that a victor might still exercise his right and was able to quote two examples from recent history where acts of treason and privateering were declared punishable by death.

He went on to relate how the right to kill had been replaced by the custom of turning enemies into slaves. This custom had, in its turn, fallen into disuse among Christians. Prisoners were now often held for ransom; they were sometimes released without ransom, or exchanged according to rank.[75] Bynkershoek also found the right to kill captives fallen into disuse. He considered it cruel and disgraceful to punish an enemy for his courage in battle.[76] Enemy property was open for capture.[77] With regard to siege warfare, Bynkershoek only addressed the matter of contraband and the supplying of a town under siege. 'Common sense and the usages of nations' asserted that it was 'not lawful to carry goods to besieged cities'.[78] Bynkershoek argued, on the

[73] Textor also referred to D. 41.1.5.7, Inst. 2.1.17 and D. 49.15.51.1 in support of his interpretation: 18.67–9.

[74] 18.70–5. Textor is in agreement with Hugo Donellus (1527–1591), *Commentaris de jure civili* 4.21 (Frankfurt, 1595–6).

[75] Bynkershoek here refers to the cartels of the seventeenth and eighteenth centuries, which regulated the exchange of prisoners.

[76] 1.3.18–22.

[77] Bynkershoek did not go into the question whether the booty fell to the captor or the state, but he did discuss whether it fell to the captor himself or to the person on whose behalf he worked, like a captain for a ship-owner: 1.20.

[78] 1.11.83–4.

basis of common sense, that it was forbidden to supply a besieged town with any goods, as one was not to know what the town was in need of.

In *Le droit des gens ou principes de la loi naturelle* (1758), the Swiss diplomat Emer de Vattel argued that public war pertained to the whole nation, not only to the sovereign. This was customary, but it was also in accordance with right reason and the precepts of the natural law. Enemy property was liable to capture.[79]

The basic right of killing all enemy subjects and capturing all enemy property was, however, mitigated. According to Vattel, the conduct of war was governed by the – natural law – principle that a belligerent had the right to do everything necessary to attain his goal. This meant that a belligerent could do whatever was necessary to weaken the enemy as long as the act was not proscribed *per se* by the law of nature. The voluntary law of nations, as he called the positive law, laid down general rules defining these actions that were considered necessary *in abstracto* – that is, without looking at particular circumstances – to defeat the enemy and that were thus acceptable. These actions permitted by the law of nations were not punishable. Even so, taking such actions as were allowed under the law of nations might in particular circumstances be unnecessary to the war effort, and thus unjustified under the law of nature. This law was, however, not enforceable in external law, but the act then must be 'condemned before the tribunal of conscience'.[80]

From all this, Vattel deduced that one had the right to kill an enemy who had taken up arms if it was necessary to prevent him from inflicting harm. As soon as the enemy had laid down his weapons, the right to kill ceased to exist. Therefore, one had to provide quarter to enemies who surrendered or accept terms of capitulation from a town even if it was 'reduced to extremities'. Only if the enemy had committed a 'grave violation of the law of nations' could death be inflicted as punishment.[81] Vattel did not justify the killing of a commander who had defended his fortress to the very last, although he acknowledged this custom had not completely fallen into disuse. He found it went against the grain of his enlightened age. Vattel quoted examples from classical, medieval and modern history where the old rule had not been applied. After all, there was some rationality in obstinate defence, which might prove beneficial for the general war effort, by delaying or exhausting the enemy. Vattel

[79] Emer de Vattel, *Le droit des gens ou principes de la loi naturelle* 3.5.69–76 (Charles G. Fenwick, trans., Classics of International Law, Washington, 1916).

[80] 3.8.136–7 and 3.9.173. [81] 3.8.138–42 and 149, about not killing prisoners of war.

also rejected using the old customary rule as a mere threat, because its non-application would make it obsolete. It was permitted to try and persuade the besieged by offering gracious terms and to threaten to sharpen them as the siege continued. But one could not go beyond making the commander a prisoner of war. Only if the obstinacy was most manifest and without any purpose, as in the event that an entire state had surrendered and one single town held out, then a subordinate officer who commanded a garrison could be threatened with death.[82] All this implied that the garrison itself and the population could never be put to death or threatened with it. On the basis of the same principle that killing could only be condoned in order to stop the enemy from doing harm, it was not allowed to kill women, children, the elderly and sick men as long as they did not take up arms. The same went for clerics, men of letters and others. Because war was the business of regular armies, all citizens who did not take up arms should be spared. This did not prevent a belligerent from capturing these people and turning them into prisoners, though Vattel recognised this was hardly ever done.[83] Vattel stated that prisoners of war could be kept in captivity until the end of the war, in order to prevent them from rejoining the war effort. At the end of the war, a ransom could be exacted as an indemnity. During war, ransom was a means to weaken the enemy. Vattel pointed to the humane custom of release or exchange of prisoners during war and the cartels of his day.[84]

Enemy property could be captured or destroyed to the extent that it served as an indemnity for the war, induced the enemy to accept peace or weakened him. All lands and movables taken from the enemy belonged to the prince upon whose authority the war was waged. He could distribute the booty. Vattel acknowledged that soldiers were sometimes permitted to pillage the towns, though this had become exceptional. Instead, it was now customary to demand contributions from the population.[85] Vattel applauded the practice of bombarding only the ramparts and fortifications and not the town itself, but he found the other course of actions justifiable if necessary to defeat the enemy.[86]

Vattel acknowledged the importance of capitulations in modern warfare. He stated that the commanders of towns and fortresses had

[82] 3.8.143. [83] 3.8.145–8. [84] 3.8.152–3.

[85] John A. Lynn, 'How War Fed War: The Tax of Violence and Contributions during the *Grand Siècle*', *Journal of Modern History*, 65 (1993) pp. 285–310.

[86] 3.9.160–72.

the right to surrender. Thereby they had to stay within the confines of their office. They were possessors, not owners, of the place. They could negotiate about the actual surrender of the town and the treatment of the garrison. The victor might make concessions as to the treatment of the citizens and the upholding of religion and of privileges. The garrison commander was allowed to surrender unconditionally, or to give himself and his soldiers up as prisoners of war. Also, he could concede that he and his soldiers would not fight during the remainder of the war.[87]

All writers emphasised that war was a public conflict between states, involving all subjects and their property. Their first and foremost concern was to strengthen the public character of war and the monopoly of the state on warfare. This explains why they all took the rule that all enemy personnel and property was liable for killing or capture as the basic precept of the laws of war. From thereon, they endeavoured to mitigate the application and the consequences of this basic rule. They did this by referring to custom and treaties and by an appeal to the precepts of natural law and right reason, and, sometimes, to honour. Their musings on the treatment of prisoners of war and unconditional surrender show that none of them was prepared to accept the old right to refuse quarter to a town that had surrendered belatedly. The same went for the newer custom to threaten the enemy commander with death, a practice Vattel expressly condemned.

Customary law and the laws of war

What can we learn from all this with regard to customary law? What were its constitutive elements? We will address this question making use of the dual notions of *usus* and *opinio iuris*. Though the latter term is a fairly recent addition to the language of international law, the awareness that both a corporal and a mental element were necessary for a custom to be law dates from Roman times.[88]

First, a word needs to be said about the actors behind the *usus* and *opinio*. During the century after Westphalia the laws of war and military law grew apart. One should be careful, however, not to overstate the consequences thereof. When current international lawyers discuss *usus* and *opinio iuris*, they refer to the behaviour and opinions of states, acting through their agents. In relation to the laws of war, these might be

[87] 2.14.207 and 2.16.262–3.

[88] D. 1.3.32 and 35; for the Middle Ages, see Ibbetson, chapter 7 in this volume.

military as well as civil authorities, but they are seen to represent the state and act in its name. Though the Early Modern Age may have marked the transition to the monopoly of the state over war, the process was, however, far from complete by the early eighteenth century. Many customs of war of the Early Modern Age can be traced back to the late-medieval codes of chivalry. These were customs developed by the members of an international and professional military class. After the Middle Ages, these customs were inherited by the new military elite of the mercenary armies. As state control over the armies grew and this military elite was incorporated into the state, these customs were adopted by the state. The great ordinances on military discipline were first and foremost concerned with matters of jurisdiction, and only gradually ventured into substantive law, often doing little but confirming, clarifying or detailing existing customs and regulations. The formal and conceptual emancipation of the law of nations and of war made it appear that the practices of military commanders and soldiers became practices of the state; but that is overstating reality. In fact, the customs of war were still very much determined by the same professional elite that had dominated them for ages and whose incorporation into the state was as yet far from complete. This was not without its practical consequences. While today's international lawyers take it for granted that state authorities dictate the behaviour of their military agents and lay down the law, during the century after 1648 it was often the other way round. The capitulations themselves offer a good illustration of this. These were agreements between military commanders, and as such, to a large extent, these commanders determined their contents. Most capitulations were not ratified by the sovereigns, but the right of military commanders to make such agreements binding upon the prince was not contested. The incorporation of the army into the state was a two-sided process.

Secondly, the customs of siege warfare were based on longstanding usage. The fundamental rules of siege warfare went back far in time and had been continuously applied and invoked since the Late Middle Ages.

Thirdly, it can be ascertained that the fundamental rules of siege warfare were broadly accepted as legally binding. But what was this acceptance based on, apart from long usage? The analysis of the practices of war indicates two bases: honour and reciprocity. The customs of war were respected because it was the honourable thing to do, as the customs themselves were designed to safeguard the professional soldier's honour. The customs of war were considered binding because they guaranteed equal treatment of the soldiers on both sides, and they guaranteed such treatment because they were considered binding. Reciprocity was at the heart of the customs of war. It came naturally to a professional warrior class, whose members all wanted to live to fight another day and were inclined to respect the other's wish to do so as well. It was also, again, a matter of honour to treat the soldiers of the enemy with the same decency as they treated yours. By the early seventeenth century, the indiscriminate character of the laws of war had also been accepted in doctrine, replacing the old idea that the laws of war only benefited the just belligerent fighting a just war.[89] Donagan refers to the laws of war as 'a kind of contractual etiquette of belligerence'.[90] Our analysis of the evolution of the customs of siege warfare makes clear that usage alone did not suffice to have a rule considered binding. The old rule about the fate of places that surrendered belatedly was not applied and sustained as a rule of law, because it was not the honourable thing to do.

Fourthly, the early modern practices of siege warfare also shed some light on the interaction between customary and conventional law. The many capitulations from the century after Westphalia not only applied and thus bear witness to the existing customs of war, they also helped form and develop those customs. The honours of war for a departing garrison were developed with time in the capitulations, up to a point where they had gained a strong enough foothold to be referred to as customary.

Let us now turn to doctrine. First, a significant difference between the pre- and post-Westphalian writers should be noted. The authors from around 1600 acknowledged that the fundamental rules of siege warfare were established practice, but that did not suffice for them. They also based these rules on the authority of classical and medieval texts. These included the Bible, the Church Fathers, the Justinian Code, the medieval canon law texts and the writings of medieval Roman and canon lawyers. This reliance upon the canon of authoritative texts was in the tradition of medieval, scholastic scholarship.

Ayala, Gentilis and Grotius had undergone the influence of humanism. To the traditional canon, they added some of the great Roman historians, particularly Livy. They furnished their argument with examples from Greek or Roman history. This not only served to indicate the longevity of a certain *usus*, but gave it authority and sanction. The humanists may have considered the authority of the traditional canon

89 Stephen C. Neff, *War and the Law of Nations: A General History* (Cambridge, 2005).
90 Donagan, 'Codes of Conduct', p. 78.

of texts no longer to be absolute and timeless. They may have understood these texts to be the fruit of human labour. But they certainly held the drafters of these texts and the historical figures of whose deeds they spoke in the highest possible regard. A usage that went back to the Greeks and the Romans was clothed with the authority of its *exemplum*, worthy of imitation and emulation.[91]

After Westphalia, arguments on the basis of textual or historical authority started to become less frequent and finally disappeared.[92] The writers continued to refer to the old texts and to examples from ancient history; but they attributed far less authority to these past authorities and displayed greater intellectual autonomy.[93] This was the outcome of the shift from the scholastic to the humanist paradigm. Consequently, a link between *usus* and Antiquity, let alone between *usus* and the *auctoritas* of the canonical texts, was no longer considered necessary. Custom became a more independent source of law.

Secondly, authors became less concerned with the longevity of a custom. References to ancient history remained popular throughout the seventeenth century, then gradually became less frequent. As the authority of the ancients faded and the self-confidence of the moderns was raised, the literal antiquity of a *usus* was not considered to offer sufficient proof of acquiescence any longer. Recent practice and acquiescence became more significant.[94] Underneath lay the awareness that customs did evolve.[95] Textor may have been keen to note that the custom of ransoming prisoners went back 300 years, but he also argued that no fixed rules on longevity could be laid down and that one instance of assent sufficed to make a custom binding upon a given state.[96]

Thirdly, tacit agreement, or tacit mutual consent, was the fundament on which the *opinio iuris* of a customary rule was based. As Grotius before, all four authors of the post-Westphalian era recognised customary law based on tacit agreement or tacit mutual consent as one of the

[91] Peter Haggenmacher, 'La pratique chez les fondateurs du droit international', in *La pratique et le droit international* (Paris, 2004), pp. 49–78, at pp. 67–70. See Gentilis 1.1.15.

[92] David Kennedy, 'Primitive Legal Scholarship', *Harvard International Law Journal*, 27 (1986) pp. 1–98.

[93] Rachel took offence at adherence to the authority of the old jurists: 2.35.1.

[94] Textor advised looking at recent practice, particularly if old examples contradicted one another: 1.19.

[95] Rachel 2.37; Textor 1.15; Bynkershoek *Ad lectorem*.

[96] Textor 1.20.

sources of the voluntary law of nations.[97] It mirrored the reciprocity that was fundamental to the workings of the customs of war in reality.

Fourthly, a distinction was drawn between particular and general customary law. Customs were based on consent. In consequence, they were solely binding upon those who had consented to them. In reality, this meant that they could hardly ever become universally applicable. Still, custom could also give rise to generally applicable law. The writers of the post-Westphalian era acquiesced to the fact that it was impossible to check whether all nations had effectively consented – as not even all nations were known, as Rachel cleverly pointed out.[98] Nevertheless, a custom could give rise to general law of nations. For Rachel and Textor, as for Grotius, a wide spread acceptance sufficed.[99] Vattel for his part based the general application of his 'voluntary law of nations' on presumed consent.[100] Rachel stated expressly that particular customary law could deviate from general law.[101]

Fifthly, doctrine acknowledged the existence of a Christian, or 'civilised', customary law of nations. In relation to the laws of war, many authors from both the pre- and the post-Westphalian periods pointed to the custom of Christians not to enslave each other, but to ransom, exchange or release prisoners. Textor considered rules that were established among the more 'cultured' or 'civilised' nations or the nations of a single continent – more particularly Europe – to be generally binding.[102] Vattel referred to customs which were generally accepted among the civilised countries of the world, or within a continent, or among the countries that had frequent intercourse with one another as a distinct category of 'particular' customary law.[103]

Sixthly, according to all authors the positive law of nations, based on human will – which they called voluntary or arbitrary – was distinct from the law based on natural reason – either natural law or the natural law of nations.[104] For Rachel, Textor and Vattel, natural law or the natural law of nations served as an autonomous body of law to judge over and criticise the existing voluntary law of nations. With Bynkershoek, reason

[97] Grotius *Prol.* 15; Rachel 2.10, 2.16, 2.28–30 and 2.42; Textor 1.3–6 and 1.8; Bynkershoek *Ad lectorem* and 2.10; Vattel *Préliminaires* 25.

[98] 2.11. [99] Grotius 1.1.14; Rachel 2.11–12 and 2.23–5; Textor 1.3.

[100] Vattel *Préliminaires* 21 and 26–7; Emmanuelle Jouannet, *Emer de Vattel et l'émergence doctrinale du droit international classique* (Paris, 1998), pp. 92–3.

[101] 2.73–4. [102] 1.3. But not Rachel 2.74. [103] Vattel *Préliminaires* 26.

[104] Natural law applies to men and nations; natural law of nations is a law applicable to nations, derived from natural law.

itself – common sense and rationality – rather than a distinct body of natural law, served this very purpose.[105] As was shown above, the precepts and dictates of right reason and nature were constantly appealed to by the great authors of the sixteenth to eighteenth centuries to mitigate voluntary law regarding siege warfare. Accordance with natural reason was certainly a criterion for judging a customary rule's fairness and desirability. However, if the law of nature was a touchstone for the fairness of a customary rule, it was not for its being externally binding. None of the authors rejected the external validity of a customary rule that did not meet the standards of natural reason. Whereas customary law was considered externally binding, law based on natural reason alone was not. It was only binding in conscience. Some authors expressly stated that customary law that deviated from the precepts of reason and nature, or even contradicted them, remained law – even though it would have to be rejected *in foro interno*. The moral deficiency of positive law was criticised, but did not undo its legality.[106]

And yet, customary law was not completely independent from natural reason. In the minds of the authors of the seventeenth and eighteenth centuries, consent to a custom was more likely if that custom was in accordance with natural reason. According to Textor, reason formed the basis of both usage and natural law.[107] With Vattel, accordance with the natural law of nations was of greater consequence to general than to particular customary law. The presumption of general consent on which the general voluntary law rested was tantamount to the rationality that came naturally to all rational human beings and to states. The general voluntary law of nations might set lower moral standards than the necessary law of nations, but it was as much the result of the dictates of natural reason. General voluntary law might differ from the necessary law of nations, but it was hard to conceive of a rule that went against natural reason that was the common source of both bodies of law.[108] Particular customs should heed natural law, but their going against the grain of the natural law of nations did not invalidate them *in foro externo*.[109]

[105] Kinji Akashi, *Cornelius van Bynkershoek: His Role in the History of International Law* (The Hague, London and Boston, 1998), pp. 21–33.

[106] Rachel 2.56 and 2.89–102; Textor 1.2 and 2.1–3; Vattel *Préliminaires* 9. On Bynkershoek, see Akashi, *Bynkershoek*, pp. 29 and 81–6.

[107] Textor 1.10–11; Jouannet, *Vattel*, pp. 72–3.

[108] Vattel *Préliminaires* 28 and 3.12.

[109] Vattel *Préface* and *Préliminaires* 9; Akashi, *Bynkershoek*, pp. 150–4; Jouannet, *Vattel*, pp. 85–104 and 153–4.

The general law of nations of Vattel and his immediate predecessors was largely the product of their own intellect. They valued practice more than the writers of older times, but it was their ambition to construct a rational and just system of law. In that context, customary law could not be divorced completely from natural law. Consent, the ultimate foundation of a customary rule, was or could be presumed general because it was reasonable and natural to consent. But, by and large, these writers did not take it upon themselves to outlaw customs that went against their understanding of natural reason. Accordance with right reason might be a criterion for the universality of a customary rule, but not for its application between states that had clearly consented to it. For these rules, it was only there to judge on the moral justice of it. While it would go too far to state that accordance with natural reason had nothing to do with *opinio iuris*, even for particular customs, the writers of the century after Westphalia surely helped doctrine underway in that direction. In the final analysis, doctrine acquiesced to the fact of life that customary law in reality was not and did not have to be in accordance with rationality and morality to be accepted by states as constituting law. Consent – the doctrinal tantamount of the reciprocal acceptance of rules from military practice – rather than reason, was forwarded as the foundation of *opinio iuris*.

In conclusion, let us bring all this to bear on the evolution of siege warfare through the Early Modern Age. In the century after Westphalia, the laws of war became more humane. A well-understood self-interest in the reciprocal preservation of life and honour had imbedded itself into the mores of a professional military class and had led to more humane customs and practices of war. The growing monopolisation of war by the state had led to distinguishing combatants from non-combatants.

The writers of the seventeenth and eighteenth centuries were not unaware of the gradual humanisation in the practices of war, but did little to further it or to vest it on strong theoretical foundations. They sat in judgment over modern practices as being in accordance with natural reason or not, but recognised that an unreasonable rule could nonetheless be binding under the positive law of nations. Moreover, notwithstanding their desire to build a rational system, they took little trouble to introduce new rules and make their own suggestions towards a more comprehensive body of law of concrete rules. Concrete regulations were the domain of the voluntary, and, even more so, the particular law of nations, and not of natural reason. This reluctance was consequential to the authors' acknowledgment that there could be consent without reason. Thereby, they jeopardised the basis from which to influence the law outside the *forum internum*.

But, even there, they did more harm than good. Because of the authors' focus on the control of the central government over war and its machinery, they largely overlooked the opportunity to introduce the distinction between combatants and non-combatants as a basic principle of the laws of war. They preferred not to make the humanisation of war their main concern, but to help underpin the process of state-building. Though for all practical purposes Vattel might come close to making the distinction between combatants and non-combatants, his fundamental principle that gave the green light to everything necessary for the war effort could always be revived to justify any attack on civilians. This allowed him to condone the practice of siege warfare, whereby citizens were made the targets of war. But its consequences were more gruesome. Once the dynastic state of the eighteenth century had given way to the nation-state and war became the affair of an entire nation, the justification for all-out war could be made on the basis of the intellectual tradition laid out by Vattel and his predecessors. In the end, mankind would have to live through the atrocities of the total wars of the twentieth century before the starvation of civilians through sieges was outlawed.[110]

110 Additional Protocol I to the Geneva Conventions, Art. 54.

9

The idea of common law as custom

ALAN CROMARTIE

Some of the extreme opacity of the idea of custom seems to be owed to two considerations. One is that custom modifies the actors who observe it; a well-established custom is not merely a constraint external to a person's character, but has a tendency, with time, to constitute an aspect of his being. Another is that customary arrangements have typically involved an interaction between two overlapping groups of people: the community within which given customs are observed and a much smaller group perhaps most neutrally described as the custodians of such arrangements, a group who are in practice charged with the articulation of the customs, and therefore with their application and development. A link between these two considerations is that the very function of the custodians is likely to demand internalisation of methods, moral attitudes, and intellectual habits appropriate to the social norms that they articulate. At all events, these generalities were true of the pre-modern common lawyers. From the perspective of a book on custom, the interest of pre-Benthamite common law thinking lies in the tension it exhibited between its accounts of what the lawyers did – the patterns of thought and behaviour that might be said to constitute a trained professional – and its attempts to identify their esoteric practice with principles engendered by the wider population.

The earliest common lawyers

No one is likely to deny that common law is the developing usage of the community of common lawyers, nor that the most appropriate word for such a thing is 'custom' (or, in Latin, *consuetudo*).[1] But, even in the homeland of the common law tradition, a claim that on the face of it

[1] A. W. B. Simpson, 'The common law and legal theory' in *Legal theory and legal history: essays on the common law* (London, 1987), pp. 359–82.

requires more argument is that this usage represents the custom of the people. There are, of course, intelligible senses in which the custom of the common lawyers could reasonably be called a popular custom: non-lawyers plainly acquiesce in what the lawyers do, and someone of a holist cast of mind might want to say that courts of law should be considered as a kind of *organ* through which the nation as a whole evolved and sustains certain practical arrangements. A positivist might prefer to see the acquiescence of the people as evidence of some kind of *delegation* of a provisional legislative power. But the earliest common law writers did not in fact explore such avenues; they were so far from admitting that common law might be a popular custom that they denied its character was customary at all.

There is convincing evidence that the idea of law as populist custom was readily available in twelfth- and early-thirteenth-century England, and that this notion was ignored, perhaps deliberately, in the common law's two earliest treatises. A well-known mid-twelfth-century work, the *Leges Edwardi Confessoris*, described how William the Conqueror 'summoned from all the counties of the country English nobles, who were wise men and learned in their *lex*, so that he might hear from them their *consuetudines*'.[2] Moreover, Englishmen who knew a little Roman law were probably familiar with the passage in the *Digest* (*Digest* 1.3.32) that argued that custom, like statute, was a possible source of *lex*, on the grounds that both custom and statute expressed the people's will. In about the year 1200, some introductory lectures in the *studium* at Northampton remarked that 'a *consuetudo* [based on reason] can abrogate *lex*, just as *lex* can abrogate *consuetudo*. For the force of *lex*, like the force of *consuetudo*, is the will of the people. *Lex* does not derive its authority from writing.'[3]

But the earliest common law writers showed no interest in *Digest* 1.3.32. The treatises we know as 'Glanvill' and 'Bracton' have always been entitled 'On the *leges* and *consuetudines* of England', but the people who produced these books made no attempt to argue that popular *consuetudo* was just as good as *lex*. They knew that English legal rules fell into the category of *ius non scriptum* – the sort of jural principles, the *Institutes* remarked (1.2.9), that usage approved (*quod usus comprobavit*) – but the usage they referred

[2] Bruce R. O'Brien, *God's Peace and King's Peace: the law of Edward the Confessor* (Philadelphia, PA, 1999), p. 159.

[3] *The teaching of Roman law in England around 1200*, ed. F. de Zulueta and P. Stein, Selden Society Supplementary Series 8 (London, 1990), p. 12.

to was primarily the usage of royal councillors.[4] The reason the bulk of that usage could be described as *lex* was its connection with the royal will. In consequence, the Roman claim that they found most appealing was the monarchist tag: *Quod principi placuit legis habet vigorem*. As Glanvill (c.1190) explained,

> Although the *leges* of England are not written, it does not seem absurd to call them *leges* – those that is, which are known to have been promulgated about problems settled in council on the advice of the magnates and with the supporting (*accedente*) authority of the prince – for this principle itself is *lex*: 'what pleases the prince has the force of *lex*'. For if, merely for lack of writing, they were not deemed to be *leges*, then surely writing would seem to supply to *leges* a force of greater authority than either the justice of him who decrees them or the reason of him who establishes them.[5]

The somewhat later 'Bracton' (?1225–50) took a not dissimilar view, but fused it with a famous definition drawn by the *Digest* (1.3.1) from Papinian: '*lex* is a general precept (*commune praeceptum*), the pronouncement of judicious men (*prudentes*) . . . the general agreement of the commonwealth (*communis rei publicae sponsio*).' He held that:

> [In England] law derives from nothing written, [but] from what usage has approved (*quod usus comprobavit*). Nevertheless, it will not be absurd to call English laws *leges*, though they are unwritten, since whatever has been rightly decided and approved with the counsel and consent of the magnates and the general agreement of the commonwealth (*communis rei publicae sponsio*), with the previous (*praecedente*) authority of the King or prince, has the force of *lex*.

It will be noted that the effect of his adjustments to Papinian was to emphasise the role of royal power. It was only after dealing with the common law's status as *lex* that he supplied the afterthought that:

> England has also many *consuetudines*, varying from place to place, for the English have many things by *consuetudo* which they do not have by *lex*, as in the various counties, cities, boroughs and vills.[6]

[4] For a helpful discussion drawing similar conclusions, but with some differences of emphasis, see J. W. Tubbs, *The common law mind: medieval and early modern conceptions* (Baltimore, 2000), pp. 4–17.

[5] *The treatise on the laws and customs of England commonly called Glanvill*, ed. G. D. G. Hall (Oxford, 1993), p. 2.

[6] *Bracton on the laws and customs of England*, ed. G. E. Woodbine, trans. S. E. Thorne (4 vols., Cambridge, MA, 1968–78), vol. II, p. 19. Papinian's *dictum* is quoted in full at *ibid.*, p. 22.

Bracton was perfectly aware that the term 'custom' could be used in a more general fashion – at one point, he remarked that 'civil law', the strictly positive part of human law, 'may be called customary right (*ius consuetudinarium*)'.[7] As he actually cited the *Leges Edwardi Confessoris*, he must additionally have known that English 'civil law' was felt by many to be populist. But he seems to have picked up from the civilians two broad assumptions about *consuetudo*. One was that it was primarily a supplement to *lex*; the other that it was in essence local. His clearest general treatment of the concept conflates a couple of civilian tags to give a somewhat grudging view of its legitimacy: '*consuetudo*, in truth, in regions where it is approved by the practice of those who use it, is sometimes observed as and takes the place of *lex*. For the authority of *consuetudo* and long use is not slight.'[8]

The Year Book period

There is no need to be surprised at Glanvill and Bracton's aversion to explicit populism. The usage that they set out to describe was after all the usage of the judges of the king, concerned, for the most part, with applying 'writs' the English crown had voluntarily made available. Moreover, their very conception of a treatise involved them in a stress upon the idea of monarchical will; part of the point of such a document was to assert for English royal law the status of the laws set forth by popes and emperors. In any case, they felt some obligation to reconcile the facts of legal practice with contemporary political/philosophical ideas that were derived from non-professional sources.

In this respect, their treatises were different from the Year Books, the slowly developing law reports (to use an unavoidable but slightly misleading expression) that are our most important source for late-medieval thinking. In the later Middle Ages, common law became a small-scale lay profession that had (to the best of our knowledge) lost touch with academic learning. At all events, the Year Books are virtually devoid of second-order statements about legal principles. For what it is worth, however, there seems to be no cogent evidence that lawyers before Christopher St German (?1460–1539) regarded their laws as consisting in populist custom. A custom immemorially observed throughout the land obtained the status of a common law, but this did not, of course,

[7] *Ibid.*, p. 27. [8] *Ibid.*, p. 22. His principal sources are *Institutes* 1.2.9 and *Code* 8.52.2.

imply that law as a whole was derived from the will of the people. Norman Doe is helpfully categorical that 'the judges do not employ the idea that the basis for the common law is the consent of the community: judicial consent alone shapes the common law'.[9] To a degree embarrassing to many later readers, the Year Book judges made no bones that they were 'making law' in their decisions.[10]

In the nature of things, the shared presuppositions facilitating their self-confidence are difficult to excavate from intra-professional sources. It does seem clear, however, that the self-understanding of the judges was bound up with a concept they called 'reason', or sometimes, more emphatically, 'common reason'. If there was some advantage in doing something new, a permissible rhetorical manoeuvre was to remind the court that 'law is reason'.[11] One possible conclusion from this language was simply that the lawyers made use of common sense with the guidance of professional tradition; another was that common law was natural law applied to English problems. Both conclusions were probably drawn, but the best evidence we have of what was going on is a pronouncement on judicial method that may, for all we know, have been eccentric. In 1468, a certain Justice Yelverton told the court of Common Pleas that:

> We will do now in this case as the Sorbonnists [theologians] and civilians do when a new case comes, for which they have no law before . . . they resort to the law of nature which is the ground of all laws, and according to that which is suggested by them to be more beneficial for the commonwealth, etc., they do, and so now will we do.[12]

This statement was later much cited, but it seems to have owed its fame to its uniqueness; other judges and reporters shied away from such attempts to characterise their method. The most we can say is that 'reason' in general functioned to justify enhancement of law's flexibility. As a formidable Chief Justice once maintained:

> Sir, the law is as I have said, and has been always since the law was first begun, and we have many courses and forms, which are held for law, and have been held and used because of reason, although the same reason may

9 Norman Doe, *Fundamental authority in late medieval English law* (Cambridge, 1990), p. 26.

10 *Ibid.*, p. 23.

11 *Year Books of the reign of King Edward the Third Years XVIII and XIX*, ed. L. O. Pike (London, 1905), p. 378.

12 Doe, *Fundamental authority*, p. 71.

> not be readily remembered; but by study and labour it may be found; and if any such course or form is and has been used contrary to reason, it is no harm to amend it.[13]

It is possible that nobody would ever have supposed that judges were the mouthpiece of populist custom if that Chief Justice, Sir John Fortescue, had not become the author of an encomium: a dialogue explicitly in praise of common law that any patriot can read with pleasure. Fortescue's famous little book, *De laudibus legum Angliae*, is not a contribution to professional literature, but a political pamphlet of the later 1460s, when Fortescue was a Lancastrian exile. Its reassuringly high praise of English institutions (composed by the employee of Margaret of Anjou, who was, of course, a hated French-born queen) was meant to be read in conjunction with a longer, duller work, *De natura legis naturae*. The latter explained in some detail that natural law prohibited female rule, or even claims transmitted through a woman (the Lancastrians, unlike the Yorkists, could trace their descent from Edward III exclusively through men). In his anxiety to show that ordinary law had nothing to do with this question, Fortescue made a very sharp distinction between the law of nature and unwritten positive law. This was a new departure; whatever precisely is made of talk of 'reason', the tendency of English professional practice was evidently to blur these categories. It had the interesting consequence that the main bulk of the unwritten law was forced into a category described as *consuetudo* (what other word could possibly be used?). But Fortescue does not seem to hold the more specific view that it is the will of the people that makes *consuetudo* a law.

The idea that Fortescue upheld a populist position is largely based upon his pamphlet's contrast between the good fortune of England, with its enlightened legal principles, and the miserable condition of the French, whose country's laws were borrowed from the Romans. He differed from Glanvill and Bracton in disapproving of the tag *Quod principi placuit legis habet vigorem*, which was the principle, he thought, explaining the miserable state of the starving French peasants. Readers have understandably supposed that his idealised account of England as a *dominium politicum et regale* – a country in which monarchs could not legislate unaided – is based on admiration for government by consent, and that the notion was derived from common law tradition. I have

[13] YB 36 Henry VI fo.25–6, pl.21.

argued in another place that the first of these assumptions is unfounded: *dominium politicum et regale* is less an ideal of government by consent than of government assisted by a council.[14] Perhaps this revisionist theory is over-pitched or otherwise mistaken. But, at all events, the Year Books offer little evidence that his political beliefs had much to do with his professional practice.

There is, however, one idea within *De laudibus* that he may genuinely have drawn from his professional experience. This was his view that common law is summarised in 'certain universals which those learned in the laws of England and mathematicians alike call maxims, just as rhetoricians speak of paradoxes, and civilians of rules of law'.[15] Rules known as 'maxims', 'grounds' or 'eruditions' in which existing learning had been unchallengeably crystallised do seem to have been growing in importance. But Fortescue distinguished this rough and ready knowledge of the law (attainable through a year of moderate labour) from the learning of the judges (which was achieved, with difficulty, in twenty).[16] The maxims were a helpful means of stating common law; he did not maintain that they themselves were natural laws or customs. The idea that these simplified rules *were* populist customs originated with the thought of Christopher St German.

Christopher St German

St German's *Doctor and Student* was first printed in 1528 and subsequently regularly republished; for most of the long period down to Blackstone, it was the only readily available attempt to state the common law's presuppositions. As St German was probably sixty-eight years old at the time of this, his earliest publication, and as his intellectual powers were evidently so remarkable, one feels some reluctance to treat his masterpiece as simply the precipitate of its immediate context. It does, however, seem likely that he had realised that certain detailed problems that the common lawyers faced – specifically jurisdictional competition with church courts and the courts of equity – required some second-order speculation.

[14] Alan Cromartie, 'Common law, counsel and consent in Fortescue's political theory', in *The fifteenth century*, vol. 4, ed. Linda Clark (Woodbridge, 2004).

[15] Sir John Fortescue, *De laudibus legum Angliae*, ed. and trans. S. B. Chrimes (Cambridge, 1942), p. 21.

[16] *Ibid.*, p. 25.

Competition with the church's canon lawyers required that he clarify the way that God's own law impinged on rights of private property; competition with the equitable courts (especially in the period when Thomas Wolsey was Lord Chancellor) required that he place limits on external interference with common law rules that seemed to cause injustice. In both areas, St German struck a balance. He did not deny that divine and natural law, unmediated by the laws of England, might sometimes provide the appropriate criterion by which to settle social disagreements, but he discovered arguments that delimited a sphere within which common law ideas were sovereign. We know, from numerous references scattered throughout his works, that there were common lawyers with a simpler attitude: they identified their 'reason' with *recta ratio*, the absolute rationality that underpinned all valid legal systems. The reasoning of qualified judges thus generated nature's law for England, and there could be no question of the Lord Chancellor discovering ways of improving its perfection.

St German took a rather different tack. He noted that English lawyers spoke of reason where others might appeal to natural law:

> It is not used among them that be learned in the laws of England to reason what thing is commanded or prohibit by the law of nature and what not: but all the reasoning in that behalf is under this manner: as when anything is grounded upon the law of nature: they say that reason will that such a thing be done and if it be prohibit by the law of nature they say it is against reason or that reason will not suffer that it be done.[17]

Though he did not contest the appropriateness of this way of talking, his intellectual breakthrough depended on distinguishing two kinds of natural law. 'The law of nature primary' did not 'command or prohibit anything save what any man who has reason, as a mere man, knows ought to be commanded or prohibited by reason'.[18] This category included large numbers of common law rules, including rules forbidding 'murther that is the death of him that is innocent, perjury, deceit, breaking of the peace and many other like'.[19] The law of nature secondary, by contrast, was an inference from primary natural law and an additional premise drawn from human institutions. What he called the 'law of reason secondary general' was deduced from the existence

[17] St German's *Doctor and Student*, ed. T. F. T. Plucknett and J. L. Barton, Selden Society, vol. 91 (London, 1974), pp. 31–3.
[18] *Ibid.*, p. 33. [19] *Ibid.*, p. 33.

of 'the law or general custom of property',[20] the human invention that replaced the primitive community of goods. The very existence of property was thus dependent on a positive custom; this was the explanation why assets such as tithes were nonetheless a matter for a secular jurisdiction.

The 'law of reason secondary particular' consisted in deductions from 'divers customs general and particular' and 'divers maxims and statutes ordained in this realm'.[21] The fact that such laws could be altered by a statute was a sign that their detailed provisions were strictly positive: the common law spokesman – the 'Student' – maintained that 'the law of reason is not of such strength and virtue that a knowledge of it would be equivalent to a knowledge of all English law', and the 'Doctor' was made to reaffirm the point:

> Although many things in English law are derived from the highest practical reason, nevertheless thou dost not pretend that the law of England can be said to be in all respects the law of reason (as some would maintain) . . . For as thou hast said above they can be changed by a statute made contrary to them; and thou affirmest that something that can be changed was certainly never the law of reason primary.[22]

St German's view of custom was unambiguously populist. He spoke of 'divers general customs of old time used through all the realm: which have been accepted and approved by our sovereign lord the king and his progenitors and all their subjects'.[23] He added that 'these be the customs that properly be called the common law'.[24] At this point, however, he faced a difficulty. In a passage which influenced Blackstone, he admitted the existence of a category of custom that was in practice only known to lawyers. These were 'divers principles that be called by those learned in law maxims the which have been always taken for law in this kingdom so that it is not lawful for none that is learned to deny them'. But though 'general custom' was their 'strength and warrant' (the Latin version has *authoritas*), these maxims were 'only known in the king's courts or among them that take great study in the law of the realm';[25] it was only in a very weak or frankly fictional sense that they could be said to have been approved by the community. He nonetheless excluded the possible way out represented by a delegation thesis, insisting that 'there is no statute that treateth of the beginning of the said customs ne why

20 *Ibid.*, p. 33. 21 *Ibid.*, p. 35. 22 *Ibid.*, p. 75. 23 *Ibid.*, p. 45.
24 *Ibid.*, p. 47. 25 *Ibid.*, pp. 57–9.

they should be holden for law'.[26] Nor was he willing to confuse the authority of maxims with their rationality. It was true that 'most commonly there be assigned some reasons or consideration why such maxims be reasonable', but this was only 'to the intent that other cases like may the more conveniently be applied to them'.[27]

St German thus held that the fruits of legal reason were usually dependent on a set of positive rules that drew authority from outside the courts. Given the Aristotelian point (then generally accepted) that systems of rules invariably break down when faced with the complexity of human situations, it might be thought he had supplied the opportunity for virtually unlimited cancellarial intervention. In fact, however, his system was defended against the threat of equitable encroachment. To begin with, the positivity of private property made it legitimate to insist on forms by which alone that property was defined; hard cases thrown up by those forms (involving, for example, the loss of a receipt) were often, it followed, beyond redress by human institutions. But, in any case, the common law possessed its own resources for dealing with inequitable results of rigorous pursuit of its procedures. St German believed that 'most commonly where any thing is excepted from the general customs or maxims of the laws of the realm by the law of reason the party must have his remedy by a writ that is called *subpoena* [that is, in Chancery]'.[28] But there were also examples where 'the parties shall be holpen in the same court and by the common law. And thus it appeareth that sometime a man may be excepted from the rigour of a maxim of the law by another maxim of the law. And sometime from the rigour of a statute by the law of reason and sometime by the intent of the makers of the said statute.'[29]

The most important of these techniques was appeal to *epicaia* (Aristotle's *epieikeia*), which

> is no other thing but an exception of the laws of God or of the law of reason from the general rules of the law of man: when they by reason of their generality would in any case judge against the law of God or the law of reason the which exception is secretly understande in every general rule of every positive law . . . if any law were made by man without any such exception expressed it were manifestly unreasonable.[30]

Of course, if *epicaia* could always be invoked, then it appeared that Chancery was needless. In practice, the courts had a rough division of

[26] *Ibid.*, p. 57. [27] *Ibid.*, p. 59. [28] *Ibid.*, p. 103. [29] *Ibid.*, p. 103. [30] *Ibid.*, p. 97.

labour, but there was little in St German's theory that either located or justified the demarcation line. St German did not consider this fact a weakness; it simply brought him, by another route, to affirming the centrality of custom. The question of whether *subpoenas* could be issued in any particular type of situation was one that was argued before the Chancellor, rather than in the courts of common law, but it was still in essence a matter that was sorted out by legal argument, and the learning of *subpoenas* could be thought of as one of the sources of the law of England. As one of St German's later pamphlets put it, 'no man ought to marvel what authority the Chancellor hath to make such a writ of *subpoena* in the king's name; for the old custom, not restrained by any statute, warranteth him by reason of his office so to do after certain grounds'.[31] The very boundaries of equity were thus a matter for the common law.

Custom and artificial reason

It is not too much to say that *Doctor and Student* supplied the essential framework for the next century of speculation. As might have been expected, the work's effects were broadly speaking twofold. On the one hand, it encouraged the spread of attitudes that emphasised the role of populist custom in the formation of the common law. In Anthony Fitzherbert's *Abridgement* (1514), the title 'custom' was concerned with purely local customs; but his successor Brooke's *La Graunde Abridgement* (presumably completed before Brooke's death in 1558) makes an extremely interesting slip. It reports a fifteenth-century judge as stating that 'the common law is the general custom of the realm', but the Year Book passage cited makes the rather different point that there are two varieties of *prescription*, one which is purely local and one 'which runs throughout the realm, and that is properly law'.[32] Brooke thus transforms a statement to the effect that popular behaviour can (by prescription) make the common law into a statement that the law is, as a whole, prescriptive.

Of course, the increasing salience of customary law owed something to the role now played by statute, especially in putting through the English Reformation. If statute had power to alter the country's religion,

[31] J. A. Guy, *Christopher St German on chancery and statute*, Selden Society Supplementary Series 6 (1985), p. 108.

[32] YB P 7 Henry VI, fo. 33, pl.27.

the obvious corollary was that the highest law was a law made by popular consent. It was therefore not surprising that populist views of the law had a particular appeal to those who wanted further reformation. By 1581, the puritan barrister Robert Snagg felt able to assert that the *lex terrae* was 'the ancient custom of the land that all *people* of several nations that at several times inhabited here liked best of'.[33] Amongst other things, this principle supplied him with a way of understanding the powers of Chancery. Snagg was troubled that the Chancellor 'had most to do and bare the greatest rule; and yet gave his judgment (as it seemed to me) as pleased himself, whatsoever the law of the land required in the case'.[34] This observation left him 'in a maze, not seeing at first how it could stand with the Great Charter that referred all judgment *ad legem terrae*', but his fundamental legal theory provided him with a natural solution:

> I found that the custom of the land, which is that *lex terrae*, allowed of that authority also, as of the rest; and that it was also a species of that general, the law of the land, which was the ancient custom of the realm.[35]

Though it was probably not coincidence that Morrice and Snagg were radical puritans, this attitude was not confined to opposition figures. During the 1590s, it was appropriated by the Anglican apologist Richard Hooker, who served a stint as Master of the Temple.[36] By 1599, a populariser with no discernible bias felt able to say that 'the common law ariseth from the people and multitude, but statute originally from the king'.[37]

One slightly later thinker took this notion rather further. The preface of Sir John Davies' *Irish Reports* (1613) treated the wisdom of unwritten law as guaranteed by popular experience: 'when a reasonable act once done is found to be good and beneficial to the people, and agreeable to their nature and disposition, then do they use it and practise it again and again, and so by often iteration and multiplication of the act it becometh a custom.'[38] The people of England had 'made their own laws out of their wisdom and experience (like a silkworm that formeth all her web

[33] Snagg, *The antiquity and original of the court of Chancery* (1654), p. 16 (emphasis added).
[34] *Ibid.*, p. 20. [35] *Ibid.*, pp. 20–1.
[36] *The Folger Library Edition of the works of Richard Hooker*, ed. W. Speed Hill, 7 vols. (Cambridge, MA, 1977–98), vol. III, p. 340.
[37] William Fulbecke, *A direction or preparative to the study of the lawe* (1600), fo.64v.
[38] J. G. A. Pocock, *The ancient constitution and the feudal law: a study of English historical thought in the seventeenth century: a reissue with a retrospect* (Cambridge, 1987), p. 33.

out of herself only)'.[39] But, though the simile is most suggestive, Davies was either unable or unwilling to work out a theory of organic specialisation that could have made some sense of judge-made law.[40] Perhaps for this reason, his thoroughly populist views were still at this stage quite unusual among professionals.

More narrowly technical thinkers appear to have taken their cue from one of the best-known *dicta* in Plowden's *Commentaries* (1571). The *Commentaries* is a complex book that nobody has adequately studied, but even a casual reading suggests a focused mind controlling the selection of its details. Plowden was perfectly aware that the law is a human creation (he sometimes referred to the 'founders'[41] of the system), but he was also much preoccupied with its relationship to absolute reason. One of the most commonly cited of the *dicta* he reports was that:

> there are two principal things from whence arguments may be drawn, that is to say, our maxims, and reason which is the mother of all laws. But maxims are the foundations of the law and the conclusions of reason and therefore they ought not to be impugned, but always to be admitted; yet these maxims may by the help of reason be compared together and set one against another (although they do not vary) where it may be distinguished by reason that a thing is nearer to one maxim than to another, or placed between two maxims.[42]

In Plowden's view, then, reason engendered legal rules that were in principle unchallengeable, but a continuing appeal directly to 'the mother of all laws' could not in practice be eliminated; the very existence of maxims gave rise to further puzzles – not least where those maxims apparently conflicted – that had to be resolved by reasoning.

Plowden was also much concerned with the relationship between unwritten and statute law, which he treated in the light of a conviction that 'the letter of the law is the body of the law, and the sense and reason of the law is the soul of the law, *quia ratio legis est anima legis*'.[43] He shared St German's stress on *epieikeia*, but his discussion of this crucial concept was more authentically Aristotelian. St German had believed that his *epicaia* was an 'exception' from the law of man by reference to some higher-order norm. Plowden inherited his interest in 'equity which is called by some epichaia [*sic*], which often puts an exception

[39] *Ibid.*, p. 34.
[40] On this, see also Pocock's subtle remarks at *Ancient constitution*, *ibid.*, pp. 265–70.
[41] 1 Plowden 368. [42] *Ibid.*, p. 27. [43] *Ibid.*, p. 465.

to the generality of the text for some reasonable cause',[44] but he referred to Aristotle's *Ethics* to show that 'in order to form a right judgment when the letter of a statute is restrained, and when enlarged by equity, it is a good way, when you peruse a statute, to suppose that the law-maker is present', partly because 'while you do no more than the lawmaker would have done, you do not act contrary to the law, but in conformity to it'.[45]

The consequence of this method was to expand the judge's room for manoeuvre by letting him impute to legislators priorities that he discerned within the legal system. Thus Plowden recorded that 'in general statutes made for the safety of inheritances, or for the public good, the expositors of them have construed them according to the course of common law', bearing in mind the principle that 'the law hath so admeasured [the king's] prerogatives that he shall not take away nor prejudice the inheritance of any';[46] not surprisingly this statement was much quoted by early seventeenth-century politicians.

Though it would be misleading to imply that there was vigorous debate about such abstract issues, there do exist some other Elizabethan texts addressing the cluster of problems raised by *epieikeia* and statutory intention. They demonstrate awareness of the danger of over-stating what a judge could do. According to *A Treatise Concerning Statutes* probably written in the 1580s:

> Whereas I have said that some statutes are constitutive of new laws, and go to the enlargement of the common law, I cannot tell how it might be taken of some, who hold the law to be so perfect and so large, as reason is in every thing and beyond reason a man cannot go.[47]

His unnamed intellectual opponents apparently referred to Cicero's *De Legibus*, where Cicero held that '*lex* is the highest reason (*summa ratio*) implanted in nature, which commands those things which ought to be done, and prohibits the opposite things. The same reason when it is confirmed and fully developed (*confirmata et perfecta*) in the human mind, is *lex*. And so they believe that *lex* is practical wisdom (*prudentia*).'[48] The author of *A Treatise Concerning Statutes* commented that:

> I know that reason may be called the mother of the law and maxims the foundations, in respect of the more part of laws; and maxims may not be

[44] *Ibid.*, p. 465. [45] *Ibid.*, p. 467. [46] *Ibid.*, p. 236.

[47] Sir Christopher Hatton, *A treatise concerning statutes, or acts of parliament: and the exposition thereof* (1677), p. 24.

[48] Cicero, *De republica: De legibus*, ed. and trans. C. W. Keyes (London, 1928), pp. 316–17.

denied, but they may be compared, and must be reconciled in every case where they seem to differ; but all this negotiation bringeth us to a less matter than that which Tully *De legibus* speaketh of *Lex est summa ratio, etc.*[49]

But this self-conscious moderate showed deep respect for the judicial function: if individual legislators were to reassemble 'for interpretation by a voluntary meeting', their views would have no legal interest, 'for the sages of the law whose wits are exercised in such matters, have the interpretation in their hands'.[50] He even held that 'if the words and mind of the law be clean contrary, that law or statute is void'. His resolution of 'one great doubt, which is, whether parliament may err or not', was thus that, 'when the matter is plain, every judge may esteem of it as it is, and being void, is not bound to allow it for good and forcible'.[51]

Thinkers in this tradition were not regarding law as simply a collection of populist customs. It does, however, seem possible that judges were seen as discerning the underlying 'reason' of such customs. Edward Hake's *Epieikeia*, a dialogue completed in 1597, has some remarks that may be relevant. Hake fully recognised the need for courts of 'conscience' like the Chancellor's, but he was anxious to maintain that 'the common law is not so severed from equity as amongst many hath been fondly conceived'.[52] Thus he held that 'no more can the words of the law without equity to direct it to the right sense thereof be said to be the law than the body of a man without reason to direct it in the actions of a man may be said to be a man'.[53] Significantly, Hake believed that custom was analogous to statute. Both raised difficulties of interpretation which had to be resolved in the same way: the lawyer was to look 'into the reason of the custom, and there you shall be satisfied (the same reason I mean as by the which by all likelihood the custom had his commencement)'.[54] In general, Hake thought that the effect of judicial decisions was to articulate the qualifications concealed within existing legal maxims. Thus in the case of 'omission of continual claim . . . the righteousness of the law doth secretly administer an exception for infants'. In time, exceptions of

49 Hatton, *Treatise concerning statutes*, pp. 25–6. 50 *Ibid.*, p. 30.

51 *Ibid.*, pp. 18–19 and 21. This passage is of course of some importance to the debate on what Coke meant in his obscure remarks on Bonham's case.

52 Edward Hake, *Epieikeia: a dialogue on equity in three parts*, ed. D. E. C. Yale (New Haven, 1953), p. 2.

53 *Ibid.*, pp. 9 and 12. 54 *Ibid.*, pp. 19–20.

this type, 'which in the beginning were *tacitae* and hidden . . . themselves became grounds or maxims as well as the principal grounds whereof they are exceptions', but they started as 'silent exceptions from the generality of law'.[55]

Hake's theory offered resources which could perhaps be taken in a populist direction. But the main thrust of his ideas was rather different. He suggested that the *common law* side of Chancery (in effect, the secretariat that issued legal writs) 'ought to be always so powerful and helpful as that a man might have from thence at all times an original writ for every particular wrong'.[56] This was, he believed, the force of Yelverton's statement that 'we must do even as the Sophonists [*sic*] and civilians . . . they resort thereupon to the law of nature which is reason and the ground of all laws and therein out of that which is most for the common wealth they make a law.'[57] At times, it was true, the lawyers referred to 'other sciences', but they could also properly be guided by principles inherent in their system: 'divers things which the common law itself is said to favour, as life, liberty, a woman's dower, infancy, coverture, privilege of arts and sciences . . . and sundry other things.' Though judgments guided by these preferences 'may be said to be the favour of the judge', they could also be described as 'the favour of the law'.[58]

This theme of Hake's attractive and subtle account of the development of legal thinking foreshadowed an intriguing shift in legal rhetoric. During the Year Book period, judicial reason could be said to be just 'common reason' – no more than common sense. From about 1600, however, apologists for common law began to speak of 'artificial' reason, the reason, that is, of an *artifex*, the master of a craft. This phrase was prominent, of course, in both the writings and judicial practice of Hake's contemporary Sir Edward Coke (1552–1634). Where Davies regarded the wisdom of the law as guaranteed by many years of popular experience, Coke insisted that it owed its excellence to having been endlessly 'fined and refined' by the lawyers, perhaps to the point where, in some circumstances, it could resist the authority of statute. Moreover, if law had been fined and refined by the lawyers, it was also true that lawyers had been moulded by the law; the sage of the law was a person who had internalised the underlying logic of the system:

[55] *Ibid.*, p. 50. [56] *Ibid.*, p. 107. [57] *Ibid.*, p. 108. [58] *Ibid.*, pp. 114–15.

> then we are said to know the law when we apprehend the reason of the law, that is, when we bring the reason of the law so to our own reason that we perfectly understand it as our own; and then, and never before, we have such an excellent and inseparable property and ownership therein, as we can neither lose it, nor any man take it away from us, and will direct us (the learning of the law is so chained together) in many other cases.[59]

Coke's copious, self-indulgent, self-assured, occasionally self-contradictory writings pose special problems of interpretation, but one way of approaching his achievement is to regard it as the final flower of a tradition that had stemmed from Plowden: a tradition whose sense of professional skills and professional resources provided a way of constructing a popular will with which the lawyers could be comfortable. Another equally plausible account would treat him as a more old-fashioned figure, a thinker who was loyal to the late medieval view that judges simply articulated reason. But, whatever view is taken of Coke's thinking, we have a moderate account of mainstream attitudes in a work by his junior colleague, Sir John Doddridge, probably drafted around 1600.[60]

Doddridge aimed at a description of the law in terms of 'general rules' of the type that were known to the Year Books (he said) as 'principles', 'grounds', 'maxims', 'eruditions' or 'positive laws'. The notion captured by these various labels was 'a conclusion either of the law of nature or derived from some general custom used within the realm containing in a short sum the reason and direction of many particular and special occurrences'.[61] Doddridge agreed with Plowden's view that a maxim was 'the foundation of law, and the conclusion of reason; for reason is the efficient cause thereof, and law is the effect that floweth therefrom.'[62] He took this to mean that:

> the common law of this land (which is often styled in our books by the name of common reason) is deduced from principles evident and known for the decision of such things as are drawn into doubt, and are unknown.[63]

[59] Edward Coke, *The first part of the institutes of the laws of England*, ed. F. Hargrave and C. Butler, 2 vols. (1832), fo.394b.

[60] Add 32,092, fos.160–200. Internal evidence (fo.160) reveals that the draft material in this manuscript was written by 1604. Most of it was eventually published in *The English lawyer* (1631).

[61] Add 32,092, fo.161v.

[62] Sir John Doddridge, *The English lawyer* (1631), p. 154.

[63] *Ibid.*, p. 62.

More precisely, the judges 'framed law upon deliberation and debate of reason . . . when present occasion is offered to use the same, by a case then falling out and requiring judicial determination';[64] a law of this type had the merit that it addressed the problems that actually arose, rather than those existing in the minds of legislators. Doddridge was thus enabled to see advantages in being 'governed by an unwritten law, not left in any other monument than in the mind of man; and thence to be deduced by deceptation [disputation, discussion] and discourse of reason: and that when occasion should be offered, and not before.' 'Hence is it', he explained,

> that the law . . . is called reason; not for that every man can comprehend the same; but it is artificial reason; the reason of such as are . . . skilful in the affairs of men, and know what is fit and convenient to be held and observed for the appeasing of controversies and debates among men, still having an eye and due regard of justice, and a consideration of the commonwealth wherein they live.[65]

Doddridge's claims for common law were thus in essence claims for the capacity of judges to act as experts on the common weal.

Common law as populist custom

This survey raises an intriguing question. During the Jacobean period, there was an intellectual tradition that had an attractive account of the development of law but seems to have been indifferent to popular consent. A century later, their views had been largely forgotten. There were, it is true, a handful of occasions on which the Georgian courts appealed to natural principles, but these appeals were felt to be exceptional events and the rhetoric of those who approved them was defensive.[66] The lawyers had lost Doddridge's self-confident assumption that an appeal directly to the 'mother of all laws' was a *routine* event in legal practice. From the standpoint of an orthodox historian of law, this shift is doubtless primarily a mark of the transition from practices based on professional consensus towards a 'modern' precedent-based system. But the strange fiction of a 'general custom' seems not to have been required by that transition and arguably made it difficult. It is natural to ask what

[64] *Ibid.*, p. 241. [65] *Ibid.*, p. 242.

[66] This is evident from the examples given in David Lieberman, *The province of legislation determined: legal theory in eighteenth century Britain* (Cambridge, 1989), pp. 89–98. At 4 Burrow 2343, Aston J cites Doddridge.

had happened; a sympathetic reader of Doddridge's work might even be tempted to wonder what went wrong.

Part of the explanation must be that the self-confidence that 'artificial reason' had encouraged invited an unwelcome politicisation. Initially, this favoured the judges' employer, the king. From *Bate's Case* (1606) to *R.* v. *Hampden* (1637–8), the constitutional cases of the first two Stuart reigns could be construed as pitting pliable judges, appealing to the *natural* rights of monarchs, against the letter of the liberties granted by custom and confirmed by statute. This seems to have been the anxiety which lay behind John Selden's legal theory, which claimed that 'name what laws you will . . . they are to be reduced to these two foundations: either ascertained by custom, or established by acts of parliament. There is not a third.'[67] In Selden's hands, this principle expressed a theory that treated the positive laws of particular nations as examples of 'permissive natural law' that found a determinate form in contractual agreements. But no such apparatus was really necessary to grasp the appeal of the certainty provided by laws that had been set in stone by popular consent.

The relatively sudden disappearance of the self-confident appeals to reason that characterised thinkers such as Coke owed less, however, to such arguments than to the outcome of the Revolution. Parliamentarianism was Cokean. In the first civil war (1642–6), the constitutional case for parliament rested on the assertion that the 'fundamental laws' enabled the two Houses (without the king's consent) to judge that those laws permitted armed resistance; in an unprecedented situation, in which the king appeared to be attacking his own people, the common law had methods enabling it to judge that an unprecedented act was legal. The constitutional royalists, by contrast, paraded their attachment to what they called 'known laws', that is, to determinate principles arrived at by consent. The Restoration settlement was a victory for 'known laws', securing the predominance of moderate royalists over Hobbesian absolutists on the one hand and defenders of rebellion on the other.

There are thus non-legal reasons why past acts of consent began to play such a significant role in English legal theory. The best attempt to integrate this stress on past consent into conventional professional thinking was the Restoration judge Sir Matthew Hale's *The History of the Common Law of England* (probably written around 1670, but unprinted until 1713). Hale was quite clear that common law consisted

[67] Pocock, *Ancient constitution*, p. 296.

in 'general customs', but he thought that judicial decisions were 'a greater evidence thereof than the opinion of any private persons'.[68] Though only acts of parliament could make deliberate changes in these customs, he knew that common law had changed through 'use and custom, and judicial decisions and resolutions'[69] as well as statutory legislation, and he accepted that the influence of Saxons, Danes and Normans 'might easily have a great influence upon the laws of this kingdom, and secretly and insensibly introduce new laws, customs and usages'[70] (the fact that so much of English law looked Norman resulted, for the most part, from 'conformation of the laws of Normandy to those of England', rather than *vice versa*).[71] Hale's picture of the legal past thus ruled out any catastrophic breaches in its essential continuity. So did his notions of adjudication. It was highly characteristic of his view of common law that he thought that, when judges decided in difficult cases, 'the rule of decision is, first, the common law and custom of the realm, which is the great substratum that is to be maintained; and then authorities or decisions of former times in the same or the like cases'.[72] To the extent that law was shaped by judges, it was unlikely to depart from the main outlines of the 'great substratum'.

By the mid-eighteenth century, this residual holism appears to have been virtually forgotten. Hale's distinction between customs and their 'evidence' in judgments was the foundation of the view that was expressed in Blackstone's *Commentaries* (1765–9). To Blackstone, it seemed obvious that common law was just a list of rules, 'a collection of customs and maxims',[73] all of which were strictly speaking 'general customs', that is to say, rules that drew their force from 'general reception and usage'.[74] Though he believed that judgments were 'the principal and most authoritative evidence, that can be given of the strength of such a custom as shall form a part of the common law',[75] he stressed that such decisions were no more than evidence; they were conceptually distinct from common law itself. He was indeed careful to rule out one possible way of softening this doctrine. He noted that some people had distinguished between 'established customs', such as the rule that, 'where there are three brothers, the eldest brother shall be heir to the

[68] Sir Matthew Hale, *The history of the common law of England*, ed. C. M. Gray (Chicago, 1971), p. 45.
[69] *Ibid.*, p. 40. [70] *Ibid.*, p. 42. [71] *Ibid.*, p. 84. [72] *Ibid.*, p. 46.
[73] William Blackstone, *Commentaries on the laws of England*, 4 vols. (1765–9), vol. I, p. 67.
[74] *Ibid.*, vol. I, p. 68. [75] *Ibid.*, vol. I, p. 69.

second', and 'established rules and maxims' of a more abstract type, such as 'that the king can do no wrong, that no man shall be bound to accuse himself, and the like', but he took

> these to be one and the same thing. For the authority of these maxims rests entirely upon general reception and usage: and the only method of proving that this or that maxim is a rule of common law, is by showing that it hath been always the custom to observe it.[76]

The principal implication of this theory was that there was no question of judicial legislation. Though it was an 'established rule' (that is, of course, a custom) 'to abide by former precedents when the same points come again in litigation', these precedents had no intrinsic legislative force.[77] When a judgment was 'most evidently contrary to reason', or to the law of God, it was permissible to disregard it, 'but even in such cases, the subsequent judges do not pretend to make a new law, but to vindicate the old one from misrepresentation . . . it is declared, not that such a sentence is *bad law*, but that it was *not law*; that is, that it is not the established custom of the realm, as has been erroneously determined.'[78] Though the 'monuments and evidences' of custom were of course extant in writing, the laws they recorded were properly '*leges non scriptae*, because their original institution and authority are not set down in writing, as Acts of Parliament are, but they receive their binding power, and force of laws, by long and immemorial usage, and by their universal reception throughout the kingdom'.[79]

Any doubt that '*general* usage' and '*universal* reception' involve expression of the *popular* will should be dispelled by a remark about the law of Rome 'as practised in the times of its liberty'. Blackstone observed that Roman law 'paid also a great regard to custom; but not so much as our law; it only then adopting it, when the written law was deficient', but added that there was authority in the *Digest* (1.3.32) for a more English view of the position:

> For since, says Julianus, the written law binds us for no other reason but because it is approved by the judgement of the people, therefore those laws which the people have approved without writing ought also to bind every body. For where is the difference, whether people declare their assent to a law by suffrage, or by a uniform course of acting accordingly?

76 *Ibid.*, vol. I, p. 68. 77 *Ibid.*, vol. I, p. 69. 78 *Ibid.*, vol. I, p. 70. Blackstone's italics.
79 *Ibid.*, vol. I, p. 64.

> Thus did they reason while Rome had some remains of her freedom . . . And indeed it is one of the characteristic marks of English liberty, that our common law depends upon custom.[80]

As might have been expected, Blackstone associated this position with a benign view of the Saxon past. He took it that the common law had had its origin in an authoritative compilation of a variety of local customs. This had been undertaken by King Alfred, but Alfred's code received a 'new edition, or fresh compilation' from Edward the Confessor.[81] It was King Edward's laws, he thought, 'which our ancestors struggled so hardly to maintain, under the first princes of the Norman line . . . which gave rise and original to that collection of maxims and customs, which is known by the name of the common law'.[82]

The problem with this nationalistic vision was that the findings of historians had forced common lawyers to jettison Hale's comforting belief that even Norman feudal law had English origins. It was accepted by the well informed that the English land law Blackstone was proposing to expound was evidently feudal in its basis and that the introduction of feudal principles had coincided with the Norman Conquest. In a remarkable sign of his commitment to the belief that valid law must rest upon consent, Blackstone felt driven to postulate an act of parliament by which the guileless English had 'probably meant to do no more than to put the kingdom into a state of defence' by consenting to 'the fiction of tenure from the crown as the basis of a military discipline'.[83] They reckoned without 'the Norman interpreters, skilled in all the niceties of the feudal constitutions, and well understanding the import and extent of the feudal terms', who 'took a handle' to bring in a fully feudal system.[84]

From the perspective of most modern readers, this desperate hypothesis seems curiously needless. As Blackstone later frankly said in a judicial context,

> The common law maxims of descent . . . and a hundred other instances that might be given are plainly the offspring of a feudal system; but whatever their parentage was, they are now adopted by the common

80 *Ibid.*, vol. I, pp. 73–4. 81 *Ibid.*, vol. I, p. 66.
82 *Ibid.*, vol. I, pp. 66–7. 83 *Ibid.*, vol. II, p. 51.
84 *Ibid.*, II 51. Blackstone's source for the postulated statute is Sir Martin Wright, *An introduction to the law of tenures* (1730), pp. 63–73; the emphasis on the role of the malign interpreters appears to be largely his own.

> law of England, incorporated into its body, and so interwoven with its policy, that no court of justice in this kingdom has either the power or (I trust) the inclination to disturb them.[85]

Blackstone was evidently in a position to rest his defence of the system on a conservative-minded pragmatism. After all, as his judgment went on to remark (in strikingly Burkean phrasing),

> the law of real property in this country wherever its materials were gathered, is now formed into a fine artificial system, full of unseen connexions and nice dependencies; and he that breaks one link of the chain, endangers the dissolution of the whole.[86]

Given the admission that so much of law was actually not customary in its origins, it would be natural to conclude that this 'artificial system' was a variety of judge-made law, whose rationality was constituted simply by the advantages derived from its coherence. He certainly held (following Coke) that 'whenever a standing rule of law, of which the reason perhaps could not be remembered or discerned, hath been wantonly broken in upon ... the reason of the rule hath in the end appeared from the inconveniencies that have followed the innovation'.[87]

Unfortunately, Blackstone appears to have believed that he had demonstrated this rationality when he had supplied a historical explanation of how a particular positive law arose. In the notoriously anomalous case of the common law rule that the half-blood cannot inherit, Blackstone admitted that 'the artificial reason of [this positive law], drawn from the feudal law, may not be obvious to everybody', but he believed he had discharged his duty when he had explained, at least to his own satisfaction, why this curious rule was originally adopted.[88] The rationale of present law was thus identified with reasoning recapitulated by historians. Doddridge's proper focus on present social needs had been displaced by a concern to reconstruct the past.

Conclusion

The purpose of this essay has been historical; it has sketched the lengthy process by which the 'reason' of the common lawyers gave way to the

[85] Lieberman, *Province of legislation*, pp. 139–40. [86] *Ibid.*, p. 140.
[87] Blackstone, *Commentaries*, vol. I, p. 70.
[88] *Ibid.*, vol. I, p. 70; for the explanation, see *Ibid.*, vol. II, p. 228, though even Blackstone saw it as 'a very fine-spun and subtle nicety' (*ibid.*, vol. II, p. 230).

presumed consent of the wider population as the ultimate criterion of the law's legitimacy. If none of the writers it mentions achieved a completely coherent conception of their law, a number of them had insights that seem worth recovering, and the story of their struggles is also theoretically suggestive. But the best way of serving an interest in the theory of custom may be to draw attention to a final historical problem. Blackstone's capacity to make sense of what the lawyers did was evidently impeded by his dogmatic view that English law consists in general customs, but nobody who reads his works is likely to suppose that his attachment to this view derived from democratic inclinations; beyond a certain patriotic libertarianism, he surely felt no personal attraction to the idea of common law as *popular* legislation. There is, however, a better way – more biographically plausible and theoretically informative – of characterising the source of his confusion.

His difficulties really stemmed from the more abstract doctrine that any positive law, by definition, was a 'rule of civil conduct prescribed by the supreme power in a state'.[89] The word 'prescribed' implied a universal promulgation before the rule in question could 'be properly a law';[90] laws must be known, and known as laws, by those that they affected. One logical implication of this dogma was that the very existence of laws made by popular usage showed that the nation as a whole must be the 'supreme power'. Another effect was, as it were, to atomise the law, transforming what Hale called 'the great substratum' into Blackstone's mere 'collection of laws and maxims'.

It was this atomisation of the content of the law that was the most significant shift between Hale's thought and Blackstone's. Hale might have agreed with Blackstone's definitions, but there are signs within his work of a resistance to their consequences. He still retained a sense of law as unified both by an order that was inherent in its subject matter and by the operations of a shared professional method. As he once explained when commenting on Hobbes, the two ideas were intimately connected: 'the same faculty of reason variously applied and directed renders this man a mathematician, a physician, a lawyer, an artificer, according as the reasoning faculty is directed or applied and habituated by use and exercise to the several objects thereof.'[91] Hale felt a need, in other words, for some residual element of artificial reason to give the common law

[89] *Ibid.*, vol. I, p. 44. [90] *Ibid.*, vol. I, p. 45.
[91] Sir William Holdsworth, *A history of English law*, 3rd edn, 16 vols. (1945), vol. V, p. 502.

legitimacy; Blackstone's equivalent to this conception was a diffuse plurality of artificial reasons, the justifications peculiar to individual rules that could be excavated by historical enquiry. It remains an open question if an 'unwritten' law can be indefinitely sustained on such a meagre basis.

10

Three ways of writing a treatise on public international law: textbooks and the nature of customary international law

AMANDA PERREAU-SAUSSINE

International law is a system of customary law. And, like all writers of textbooks on customary law, scholars of international law find themselves in a curious position: it is philosophically impossible to treat customary law as a system of clear, settled rules since there is no way of settling the correct text or formulation of those rules. As Brian Simpson writes in an essay on English common law,

> we all know that no two legal treatises state the law in the same terms, there being a law of torts according to Street, and Heuston, and Jolowicz and James and the contributors to Clerk and Lindsell, and we buy them all *because* they are different. And what is true of the academics is true perhaps even more dramatically of the judges, who are forever disagreeing, often at inordinate length ... As a system of legal thought the common law then is inherently vague; it is a feature of the system that uniquely authoritative statements of the rules which, so the positivists tell us, comprise the common law, cannot be made.[1]

What is true of English law is at least as true of public international law, on which not only academics and individual judges but also tribunals and courts disagree, similarly often at inordinate length.

This essay argues that one of the most fundamental differences between various treatises on international law stems from diverging assumptions about what renders a statement of a rule of international law correct or authoritative. These assumptions reflect three distinctive accounts of the nature of international law, and more specifically of the

[1] Brian Simpson 'The common law and legal theory' in Simpson ed. *Oxford essays on jurisprudence II* (1977) 77 at pp. 89–90.

relationship between reasoned argument and the practices of states. My focus is on English textbooks of enduring influence dating from the mid-nineteenth until the mid-twentieth century.

Sceptical accounts of the nature of customary international law

Disagreements among academics and judges about the nature and content of rules of common law, argues Simpson, mark the disintegration of the shared ethos of a closed, decadent and self-interested caste of lawyers. For a sceptic like Simpson, rational principles that purportedly emerge from within the common law are Roman law imports from Justinian's *Institutes* (and so Gaius' *Institutes*). Treatises on the common law like Hale's *Analysis of the Laws of England* and Blackstone's *Commentaries*, far from being examplars of an English common law tradition, 'do not arise from the common law' (although 'it is striking that once English law had been expressed in the language of the scholar and the gentleman, as civil law previously had been, common law legal writing took on a literary character it had previously lacked').[2]

An equivalent account of international law, one often met in writing by international relations scholars, treats international law as a tradition ornamented with the scholarly language of a civilian tradition but one guided and sustained by the closed and at worst self-interested practices of senior jurists and judges:

> There is a sense in which peace and co-operation between nations or classes or individuals is a common and universal end irrespective of conflicting interests and politics. There is a sense in which a common interest exists in the maintenance of order or 'law and order' within the nation. But as soon as the attempt is made to apply these supposedly abstract principles to a concrete political situation, they are revealed as the transparent disguises of selfish vested interests.[3]

Sceptical accounts such as this have fed back into the self-understanding of some international lawyers.[4] International law, the argument might

[2] Brian Simpson 'The rise and fall of the legal treatise: legal principles and forms of legal literature' 48 *University of Chicago Law Review* (1981) 632 at pp. 641, 658, 655.

[3] E. H. Carr *Twenty years crisis* (1939) at p. 111.

[4] Cf. Thomas Franck, arguing that '[V]ogue-ish legal thinking, dominated by the school of policy science, has professed its normativity even while advancing a theory of creative interpretation of positive law that is nihilist in all but name.' 'The case of the vanishing treatises' 81 AJIL (1987) 763 at p. 766.

go, has continued throughout the twentieth century to be taught and developed by an unusually small group of influential scholars who combine their roles as academics with positions as advocates, arbitrators and judges. This international set of scholar-preachers shares the same teachers (one influential teacher's student often becoming the teacher of a subsequent generation) and sustains a common international understanding thanks to peer pressure accumulated as these international lawyers mix at regular international meetings and tribunals.

One way of developing this sceptical account of international law sees it as reflecting the very nature of every legal system: for such sceptics, legal (and moral) principles will be *inevitably* a piecemeal expression of the interests of a ruling elite. (A classical Marxist account of law would fall within this category.)

Other sceptics believe that a legal system *could* be built and based upon rational moral principles but that this could be the case only with comprehensive systematisation, with a 'complete code'. Wholescale codification was of course the end sought by late-eighteenth- and early-nineteenth-century law reformers. In 1792 the French Convention resolved to create a Declaration of the Rights of Nations.[5] In England, Bentham had ambitious codification plans for both English and international law, each code to be structured around his master principle of utility.[6]

But any project aiming at total codification is doomed to fail. No written law *can* give exhaustive directions on its own interpretation, so customary rules and practices will be needed not just to resolve 'a fault that codification has made'[7] but to guide judicial interpretation – and these guiding customary rules and practices will themselves be subject to change and development through interpretation. To argue that a particular formulation is the correct view of a rule of customary law, as do teachers, textbook-writers, judges and counsel, is, as Simpson argues, 'to

[5] Although, having charged Abbé Grégoire to draft the declaration, in 1795 the Convention rejected the principles he laid out as a twenty-one article code.

[6] Simpson similarly suggests – although one suspects with a twinkle – that wholescale codification of a legal system, accompanied with a ban on law reporting (and, in the case of the common law, with a demoting of the status of the judiciary), *could* reduce customary law to a set of clear, settled rules (although 'to portray the common law as actually conforming to this ideal is to confuse the aspirations of those who are attempting to arrest the collapse of a degenerate system of customary law with the reality'). 'The common law and legal theory' (above, note 1) at p. 99.

[7] Oppenheim *Treatise I* section 34 p. 41.

participate in the system, not simply to study it scientifically'.[8] Codify it, repeal it, abolish it; some form of customary law will inevitably reappear.

The only question for a textbook writer is that of what view to take, what account to assume of the nature of this customary law. For a sceptic, as sketched above, customary law is but a disguise for the furtherance of writers' or judges' motives, motives which are usually self-interested and 'sinister'. Although the result would be entertaining and perhaps revealing, no English nineteenth- or twentieth-century textbook writer has attempted to write a treatise on international law from a sustainedly sceptical perspective. But there are three other accounts of the nature of customary law which do underpin rival English treatises on international law. According to the first, rules of customary law become manifest or emerge thanks to a spirit sustaining that customary system and those who deliver its rules: this account I call that of midwives. According to the second 'natural law' account, rules of customary law are elaborations of principles of justice or natural law (including a principle recognising the moral value of a stable system of rules). And, according to the third account, which I call that of noble liars, arguments in terms of rules of customary law veil law-making by benign (*not* self-interested) writers or judges.

Pollock and Hall: two midwives' accounts of international law

On the view of customary law taken by those I call midwives, the role of a textbook writer is to contemplate and immerse himself in the traditional practices and customs manifest in scholarly writings, treaties, the diplomatic practices of states, and possibly areas of domestic law. Just as a midwife hopes to stand by at the birth of a baby, intervening as little as possible and ideally not at all, so a midwife of customary law believes that customary rules emerge from legal practices and customs and that as they emerge the rules will point their own way out of any apparent internal conflict. For a midwife, there can be no real 'founders' of a legal system: the reasoning of a Hale or a Blackstone plays at most a formal role, drawing on civilian structures or schemes to assist at the delivery of principles from within customary practice itself. On this account, knowledge of legal principles is unattainable without understanding their variable manifestations or actualisations in a wide range of sources: lawyers' reasoning can only be guided by customary understandings,

[8] Simpson 'The common law and legal theory' (above, note 1) at p. 97.

and the relevant principles will necessarily be manifest in or emerge from a careful study of customary practices. Such understandings of customary law assume that legal development or evolution is graced, guided and constrained by a benign spirit (rather than the sinister ethos traced by sceptics as underpinning customary law).

The main difficulty for a midwife of customary law arises as soon as reason becomes involved, even if only to articulate the relevant legal principles, those principles are exposed to question. The midwife's account of rules of international law follows practice, taking traditional, enduring and widespread belief as providing the ultimate criterion of legal validity. For a consistent midwife, it makes no sense to talk about the correctness or otherwise of these beliefs. So, if substantive questions arise about their rationality or justice, to evade these questions requires a self-consciously irrational preparedness to hold two contradictory beliefs in one's mind simultaneously and accept both, an Orwellian 'double-think'.

International law as the deliverances of a civil law tradition

An account of international law offered by Frederick Pollock exemplifies the midwife's approach. While recognising that Grotius' name 'must always be pre-eminent when we speak of the establishment of the law of nations as a distinct body of doctrine', Pollock's essay emphasises Grotius' role not as a 'founder' but as an important late voice in an ongoing tradition. 'We should go far astray', he instructs his readers, 'if we supposed that Gentili or Grotius revived the Roman lawyers' conceptions of *ius naturale* and *ius gentium* for a world which had forgotten them.' Since Grotius, '[m]any different theories have ... been put forward, generally determined by the contemporary fashion in moral philosophy, or by the writer's own philosophical predilections, rather than by any specific and appropriate development from within'.[9]

So, for Pollock, appropriate developments of international law are built around the venerable principles of canon and civil law and on Aristotelian and later Greek philosophy – and *not* 'the contemporary fashion in moral philosophy' or a writer's 'own philosophical predilections'. Developments building on these traditional sources believed to be 'little short of sacred' would count as appropriate, internal developments; those building on contemporary philosophical practices would not.

[9] Pollock 'The sources of international law' 72 LQR (1902) 418.

But, in assuming that *traditional and widespread belief* is the fundamental criterion for the validity of a rule of international law, the 'double-think' difficulty appears. On the midwife's own account, if the popularity of a modern fad proves enduring, becoming internalised by practitioners and scholars, that same account will have to be accepted at some point in the future as providing the touchstone for contemporary rules. On Pollock's own account, his attachment to Roman law as at the core of international law can be undermined by rival fashionable principles if and when the latter themselves become widely adopted as 'little short of sacred'. While a positivist account of international law like Oppenheim's was breaking with the traditional approach of treatise writers at the time Pollock was writing, Pollock's own defence of the centrality of Roman law principles to international law itself would become incorrect viewed with the hindsight of another century in so far as this 'new' positivist view has come to be widely accepted.[10]

International law as the deliverance of an English legal tradition

William Hall's position in his *Treatise on International Law* is also that of a midwife, although the tradition from which Hall delivers principles of international law is a resolutely English one. Existing rules of international law, argues Hall, are *not* 'an imperfect attempt to give effect to an absolute right which is assumed to exist and to be capable of being discovered': they are rather 'the sole standard of conduct or law of present authority; and changes and improvements in those rules can only be effected through the same means by which they were originally formed, namely, by growth in *harmony with* changes in *the sentiments and external conditions of the body of states*'.[11]

Recognising that 'the accepted principles of international law sometimes lead logically to incompatible results', Hall argues that 'it is evident that as neither of two ultimate principles can control the other, and reconciling legislation at the hands of a superior is from the

10 Cf. Nigel Simmonds *The decline of juridical reason* p. 118: 'It becomes hard to say whether legal positivism is true or false. The message of this book is, in a sense, that it is neither: legal positivism is an attempt to reinterpret traditional institutions and patterns of reasoning along lines consistent with a changed and changing situation.' Simmonds does, however, go on to argue that '[w]hether or not that reinterpretation should be resisted is another question', as such raising the question addressed in different ways by my natural lawyers and noble liars (text below).

11 *International law* (8th edn, ed. Pearce-Higgins) p. 1 (my emphasis).

nature of the case impossible, there is nothing but bare practice which can fix at what point the inevitable compromise is to be made'.[12] Consequently, an international lawyer's focus needed to be exclusively on '*authoritative international usage*', qualified in two ways: 'unanimous opinion of recent growth is a better foundation of law than long practice on the part of some only of the body of civilised states', but the usages of some *states 'to whom the moulding of law has been committed'* must be taken 'to have preponderant weight'.[13]

Despite his expressions of misgiving, Hall's position is that of a classic pragmatist with deep faith in the good sense of the practices of British and (to a lesser extent) American lawyers. Their practices could be relied upon to deliver whatever principles were needed by international lawyers. Thus in his Preface, Hall makes a broader claim about the direction he expects states' practice to take, a claim characteristic of the wearily qualified optimism of the midwife:

> In a community, as in an individual, passionate excess is followed by a reaction of lassitude and to some extent of conscience. On the whole the collective seems to exert itself in this way more surely than the individual conscience; and in things within the scope of International Law, conscience, if it works less impulsively, can at least work more freely than in home affairs ... [I]t is a matter of experience that times, in which International Law has been seriously disregarded, have been followed by periods in which the European conscience has done penance by putting itself under straiter obligations than those which it before acknowledged. There is no reason to suppose that things will be otherwise in the future. I therefore look forward with much misgiving to the manner in which the next great war will be waged, but with no misgiving at all as to the character of the rules which will be acknowledged ten years after its termination, by comparison with the rules now considered to exist.[14]

But again the 'double-think' difficulty arises. Hall's weary optimism, his defence of the enduring nature of the rules of international law articulated in his treatise, is no more consistent with his emphasis on the exclusive relevance of state practice than is Pollock's defence of the enduring centrality of principles of Roman law.

[12] *Ibid.*, p. 6. [13] *Ibid.*, pp. 11, 12–13.

[14] 'Preface to third edition' (1889) at p. xxvi of the eight edition.

Two natural lawyers' accounts of international law

A second view of international law underlying some English treatise writing on international law is that of a natural lawyer. With midwives, a natural lawyer believes that shared practices and traditional customs are an articulation of and indeed prerequisite for her legal, political and moral reasoning. But she agrees with sceptics that customary practices can also act as a dangerous shackle. On her account, lawyers must reject on their demerits those customary practices which are inimical to legal, moral and political reasoning. This discrimination between valuable and dangerous customs will be made in terms of natural laws or principles of justice. Although natural lawyers tend to be presented (at least by their critics) as idealists, she will argue that her natural laws are *not* ideal standards imposed on a set of alien practices, but instead that they are rules manifest within and learnt from engagement with the set of customary rules with which she is working.[15] Her account of customary law will be structured around these rules of natural law, conferring a higher legal status on customary rules in which these natural laws are manifest.

A natural lawyer might argue that the venerable age of a particular set of principles is itself strong (perhaps even the best) *evidence* for its wisdom, but she would not take continued acceptance as itself sufficient ground for finding a particular theory of natural law or justice philosophically compelling. Most natural lawyers aspire to discern a set of a few core natural laws rooted in human nature: these laws are treated as capable of development in and through customary and positive law – through the study of which they will be discerned – but as laws which cannot be changed antithetically.

A natural law of variable content

This belief in enduring natural laws is defended by James Brierly in his *The Law of Nations*, asserting that 'a rational universe, even if we cannot prove it to be a fact, is a necessary postulate of both thought and action':

[15] Hence a natural lawyer will reject the account of her position assumed by Simpson, for whom 'verification by reference to cases' is 'antithetical to [the spirit] of the natural lawyers'. ('The rise and fall of the legal treatise' at pp. 668, 672.) My natural lawyers claim that reflection on practice – including on case law – is a necessary prerequisite for understanding principles of natural law.

> Modern legal writers, especially in England, have sometimes ridiculed the conception of a law of nature, or they have recognized its great historical influence but treated it as a superstition which the modern world has rightly discarded. Such an attitude, however, proceeds from a misunderstanding of the medieval idea; for under a terminology which has ceased to be familiar to us the phrase stands for something which no progressive system of law either does or can discard.[16]

For Brierly, the range of cases and rival positions which natural law arguments have been used to support is not an argument against the conception of natural law itself: 'there was nothing arbitrary about the conception itself, any more than a text of Scripture is arbitrary, because the Devil may quote it.' Brierly is ambiguous on whether or not his natural laws can change antithetically, echoing thinkers like Rudolf Stammler: 'what we have a right to believe in today is a law of nature *with a variable content*.' What *is* reasonable or what the law of nature enjoins 'cannot receive a final definition: it is always, and above all in the sphere of human conduct, relative to conditions of time and place' and as such can only be understood through careful study of practice and custom.[17]

In this respect, the line between Brierly's natural law account and that of a midwife may seem a fine one: Brierly's natural laws, like the midwife's rules of customary law, emerge from and are manifest within customary practice. But Brierly would emphasise that his natural laws have, as such, a special status *within* a system of customary law: they provide guiding, structuring and conflict-resolving rules of reason.

An Anglican civilian's natural law

Sir Robert Phillimore was 'the last of the great Civilian practitioners'.[18] He was at least as eminent as an ecclesiastical and civil lawyer as he was as an international lawyer; for him, as for his contemporaries, the three fields were intimately linked.[19] For Phillimore, international law is

[16] Brierly *The law of nations* (1st edn, 1928) pp. 14, 9.

[17] *Ibid.*, pp. 12, 14–15.

[18] John Baker 'Sir Robert Phillimore and the last practising Doctors of Law' 4 *Ecclesiastical Law Journal* (1996–7) 709–19 at p. 711.

[19] He is best known for his 2,500-page, two volume *Ecclesiastical law of the Church of England* (1873–6), which aims to systematise English canon law. He labelled himself a 'liberal Conservative', defending constitutional monarchy against the republicanism of the radicals; Doctors' Commons ('at a time when it was already doomed' – Baker p. 712); and a high vision of the catholicity of the Church of England against both

ultimately based on divine law of which custom and usage – in particular civil law – are 'natural' manifestations.[20] The 'noble profession' of the civilian and scholar of the law of nations had of its essence required earlier generations to apply 'the laws of natural justice to nations, and to enforce the sanction of individual morality upon communities'.[21] Private international law similarly stems from 'permanent and invariable relations, laid in the necessities and nature of man', relations that 'may be modified, but cannot be annhilated, by positive law'. In striking contrast to Brierly's account, Phillimore's natural laws are eternal ones. These 'natural necessities' by definition will be best discerned by communities which, by the grace of God, have been able to accrue the relevant insight: just as the 'more cultivated the mind of the individual, the more accurate will be his judgments as to what is just' so, argues Phillimore, 'the more cultivated the mind of a people, the deeper will be their insight into the true nature of legal relations, and the better will be their general definitions of what is just, or, in other words, their laws'.[22]

In his *Commentaries on International Law*, Phillimore offers a rich, scholarly overview of both public and private international law, drawing in particular on his detailed knowledge of civil law and his wide practical experience as an advocate. As sources of international law, Phillimore lists:

1. The 'principles of Eternal Justice implanted by God in all moral and social creatures, of which nations are the aggregate, and of which governments are the International Organs'.
2. Scripture, as 'enforcing and extending these principles of Natural Justice'.

Protestant Anglicanism and Roman Catholicism (on which see Norman Doe, 44 *Dictionary of National Biography* pp. 78–80).

20 International law is 'not enacted by the will of any common Superior upon earth, but . . . is enacted by the will of God; and it is expressed in the consent, tacit or declared, of independent Nations . . . Custom and usage, moreover, outwardly express the consent of nations to things which are *naturally*, that is by the law of God, binding upon them. But it is to be remembered that in this latter case, usage is the effect and not the cause of the Law. International Jurisprudence has received since the civilization of mankind, and especially since the introduction of Christianity, continual culture and improvement; and it has slowly acquired, in great measure and on many subjects, the certainty and precision of positive law.' 'Preface to first edition', reproduced in the third edition at pp. xv–xvi.

21 Preface, vol. I at p. xxxvi.

22 'Preface to first edition', reproduced in the third edition at pp. ix–x (noting that 'legal relations' was replaced by 'jural relations' in the Preface to the second edition).

3. 'Reason, which governs the application of these principles to particular cases, itself guided and fortifed by a constant reference to analogous cases and to the written reason embodied in the text of the Roman Law, and in the works of Commentators thereupon.'
4. 'The universal consent of Nations, both as expressed (1) by positive compact or treaty, and (2) as implied by usage, custom, and practice: such usage, custom and practice being evidence in various ways – by precedents recorded in History; by being embodied and recorded in Treaties; in public documents of State; in the Marine Ordinances of States; in the decisions of International Tribunals; in the Works of eminent writers upon International Jurisprudence.'[23]

In the diversity of sources on which the volumes draw, the *Commentaries* remain a rich resource for contemporary writers on international law in a way in which – as we will see below – the early editions of Oppenheim's *Treatise* do not. His 'List of authorities' at the beginning of his first volume starts with Aeschines and Demosthenes' *Orationes duae contrariae*, Ahrens' *Cours de Droit naturel*, *Allegemeine Geschichte*, Amédée Félix, *Ancillon über den Geist der Staatsverfassung*, *Annals of Congress*, *Annuaire historique universel*, *Annuaire des Deux Mondes*, *Annual Register*, Archbold's *Criminal Law* and Aristotle's *De rhetorica* and *Ethica*, continuing over nine pages to conclude with Zachariä and Zouche. This is followed by a one-and-a-half-page list of English and American reports and then a three-page list of 140 British and American cases.

Phillimore's sources are those of a scholarly English civilian practitioner, for whom it goes without saying – as for Pollock or (to a lesser extent) Hall – that the classical traditions in which he had been trained (in Phillimore's case at Christ Church in Oxford), tempered by good argument (often taken as manifest in Anglo-American case law), were in themselves sources of international law. His readers, he hopes, will be encouraged to write 'a better treatise upon the same subject . . . profiting by what may be useful, avoiding what may be erroneous, supplying what may be defective': it is 'by such gradual additions and painful accumulations that the edifice of this noble science may one day be completed, and the Code of International Jurisprudence acquire in all its branches the certainty and precision of Municipal Law'.[24]

[23] Phillimore *Commentaries* (3rd edn, 1879) vol. I, p. 68.
[24] 'Preface to first edition', reproduced in the third edition at p. l.

While recognising that Phillimore was 'an influential and well-respected practitioner and Judge of the High Court of Admiralty', Martti Koskenniemi dismisses Phillimore's *Commentaries* as texts that 'oscillate between an old-fashioned, religiously inclined naturalism and what to Continental eyes was a haphazard collection of precedents from diplomatic and judicial practice, heavily weighted in favour of its author's imperial homeland'.[25] Koskenniemi treats Phillimore's text as 'haphazard' rather than systematic because the principles around which the volumes are structured (Anglo-Catholic tenets integrated with classical Greek and civil law principles) are ones which could not possibly 'emerge' from the materials: Koskenniemi implies that they are not only old-fashioned but untenable and as such incapable of 'structuring' any satisfactory treatise. On a glance at the sample of authorities listed above, Koskenniemi might seem to be right.

Such objections are of course substantive and not simply formal ones about the consistency and coherence of Phillimore's system. Phillimore himself explicitly presents his *Commentaries on International Law* as 'an endeavour, upon a larger scale than has hitherto been attempted in England, to reduce, in some measure at least, to a system, the principles and precedents of International Law', a task 'which the very nature of the materials renders extremely hard: inasmuch as it is very difficult so to arrange them as to avoid on the one hand a vague unsatisfactory generality, and on the other an appearance of precise mathematical accuracy, of which the subject is not susceptible'.[26]

What makes Phillimore's account of international law that of a natural lawyer – rather than the 'haphazard' account of a midwife – is the fact that he aims to draw on reasoned arguments and moral principles to temper his detailed discussions of practice.[27] His theory of natural law is a scholarly high Anglican one – one with faith in the wisdom of the teachings and doctrine of the Church of England understood as part (a particularly reliable part) of a universal church. His work on ecclesiastical

[25] Martti Koskenniemi 'Hersch Lauterpacht (1897–1960)' in Jack Beatson and Reinhard Zimmermann eds. *Jurists uprooted: German-speaking emigré lawyers in twentieth century Britain* (Oxford, 2004) pp. 601–61, at p. 610.

[26] 'Preface to first edition', reproduced in the third edition at p. l.

[27] Although underplaying the High Anglican aspect, Michael Lobban categorises Phillimore's *Commentaries* more appositely than Koskenniemi as setting out 'a Grotian natural lawyer's view' of international law as 'rooted in justice and reason, but expressed in custom'. Michael Lobban 'English approaches to international law in the nineteenth century' in Matthew Craven, Malgosia Fitzmaurice and Maria Vogiatzi eds. *Time, History and International Law* (Leiden, forthcoming 2006), text at notes 13–15.

law, in the accurate words of one biographer, offers 'a formidable statement of the high Church view of nationality and internationality': his *Commentaries* aspired to be 'international' in the same sense.[28]

It was primarily the civil law tradition rather than the common law that Phillimore believed reflected insight into 'the true nature of legal relations'.[29] The jurisprudence of the Digest, 'considerably modified by custom, convention, by the usages of Christendom ... had for centuries commanded the veneration of mankind, whose natural rights it had investigated with impartiality and explained with precision'. For Phillimore, civil law was the most reliable source for a fleshing out or development of basic principles of natural law, reliable not only because of its age but also because the links could be clearly made out between accrued tradition and those fundamental principles:

> It was richly stored with comprehensive principles of written reason, of the science and philosophy of law. It was the collected experience of an empire which had included under its dominion the whole civilised world, and it was further recognised at the epoch of the revival of classical literature, by the clearness of its style and the beauty of its language. Accordingly, from Grotius to Lord Stowell, it became the basis of all the great labours of jurists.[30]

Phillimore's account of international law, then, is that of a natural lawyer: the treatise writer must discriminate between valuable and dangerous customs, and that discrimination must be made in terms of natural laws, principles of justice themselves manifest within and learnt from engagement with customary rules in general and – in Phillimore's case – developments of Roman law in particular.

[28] Doe (above, note 20) at p. 79, highlighting Phillimore's 'striking analogy of the nature of the Ottoman Empire's relation to the Concert of Europe which was much used during the various phases of the European Question in the 1870s'.

[29] '[T]he Common Law of England is, to a certain extent, like the territory in which it prevails, of an *insulated* and peculiar character. It must be acknowledged that it has borrowed less than any other State in Christendom from the jurisprudence of ancient and modern Rome. The fountains of wisdom, experience and written reason, at which the European continent in former and America in later times have so largely drank, were passed by in England with a hasty and scanty draught.' *Civil and canon law* p. 4.

[30] *Ibid.*, pp. 16–17.

Two noble liars' accounts of international law: Holland and Oppenheim

A fourth and final view of customary law shares the natural lawyers' belief that discrimination is required between customary practices that should be treated as giving rise to fundamental rules and those that should not. But this group, which I will call that of noble liars, believes that no sufficiently justifiable natural laws or fundamental moral principles have yet been found. Consequently, for noble liars, discrimination among customary practices relies at root on a decision that aspires to nobility but is ungrounded in justified moral principles: it relies on *political rather than rational* judgment.[31] For noble liars, analysis of customary practices cannot really offer a set of rational principles, but in so far as (and only in so far as) some set of principles is needed to sustain legal and political stability, that set should be imposed as if it did actually underpin customary law. The noble liar – or in contemporary terms 'spin doctor' – deliberately weaves a misleading story in defence of his politically noble position. This spirit is expressed vividly by Montesquieu, writing in his *Persian Letters* that 'justice is eternal and does not depend on human conventions; and, if it were to, this would be a terrible truth, one which one would have to hide from oneself'.[32]

Holland on the scaffolding needed for the building of international law

Two short books on international law by Thomas Holland[33] emerge from an intellectual tradition that represented much that 'liberal conservative' practitioners like Phillimore opposed. Holland never practised as an advocate or judge. Elected to a fellowship of All Souls in 1875, he was best known for his *Elements of Jurisprudence*, widely used until soon after his death as the standard textbook on analytical jurisprudence

[31] Cf. Jeremy Waldron 'Legal and political philosophy' in Coleman and Shapiro eds. *The Oxford handbook of jurisprudence and philosophy of law* (2002) 352 at p. 377: 'In the contested issues of politics, objective truth never manifests itself *in propria persona*; it presents itself always as someone's opinion, usually someone's contested opinion; and it cannot be made politically effective, nor the condition for any political action unless someone's determination is taken for practical purposes as the truth of the matter.'

[32] '[L]a justice est éternelle et ne dépend point des conventions humaines; et, quand elle en dépendrait, ce serait une verité terrible, qu'il faudrait se dérober à soi-même.' *Lettres Persanes: LXXXIII.*

[33] 27 *Dictionary of National Biography* pp. 699–700.

(outlining elements of the work of Jeremy Bentham and John Austin). His posthumously published *Lectures in International Law* were given as Chichele Professor of International Law at Oxford (a chair to which he was elected in 1910).

Although in no sense a textbook in the league of Phillimore, Hall or Oppenheim, the second lecture in his book (on the sources of international law) gives a very clear sense of the difference between his vision of international law and that of Phillimore. While for Phillimore international law was built around the principles fundamental to a 'community' of Christian civil and canon lawyers, for Holland both civil and canon law were 'withdrawn' at the Reformation and natural law arguments were needed as a 'noble lie' to *create* the community that could give rise to the traditional practices assumed by a midwife:

> A system of law had to be constructed which was not, like all other systems of law, supported by the force of a political society. The talk about a Law of Nature disguised this lack of a firm foundation and so far supplied its place as to facilitate the formation of a gradually solidified structure of public opinion.[34]

After the Reformation, Holland argues, natural law was invoked as 'a legal fiction':

> The talk about it no doubt served a useful purpose. What was written about it ... was a convenient, though merely temporary, scaffolding employed while the edifice of international law was a-building, the two pillars which used to support it [civil and canon law] having been withdrawn. (Like the wooden 'centering' upon which an arch is put together, stone by stone, but which is knocked away as soon as the arch is strong enough to span the air by virtue merely of its own proper strength.)[35]

Holland asserts that, in dealing with any uncodified system of law, a student requires 'scientific equipment' to enable him 'to cut a path for himself through the tangled growth of enactment and precedent, and so to codify for his own purposes'.[36] In the case of international law, Holland argues that the task of a contemporary writer is to present a reader with this 'equipment' by tracing 'the axioms of the science and the doctrines of received text-writers'.[37] While the relevant materials 'can only be presented by History', the 'task of Jurisprudence' is one

[34] *Ibid.*, pp. 18–19. [35] Holland *Lectures in international law* p. 18.
[36] Holland *Elements of jurisprudence* (7th edn, 1895) p. 1. [37] *Ibid.*, p. 379.

'which only begins when the facts begin to fall into an order other than the historical, and arrange themselves in groups which have no relation to the varieties of the human race':

> In the satisfaction of their needs mankind have seldom seen clearly the ends at which they were aiming, and have therefore in reaching after those ends invented a vast variety of perverse complications. The unity, in short, which it is the business of Jurisprudence to exhibit as underlying all the phenomena which it investigates, is the late discovery of an advanced civilisation, and was unperceived during much of the time during which those phenomena were accumulating.[38]

Holland's 'axioms' are not discerned through careful study of customary practices: they are the fruits of 'scientific' and logical reflection on the 'needs of mankind', tools with which the Jurisprude must be equipped *before* venturing into a jungle of customary law. Nowhere does Holland defend or aim to justify these axioms. On one reading, his 'scientific axioms' are simply rival principles of natural law; on a second interpretation, just as, as he had argued, the noble lie of natural law had been needed in the past to transform public opinion, so Holland believed his set of scientific principles was needed to solidify turn-of-the-century public opinion.

Rather than developing these two interpretations of Holland's work, my focus here will be on the analogous interpretations possible of the far more influential account of international law offered in Oppenheim's *Treatise*. Holland's earlier *Studies in International Law* were published in 1898, three years after Oppenheim's arrival in England – and the year in which Oppenheim was appointed as a lecturer in international law at the LSE.[39] Oppenheim (1858–1919) initially lectured at the University of Freiburg im Breisgau and then at Basel, becoming well known for his work on criminal law, but also teaching the philosophy of law, constitutional law and international law. At the age of thirty-seven, he moved to

[38] *Ibid*., pp. 11–12.

[39] Oppenheim lists Holland's *Studies* and his *Elements of jurisprudence* as books 'very often referred to' in his own *Treatise* (and as such ones for which he uses abbreviations: see the first edition at pp. xi–xii), but he does not discuss Holland in his summary of British treatises on international law or in his discussion of early-twentieth-century developments in international law (see the first edition at pp. 87, 90–3). Holland is mentioned *only* twice in the first volume, both times in short bibliographical references to legal positivist discussions in the *Studies*, one on the 'Relations between international and municipal law' (*Treatise I* p. 25, citing *Studies* pp. 176–200) and the other on 'The science of the law of nations' (*Treatise I* p. 76, citing *Studies* pp. 1–58 and 168–75).

England and 'since he could not hope to continue his criminal-law studies in a common-law system, he instead turned his attentions to the universal topic of international law, which transcended all common- or civil-law boundaries'.[40] He arrived to live at the Albany in Picadilly in 1895, the year in which the LSE was founded. In 1908, he was (apparently with reluctance on his part) elected to the Whewell Chair of International Law at Cambridge on the strength of the impression made by the first edition of his *Treatise* on the retiring Whewell Professor, John Westlake.[41]

Oppenheim on the background ideals needed by an international lawyer

What distinguishes the early editions of Oppenheim's *Treatise* from those of its rivals above? Oppenheim himself claims in the first edition that there is 'no English treatise which provides such a bibliography' as those printed at the start of each section (giving lists of treatises and monographs). While Oppenheim's choice of format (giving bibliographical lists) and the structure of his book *were* different from those found in Phillimore or Hall, Oppenheim's format and structure closely follows standard German treatments of the time.[42] And Oppenheim's range of references is far narrower and thinner than that found in Phillimore: Oppenheim's table of cases in the first volume of his *Treatise* is only one side long, citing fifty-four cases – as against, for example, nine sides of cases cited in only the first of Phillimore's four volumes. Oppenheim himself acknowledges in his *Treatise* that: 'Generations to come will consult Phillimore's volumes on account of the vast material they contain and the sound judgment they exhibit.'[43]

But what did distinguish Oppenheim's *Treatise* from those by Phillimore or Hall is that it offered an explicitly positivist account of international law. For Oppenheim, international law must be treated as

[40] J.L. Brierly, 'Oppenheim, Lassa Francis Lawrence (1858–1919)' 41 *Dictionary of National Biography* pp. 899–900. How far if at all anti-Semitism influenced the move is unknown. Brierly writes that 'His was not a strong constitution, and he felt that the English climate and mode of life would suit him. It was also convenient in that his brother had been living in London for some time.'

[41] 'Oppenheim was not originally a candidate for the post, but on Westlake's insisting on his standing he finally consented to do so and was elected.' Whittuck, 1 BYIL 1 at p. 6.

[42] Reisman notes that Oppenheim 'largely follows the table of contents of Johann Bluntschli's work on international law' (*Lassa Oppenheim's nine lives* at p. 263).

[43] Oppenheim *Treatise I* (1st edn) at section 59 p. 91.

inherently separable from moral principles, natural law and national legal systems:

> If we exclude the law of nature and what is called 'natural' international law altogether, and if we consider international law real law, the method to be applied by the science of international law can be no other than the positive method . . . The positive method is that applied by the science of law in general, and it demands that whatever the aims and ends of a worker and researcher may be, he must start from the existing recognized rules of international law as they are to be found in the customary practice of the states or in law-making conventions.[44]

For a natural lawyer like Brierly or Phillimore, international law is best understood as the development or fleshing out in customary law of under-determined principles of natural law. But, like Holland, Oppenheim argued that natural law theories had been politically necessary to nurture international law, but that this noble lie was no longer needed:

> The Law of Nations supplied the crutches with whose help history has taught mankind to walk out of the institutions of the Middle Ages into those of modern times . . . We know nowadays that a Law of Nature does not exist. Just as the so-called Natural Philosophy had to give way to real natural science, so the Law of Nature had to give way to jurisprudence, or the philosophy of the positive law. Only a positive Law of Nations can be a branch of the science of law.[45]

Oppenheim fears that basing international law on natural law arguments can offer 'a breach through which the deniers of the law of nations can easily come in and attack the very existence of international law': they are 'not only without any value whatever, but directly detrimental' because they distract a writer from what should be a focus on real practice, real facts, and so real law. A theory of natural law 'weakens the eyes of those who profess it', it 'prevents the criticism of the existing positive law' and 'constantly mixes up the past, the present and the future': its place 'is no longer in our textbooks, law schools, and universities, but in the museums where the scientific tools are preserved with which future generations did their best to lay the foundation of our

[44] Oppenheim 'The science of international law: its task and method' 3 AJIL (1908) 313 at p. 333.

[45] *Treatise I* (1st edn) at sections 53 and 59.

present scientific knowledge'.[46] Not only are natural law theories untenable,[47] they also obscure the real foundations of international law:

> It requires much more scientific skill to expose the real existing rules of international law, to lay bare their history and real meaning, and to criticize them in the light of reason, justice, and the requirements of the age, than to teach the rules of the law of nature in the clouds.[48]

The customary practice of states, asserts Oppenheim, just *is* a matter of rules, rules whose existence is a matter for *empirical* observation. As an example, Oppenheim offers Great Britain, where 'a good many rules of law rise every year from Acts of Parliament. "Source of law" is therefore the name for a historical fact out of which rules of conduct rise into existence and legal force.'[49] Yet elsewhere Oppenheim acknowledges that historical 'facts' generate rules thanks to pre-existing customs on what constitutes a source of law, so 'all statute or written law is based on unwritten law in so far as the power of Parliament to make statute law is given to Parliament by unwritten law'.[50] And customary or unwritten international law exists 'when a clear and continuous habit of doing certain actions has grown up under the aegis of the conviction that these actions are, according to International Law, obligatory or right'.[51]

What then is this crucial 'conviction' which transforms customary usage or habit into an obligatory rule? Oppenheim argues that usage is transformed into a moral rule 'if by *common consent* of the community it applies to conscience and to *conscience only*; whereas, on the other hand, a rule is a rule of law, if by *common consent* of the community it shall eventually be *enforced by external power*'.[52] A practice or usage of states is

[46] Oppenheim 'The science of international law' at p. 329.

[47] A claim which Oppenheim backs up by arguing both that 'the innumerable systems' of natural lawyers conflict, and that 'it is impossible to find a law which has its roots in human reason only and is above legislation and customary law': 'The science of international law'at p. 330.

[48] *Ibid.*

[49] *Treatise I* (1st edn) at section 15: 'Just as we see streams of water running over the earth, so we see, as it were, streams of rules running over the area of law'; rules of law 'rise from facts in the historical development of a community'.

[50] *Treatise I* (1st edn) at section 4. [51] *Ibid.*, section 17.

[52] *Ibid.*, section 4 (my emphasis). By enforcement, Oppenheim explains that, given 'the absence of a central authority for the enforcement of the rules of the Law of Nations, the States have to take the law into their own hands. Self-help, and intervention on the part of other States which sympathise with the wronged one, are the means by which the rules of the Law of Nations can be and actually are enforced.' *Ibid.*, section 9.

transformed into a moral rule if 'common consent' recognises it as a rule but not an enforceable one: common consent distinguishes rules that a state may defend with force (rules of international law) from moral rules (which states may not in law use force to defend). And how is this crucial 'common consent' to be discerned? For Oppenheim, it is not found in the scholarly Anglican and civilian consensus of Phillimore, nor in the contemporary Anglo-American consensus of Hall, but in

> the express or tacit consent of such an overwhelming majority of the members that those who dissent are of no importance whatever, and disappear totally from the view of one who looks for the will of the community as an entity in contradistinction to the wills of its members. The question whether there be such a common consent in a special case, is *not a question of theory, but of fact only*. It is a matter of observation and appreciation, and not of logical and mathematical decision, just as is the well-known question, How many grains make a heap?[53]

Oppenheim contends that the contents and existence of rules of international law can be determined as a matter 'of fact only', without involving evaluation on the part of the writer. Discerning these facts will require reference to states' views – which themselves *will* often be manifest within particular moral or political or domestic legal arguments – but that discernment itself remains. Oppenheim treats social reality as a matter of fact from start to end – although those facts include the meanings or subjective intentions with which particular governments, diplomats, legislators or courts act.[54]

Yet, in focusing on the understandings and judgments of state officials, Oppenheim is not concerned with the non-arbitrary verification of an empiricist: he is acting as an interpreter, aiming to tease out shared meanings, understandings and judgments. He aims to attain a greater clarity of understanding than the officials involved – an understanding

[53] *Ibid.*, section 11.

[54] For Oppenheim, although Phillimore was 'a powerful author . . . who may on the whole be called a Positivist of the same kind as Martens and Klüber', he 'applies the natural Law of Nations to fill up the gaps of the positive'. As such, Phillimore's *Commentaries* were inadequate, based ultimately on 'no real Positivism since these authors recognised a natural Law of Nations, although they did not make much use of it'. *Treatise I* (1st edn) at section 59 pp. 91–2, continuing: 'Real positivism must entirely avoid a natural Law of Nations.' Even the celebrated textbook by his former teacher, Bluntschli, 'must, in spite of the world-wide fame of its author, be consulted with caution, because it contains many rules which are not yet recognised rules of the Law of Nations': *Treatise I* (1st edn) at section 59 pp. 92–3.

that enables him to show not only 'how things have grown in the past, but also to extract a moral for the future out of the events of the past'. Five morals, Oppenheim argues, 'can be said to be deduced from the history of the development of the Law of Nations':

1. first, and principally, that international law can exist 'only if there is an equilibrium, a balance of power, between the members of the Family of Nations';
2. that international politics, and in particular the use of force, should be conducted 'on the basis of real State interests' *rather than* to preserve dynasties or to act 'in favour of legitimacy';
3. 'that the principle of nationality is of such force that it is fruitless to stop its victory', so international politics should 'enforce the rule that minorities of invididuals of another race shall not be outside the law, but shall be treated on equal terms with the majority';
4. that 'every progress in the development of International Law wants due time to ripen', although the establishment of the Permanent Court of Arbitration in The Hague and the codification of parts of the Law of Nations (which 'will in due time arrive' following the Geneva Conventions on land warfare) will 'make the legal basis of international intercourse firmer, broader, and more prominent than before'; and
5. 'that the progressive development of International Law depends chiefly upon the standard of public morality on the one hand, and, on the other, upon economic interests', and that it may 'fearlessly be maintained that an immeasurable progress is guaranteed to International Law, since there are eternal moral and economic factors working in its favour'.[55]

Oppenheim later added two more morals, both defending a notion of an international rule of law: one new moral connects the progress of international law with the 'victory everywhere of constitutional government over autocratic government, or, what is the same thing, of democracy over autocracy'; the other links the progress of international law with the 'prevailing' of 'the legal school of international jurists' (who aim at 'codification of firm, decisive, and unequivocal rules of International Law' and work for the establishment of international courts') over the 'diplomatic school' (which 'considers International

[55] *Ibid.*, section 51.

Law to be, and prefers it to remain, rather a body of elastic principles than of firm and precise rules').[56]

These morals show how Oppenheim's work was consciously intended to *alter* state officials' actions (often radically) in so far as his 'morals' would be internalised as their own self-interpretations: no more striving at hegemony nor use of force to preserve dynasties or to restore a legitimate successor; minorities to be treated on equal terms with the majority; the Court of Arbitration and general codification projects to be supported with fearless confidence that international law (and, with the later morals, the rule of international law more generally) will 'progress'.

Indeed, Oppenheim treats it as a 'grave sin of method' in treatise-writing to 'pile case upon case ... without sifting them and without abstracting the rules they are supposed to bring into view', a practice that is 'without any value for the science of international law, unless it is done only for the purpose of collecting material'.[57] A writer who avoids this 'sin' *must* 'sift' and evaluate cases in the light of a liberal internationalist vision.

What then is the point of Oppenheim's repeated insistence that he is acting as a scientific observer, delivering rules of international law which do *not* rely on – and are necessarily separable from – any moral or political principles? One way of understanding Oppenheim's separability claim is as an insistence on the separation of correct, objective principles which *are* a source of scientific law from the conventionally accepted but unfounded principles of natural lawyers. In Oppenheim's case, these scientific principles build on his belief in there being a society of states, in the importance of a balance of powers, and his 'faith in the progress of nations towards peace and civilization'. The science of

56 For a thought-provoking (and generally sympathetic) discussion of Oppenheim's morals, see Benedict Kingsbury 'Legal positivism as normative politics: international society, balance of power and Lassa Oppenheim's positive international law' 13 EJIL (2002) 401; and a series of essays on Oppenheim by Matthias Schmoekel: 'The internationalist as a scientist and herald' 11 EJIL (2000) 699 at pp. 699–700; 'The story of a success: Lassa Oppenheim and his "International Law"' in Michael Stolleis and Masahuru Yanagihara eds. *East Asian and European perspectives on international law* (Baden-Baden, 2004) p. 57; 'Lassa Oppenheim' in Jack Beatson and Reinhard Zimmermann eds. *Jurists uprooted: German-speaking emigré lawyers in twentieth-century Britain* (Oxford, 2004) p. 583; and 'Consent and caution: Lassa Oppenheim and his reaction to World War I' in Randall Lesaffer ed. *Peace treaties and international law in European history* (Cambridge, 2004) p. 270.

57 Oppenheim 'The science of international law' at pp. 340–1.

international law can be conducted 'only by those workers who are imbued with the idealistic outlook on life and matters':

> International law is at present an unfinished and uncrowned system and building. He who has no faith in the possibility of accomplishing it is not wanted among us. We require men possessed of that idealism which sits down to historical research because it sees the present and the future in the past, and the past in the present and future, although it does not confound them; which criticises the existing law for the purpose, not of pulling it to pieces, but of preparing its improvement and its codification; which believes in the good instincts of the masses and therefore helps to popularize international law in the hope of thereby improving international relations and working for the cause of peace.[58]

So Oppenheim's account of international law *does* depend upon and is structured around specific moral and political principles, principles that he believes would lie at the core of the international practices of an imagined world of 'peace and civilization' – even if not at the core of the current, real one. As such, his principles are utopian ones in the true sense of More's word: they belong to 'no-place', to a world other than our own. Oppenheim relies on those utopian principles to structure his account of the international law which he hopes will transform the illiberal practices of states in his own time.

Oppenheim seems to equate the scientific principles on which he builds his account of the rules of international law with what he believes are justified or truly moral principles or 'ideals'. Does this make his 'science' simply a rival natural law theory, one more progressivist or less conservative than Phillimore's?[59]

Oppenheim's insistence on the separability of his legal account from moral claims seems best understood as a noble lie, a *political* claim which he knows is untrue. He believes his utopian ideals need to be disguised or hidden as the science of international law will succeed only if 'all authors endeavour to write in a truly international and independent spirit, and . . . to *keep in the background* their individual ideas concerning *politics, morality, humanity, and justice*'.[60]

[58] *Ibid.*, pp. 355–6.

[59] This seems to be the category into which Brierly would place Oppenheim (text above, pp. 235–6).

[60] Oppenheim 'The science of international law' at p. 354 (my emphasis).

A classical noble liar would see her noble lie as one which it is hoped philosophers will one day find a convincing way of justifying. In the meantime, her separability claim encourages commitment to her account of international law (and so, in effect, to enlightened principles and ideals) while reassuring governments of the separability of law from contentious moral principles and ideals. Scientific international law would then encourage a gradual conversion from conventional practices into enlightened ones respecting Oppenheim's 'background' ideals (for which no sufficient justification has yet been found): the grounds of political or moral and legal judgment (*mores* and enlightened principles) will eventually coincide as law transforms discordant conventional practices and beliefs into the harmonious enlightened ones of his utopia.[61]

This is the picture of Oppenheim presented unwittingly by Schmoekel, who argues that Oppenheim 'had to discuss the principles so that the new law became intelligible'. For Schmoekel, it 'is of little importance whether science is regarded as an independent source of law or – as Oppenheim did – as a means to perceive the law so that it gradually becomes accepted through consent or custom'.[62] The summary of Oppenheim's position is apposite, but the comment seems less so: as we have seen, Oppenheim argues that common consent to enforcement is the only marker that distinguishes a rule of international law from other customary rules and habits. If the principles 'perceived' by Oppenheim are not yet accepted, let alone accepted as enforceable principles, then on Oppenheim's own definition they are at best political or moral *rather than* legal principles.

For Oppenheim, moral rules result from a concordance of free, conscientious opinions: a rule 'is a moral rule, if by common consent of the community it applies to conscience and to conscience only'.[63] On Oppenheim's own account of the common consent or opinion needed to justify a moral rule, he seems to have thought that a satisfactory justification for his liberal principles would be found when, and only when, those principles came to be widely accepted – something which would happen when, and only in so far as, public opinion came to be

[61] Opinions of 'famous writers', he explains, 'may influence the growth of International Law' by 'creating usages which gradually turn into custom'. *Treatise I* (1st edn) at section 19 p. 24.

[62] Schmoekel 'Consent and caution' (above, note 56) at p. 288 and n. 127.

[63] E.g. *Treatise I* (1st edn) at section 4 p. 8.

transformed in line with his fifth moral.[64] And, for Oppenheim, the best hope for this transformation was through the teachings of his textbook.

Conclusion: morals for contemporary writers on customary international law

This essay has suggested that influential English treatises on international law rely on three strikingly different assumptions about what renders a statement of international law correct or authoritative. These assumptions reflect distinctive accounts of the nature of international law, and more specifically of the relationship between reasoned argument and the practices of states. Hall, Phillimore and Oppenheim were all knowledgeable scholars of international law yet they assumed different criteria for the ultimate validity of rules of international law. Could any moral be drawn by contemporary writers on which approach is best? How is the superiority of one account, one interpretation, one set of principles to be shown?

If one follows Charles Taylor in his essay on 'Interpretation and the Sciences of Man', then one must turn to the classical argument that 'from the more adequate position one can understand one's own stand and that of one's opponent, but not the other way around'. But, as Taylor acknowledges, this argument only has weight for those in the superior position. Those in the less adequate position will be told that it is not simply that they do not understand, but that they will need to change themselves *in order* to understand: 'Our capacity to understand is rooted in our own self-definitions hence in what we are.'[65] Must the last word be Simpson's suggestion that fellow lawyers and students will buy different textbooks on the same subject simply *because* they are different?

Pollock and Hall seemed to assume that the continued acceptance of a rule of customary international law manifests the benign spirit sustaining an international legal system. As a midwife hopes to intervene as

[64] As Kingsbury highlights, Oppenheim's view of the role of public opinion in international law matters 'was at the cautious end of the spectrum prevalent in late-Victorian and early Edwardian England: a liberal disposition to regard it as part of achieving progress in law and public policy, epitomized by Dicey's *Law and public opinion in England*, but a lack of conviction that a truly international public opinion was really possible.' 'Legal positivism' (above, note 56) at p. 411, referring to Carty *The decay of international law* (Manchester, 1986) at p. 90.

[65] Charles Taylor 'Interpretation and the sciences of man' pp. 53–4.

little as possible at the birth of a baby and ideally not at all, so these midwives of customary international law believe that the relevant rules will emerge from legal practices, as they do so pointing their own way out of any apparent internal conflict: on such accounts, the treatise writer's influence reflects and can be but a product of influences at play within a professional tradition; a tradition focused on resolving practical problems. The treatise is a training manual, designed to familiarise students – and the more forgetful practitioner – of past practice. Any grander ambitions to articulate fundamental principles prior to and constraining of practice are misplaced.[66]

Pearce Higgins took on the task of editing what proved to be the final two editions[67] of Hall's *Treatise*, explaining that it was because Hall 'went below the surface of positive rules and examined and criticised the principles upon which they purported to be based, that his work remains of such permanent value to students of International Law'.[68] Driving his fondness for those criticisms, according to McNair, was Higgins' 'desire to introduce a breath of realism into the rather academic and idealistic atmosphere which marks much of the literature of international law': he was 'attracted by what has been called Hall's *méthode historico-pratique*, by his cautious scepticism concerning idealistic proposals, and by his frequent but discriminating preference of the British view upon any incident or practice or rule where there was room for legitimate doubt'.[69]

For Oppenheim, although Hall was 'an excellent international jurist' and his treatise 'one of the best books on the Law of Nations that have

[66] Cf. James Crawford, arguing that just as 'art critics may influence the development of painting in a variety of ways, but it would be misleading to write a history of art by reference to their work', so the 'professional tradition of international law in Britain' has remained 'essentially distinct' from the 'secondary literature' of international law scholarship. James Crawford 'Public international law in twentieth-century England' in Beatson and Zimmerman eds. *Jurists uprooted: German-speaking emigré lawyers in twentieth-century Britain* (Oxford, 2004) p. 681 at pp. 693, 695. Although Ian Brownlie also insists, throughout the eight editions of his influential contemporary textbook, on a preference for 'practice over theory' (*International law* (8th edn) p. 34), his adoption of a midwife's position is a politically strategic one: in a recent lecture, his position is that of a progressivist noble liar. See Ian Brownlie 'Does international public order include the rule of law?' (Lauterpacht Research Centre for International Law, Cambridge, 22 October 2004).

[67] 7th edn, 1917; 8th edn, 1924, both Clarendon, Oxford.

[68] Preface to eighth edition, p. ix.

[69] McNair, obituary for Pearce Higgins, 22 *Proceedings of the British Academy* (1935) at p. 14.

ever been written',[70] his focus on the practice of English courts and the interests of the UK was a 'grave sin of method': Oppenheim numbered Hall among those jurists who 'fall on their knees and worship the decisions of the courts of their own country, while they abuse the differing decisions of foreign courts'.[71] And this 'sin of method' was aggravated by a second: as noted above, according to Oppenheim, Hall and writers like him 'pile case upon case ... without sifting them and without abstracting the rules they are supposed to bring into view', a practice which is 'without any value for the science of international law, unless it is done only for the purpose of collecting material'.[72]

Oppenheim's two criticisms of Hall sit ill together: he criticises Hall both for preferring decisions of British courts over those of other countries *and* for failing to 'sift' cases. The two criticisms are compatible only for one who shares Oppenheim's conviction that an account of international law must be structured around explicitly internationalist convictions, for one who believes that the only way a writer can really 'sift' cases on points of international law is by using a set of internationalist principles.[73]

Every treatise writer aims to sift cases and decisions to bring out a correct understanding of the rules of customary international law. In so far as the resolution of cases, of practical problems, requires systematised argument, every practitioner will also draw on some of the rival principles, criteria and arguments that structure contemporary textbooks. The question here is that of whether, and if so how, these structuring principles and arguments are justified.

For noble liars like Holland or Oppenheim, arguments in terms of the continued acceptance of a rule of customary law veil law-making by benign jurists and judges. These lawyers rely on their ideals, ideals for which they fear they cannot offer a convincing justification or at least not one that will be widely accepted: as such, their ideals need to be

[70] Oppenheim *Treatise I* (1st edn) at section 59 pp. 92–3.

[71] Oppenheim 'The science of international law: its task and method' 3 AJIL (1908) at 340–1.

[72] *Ibid.*

[73] For Oppenheim, a compelling account of international law must be motivated by 'the conviction that all the civilised States form one Community throughout the world in spite of the various factors which separate the nations from one another; the conviction that the interests of all the nations and States are indissolubly interknitted, and that, therefore, the Family of Nations must establish international institutions for the purpose of guaranteeing a more general and a more lasting peace than existed in former times'. Oppenheim *The League of Nations and its problems* (1919) p. 12.

disguised. Noble liars purport to offer an account of international law separated from contentious moral principles and utopian ideals – while structuring that very account in line with their liberal internationalist ideals. Their 'scientific' international law, they hope, will encourage a gradual transformation of discordant conventional practices and beliefs into the harmonious enlightened ones of their utopia.[74]

Here, then, my argument is converging with that of Oppenheim's later editor, Hersch Lauterpacht: 'Being unable to afford the consistency of totally ignoring both private and natural law, [modern positivist writers] put in their place "the reason of the thing", "the demands of logic", and "the principles of general jurisprudence" . . . – the very natural law from which they wish to purify the science of international law'[75] For natural lawyers like Phillimore and Brierly, the principles of natural law can only be understood through and drawn out of careful study of practice, but this study cannot be as passive as it is presented as being by the midwife: it must involve active attention, 'sifting' and interpretation. Reciprocally, for the natural lawyer, the continued acceptance of a rule of customary law is itself evidence of its links with anchoring principles of justice or natural law. Those principles include one recognising the moral value of a stable system of rules – something which the natural lawyer would argue that a noble liar undermines in imposing alien, utopian principles on a set of customary practices. Legal positivists like Oppenheim claim their accounts of international law focus only on hard facts and avoid all reliance on utopian ideals. The reverse is closer to the truth.

[74] Opinions of 'famous writers', he explains, 'may influence the growth of International Law' by 'creating usages which gradually turn into custom'. *Treatise I* (1st edn) at section 19 p. 24.

[75] Lauterpacht *Private law sources and analogies of international law* (1927) p. 33. In this early essay, Lauterpacht treats natural law as 'a purely abstract philosophy of law'; his later 'Grotian' account of natural law is closer to that outlined in the text.

11

Custom, common law reasoning and the law of nations in the nineteenth century

MICHAEL LOBBAN

The common law has long been explained as a customary system of law, rooted in consent, whose rules are both consonant to reason and flexible, allowing the law to develop in accordance with the 'felt necessities' of the community.[1] As such, it seems to have much in common with a law of nations founded on the consent of nations as well as reason, manifested in part by developing customary practices in the international community. Indeed, lawyers have gone so far as to state simply that the law of nations is part of the common law. In the words of Lord Denning:

> Seeing that the rules of international law have changed – and do change – and that the courts have given effect to the changes without any Act of Parliament, it follows to my mind inexorably that the rules of international law, as existing from time to time, do form part of our English law.[2]

Yet such a view has not been universally subscribed to. Many judges have taken a narrower approach, requiring norms of international law to be positively incorporated before they bind at common law. Nourse LJ, for instance, felt that established rules 'derived from one or more of the recognised sources of international law' are binding only when they have 'been carried into English law by statute, judicial decision or ancient custom'.[3]

It will be suggested in what follows that in the late eighteenth and nineteenth centuries – when the relationship between common law and international law was first extensively explored – common lawyers generally preferred the approach suggested by Nourse. Unlike international

[1] O. W. Holmes, *The Common Law* (Boston, 1881), pp. 1–2.

[2] *Trendtex Trading* v. *Bank of Nigeria* [1977] 1 QB 529 at 554G. See also *R* v. *Jones (Margaret) and Others* [2005] QB 259 at 272.

[3] *J. H. Rayner (Mincing Lane) Ltd* v. *Department of Trade and Industry* [1989] Ch 72 at 207.

lawyers, who argued that customary norms grew out of developing practices which became binding as a result of general use, common lawyers did not feel that community practices could by themselves generate binding norms. In their view, while community custom provided the historical foundation of the common law, its development was the preserve of judges. Community practices were only permitted to derogate from the common law where they were ancient and unchanging; and old common law could not be abrogated by new custom. Equally, although judges could incorporate newer customs and practices – whether domestic or international – in developing the common law, their authority and validity derived from the judicial decision and not from the custom itself. As shall be seen, the judges' attitude to their own custom informed their view of the law of nations. It was regarded as a source of law, to be incorporated when occasion suited; but it was not law itself.

The common law and custom

Common lawyers spoke of two kinds of custom. The first kind was 'general custom', or the common law in general. It was not made up of popular customs, but of 'legal customs' manifested 'in the records of the several courts of justice', and whose validity was determined by the judges.[4] As Thomas Hedley explained in 1610:

> the common law is a reasonable usage, throughout the whole realm, approved time out of mind in the king's courts of record which have jurisdiction over the whole kingdom, to be good and profitable for the commonwealth. But here because I make custom a part in my definition of the common law, I would not be mistaken, as though I meant to confound the common law with custom, which differ as much as artificial reason and bare precedents . . . [Common law] hath not custom for [its] next or immediate cause, but many other secondary reasons which be necessary consequence upon other rules and cases in law, which yet may be so deduced by degrees till it come to some primitive maxim, depending immediately upon some prescription or custom, in which secondary reasons and consequence appear as much art or learning, wisdom and excellency of reason as in any law, art of profession whatever.[5]

[4] *Commentaries on the Laws of England* (Oxford, 1765–9), vol. I, pp. 63–8.

[5] Elisabeth R. Foster (ed.), *Proceedings in Parliament 1610* (2 vols., New Haven, 1966), vol. 2, pp. 175–6. See also M. Lobban, *A History of Legal Philosophy in the Common Law World, 1600–1900* (forthcoming, 2006), pp. 36–7.

The common law was not developed in the community by the people, but was developed in court by the 'artificial reason' of judges.

Since custom was assumed to be the foundation rather than the animating spirit of the law, it was not much discussed. As Gould J observed in 1788, 'it was a singular task to be called upon to prove the general common law of the land: that depends on general knowledge, it being universally exercised, or so understood'.[6] Seeing community custom as foundational encouraged a conservative approach to fundamental questions. When Victorian and Edwardian women claimed the right to vote by invoking occasional medieval examples of female election, judges answered that 'uninterrupted usage' of exclusive male participation stood against them.[7] 'Only the clearest proof that a different state of things prevailed in ancient times could be entertained by a Court of law in probing the origin of so inveterate an usage', Lord Loreburn ruled in 1909: 'numberless rights rest upon a similar basis. Indeed, the whole body of the common law has no other foundation.'.[8] Attempts to invoke a developing usage which went against established principles did not go down well. Thus, in 1765, the King's Bench rejected an argument defending general warrants on the grounds of long usage by holding that 'no Usage or Custom whatever, can ever establish anything that is in its first Principles illegal'.[9]

The second kind was 'particular customs'. These were local community practices in derogation of the general common law. Local custom was invoked when rights were claimed for a distinct community, which rested on immemorial usage. No new custom could arise in derogation of the common law. Old ones which survived were presumed to be the remnants of community practices which predated the creation of a national, common law. Unlike the 'general custom' of the common law, they had to be pleaded and proved. Moreover, there were settled criteria customs had to satisfy to be valid. First, they had to be ancient and continuously practised. Although in theory customs had to be immemorial, it was accepted that it would be unreasonable to expect proof of the existence of a custom before the time of legal memory. Instead, proof was required 'as far back as living memory goes, of a

[6] *Steel* v. *Houghton* (1788) 1 H Bl 51 at 53.

[7] *Chorlton* v. *Lings* (1868) LR 4 CP 374 at 383.

[8] *Nairn* v. *University of St Andrews* [1909] AC 147 at 160, *per* Lord Loreburn LC. See also *Bebb* v. *Law Society* [1914] 1 Ch 286 at 297.

[9] James Oldham, *The Mansfield Manuscripts and the Growth of English Law in the Eighteenth Century* (2 vols., Chapel Hill, NC, 1992), vol. I, p. 204. The case is reported in 3 Burr 1742.

continuous, peaceable, and uninterrupted user of the custom'.[10] If it could be shown that the right claimed could not have been exercised in 1189, then subsequent usage could not establish it.[11] But this did not mean that customary rights were wholly static, for one was permitted to use modern methods to exercise a right which could be ancient.[12]

Secondly, to be valid, customs had to be certain, '[b]ecause if it be not certain, it cannot be proved to have been time out of mind; for how can anything be said to have been time out of mind when it is not certain what it is?'[13] It had to be certain which particular individuals were entitled to them, for 'what is common to all mankind, can never be claimed as a custom'.[14] The need for certainty was often stressed to protect those over whose land customary rights were claimed. Thus, in *Blewett* v. *Tregonning* (1835), an attempt to claim a customary right to collect sand blown onto the plaintiff's land failed, since such a right might end with all the plaintiff's soil being removed.[15] But where a custom was 'seasonably' exercised – such as dancing round a Maypole once a year – it was permitted, being certain in scope.[16]

Thirdly, customs had to be reasonable in the eyes of the court. In Matthew Bacon's words, 'every custom which appears to have been unreasonable in itself, as being against the good of the commonwealth, or injurious to a multitude, though beneficial to a particular person, or owe its commencement to the arbitrary will and oppression of a powerful lord, and not to the voluntary agreement of the parties, is void'.[17]

[10] *Bastard* v. *Smith* (1837) 2 Moo & Rob 129 at 136.

[11] See, e.g., *Simpson* v. *Wells* (1872) LR 7 QB 214.

[12] *Mercer* v. *Denne* [1905] 2 Ch 538 at 581 (CA) (concerning the drying of fishing nets using modern methods). It should be noted that courts were to consider the reasonableness of a custom *at its inception* (*ibid.*, 557; cf. *Tyson* v. *Smith* (1838) 9 A & E 406 at 423).

[13] *Broadbent* v. *Wilks* (1742) Willes 360 at 361.

[14] *Fitch* v. *Rawling* (1795) 2 H Bl 393 at 398. See also *Selby* v. *Robinson* (1788) 2 TR 758; *Edwards* v. *Jenkins* [1896] 1 Ch 308.

[15] *Blewett* v. *Tregonning* (1835) 3 Ad & E 554. Cf. *Wilson* v. *Willes* (1806) 7 East 121; and *Sowerby* v. *Coleman* (1867) LR 2 Exch 96.

[16] *Hall* v. *Nottingham* (1875) 1 Ex D 1; *Mounsey* v. *Ismay* (1863) 1 H & C 729. See also *Abercromby* v. *Fermoy Town Commissioners* (1900) 1 IR 302 at 314, where Holmes LJ, protecting the rights of the inhabitants of the town to a promenade, noted that 'our law has always recognised that the people of a district – a town, a parish, or a hamlet – are capable of acquiring by dedication or custom, certain rights over land which cannot be gained by the general public'.

[17] M. Bacon, *A New Abridgment of the Law* (London, 1832), vol. 2, p. 567.

Thus, in 1676, a custom of Canterbury to ride Skimington – to shame a cuckolded husband – was held ill.[18] What criteria were used to determine whether a custom was reasonable? In 1907, Parker J ruled that it involved an appeal to higher criteria than the rules or maxims of the common law (since local customs were permitted to derogate from them), but it did not involve an appeal to the reason of the average human being. In his view, to be valid, a custom 'must be such that, in the opinion of a trained lawyer, it is consistent, or at any rate, not inconsistent with those general principles which, quite apart from particular rules or maxims, lie at the root of our legal system'.[19]

Besides such communal, customary rights, rights over the property of others – such as to take profits from the soil of another, as by grazing one's beasts or digging in the soil – could be acquired by freeholders by prescription.[20] Although often regarded as customary by their claimants, these rights were seen by courts as property rights originating in lawful past grants.[21] If no particular grant could be produced, the claimant had to show that the right had been held since time immemorial by the person seised in fee of the land in question, and his predecessors.[22] The right did not come merely from enjoyment for a given period, however long, but 'on the assumption, when possession or enjoyment had been carried back as far as living memory would go, that a grant had once existed which had since been lost'.[23] Although rights to *profits à prendre* could be claimed as a matter of custom (rather than prescription) by copyhold tenants,[24] there was also a presumption

[18] *R* v. *Roberts* (1676) 2 Keb 578.

[19] *Johnson* v. *Clark* [1908] 1 Ch 303 at 311. In this case, he held void a custom which allowed a married woman to dispose of her real property with the consent of her husband but without her separate examination 'as conflicting with the general principle of the common law that an exercise of free will was essential to alienations and contracts, and that a married woman was not in a position to execrise such free will' (at 318).

[20] *Grimstead* v. *Marlowe* (1792) 4 TR 717 at 718; *Hardy* v. *Hollyday* (1763) 4 TR 718. The rule derived from *Gateward's Case* (1608) 6 Co Rep 59b. See also *Constable* v. *Nicholson* (1863) 14 CB NS 230 at 240.

[21] See *Gateward's case* (1608) 6 Co Rep 60b.

[22] That is 'tous ceux que estate il ad' (all those whose estate he had), from whence came the expression to 'prescribe in a que estate'.

[23] *Bryant* v. *Foot* (1867) LR 2 QB 161 at 179.

[24] 'For a copyholder hath a customary interest in the house, &c and therefore he may have a customary common in the lord's wastes; and in such case he cannot prescribe in the name of the lord, for the lord cannot claim common in his own soil, and therefore of necessity such custom ought to be alledged.' *Gateward's Case* (1608) 6 Co Rep 60b.

of a past grant in these cases,[25] since (as Lord Cranworth observed in 1861) the relation between lord and tenants 'must have had its origin in remote times by agreement'.[26]

As they did with proof of custom, so courts relaxed the rule according to which the prescriptive right should have been shown to have existed since 1189. In the late eighteenth century, judges began to tell juries that they could infer a lost grant or deed from twenty years' uninterrupted enjoyment. Judges soon came to treat twenty years' user as conclusive, so that a jury could find the right to exist even if they had no belief that any grant had ever been made;[27] and the Prescription Act of 1832 enacted that it was only necessary to show twenty years' use in cases of rights of way or easement, and thirty years in case of claims to *profits à prendre*.[28] But no amount of prescription could give validity to any right which was not capable of being granted.[29] In contrast to local customs, which by their nature were incompatible with the common law, rights acquired by prescription had to be lawful. Unlike local customs, by contrast, rights acquired by prescription did not have to pass a reasonableness test.

Local customary practice thus could not generate new law. Although new rights could be acquired by prescription, it was on the assumption of a positive grant of rights over property which the courts would recognise. But, where a customary right was claimed in the community, it had to be ancient and reasonable by the criteria of the judges.

The common law and the custom of merchants

Although the judges' view of how to handle local customary law encouraged a static approach, the common law was famously a system which grew to reflect the needs of the age. In developing it, judges often drew

25 For another customary economic right which the court sought to root in a grant or agreement, see *Tyson* v. *Smith* (1838) 9 Ad & E 406 at 425–6.

26 *Marquis of Salisbury* v. *Gladstone* (1861) 9 HLC 692 at 701–2.

27 See *Holcroft* v. *Heel* (1799) 1 B & P 400; *Campbell* v. *Wilson* (1803) 3 East 294; notes to *Yard* v. *Ford* 2 Wms Saund 172; *The King* v. *Joliffe* (1823) 2 B & C 54 at 59; *Jenkins* v. *Harvey* (1835) 1 CM & R 877 at 894; *Shepherd* v. *Payne* (1864) 16 CB NS 132. But contrast Lord Ellenborough's comments in *Hendy* v. *Stephenson* (1808) 10 East 55 at 60. The notion that the legal presumption is not to be displaced by showing no grant was in fact made was affirmed in *Dalton* v. *Angus* (1881) 6 App Cas 740.

28 2 & 3 Will. 4, c. 71.

29 See *Lockwood* v. *Wood* (1844) 6 QB 50 at 64; *Attorney General* v. *Mathias* (1858) 4 K & J 579.

on customary practices outside the court as a source when making decisions. This is most clearly seen in their use of the custom of merchants. To some, the law of merchants appeared to be 'a branch of the law of nations' applied by the common law.[30] As Blackstone put it:

> the affairs of commerce are regulated by a law of their own, called the law merchant, or *lex mercatoria*, which all nations agree in and take notice of. And in particular the law of England does in many cases refer itself to it, and leaves the causes of merchants to be tried by their own peculiar customs.[31]

But this was misleading. While the law of merchants was a part of the common law, it was so in the same way that 'general' customs were, and not in the way that 'particular' customs were. That is, once a customary rule had been incorporated into the common law by judicial pronouncement, it became a matter under the control of the judges of Westminster Hall, rather than a matter of customary fact whose existence was to be proved by merchants. As Lord Mansfield put it, once a point of commercial law was 'solemnly settled, no particular usage shall be admitted to weigh against it: this would send everything to sea again.' Foster J added:

> This word custom is apt to mislead our ideas. The custom of merchants, as far as the law regards it, is the custom of England; and therefore Lord Coke calls it, very properly, the law-merchant. We should not confound general customs with special local customs.[32]

Once a point of commercial law was settled, it could be extended by the judges in the same way that other rules were extended – by analogy with existing rules or by invoking commercial convenience – without needing to take evidence of commercial practice. It was in this way that late-eighteenth- and early-nineteenth-century judges developed rules establishing which kinds of financial instruments were negotiable.[33] But, where they were in doubt with regard to newly developing instruments, they continued to resort to evidence of commercial custom before recognising them.[34]

[30] 4 *Comm.* 67. [31] 1 *Comm.* 263–4.

[32] *Edie and Laird* v. *The East India Company* (1760) 1 W Black 295 at 298, 299. See also *Brandao* v. *Barnett* (1846) 12 Cl & F 787 at 805.

[33] *Miller* v. *Race* (1758) 1 Burr 452 at 457; *Wookey* v. *Pole* (1820) 4 B & Ald 1; *Gorgier* v. *Mieville* (1824) 3 B & C 45.

[34] See Lord Esher's comments in *Picker* v. *The London and County Banking Company* (1887) 18 QBD 515 at 517–18 and in *Hogarth* v. *Latham & Co.* (1878) 3 QBD 643 at 651. See also *Bechuanaland Exploration Company* v. *London Trading Bank Ltd* [1898] 2 QB 658; and *Edelstein* v. *Schuler & Co.* [1902] 2 KB 144 at 155.

In the later nineteenth century, a dispute emerged over whether the law merchant was a fixed and ancient or an expanding and modern set of rules. In deciding in 1873 that debenture bonds could not be regarded as negotiable, since they were 'only of recent introduction', Blackburn J took the former approach. For him, current commercial practices could not be part of the 'ancient' law merchant.[35] But, two years later, Cockburn CJ condemned the 'view that the law merchant . . . is fixed and stereotyped, and incapable of being expanded and enlarged so as to meet the wants and requirements of trade'. There was no reason why new usages should be less eligible for incorporation into the common law than older ones:

> While we quite agree that the greater or less time during which a custom has existed may be material in determining how far it has generally prevailed, we cannot think that, if a usage is once shewn to be universal, it is the less entitled to prevail because it may not have formed part of the law merchant as previously recognised and adopted by the Courts.[36]

His view was not that new customs could overturn what had been incorporated into the common law and change its course, but rather that new customs could still be incorporated into it.[37]

Cockburn did not dissent from the view that the control of these commercial customs was for the judges. This can be seen from a test case on the practice of insurance average adjusters. In *Atwood* v. *Sellar*, the owners of a ship which had been damaged in a storm sought to have the cost of repairs treated as general average (and so to be paid for by all those who had a share in the adventure) rather than as particular average (to be paid by the party suffering the loss). At the trial, it was shown that the practice of English average adjusters over eighty years had been to regard this as particular average. Nonetheless, a majority of the Queen's Bench Division, including Cockburn, found that there was already a settled common law which established that this was general average, which could not be dislodged by later commercial practice. Since the practice went against the principles of the law of general average, '[i]t is not a custom which can be presumed to have had a legal origin'.[38] The

[35] *Crouch* v. *The Credit Foncier of England, Limited* (1873) LR 8 QB 374.

[36] *Goodwin* v. *Robarts and Others* (1875) LR 10 Ex 337 at 346, 356.

[37] For another view of the expansive nature of both the law merchant and the common law, see Bigham J in *Edelstein* v. *Schuler & Co.* [1902] 2 KB 144 at 155. See also *Rumball* v. *The Metropolitan Bank* (1877) 2 QBD 194.

[38] *Atwood and Others* v. *Sellar & Co.* (1879) 4 QBD 342 at 363.

decision was controversial for the real aim of the litigation was to make English law conformable with foreign practice, and thereby 'more consonant with strictly logical principles'. The dissenting Manisty J was unconvinced by the majority, finding himself 'at a loss to comprehend how the law of any particular nation as to general average can be arrived at except by ascertaining what has been, as a matter of fact, the usage and practice in such particular nation with regard to it'.[39]

Besides incorporating rules from the custom of merchants into the common law, judges in commercial cases interpreted contracts in the light of commercial custom, on the understanding that contracts incorporated – often by implication – the customs of the trade.[40] When commercial parties contracted on terms which contradicted common law rules, judges tested the terms by invoking notions of reasonableness which they used in other areas of custom. In *Robinson* v. *Mollett*, for instance, the House of Lords held invalid a custom (which went against a settled rule in the law of agency) among London tallow brokers to sell to their principals tallow which they had themselves already bought. In his advice to the Lords, Brett J held that, when a custom developed which was so one-sided to be fundamentally unjust – when it contradicted 'the fundamental ethical principles of right and wrong' – it would not be upheld.[41] But otherwise, mercantile business was to be left as free as possible.

Judges were thus enthusiastic about incorporating customary practices into the common law when they were beneficial to the community, and when they were turned into legal rules subject to their control. The customary norms were not considered to be binding of themselves: they were a source of law, rather than law itself. With these views of custom in mind, we can now turn to how they saw the customary system of international law.

The common law, reason and the law of nations

Common lawyers, who saw their system as founded on reason, were happy to invoke the law of nations, insofar as it was also based on natural

[39] *Atwood and Others* v. *Sellar & Co* (1879) 4 Q.B.D. 342 at 352, 349–50.

[40] E.g. *Hutton* v. *Warren* (1836) 1 M & W 466; *Brown* v. *Byrne* (1854) 3 E & B 703. See also the use of evidence to establish what the custom of the trade was in insurance cases: e.g. *Camden* v. *Cowley* (1763) 1 W Black 417, Oldham, *Mansfield Manuscripts*, p. 500; *Noble and another* v. *Kennoway* (1780) 2 Dougl 510.

[41] *Robinson* v. *Mollett* (1874–5) LR 7 HL 802 at 818.

law or reason. Both common lawyers and international lawyers resorted to arguments from reason, and both were sceptical about the ability of pure natural reason to solve current problems. But they took divergent approaches to resolving this problem. 'To be sure', Bynkershoek wrote, 'reason remains immutable, but when reason argues in behalf of both sides so that it is doubtful where the preponderating weight lies, we must appeal to custom for a decision.' By this he meant recent rather than distant practice.[42] By contrast, common lawyers ever since Coke had stressed the 'artificial' reason of the law, which was in the control of lawyers; and which did not look to custom for enlightenment.

When common lawyers invoked the law of nations as a source in their reasoning process, they often referred to it as if it were the same as the law of nature, to which they occasionally made reference when they were short of arguments from authority. In 1758, for instance, Sir Richard Lloyd argued in an insurance case that the question 'must be determined by the law of nature and nations, or rather by the law of right reason, which becomes the law of nations, when determinations are made in cases which happen to arise'.[43] More frequently, they considered the law of nations as allowing the court to determine according to 'the reason of the thing'.[44] In the eighteenth century, this treatment of the law of nations was found especially in cases involving ambassadorial privileges, which saw the clearest declarations that 'the law of nations, in its full extent was part of the law of England'[45] – a proposition which Blackstone famously repeated.[46] This principle was invoked to justify a narrow interpretation of the Diplomatic Privileges Act of 1708.[47] In stating that the law of nations was part of the common law, judges could treat the Act as merely declaratory of rights which already existed, rather than as creating new statutory ones.[48] In determining the reach of those rights, judges looked to what protection reason suggested

42 Cornelius Van Bynkershoek, *Quaestrionum Juris Publici Libri Duo*, trans. Tenney Frank (Oxford, 1930), p. 7.

43 *Goss* v. *Withers* (1758) 2 Kenyon 325 at 336.

44 Sir Robert Phillimore, *Commentaries upon International law* (2nd edn, London, 1871), vol. I, p. 29.

45 Quoted by Lord Mansfield in *Triquet* v. *Bath* (1764) 3 Burr 1478 at 1481.

46 4 *Comm.* 67. See on this the comments of Hersch Lauterpacht in E. Lauterpacht (ed.), *International Law: Being the Collected Papers of Hersch Lauterpacht*, vol. 2, *The Law of Peace, Part 1 International Law in General* (Cambridge, 1975), p. 538.

47 7 Ann., c. 12. See also *Mattueof's Case* (1709) 10 Mod 4.

48 See e.g. *Lockwood* v. *Dr Coysgarne* (1765) 3 Burr 1676. See also *Heathfield* v. *Chilton* (1767) 4 Burr 2015; *Viveash* v. *Becker* (1814) 3 M & S 284.

ambassadors needed. Thus, Abbott CJ found in 1823 that the act did not grant exemption from taxation to the private property of an ambassador's servant, since this was unrelated to anything necessary to the rank of an ambassador.[49]

When reasoning on the nature of the problem before them, English judges were prepared to refer to the opinions of foreign jurists who were not themselves regarded as binding or authoritative. This can be seen from litigation in 1844, when the Duke of Brunswick (whose government had been overthrown in 1830, pursuant to a decree of the German diet) attempted to sue the King of Hanover (who was also the British Duke of Cumberland) for his part in the affair. It had already been settled that a foreign sovereign could sue and be made subject to cross bills in English courts, on matters recognised by English law.[50] But could he be sued for acts he committed? According to Lord Langdale, 'there is no English law applicable to the present subject, unless it can be derived from the law of nations, which, when ascertained, is to be deemed part of the common law of England'. Where (as here) there was no settled usage reflecting the common consent of nations, the decision had to be 'according to such light as may be afforded to us by natural reason, or the dictates of that which is thought to be the policy of the law'.[51] For help, he turned to the writings of international jurists, including Bynkershoek. Discussing the question of what to do with a foreign prince who committed a crime in another state, Bynkershoek found that since precedents from international practice were indecisive, 'reason alone remains to be consulted'. He therefore drew an analogy between a monarch and an ambassador: if the latter was inviolable, so should the former be.[52] Even if the sovereign acted 'after the manner of a robber', attacking the life, property or chastity of anyone in the host country, which might justify his arrest and execution, punishment should 'be done by a mob rather than through duly constituted process

[49] *Novello* v. *Toogood* (1823) 1 B & C 554.

[50] See *Colombian Government* v. *Rothschild* (1826) 1 Simons 94; *Hullett* v. *The King of Spain* (1828) 2 Bligh NS PC 31; *South African Republic* v. *La Compagnie Franco-Belge du Chemin de Fer du Nord* [1898] 1 Ch 190.

[51] *Duke of Brunswick* v. *King of Hanover* (1844) 6 Beav 1 at 45.

[52] Cornelius van Bynkershoek, *De Foro Legatorum Liber Singularis: A Monograph on the Jurisdiction over Ambassadors in Both Civil and Criminal Cases* (2nd edn, Oxford, 1946), p. 20. At p. 21, he observed: 'If you should say that when it comes to the law of nations, argument cannot be based on analogy, I should rejoin that this question cannot be settled in accordance with international law on account of the lack of examples through which the agreement of the nations can be proved.'

of law'. Langdale considered the ambassadorial analogy but found it indecisive. He was, however, swayed by the argument implicit in Bynkershoek's last phrase, and concluded:

> that offences committed by sovereign princes in foreign States ought rather to be treated as causes of war, than as violations of the law of the country where they are committed, and ought rather to be checked by vengeance, and making war on the offender, than by any attempt to obtain justice through lawful means.[53]

Considering the practical and political consequences, 'it ought to be considered as a general rule, in accordance with the law of nations, that a sovereign prince, resident in the dominions of another, is exempt from the jurisdiction of the courts there'.[54] This decision was upheld by the Lords, who ruled that a foreign sovereign could not be made liable in English courts for his acts done as a sovereign abroad.[55]

Reasoning from the nature of sovereign power, with the help of the opinions of jurists, also helped determine the point that a sovereign, while able to sue in English courts, could not use them to vindicate his sovereign powers. This was seen in *The Emperor of Austria* v. *Day* in 1861, where the plaintiff sought an injunction to prevent the revolutionary nationalist Louis Kossuth printing his own Hungarian banknotes in order to undermine the emperor's currency. The case raised the question of whether a sovereign could sue in an English court to assert a prerogative or sovereign power. Counsel for the emperor had argued that, since international law recognised the right of a sovereign to issue money, and since international law was part of domestic law, the right should be protected by the Chancery. Although the court found that the emperor could sue on behalf of his subjects (and obtain an injunction to protect their property), its jurisdiction could not be used to protect

[53] *Duke of Brunswick* v. *King of Hanover* (1844) 6 Beav 1 at 49. See also Zouch's view that 'if it appears better to inflict immediate punishment upon a king, that is taken in a foreign country, plotting against the state, it suits better with the law of nations to proclaim war against them, and declare them open enemies, and then one may safely kill them without waiting for any judicial process'. Richard Zouch, *A Solution of an Ancient and Modern Question; or a Dissertation Concerning the Proper Judge of a Criminal Ambassador* (London, 1717), p. 85.

[54] *Duke of Brunswick* v. *King of Hanover* (1844) 6 Beav 1 at 51.

[55] *Duke of Brunswick* v. *King of Hanover* (1848) 2 HLC 1. For another case confirming sovereign immunity, and where arguments were drawn from the nature of sovereignty, analogy with ambassadors, and the opinions of foreign jurists, see *The Parlement Belge* (1880) LR 5 PD 197.

prerogative rights. As Turner LJ saw it, prerogative rights were of the same nature as acts of state, which were not enforced by English municipal courts.

> If the subject of one State infringes the prerogative of the sovereign of another State, the remedy, as I apprehend, lies in an appeal by the offended sovereign to the sovereign of the State to which the offender belongs, and if redress be unjustly refused, the refusal may, I apprehend, even be made the ground of war. This, I think, may be gathered from Vattel, and it seems to me important to be adhered to; for the prerogative of peace and war belongs to the sovereign of every State, and it can hardly be denied that the interference of the municipal courts in such matters may tend very much to embarrass if not to fetter the free exercise of these latter prerogatives.[56]

Reasoning on the nature of the problem also helped determine the boundary between what was law for the courts to determine and what was a matter for political determination. Despite Blackstone's wide statement, it was evident that the law of nations comprised matters which were beyond the control of any court. This can be seen from the contrast put by Robert Chambers, the second Vinerian professor:

> [W]hilst the subjects of each state are governed by these its positive institutions, as the *rule* of their *civil conduct*, and we owe an obedience to the laws of God and of nature, as the *rule of their moral behaviour*, the state itself considered as a single person is bound to observe a certain rule of *political conduct* (if I may so speak) called the *law of nations*.[57]

This meant, for instance, that 'a *political* treaty, between sovereigns, cannot be the subject of municipal jurisdiction; but that its observance, or neglect, must depend on that respect which the parties bound thereby can be made to feel for the *ius gentium*'.[58]

The boundaries between the political and the legal were made clearer in the early nineteenth century, when the question was raised as to who was to determine whether a state existed. Considering the law of nations as an abstract science, it was possible to argue that the existence of states

[56] *The Emperor of Austria* v. *Day and Kossuth* (1861) 3 De GF & J 217 at 251–2.

[57] Robert Chambers, *A Course of Lectures on the English Law Delivered at the University of Oxford, 1767–1775*, 2 vols., ed. Thomas M. Curley (Oxford, 1986), vol. I, p. 91.

[58] 1 Ves Jun Supp 149, commenting on *Nabob of the Carnatic* v. *The East India Company* (1793) 2 Ves Jun 56. See also *The Secretary of State for India* v. *Kamachee Boye Sahaba* (1859) 13 Moo PC 22.

could be determined by reason alone, and hence be within the jurisdiction of domestic courts. International lawyers after all did give abstract definitions of what constituted a state, referring to concepts such as independent self-government,[59] or shared territory bound under a common system of laws, habits, customs and government.[60] Some judges therefore tried to make the existence of a state a matter of judicial determination. In 1826, Best CJ held that in the case of countries which had not been formally recognised but 'which conquest and commerce have made us acquainted with', evidence could be given to prove their existence:

> The proof necessary to establish the fact of the existence of such states is, that they are associations formed for mutual defence, who acknowledge no other authority but that of their own government, observe the rules of justice to the subjects of other states, live generally under their own laws, and maintain their independence by their own force.[61]

Best's view was not, however, taken up by his fellow judges.[62] For Lord Eldon, 'it was extremely difficult to say, a judicial Court can take notice of a Government, never authorized by the Government of the Country, in which that Court sits'.[63] The difficulty of the issue was made apparent in the years after 1810, when rebellions erupted throughout Latin America, and the question whether the rebels had created independent states meriting recognition was much debated in parliament. As long as it was unclear whether Spain would be able to reassert its authority, the British government desisted from recognising the new states, even though private individuals traded with the new governments. Under such circumstances, could courts pre-empt the decision, when the matter was raised in civil litigation? Eldon doubted it: 'What right have I, as the King's judge, to interfere upon the subject of a contract with a country which he does not recognize?'[64] It thus came to be generally accepted that courts would not enforce contracts with

[59] E. de Vattel, *The Law of Nations or the Principles of Natural Law*, trans. Charles G. Fenwick (Washington, DC, 1916), p. 18

[60] Phillimore, *International Law* (2nd edn, 1871), vol. 1, p. 81. See also Sir William Scott's judgment in *The Helena* (1801) 4 C Rob 4.

[61] *Yrisarri* v. *Clement* (1826) 3 Bing 432 at 437–8.

[62] *Ibid.*, 440. The question was not necessary for the determination of the case.

[63] *City of Berne* v. *The Bank of England* (1804) 9 Ves Jun 347 at 348. See also *Dolder* v. *Bank of England* (1805) 10 Ves Jun 353, 11 Ves 284.

[64] *Jones* v. *Garcia del Rio* (1823) Turn & Russ 297 at 299.

unrecognised states,[65] and some judges even referred to the Foreign Office to confirm whether a state had been recognised.[66] The doctrine became settled that the factual question of who was sovereign and what was sovereign property was a matter for political determination.[67] Courts would take judicial notice of the status of foreign governments, having where necessary sought information from the government.[68] Where the existence of a state was at issue, the courts thus treated it as a factual matter determined by international politics, rather than as a legal issue which they could settle.

In taking this approach, they followed the view of international jurists who saw the recognition of states as an act of political judgment, manifested by treaty, and not as a judicial act. In doing so, they also accepted the idea found in these texts that the law of nations was a fluid matter, made up as much of political judgments made by statesmen, as of juridical matters debated in court. By the late eighteenth century, writers on the law of nature made it clear that the law of nations was not universal. Robert Plumer Ward, for instance, observed in 1795, 'it was not reasonable to expect, that the intercourse between the Spaniards and the Mexicans should be governed by the same customs as the intercourse of Nations in Europe'.[69] The law of nations had a more limited ambit: 'when we see [nations] governed by the same customs, arising from climate or geographical situation, and bound together by *one common Religion*; then, may we fairly suppose that they agree, tacitly or expressly, to obey the same law of Nations.' By this view, the law of nations was not a matter of abstract definition to be discovered by reason. It was a matter of convention, which reflected economic intercourse and common culture. Different nations therefore 'took their place in the European

[65] See also *Thompson* v. *Powles* (1828) 2 Sim 194 at 213. In this case (at 203) counsel for the defendant (Pepys) argued that contracts for supplying unrecognised states with money was illegal: 'It must be looked at as a question of international law.' But Shadwell VC ruled that 'this is a contract entered into by the Plaintiff for the purpose of purchasing that which, by the law of the land, he could not purchase'.

[66] *Taylor* v. *Barclay* (1828) 2 Sim 213 at 220.

[67] See also *Mighell* v. *Sultan of Johore* [1894] 1 QB 149; *Statham* v. *Statham and His Highness the Gaekwar of Baroda* [1912] P 92.

[68] See *Foster* v. *Globe Venture Syndicate, Limited* [1900] 1 Ch 811; *Duff Development Company Limited, Appellants* v. *Government of Kelantan* [1924] AC 797. See also *Mighell* v. *Sultan of Johore* [1894] 1 QB 149 at 158.

[69] R. P. Ward, *An Enquiry into the Foundation and History of the Law of Nations in Europe, from the Time of the Greeks and Romans, to the Age of Grotius*, 2 vols. (Dublin, 1795), vol. 1, p. 82. Contrast Emmerich de Vattel, *The Law of Nations* (London, 1797), p. 467, speaking of Mexicans recognising ambassadors; see also *ibid.*, p. 431, on Algiers.

Republic' at different times: 'the steps have been very gradual, and the manner by Treaty.'[70] It was this which explained the doubts which remained over the Ottoman Empire's place within the European system,[71] and which served to exclude 'uncivilised' polities from the international system throughout the nineteenth century.[72]

The common law and the force of treaties

Besides reason, the second key source of the law of nations were treaties. Blackstone's brief discussion suggested that treaties bound in domestic law by the act of the sovereign alone. 'It is by the law of nations essential to the goodness of a league, that it be made by the sovereign power', he wrote, 'and then it is binding on the whole community.' The check imposed by the constitution against the abuse of this power was the ability to impeach the king's advisers.[73] From the early nineteenth century, however, it came to be argued that the signing of treaties was a political matter under the control of the sovereign which did not bind in English law until incorporated by legislation. The development of this doctrine reflected both an understanding of international law as involving matters properly political and a narrowing of the prerogative powers of the crown.

The notion that the crown could by treaty neither impose new charges, nor interfere with the rights of its English subjects, was not difficult to establish, given that it was a settled constitutional principle that changes in law or in taxation needed parliamentary consent.[74] But it was more contentious whether the crown could acquire new territories (which might involve costs on the British taxpayer) or cede territory by its prerogative. Concerns were raised in parliament both over the peace of 1783, under which the crown ceded sovereignty over its thirteen American colonies, and over the cession of sovereignty over the

70 Ward, *Enquiry*, pp. 97–8, 100.

71 It was excluded from the Congress of Vienna of 1815, but its independence was guaranteed by the Treaty of Paris in 1856.

72 See Antony Anghie, 'Finding the Peripheries Sovereignty and Colonialism in Nineteenth Century International Law', *Harvard Journal of International Law*, vol. 40 (1999) 1–80.

73 1 *Comm*. 249.

74 See Sir Robert Phillimore's judgment in *The Parlement Belge* (1879) 4 PD 129 at 154. See also *Attorney-General for Canada* v. *Attorney-General for Ontario* [1937] AC 326 at 347; *Maclaine Watson* v. *Department of Trade* [1988] 3 WLR 1033; and L. Oppenheim (ed.), *The Collected Papers of John Westlake on Public International Law* (Cambridge, 1914), p. 499.

Orange River Colony in 1854. In the latter case, the Attorney General, Sir Alexander Cockburn, told the House of Commons that, where a territory was conquered, it was subject to the crown's absolute sovereignty, though where territories were settled there was 'considerable difference of opinion' over whether the crown could cede them without legislation.[75] The view came to be accepted in the nineteenth century that the crown could not cede territories which had come under parliamentary jurisdiction without legislation.[76] In this area, the crown's power was diminished and that of parliament increased; though the process was driven as much by the opinion of constitutional experts and the practice of governments, as it was by the meagre amount of case law.[77] Moreover, the matter often remained moot. Thus, in 1892, the Judicial Committee of the Privy Council refrained from determining whether the crown could compel its subjects to obey the provisions of a treaty ending a war, when to do so would remove property rights without legislative assent.[78]

Just as constitutional lawyers defined the crown's power to cede territory more precisely, so its power to provide for the extradition of aliens by treaty was also rethought. In the late eighteenth and early nineteenth centuries, the view was taken that wanted criminals could be extradited as a matter of comity. Drawing on a number of seventeenth-century cases of extradition to Ireland,[79] the Court of Exchequer observed in 1749 that 'the government may send persons to answer for a crime wherever committed, that he may not involve his country; and to prevent reprisals'.[80] In an opinion given in 1792, Serjeant Hill stated that the crown had power to extradite aliens, 'for this is warranted by the practice of nations, and is therefore not part of the legislative power, but of the executive, which is vested solely in the king'.[81] In 1811, in *Mure* v.

[75] *Parliamentary Debates*, 3rd Ser., vol. 133, col. 82. Where territory was settled, the settlers were regarded as having brought their common law rights with them.

[76] See *Damodhar Gordhan* v. *Deoram Kanji* (1875) 1 App Cas 332. See A. D. Macnair, 'When Do British Treaties Involve Legislation?', *British Yearbook of International Law*, vol. 9 (1928) 59–68.

[77] Thus, the decision to seek parliamentary confirmation of the cession of Heligoland in 1890 and of the ratification of cessions in the Entente Cordiale in 1904 demonstrated a developing constitutional consensus.

[78] *Walker* v. *Baird* [1892] AC 491. Cf. A. V. Dicey, *Introduction to the Study of the Law of the Constitution*, ed. E. C. S. Wade (10th edn, London, 1959), p. 465.

[79] *Colonel Lundy's Case* (1690) Holt KB 333, 2 Vent 314; *R* v. *Kimberley* (1728) 2 Stra 848.

[80] *East India Company* v. *Campbell* (1749) 1 Ves Sen 246 at 247.

[81] Quoted in Edward Clarke, *A Treatise upon the Law of Extradition* (2nd edn, London, 1874), p. 26.

Kaye Heath J observed that criminals were always punished by the *lex loci* of the place where the crime was committed and that 'by the comity of nations the country in which the criminal has been found, has aided the police of the country against which the crime was committed'. Recalling a ship where a rebellious Dutch crew was returned to Holland, he stated 'the same has always been the law of all civilized countries'.[82]

But this view was challenged by Sir Samuel Romilly in parliament in 1818,[83] and by the law officers in 1836, in advising that Spanish transportees shipwrecked in the Bahamas were not to be returned to Spain, but were to be treated as free agents.[84] The matter was debated again in 1842, after a slave-carrying brig, the *Creole*, sailed into Nassau, after the slaves had rebelled and killed one of the owners. Debating whether the slaves could be extradited for the killing, Lord Brougham declared that the government had no right under municipal law to hand them over. 'Whatever right one nation had against another nation – even by treaty', he said, 'there was, by the municipal law of the nation, no power to execute the obligation of the treaty.'[85] The law lords agreed that there was no right of securing and deporting persons accused of crimes in foreign countries.[86] Thus, by the middle of the nineteenth century, it was clear 'that the Crown may make treaties with foreign States for the extradition of criminals; but those treaties can only be carried into effect by Act of Parliament.'[87] This meant that the extradition provisions of the 1842 Ashburton treaty with the United States and the provisions of a treaty with France in the following year needed ratification by parliament before becoming effective.[88]

Once a treaty was incorporated into the law, it was for the courts to determine its meaning and application. In *In re Tivnan*, the Queen's Bench had to interpret the 1842 treaty by which the parties had agreed to extradite those accused of piracy 'committed within the jurisdiction' of either party who 'should seek an asylum' in the jurisdiction of the other. The case concerned the acts of confederate sailors who had seized a federal ship. In the view of Blackburn J, '[t]he treaty is an agreement between those high contracting parties, and is to be construed according

82 *Mure* v. *Kaye* (1811) 4 Taunt 34 at 43–4.

83 *Parliamentary Debates*, vol. 38, col. 528 (5 May 1818). This was in debates on the Aliens Bill.

84 William Forsyth, *Cases and Opinions on Constitutional Law* (London, 1869), p. 341.

85 *Parliamentary Debates*, 3rd Ser., vol. 60, col. 318 (14 February 1842).

86 *Ibid.*, 326. 87 Forsyth, *Cases and Opinions*, p. 369. 88 6 & 7 Vict., cc. 75–6.

to the same rules as a contract between two subjects'.[89] In his view, the aim of the treaty was to bring to justice those who would otherwise escape it. It thus only applied to acts which amounted to municipal piracy, rather than to piracy on the high seas, which constituted piracy by the law of nations. Since piracy by the law of nations was triable in all countries, it was held by the majority not to be the subject of the exclusive criminal jurisdiction which they felt was covered by the treaty. In this judgment, the notion that, by the law of nations, a pirate could be tried anywhere was taken to be 'good English law'; and this principle of domestic and international law was taken as a context in which to read the meaning of the treaty.

The common law and developing international custom

The third source of international law was custom. Nineteenth-century common law courts handled developing international customary practices in the same way that they treated the developing custom of merchants, incorporating developing practices into law which they felt were convenient, but often doing so on the basis of analogy with English law rather than directly incorporating international practice. Thus, mid-nineteenth-century courts incorporated the developing rule that successor states obtained the rights and were bound by the obligations of *de facto* predecessors. In 1851, in *The King of the two Sicilies* v. *Willcox*, where the restored Sicilian government sought the return of moneys raised by a predecessor revolutionary government, Lord Cranworth found for the legitimate government by drawing an analogy between governments and corporations which were separate from the individuals of whom they were from time to time composed.[90] By contrast, in 1865, in *United States of America* v. *Prioleau*, Wood VC made more explicit reference to international jurists, when he drew on a text of Wheaton[91] to hold that the rights of a successor *de jure* (federal) government were subject to obligations incurred by the predecessor *de facto* (confederate) one. But his decision was also influenced

[89] *In re Tivnan* (1864) 5 B & S 645 at 686–7.

[90] *King of the two Sicilies* v. *Willcox* (1851) 1 Sim NS 301 at 320. The notion of a foreign monarch being a corporation sole (as the English king was) had been mentioned by Brougham LC in *King of Spain* v. *Hullett* (1833) 7 Bli NS 359 at 388.

[91] Henry Wheaton, *Elements of International Law*, ed. George Grafton Wilson (Oxford, 1936), p. 43 (section 31), citing Grotius, *De Jure Belli ac Pacis*, 2.14.16.

by considering the practical consequences. If the plaintiff were right, he noted, 'no dealing with a *de facto* Government would ever be possible'.[92] Yet, during the civil war, the confederate government 'exercised the power of levying taxes, and enjoyed belligerent rights' against the federal states. It was not open in such a situation for neutral states to decide which was the only lawful government. They had to 'protect their subjects, and cannot allow a Government which succeeds to the property of a *de facto* Government to displace rights acquired by their people'.

If they were prepared to incorporate developing international rules, courts remained unwilling to let them unsettle domestic constitutional rules. This can be seen from their approach to cases at the end of the century where plaintiffs sought to make claims which held the British government liable for the debts of predecessor regimes in South Africa. In *Cook* v. *Sprigg* in 1899, where the plaintiff claimed mineral rights granted to him before the British annexation of Pondoland, the Privy Council held that, while there might be 'well-understood rules of international law' that a change of sovereignty by cession ought not to affect private property, 'no municipal tribunal has authority to enforce such an obligation'.[93] In the court's view, the plaintiff's right to have his private property respected derived from a bargain between sovereigns, which could only 'be enforced by sovereign against sovereign in the ordinary course of diplomatic pressure'. This was to suggest that, while English courts would require foreign governments (as plaintiffs) to recognise the right derived from their predecessors, any international obligation on a sovereign to respect earlier rights could only be enforced by international sanctions. The decision also endorsed the constitutional rule that the British sovereign could not be sued in court.

Six years later, in *West Rand Central Gold Mining Company, Limited* v. *The King* in 1905, the plaintiffs sought a petition of right to obtain compensation for gold seized by the government of the annexed South African Republic, under laws which required its restitution. Counsel for the company cited jurists who held that the sovereign of a conquering

92 *United States of America* v. *Prioleau* (1865) 2 Hemming & Miller 559 at 564. See also *Republic of Peru* v. *Dreyfus Brothers & Co* (1888) 38 ChD 348 at 355, where the passage from Wheaton was quoted in full. See also the discussion in John Westlake, *International Law*, Part I, *Peace* (Cambridge, 1904), pp. 74–83, and William E. Hall, *A Treatise on International Law* (4th edn, Oxford, 1895), pp. 96ff.

93 *Cook* v. *Sprigg* [1899] AC 572 at 578.

state was liable for the obligations of the conquered state, and that obligations derived from international law had to be protected in domestic courts. The King's Bench was unconvinced. Lord Alverstone CJ considered international law much less certain than domestic law, with jurists often expressing 'their views as to what ought to be' law, rather than what was law.[94] In any event, he found no jurist who unequivocally stated that a successor state was liable for the internal debts of the antecedent state. 'But whatever may be the view taken of the opinions of these writers', he noted, 'they are, in our judgment, inconsistent with the law as recognised for many years in the English Courts.'[95] This law was that a conqueror could impose such terms as he wished.[96] Turning to whether a petition of right would lie, Alverstone ruled against the plaintiffs on the authority of *Cook* v. *Sprigg*:[97] 'matters which fall properly to be determined by the Crown by treaty or as an act of State are not subject to the jurisdiction of the municipal Courts.'[98]

According to John Westlake, this decision of the King's Bench 'was made necessary by a British rule excluding any rule of international law'; and, in his view, Alverstone's understanding of international law was faulty.[99] Alverstone's view is perhaps best seen as reflecting the cautious approach to incorporation shared by many of his nineteenth-century predecessors. He was, to begin with, highly sceptical about the value of juridical opinion:

> the international law sought to be applied must, like anything else, be proved by satisfactory evidence, which must shew either that the particular

94 *West Rand Central Gold Mining Company, Limited* v. *The King* [1905] 2 KB 391 at 401–2.

95 *Ibid.*, 406.

96 He cited eighteenth-century authorities: *Campbell* v. *Hall* (1774) 1 Cowp 204; *Anonymous* (1722) 2 P Wms 75.

97 The decision in this case may have been informed by the conclusions of a commission appointed to examine the maintenance of concessions granted by the former South African Republic, which reported (following *Cook* v. *Sprigg*) that a state which annexed another was not legally bound by the contracts of the conquered state: PP 1901 [Cd 623] XXXV 7, p. 7. See also J. Westlake, 'The Nature and Effect of the Title by Conquest', in Oppenheim, *Collected Papers*, pp. 475–89.

98 [1905] 2 KB 409.

99 Oppenheim, *Collected Papers*, 515n. According to Lauterpacht, *International Law*, p. 116, 'it is doubtful whether [Alverstone's] dictum would even at that time have been accepted by an international court'. Alverstone's statement about the place of international law has nonetheless long been quoted by those who assert that 'Britain essentially adopts a monistic approach to customary international law'. Rebecca M. M. Wallace, *International Law* (4th edn, London, 2002), p. 38.

> proposition put forward has been recognised and acted upon by our own country, or that it is of such a nature, and has been so widely and generally accepted, that it can hardly be supposed that any civilized State would repudiate it.[100]

While the latter might include *practices* which had gradually grown, it did not include 'opinions of text-writers upon a question as to which there is no evidence that Great Britain has ever assented, and a fortiori if they are contrary to the principles of her laws as declared by her courts'.[101] Where there was universal assent, international law would be 'acknowledged and applied by our municipal tribunals *when legitimate occasion arises*'.[102]

Conclusion

If Lassa Oppenheim was to give the most important expression in the twentieth century of the notion that international law was a source of English law without being itself part of it, he was putting into words an assumption generally shared by nineteenth-century common lawyers.[103] The common law remained a customary system, uncodified, uncertain, fluid and developing. But it was the custom of the English courts, not of the English people; and the materials which judges sought to explain and elaborate were those which had been incorporated into the system by their own decisions. They were content to treat the law of nations as part of their system insofar as it was a system of reason. As with their use of the law of nature, it was drawn on not for the moral content of its precepts, but as a means of reasoning on the nature of the problem. In novel cases where English law offered no clear answers, courts (particularly before the mid-nineteenth century) were content to draw on the classic natural law works of Grotius, Bynkershoek or Vattel.

However, insofar as the law of nations was made up of contingent and changing state practice, it was not regarded as of itself part of the

[100] *West Rand Central Gold Mining Company, Limited* v. *The King* [1905] 2 KB 391 at 407.

[101] *Ibid.*, 408.

[102] Cf. *Mortensen* v. *Peters* (1906) 8 F (JC) 93 at 101: 'It is a trite observation that there is no such thing as a standard of international law extraneous to the domestic law of a kingdom, to which appeal may be made. International law, so far as this Court is concerned, is the body of doctrine regarding international rights and duties of states which has been adopted and made part of the law of Scotland.'

[103] See Perreau-Saussine, chapter 10 above.

common law. In an age when international lawyers increasingly focused on matters of state practice, judges often became more sceptical about the authority of their opinions. Clearer lines were drawn between what was political – including treaties – and what was properly legal. In the latter area, courts were prepared to incorporate developing rules as and when they saw fit; but they were equally determined not to incorporate rules which might threaten established common law doctrine.

12

Custom in international law: a normative practice account

GERALD J. POSTEMA

A troubled concept

"Custom is not a special department or area of public international law: it *is* international law."[1] So writes Ian Brownlie; yet, writers on international law now widely declare customary international law to be dead or at least in mortal crisis. Such disputes over its viability, of course, stem from differences of political principle and partisan geopolitics, but they also stem from genuine confusion about the nature of custom and its role in the international legal order.

For example, according to the International Court of Justice, it is "axiomatic" in international law jurisprudence that customary international law is found "primarily in the actual practice and *opinio juris* of States."[2] To determine whether legally recognized custom exists on some matter, the Court added later:

> [n]ot only must the acts concerned amount to a settled practice, but they must also be such, or be carried out in such a way, as to be evidence of a belief that this practice is rendered obligatory by the existence of a rule of law requiring it . . . The States concerned must therefore feel that they are conforming to what amounts to a legal obligation.[3]

What is here said to be *axiomatic* in international law jurisprudence is the familiar additive understanding of custom: custom is analyzed into behavior or usage (*usus*) plus belief or conviction of (legal) necessity (*opinio juris sive necessitatis*). *Usus* is necessary, it is said, to distinguish custom from merely ideal standards, while *opinio juris* is necessary to

[1] I. Brownlie, *The Rule of Law in International Affairs* (The Hague: Martinus Nijhoff, 1998), 18.

[2] *Libya* v. *Malta (Continental Shelf)*, ICJ Reports (1985), para. 27.

[3] *North Sea Continental Shelf*, ICJ Reports (1969), para. 77.

distinguish legal custom from other regularities, rules, and routines "motivated only by considerations of courtesy, convenience or tradition".[4] *Opinio juris* – the "subjective" or mental element – is said to transform mere "objective" usage into a norm of international law.

Despite its "axiomatic" status, this additive understanding is of relatively recent vintage (considering the long history of jurisprudence). Sometimes, the additive conception is traced to writers at the dawn of the modern era like Suarez, but this is a mistake. Suarez acknowledged that *consuetudo* has a "factual" and a "juridical" element, but his was not an additive conception of custom for two reasons. First, the juridical element in Suarez's view was the obligation itself, not some subjective or mental element. Secondly, although Suarez quoted with approval Isidore's claim that legal customs are rules "accepted as law,"[5] he did not understand this to suggest the additive conception. According to Suarez, Isidore meant merely to say that unwritten customary rules must be treated just like formally legislated rules. This has nothing to do with what was in the minds of those who followed the rules and everything to do with how they were properly to be used. In this respect, Suarez simply followed established Roman law doctrine: "Deeply rooted custom is [to be] observed as a statute."[6] "Those rules which have been approved by long established custom ... are no less to be obeyed than laws which have been committed to writing."[7]

If D'Amato is right, the additive conception took hold in the nineteenth century through the efforts of Historical School of jurisprudence.[8] Oddly, however, although the Historical School has largely vanished from the jurisprudential scene, the conception of custom it sired remains. Its survival may be due to the ascendance in the twentieth century of the concept of consent as a core foundational concept of the international legal order, but consent theory does not fit comfortably with the additive conception as the latter is widely understood and deployed; moreover, consent theory has been losing steam recently. Thus, the additive conception increasingly appears to be a practical test for international custom without theoretical foundations.

[4] *Ibid.*

[5] F. Suarez, '*A* Treatise on Laws and God the Lawgiver' in *Selections from Three Works of Francisco Suarez,* trans. G. Williams, A. Brown, and J. Waldron (Oxford: Oxford University Press, 1944), 444–7.

[6] *Dig.* 1.3.32.1. [7] *Dig* 1.3.35.

[8] A. A. D'Amato, *The Concept of Custom in International Law* (Ithaca: Cornell University Press, 1971), 47–9.

Moreover, the additive conception itself needs clarification in several respects. First, it is not clear whether it is offered as an analysis of custom *in general*,[9] or as an account of *legal* customs, in particular, binding customs *of international law*. Secondly, custom is said to "result from," or to be "looked for," or "found in," the two elements, but international law jurisprudence rarely explicates this relationship. Is it (1) a metaphysical relation (the elements *constitute* custom, make it what it is; or, more weakly, they constitute what philosophers call the supervenience base of customary norms)? Is it (2) an epistemological relation (these elements *mark* certain phenomena as customary norms, or customary norms of international law, and thereby help us locate such norms in a community)? Or, is it (3) a normative relation (the elements *justify* or *ground* customs or customary legal norms)? One often finds versions of two and even all three of these at work at the same time in writing on the nature and formation of custom in international law.

In recent years the additive account has come under heavy fire. Some commentators now celebrate (or regret) the emergence of a "modern" conception of custom in international law which abandons the dualism.[10] On this view, *usus* is said to be unnecessary, *opinio* is sufficient. But this modern conception is no more firmly rooted theoretically than the additive conception; indeed, it is not even clear that it has abandoned the additive analysis. What is said to be sufficient for the formation of custom in international law is not the relevant international actors' *conviction* that they are bound to act in a certain way (a "subjective" element), but their *public articulation* of a standard which then attracts *public affirmation* by (some) other actors. This proposal has attracted serious practical and moral objections. For example, some argue that talk is cheap without some demonstration of *bona fides* in action; others ask who is authorized to articulate these standards and whose affirmations count. But, more fundamentally, it seems conceptually confused. First, while it takes formal legislation by an assembly as its model, it ignores the institutional structure without which the model is empty. Secondly, it confuses the *usus–opinio* distinction with a distinction between two ends of the spectrum of elements of *usus*. Writers on

9 Compare Hart's analysis of conventional social rules. H. L. A. Hart, *The Concept of Law*, eds. J. Raz and P. A. Bulloch (2nd edn, Oxford: Clarendon Press, 1994), 56–7, 88–90.

10 See J. P. Kelly, "The Twilight of Customary International Law," *Virginia Journal of International Law*, 40 (2000), 449–543; A. E. Roberts, "Traditional and Modern Approaches to Customary International Law: A Reconciliation," *American Journal of International Law*, 95 (2001), 757–91.

custom in international law agree that "*usus*" includes *deeds* – public, non-verbal behavior of international actors – but they disagree strongly about whether it should also include *words* – the resolutions, declarations, and the myriad other forms of verbal behavior that also surround international custom. Many argue that speech in public is a kind of acting and usually an important part of "practice." Many additive theorists argue that *usus* consists of all relevant constituents on the spectrum from pure deed to pure word;[11] and *opinio juris* is often taken to be the subjective element that is typically inferred from or presumed on the basis of this *usus*. To confuse matters further, other theorists (e.g., D'Amato) equate *opinio juris* with *word*, that is, anything on the *usus* spectrum other than mere behavior. As a result, it is unclear whether the modern conception has merely taken a stand about the relative importance of certain components of the usage element, or rather has abandoned that element entirely for the "subjective" element, let alone whether such a proposal is conceptually coherent.

The normativity of custom

Two further questions have proved especially troubling for theorists of custom in international law. One concerns the nature and ground of its normative force. Among those who embrace the additive conception, the view seems to be that *usus* and *opinio juris* each play a role in grounding custom's normativity, but rarely is this role articulated or explained. Only traditional consent theory seems to offer an explanation, namely, that, if *opinio juris*, understood as the explicit or tacit consent of parties, is added to *usus*, then the custom is binding. Yet, this theory is widely and justly thought to be unable to account for the realities of modern international law, much of which is not strictly consensual. So, we still need an account of custom's normative force (as *custom*, and as *international legal* custom).

There is even greater disagreement over the alleged *scope* of customary norms of international law. Increasingly over the last half-century, many (but surely not all) rules of customary international law have come to be seen as binding universally (to impose so-called obligation *omnium*), regardless of whether the parties subject to them have signed on (some leeway being given to "persistent objectors"). But many wonder how

[11] M. Akehurst, "Custom as a Source of International Law," *British Yearbook of International Law*, 47 (1976), 1–53.

these norms can extend to parties who were not involved in their formulation. If this extension of the norm is well grounded, why is an exit option available to persistent objectors? The problem of scope gets worse once we consider alleged principles of humanitarian, human rights, and environmental law. The legal force of these principles is often said to depend on their status as international custom, because customary international law in many countries is treated as part of domestic law without explicit legislation and in some countries even overrides contrary domestic law.[12] However, if they are to be considered principles of customary international law, new problems arise because these principles are said to hold not merely *inter se* – between discrete parties or states – but rather *erga omnes*: binding all states, and entailing rights held against all, including rights against *all* states to protect right-holders, regardless of their specific relationships to the right-holders or the alleged violators. In the words of the ICJ, these are "obligations of a State towards the international community as a whole."[13] Can any sense be made of the notion of *erga omnes* obligations in a regime of custom, or in a regime of customary *international* law?

We will address these questions, but first we need to take a close look at the notion of custom and the way custom is thought to work in the global legal order. For purposes of this study, I will take at face value the following claims: (a) that there is currently in place a credible international legal order, which, while differing in important respects from domestic legal systems, bears important analogies of form and function to them; (b) that customary rules and standards offer a distinctive kind of norm of the international legal order; (c) that "custom" is used in this context not merely as a term of art, but rather refers to what are properly regarded as customs, distinguishable from other sorts of social rules by features traceable to the special sort of social environment in which they thrive. These assumptions determine the structure of the following discussion. I first offer an account of the nature of custom considered in general. I argue that customs taken generally are best understood as a certain kind of normative practice (namely, practically oriented, discursive, normative practice). I then argue that the special sort of customs

[12] See T. Meron, *Human Rights and Humanitarian Norms as Customary Law* (Oxford: Clarendon Press, 1989); and J.-M. Henckaerts, "Study on Customary International Humanitarian Law: A Contribution to the Understanding and Respect for the Rule of Law in Armed Conflict," *International Review of the Red Cross*, 87 (2005), 175–212.

[13] *Barcelona Traction, Light and Power Company, Ltd*, ICJ Reports (1970), para. 33.

that I shall call convention-customs take their shape from the interactive social environment in which they operate. Finally, I argue, briefly, that the global legal order has the characteristics of such an interactive social environment, and, thus, that it is reasonable to regard customary international law as a regime of convention-customs.

The concept of custom

What we are inclined to call customs come in a wide variety of forms. Moreover, paradigm cases of custom for some of us might be marginal for others. This is due to the fact that customs vary along several dimensions. James Bernard Murphy's contribution to this volume explores insightfully two such dimensions: the *natural* or habitual and the *conventional.*[14] Customs are more or less habit-like in the degree to which they tend to be instinctive, intuitive, tacit, reflex-like, and spontaneously pleasurable. Unlike some habits, customs are not merely acquired, but learned social behavior, and, although unreflective, they are to a degree accessible to explicit attention and even to adjustment upon reflection. On the other hand, customs are convention-like to the degree that they seem variable (across people and times) and artificial; they may be explicitly designed. It is important to understand that, for Aristotle (to whose views Murphy gives voice), custom must not be equated with either habit or convention. Not all habits are customs, even though customs have a habit-like dimension; likewise, customs are convention-like, but not to be identified with explicitly designed and imposed conventions, so not all conventions are customs. Customs vary in the degrees to which they are habit-like and convention-like. Moreover, customs have a dynamic character. Conventions may be "naturalized" over time, beginning as stipulated conventions, settle in as familiar custom and eventually become so deeply bred in the bone that they feel like "second nature." (Pascal was inclined to add that nature was simply "second custom."[15])

These dimensions, long the subject of philosophical discussion, shape our concept of custom. Two other dimensions, implicit in Murphy's discussion, also shape our concept: the *social* and the *normative.* I propose to focus on these dimensions, without, I hope, losing sight

[14] See Murphy, chapter 3 above.

[15] B. Pascal, *Pensées*, ed. T. S. Eliot, trans. W. F. Trotter (New York: E. P. Dutton, 1958), §93.

of the other two. A signal feature of custom is that it is a *practiced norm of a community*. That is to say, first, customs are a certain species of *norm*. Customs are primarily concerned with (social) behavior, but they are not (merely) *patterns of* behavior; rather they set *standards for* behavior, standards of correct and incorrect behavior, and thus purport to guide that behavior and provide bases for its assessment. Thus, mere regularities of behavior taken alone – the *usus* or "state practice" of international law discourse – not only fail to constitute customs of international *law*, they fail to constitute customs of *any sort*, including those of "comity," because they fail to constitute *norms*.

Norms guide behavior by guiding authors of that behavior. Agents are creatures capable of grasping and being grasped by norms, creatures responsive to norms in virtue of the fact that they are capable of holding themselves and others to the standards set by the norms for their behavior. To be guided by a norm involves more than merely behaving in a way that in fact conforms to a pattern or norm. (Fido, walking along the road facing traffic, may conform to the relevant pedestrian norm, but for all we know he is not guided by it.) It is not even enough that the behavior is performed because it exemplifies a pattern, as, for example, the legendary "bee-dance" by which a scout indicates to other bees where rich fields of pollen can be found. In this case, the component bits of the bee-dance are individuated and explained as moves in the patterned whole and, in a straight-forward sense, performed because they are parts of that whole;[16] nevertheless, the bee is not guided by the norm of the bee-dance. The behavior is oriented to the norm, but not guided by it. On the other hand, we go too far if we say that a norm guides only insofar as the agents act from a conception of the norm they explicitly entertain, for then rarely would behavior of rational human agents be norm-guided. Norm-guided behavior is such that the agent grasps the norm to the extent that she understands (fallibly) that acts in accord with it *ought to* (*must*) be done. (To this extent, the notion of *opinio ... necessitatis* is on the right track, although as we shall see it is a mistake to think of it as an *opinio* – belief or conviction.) Norm-guided behavior is self-regulating behavior, even if the agent is not able explicitly to express adequately the norm by which she regulates the behavior. We will explore the normative dimension of custom in the next section,

[16] W. Sellars, "Some Reflections on Language Games," in W. Sellars, *Science, Perception and Reality* (New York: Humanities Press, 1963), 324–7.

but first we need to bring into the picture the remaining dimension of custom.

Customs are social norms, that is, first, they are norms governing social interactions. Secondly, they are *practiced* or generally followed *in some community*. Not all norms are practiced, of course. The principle of respect for basic human dignity and freedom judges all forms of slavery unjust, yet slavery was long practiced and condoned. That fact may not threaten the status of that principle qua norm, but it undermines its claim to be a *customary* norm in the communities in which slavery was widely practiced. Customs are not only norms *for* members of a given community, but are actually followed (to some degree) in the community.

Thirdly, customs are social norms in the sense that they are norms *of* some community. They tend to be taught by others who have mastered the norms. The patterns of behavior and judgment practiced by members of the community are learned through explicit or implicit induction into the community's practice and learners acquire not only a shared sense of what is to be done, but a sense that it is shared, a sense that may be no more evident to them than a horizon of their deliberations and judgments. Thus, customs are not merely rules followed by most individuals as a matter of personal policy, nor are they standards of which it just happens to be true that most members of a community follow them (perhaps out of independent conviction). Such standards, even if very widely followed in the community, would be norms *in* the community, perhaps, but not norms *of* it, because their being practiced in the community figures in no way in their status as binding norms – that is, in the best account of their binding force.

We must be careful not to overstate the matter here. Even principles that seem to claim our allegiance without regard to whether they are practiced in our communities may nevertheless depend on conventional or customary elements to make their claim concrete. For example, it may be true that general principles of morality require respectful and honest behavior, but it may not be possible to determine what behavior is properly respectful or honest in the absence of social forms and customs. Insofar as morality is a mode of living and acting together, as opposed to a mode of directing one's soul for the approval of heaven, morality, and especially political morality, must have a substantial public, conventional, or customary dimension.

Customs, then, are a particular kind of social norm, which are such that their being practiced in some community is of central importance.

Understanding why this is so is critical to understanding the nature and normative force of custom. I will turn to this question in the next but one section of this chapter. But first we need to explore more carefully the idea of normativity at work in this notion of custom.

Custom and deliberative normative practices

As we have seen, Suarez maintained that custom (*consuetudo*) involves a "factual" and a "juridical" element.[17] The former consists of regular voluntary actions (of most members of the community in question), which he called *mos* or *usus*. Under favorable circumstances, he argued, *usus* produces in practitioners a "physical effect," namely, a *habit* or *inclination* to perform actions of the same kind in future. Similarly, under (possibly other) favorable conditions, it produces a "moral effect," namely, an *obligation* (or binding rule) to follow the *usus*-based pattern. For Suarez, these are not independent elements which, when combined, form the binding custom; rather, the regularities of behavior, in certain conditions, "bring [a norm] into being." While Suarez thought the relationship between *usus* and habit was causal, he took the relationship between *usus* and its moral effect to be *rational*, a matter of grounding (which for Suarez was normative and ontological). And this grounding depended on the context in which the behavior took place. This is not yet a robust theory of custom, but it sets off the quest for one on the right foot. To understand international law custom we must locate the relevant *usus* in its norm-generating context. To begin, we must explore the core notion of *normative practice*.[18]

Normative practice

The *usus* of those who follow customs is distinguished from other regularities of behavior by the mode of engagement or participation of custom-following agents in a normative practice, a practice characterized by three essential, interrelated features: mutual commitment, a notion of correct use, and common resources – commitment, correctness, and commons.

[17] Suarez, *On Laws and God the Lawgiver*, 445–7.

[18] On the notion of normative practice see R. Brandom, *Making It Explicit* (Cambridge, MA: Harvard University Press, 1994) and R. Brandom, *Articulating Reasons* (Cambridge, MA: Harvard University Press, 2000).

Parties engaged in a normative practice are rational agents in a strong sense. They have intentional states like beliefs and attitudes, and form and revise them and act on them in a way that satisfies conditions of rationality, but, more importantly, they *avow* these intentional states, actions, and judgments.[19] They acknowledge them as their own, accept responsibility for them, and submit themselves to criticism from others regarding them. Such agents undertake *commitments* (or find themselves committed) to judge certain performances as appropriate, licit, or required, and other performances as out of bounds or prohibited; commitments to act when the occasion arises in accord with these judgments; and commitments to challenge behavior that falls short of these judgments and to recognize appeals to the judgments as vindications of their actions or their criticisms of the actions of others.

The notion of commitment involved here differs sharply from the usual understanding of *opinio juris* in the international law jurisprudence, and, although it is broadly in the spirit of Hart's notion of the "internal attitude,"[20] it breaks decisively with the way it is typically understood at two crucial points. First, commitment is not a matter of accepting, assenting to, or some other way of attaching oneself to some general proposition, either one that describes convergent behavior in the community in question or one that articulates a rule or principle. Rather, it is a mode of participation in an activity of a certain kind. Secondly, commitment is not reducible to some actual attitude, belief, desire, or will of a participant in the activity. Although it involves attitudes of participants, it is not simply an intentional state or a matter of individual psychology, an "inward" relationship between the person and some object of intention (e.g., proposition, fact, or state of affairs). Commitment, rather, is essentially *normative* and *intersubjective* – a mode of acting by a strongly rational agent who occupies a status constituted by normative relations among participants in a practice.[21]

Commitments are irreducibly normative: they involve taking responsibility for one's actions, judgments, and attitudes, and recognizing the standing of others to hold one to this responsibility and to assess one's actions and judgments in light of that responsibility. The scope and content of the commitment is settled, not by the narrow content of one's mental states, but rather by proprieties of the practice in which one takes

[19] P. Pettit, "Collective Persons and Powers," *Legal Theory*, 8 (2002), 461.
[20] Hart, *Concept of Law*, 56–7, 88–90, 102–4, 115–16.
[21] Brandom, *Making it Explicit*, 626–7.

part – how participants *ought to act*, what is *to be* done, in the practice, not how one thinks or feels one ought to act. Commitments always have the potential to outrun what one explicitly entertains or acknowledges. For example, if I acknowledge *P*, it may be true that I am thereby committed also to acknowledge *Q*, but, of course, I may fail to do so. *Correct* understanding of *P* makes it the case that I *ought to* acknowledge *Q*. Hence, commitments presuppose standards of correctness.

Furthermore, commitments are *mutual*, arising from normative relations among participants, from their reciprocal recognition of the other participants' standing. To take responsibility for one's actions and judgments is to acknowledge that one's actions or judgments can go wrong, fall short of implicit standards of correctness. But this calls for the participation of others also deploying those standards; for without them, without their check on the congruence of action or judgment with implicit standards of correctness, it would not be possible for one to distinguish between seeming to act or judge correctly and actually doing so. And, without the traction necessary to distinguish between *seems* and *is*, the notion of *mistake* is emptied of all content, and with it the notion of normativity itself.

Finally, normative practices constitute a kind of *commons* on which their participants draw. This is true in two respects. First, normative practices involve participants' reciprocal recognition of standing to judge what they are doing and why. From their point of view, what is decisive is not what any one party says or thinks about this, or even what most (or even all) of them say or think about this, but rather what they *are actually doing*. This is a direct implication of the crucial fact that what any of them say or think is subject to standards of correctness implicit in the practice, standards anyone familiar with the practice can deploy to assess what is said or thought. That is, it is entailed by the fact that the recognition of standing to hold participants to their commitments is mutual and reciprocal. No one, not even the entire community, has an unchallengeable, final say on what the norms of the practice are. The standards of the practice do not exist "in the heads" of participants, but in the practice. The activity, rather than any articulated account of it, is the fundament – the commons from which all the participants draw and to which they all contribute (by their doings, thinkings, and sayings). All accounts or formulations are ultimately accountable to this commons.

Secondly, what is crucial for successful participation in the practice is mastery of a discipline and acquiring the capacities of perception, articulation, inference, and judgment necessary for such mastery. These capacities are common, acquired through and passed on by participating in the practice, not merely by imitating the habits of others, but by learning how it is done – like learning to play jazz, or sing musically, or make sense of a philosophical argument, or speak a language. To master this discipline is to develop capacities to move comfortably and creatively in a common world.

Deliberative practices

Normative practices come in many forms, from techniques of counting and measuring to language games to playing chess and playing jazz to explicit construction and analysis of logical inferences. Customary norms, the object of our inquiry here, are addressed to creatures subject to the power of reasons; they guide the action of such agents through offering them reasons for action. Agents subject to the power of reasons are able to hold themselves and others to the requirements that the norms impose on them. Thus, customary norms are embedded in a species of normative practices, namely, deliberative practices, which have two defining features: they are essentially discursive and practically concrete. *Discursive* normative practices are in the business of offering, exploring, and assessing reasons and arguments. The contents of its norms are determined by the role they play in networks of reasons and argument – we find out what they require for action not by intuition or perception, but by exploring the reasons and arguments for them and the reasons they provide for other actions and judgments. The discipline mastery of which is required for full participation in these custom-forming normative practices is a discipline of deliberative reasoning. Discursive practices make possible thoughtful, public adjusting of norms to changing circumstances, renegotiating on the ground, as it were, the terms of commitments within the practice.

The discursive normative practices which give shape to customary norms are also *practical* and *concrete*. They are practical as opposed to theoretical, concerned with what is to be done in the world, rather than merely with how we are to think and speak about the world. But custom-shaping normative practices are also practical in a deeper sense, and, as a result, customary norms have a distinctive practical concreteness: they are anchored to concrete (albeit discursively articulated) deeds in the world. Custom-shaping normative practices require mastery, not of abstract rules, or of tracing presuppositions and implications, but of rules-in-action, of grasping the custom-relevant significance of actions in their concrete circumstances, and of judgment applying the rules. Because the practice is discursive, mastery of inference and argument is indispensable, but mastery of articulation and application, two key modes of judgment, is the hallmark of skilled wielders of custom.

Deeds, words, and custom

Unlike legal systems with formally defined institutions for making and changing legal norms, customary regimes cannot admit a sharp distinction between the formation and the application of their norms.[22] It is *deeds* that create customary norms, but deeds also sustain them, refine them, and replace them with other customs. Although a robust notion of violation is a necessary condition of a customary regularity functioning as a norm – it must be possible to say with Hamlet, "it is a custom more honored in the breach than the observance" – yet, change typically comes through the same kind of actions that might as easily be seen by some participants as violations: *ex iniuria ius oritur*. This is a consequence of the practical concreteness of customary normative practice.

But, in discursive normative practices, words are as important as deeds; both are aspects of an essentially public mode of participation. Through deed and word, custom-forming commitments are undertaken, recognized, affirmed, challenged, revised, and extended. Moreover, participants' deeds and words are constituent elements of the deliberative practice, not merely evidence of the mental states of participants. In the formation of custom, deed and word work together: through articulating claims and responses, the deed takes on custom-relevant significance. Behavior viewed apart from such articulations is "a deed without a name".[23] Thus, whether the action of a state counts as a juridical claim or an act of comity, or whether silence on the part of other potentially interested parties counts as a response to the claim, let alone as acquiescence to or protest against it, is never a function of the mental state of the agents or observers (their *opinio – juris* or otherwise), but of their correct articulation and defense as dictated by proprieties of the background normative practice.

[22] M. H. Mendelson, "The Formation of Customary International Law," *Recueil des cours*, Académie de droit international, vol. 272 (The Hague: Martinus Nijhoff, 1999), 175.

[23] Macbeth, IV, I, 44.

The public nature of the participation is crucial. For some purposes, of course, sincerity will be important, but on the whole it is the performance and its public significance – how it is best understood – that is paramount. Equally important is the systemic integration of word and deed. On Hart's view, a set of social rules exists in a community if (nearly all) members of the community individually "accept" each rule in the set on its own terms.[24] However, on the normative practice account, customs are not discrete objects of individual acceptance; rather, they are stable nodes in a dynamic discursive network. Their existence and normative force depend on their place in this network, and their ability to guide members of the community depends on mastery of the deliberative discipline of the practice. Customary norms make practical sense in the context of a discursive normative practice. The content, proper scope, and normative force of a customary norm is a function of its place in this network of norms and (as we will see shortly) in the network of expectations it underwrites. Customary norms are established and mature in a community not by repetition, but by integration. And, because of the intensely practical orientation of custom's normative practice, this integration is not an abstract, theoretical matter, but rather a matter of adjustment and accommodation of action and mutual expectations. Integration is part of the process of custom-formation, a process that is discursive, but always also public and intensely pragmatic.

It should now be clear that we must reject the additive conception of custom. The *usus* characteristic of a normative practice is inseparable from the commitments of participants in the practice and their mastery of its distinctive discipline. Thus, it will usually be possible to identify the pattern in the conduct of participants only through exercise of the discipline of the practice. While any aggregation of behavior instantiates an indefinite number of patterns, the practice-relevant pattern is that pattern correctly identified as such, and to make that judgment requires a degree of mastery of the discipline characteristic of that practice.

The social environment of custom

Material and deliberative interdependence

To understand custom in international law, we need to consider the social environment in which customs typically function and to which

[24] Hart, *Concept of Law*, 91–9.

they are directly responsive. The International Law Association's Committee on the Formation of Customary International Law points us in the right direction when it asserts that a rule of customary international law is a rule "created and sustained by the constant and uniform practice of States and other subjects of international law in or impinging upon their international legal relations in circumstances which give rise to a legitimate expectation of similar conduct in the future."[25] If Hume and Fuller are to be believed, actions tend to give rise to legitimate expectations of similar future conduct in social environments characterized by thick networks of interdependence and in so doing facilitate social coordination.[26]

Some customs may thrive outside this kind of social environment.[27] They may begin their social lives doing important work of social coordination, but over time settle in as autonomous patterns of behavior, meaningful in their own right, perhaps, and they may even sink deep into near-habit. Other customs may not seem to solve any antecedent coordination problem, or, like games, only "solve" those they first create. An explanation of this phenomenon is not hard to find: human beings not only crave social interaction, they crave rules, especially rules they can follow together. Human beings want what they do to add up to something. Rules lend significance to discrete bits of behavior, relating them internally to other such bits, and bringing us together across gaps of time and subjectivity. Nevertheless, there is a very large sub-class of customs that take distinctive shape from adaptations to a social environment characterized by interdependence. The International Law Association suggests that customs in the international legal order, or at least the most important ones, are of this kind. I propose to focus our attention on this class of what I will call convention-customs.

There are material and deliberative dimensions of the interdependence that Hume and Fuller call to our attention. First, conditions of *material interdependence* obtain when resources are relatively scarce,

[25] See International Law Association, Committee on Formation of Customary (General) International Law, "Final Report of the Committee: Statement of Principles Applicable to the Formation of General Customary International Law" (2000), http://www.ila-hq.org/html/layout_committee.htm, 8; Mendelson, "The Formation of Customary International Law," 188.

[26] D. Hume, *A Treatise of Human Nature*, eds. D. F. Norton and M. J. Norton (Oxford: Oxford University Press, 2000), 311–30; L. L. Fuller, "Human Interaction and the Law," in *The Principles of Social Order: Selected Essays of Lon L. Fuller*, ed. Kenneth I. Winston (Oxford: Hart, 2001), 232–66.

[27] A. Marmor, *Positive Law and Objective Values* (Oxford: Clarendon Press, 2001), 10–19.

demands on them are many and various, and social interaction is congested, so that parties find themselves in frequently recurring situations making conflicting demands on the same scarce resources. Typically, the outcomes of their interaction are products of their aggregated actions, such that different combinations of actions are likely to yield qualitatively different results as judged in light of the parties' aims. Thus, to realize almost any aim, parties must rely on the cooperation of the natural and the social world. This cooperation is all the more difficult to achieve because the demands on the scarce resources are often in conflict.

The interdependence of mutually aware, strong, rational agents also has a *deliberative* dimension. Fuller argues that customs arise "out of situations of human interaction where each participant guides himself by an anticipation of what the other will do and will expect him to do".[28] Since the outcome of an agent's action depends on the actions of others, it is necessary to anticipate the behavior of others. Anticipations of the behavior of other strong, rational agents are very different from predictions of the behavior of denizens of the natural world. First, nature is fundamentally indifferent to our deliberations, but other rational agents often are not. In a social world characterized by thick deliberative interdependence, people respond to an environment consisting of other people responding to their environment, including the responses of the first group.[29] Caught in this deliberative net, it is often necessary for one to know not only what others *have done*, but also how they understand what they have done, what they expect me to do, how they expect me to understand what I and they have done, and how they reason to those understandings and expectations. Secondly, such agents are capable of taking responsibility for their actions and held to standards of correctness. Success in interactive deliberative reasoning to any substantial degree depends on the availability of a common world in which deeds, strategies, and the parameters of their interaction have common labels – mutually recognized significance – and on their ability to make their way around in this common world. Discursive, practically oriented, normative practices provide such a common world and common techniques for getting around in it.

In view of this deliberative interdependence, and the role of mutual expectations in it, it is not surprising that many theorists define social

[28] L. L. Fuller, *The Anatomy of Law* (Westport, CT: Greenwood Press, 1968), 73.

[29] T. Schelling, *Micromotives and Macrobehavior* (New York: Norton, 1978), 14.

rules, conventions, and customs as clusters of self-fulfilling expectations, but this is a mistake. Expectations can no more constitute a norm than any other belief, desire, disposition, or other intentional state can. Nested expectations, like patterns of behavior, have practical significance only if they figure in practical reasoning in a certain way. Because expectations and past behavior give strong reason to believe that other parties, on whom one depends, are minded to behave in a certain way in future (e.g., to comply with a certain norm), and behavior in accord with that norm is likely to promote cooperation of the kind and in the direction sought, one also may have reason to comply. So, while it is a mistake to say that a norm or rule *is* or *consists in* a system of nested expectations, it is accurate to say that norms or rules arise in and are *sustained by* such a system of expectations. Moreover, systems of nested expectations are not spontaneous natural facts, but *achievements*, the products of more or less self-conscious mutual accommodation and adjustment of expectations and actions of interdependent agents interacting over time.

The normative force of custom

This understanding of the social environment of custom provides an explanation of the fact that customs are norms of a community. The explanation ties the existence of community practice to the normative force of convention-customs, although not, perhaps, in the way many have thought. I will focus on two important consequences of locating custom in this kind of social environment.

First, the normative force of social rules operating in conditions of material and deliberative interdependence is conditional, characterized by an essential *mutuality*. I mean by this that the point of complying with such rules for any party governed by them depends on (a sufficient number of) others in the neighborhood doing so as well, and this dependency is mutual among parties involved. It is tempting to say that, in circumstances of interdependence, one's reason for complying lies in the fact that others comply with a social norm, and that they reasonably expect one also to comply. Hart, for example, characterized conventional social rules as those rules that members of a community follow in part because others regularly follow them.[30] But this way

[30] Hart, *Concept of Law*, 255.

of speaking is at least misleading. Strictly speaking, the behavior or expectations of others are not among one's reasons (or even part of one's reason) to follow a customary norm, but rather they are conditions of the norm's having whatever point or reason it has. We can understand this as follows.

The case for the practical force of customary norms characterized by mutuality has the following distinctive structure. (a) Agents subject to the norms have some substantive reason to cooperate or to coordinate their social interaction. The reason arises from some aim or end (which can be merely self-regarding, or other-regarding, or common) that can be realized only with the coordinated efforts of others. (b) General compliance with the norm, while not necessarily the only way to achieve this coordination, is adequate to the purpose. (c) So, each party governed by the norm has reason to follow the norm, *on the condition* that there is general compliance with the norm (and, under the circumstances, focusing cooperation around a different norm is unlikely or too costly to undertake). Sometimes the compliance of others with the norm is part of the very point of the norm – for example, if the aim is in part to do something *together* – but it need not be. If not, then general compliance is not part of the reason for one's complying with the norm, but it is still a *condition* of its *having* a point or reason. Not all norms, and perhaps not all social rules, are conditional on mutuality in this way, but convention-customary norms are.

Secondly, we can now say something about the generality or *scope* of the normative force of convention-customs. Our question is: who falls within its sway when a custom is in force in a particular community? Consent theory, of course, says that one is bound to follow a norm only if one accepts it, or agrees to be bound by it. This is implausible as a general view of customs, because it makes their normative force strictly a matter of individual subscription. Explicit contracts and treaties have this character, perhaps, but many customs, including convention-customs, do not, for in many such cases the customs are binding whether or not one explicitly subscribes. Still, it seems right to insist on an element of voluntariness in the account of the normative scope of custom. In the above account, we have the resources for a quite different, less atomistic, account of the scope of customary norms, which nevertheless captures some of the attraction of the consent approach. I cannot hope to tell the whole story here, but I can mark certain major plot lines.

To begin, recall that customary norms are embedded in deliberative normative practices. Parties to such practices undertake commitments, but, as we have seen, commitments are not unilateral acts or attitudes, but normative relations between participants. One takes responsibility, but this involves according standing to others to assess one's performance of those responsibilities on condition that they reciprocally accord one standing to assess their responsibility-taking (including their assessments of one's own commitments and actions). Thus, the scope and content of the norms, determining that for which one is responsible, is never merely up to any single party. The norms to which parties are committed are norms of the community of the practice – not in the sense that they are norms every participant agrees upon, but rather in the sense that they are norms implicit in the practice in which they participate together, to which they are mutually committed. Norms of the practice-community bind each participant in virtue of his or her being a member of that community. Thus, norms of a customary regime, embedded in a normative practice of this kind, bind from whole to part: being norms of the whole, they bind each in virtue of being members of that whole, not in virtue of any form of merely individual subscription.

Now consider those normative practices that function in conditions of material and deliberative interdependence. As we have seen, the practical force of customs embedded in such practices is a function of the ends to which custom-directed cooperation is directed plus the fact that following the norm, given assurance of broad compliance with it in the community, will contribute to that cooperation. Where there is assurance of mutual compliance with the customary norm, each has a substantial reason to do his or her part in the custom-shaped cooperative enterprise. It is tempting to speak of "mutually beneficial cooperation" here, but we must keep in mind that this argument scheme is broad enough to include cases in which the "benefit" to individual parties is measured not in terms of service to private ends or interests of participants, but rather in terms of service to common ends. Under conditions of mutuality, individual parties cannot hope unilaterally to achieve the ends served by the custom. One is dependent on the cooperation of others, as they are on one. Threat of sanctions for defection may secure cooperation, but, in the absence of coercion, expressed and publicly assured trust-building compliance is obligatory. (And, typically, coercion is justified as enforcement of this obligation.) Again, the custom's obligation arises from the commitments and actions of the community as a whole and an individual's part in them. The norms are community norms, not rules of individual subscription.

Of course, cooperative enterprises are always vulnerable to the temptations of free-riding. Yet, the reasonableness of the free-rider strategy is not as obvious as it might first appear. If, for example, the end to be served by cooperation is a common goal – i.e., one which, as parties would say, is *mine* (in part, perhaps) because it is *ours* – then taking a vacation from doing one's part in the common enterprise is deeply in tension with the ground for the goal, and rational only if other more pressing goals are served by defecting. It would appear that free-riding will have a coherent rational appeal only for those cooperative enterprises that promise to serve overlapping or convergent ends or interests of community members. In such cases, while free-riding is not rationally incoherent, it is a threat to the enterprise in a way that all parties can easily recognize. Typically in such cases, there is nothing special about the person (or her situation) who chooses to free-load, and so whatever can be said in favor of her doing so, can equally be said in favor of any other party doing so. The party considering the free-rider option proposes (secretly, of course) to make a special exception of himself, accepting the benefits of the cooperation of others while withholding as much of his contribution to the cooperative effort as he can without detection. Simple considerations of fair play and reciprocity would seem to prohibit such free-riderism.

However, this argument moved too quickly, for there may be conditions in which the defector can justify his defection by pointing to some load-bearing difference between his situation and that of most other parties. He might argue, for example, that he does not stand to benefit (or benefit enough, relative to the benefits others will reap) from successful cooperation. If the defector can successfully make this argument, then fair-minded participants must acknowledge that it is not the defector who exploits the cooperation of the others, but rather the cooperators who exploit this individual. His defection is not free-riding, and holding him to his alleged "obligation" in the cooperative enterprise is unwarranted. Despite falling within the scope of the customary norm, this party falls outside its normative force. A fairer cooperative enterprise would recognize in some systematic way the legitimacy of such defections.

One way it might do so, while holding potential free-riders to their obligations, would be to develop a way publicly to recognize conscientious defection from the custom as it is forming. Of course, to block free-riderism, objectors would have to be excluded from enjoying the benefits of the emerging cooperative custom as well. For example, the defector could be required to extend reciprocally to all others the right to ignore the customary norm when it might work to the benefit or protection of the defector. Where there is a public device for recognizing conscientious defection from customary rules, subject to the condition of reciprocity, it would be reasonable to assume that parties who did not exercise the option judged that benefits of cooperation were sufficient to warrant their voluntary participation.

On this way of construing their normative force, customary norms are regarded consistently as norms of the community and in virtue of that fact binding on its individual members or participants; the obligations are not a matter of individual subscription, yet the voluntary choice of parties is respected by making publicly available the option of conscientious defection. Of course, this condition must be a part of the community's practice; conscientious defection is not a unilateral act, but must be a matter of recognition within the practice-community, regulated by that practice.

It is reasonable, however, that for some customary norms of a community the conscientious objector option might not be open. Some customary norms might properly be thought to serve goods or ends the reasons for which are not exhausted by considerations of the benefits enjoyed by individual members. They may be goals tied to common values rather than convergent interests – values so fundamental that the community might regard them as defining minimal conditions of membership in the community. Or the customary norms may articulate general moral principles that are not fundamentally customary, but depend on customs for their concrete force in the community in question. In either case, it might be entirely appropriate to insist that all members adhere to them, regardless of their individual assent. Adherence to these customary norms, it might be argued, is a condition of continued membership. They might properly be regarded as binding *erga omnes*.

Of course, it is not hard to imagine that some parties may wish to remain active members, at the same time ignoring such obligations when they can get away with doing so. So, customary norms binding *erga omnes* may nevertheless be all too often honored more in the breach than in the observance. *Usus* inconsistent with these norms, however, would not be enough to undermine their secure status as norms of the community. Like all customs embedded in robust discursive normative practices, what is crucial is the discursive response to the deviations, the way the deviations are properly viewed and assessed both by deviators and others according to standards implicit in the practice. Among the most important considerations to be weighed and debated will be claims that the values served by the cooperation-structuring customs are common or public values and that they are fundamental to membership in the community in question. If this issue cannot be put on the agenda for deliberation within the practice, and if it is not possible for there to be wide participation in deliberation about it, then parties are entitled to doubt the *bona fides* of those who insist on the customs as binding in the name of the community as a whole.

Custom in the global environment

Thus far I have elaborated a conception of a certain kind of custom, convention-customs, familiar in our daily lives. The question for us now is whether this account can illuminate customary international law. The social environment in which customary international law functions is not one of interacting human beings, but one in which the actors involved are primarily *nation-states* and to a lesser extent other corporate or institutional entities (NGOs, multinational corporations, etc.).[31] The apparent disanalogies between ordinary human agents and interactions and international actors and the global environment are obvious, but I think they are not sufficient to make us skeptical of using the normative practice conception of custom to advance our understanding of customary international law. In this concluding section, I briefly sketch some reasons for resisting this skepticism.

Custom and the limits of community

First, it might be argued that the infrastructure needed for convention-customs to arise does not exist in the global domain; in particular, the community available to international actors is not rich enough to foster and sustain customs as understood above. Far from the robust community needed for convention-customs, a skeptic might argue, the global environment in which legal customs must function is a chaotic multiplicity of communities, groups, and nations, lacking deeply shared values, fundamental communal bonds, or a strong sense of common

[31] A. Cassese, *International Law* (2nd edn, Oxford: Oxford University Press, 2005), 3–4.

identity. To answer this objection, look again at the kind and extent of community presupposed by my account of convention-customs.

To begin, we can note that the conditions of interdependence necessary for convention-customs do not require such robust communal relations. There is little doubt that actors in the modern global environment interact in conditions of material interdependence, so the interesting question is whether deliberative interdependence obtains in this environment. That depends on how actors in it are conceived, of course, but even the most skeptical writers are willing to accept that such actors are strategically rational agents – i.e., they are aware of themselves and other actors not only as predictable intentional agents, but as mutually aware rational agents capable of reasoning to an understanding of the strategies other actors choose to follow. This is sufficient for deliberative interdependence, as long as the actors interact enough over time for there to develop an "informational commons" of shared experience. This commons can develop without every actor interacting regularly with every other actor who participates in it. It is sufficient that their participation overlaps, in the sense that between any two participants there is a series of intermediaries linking them through whom the results of immediate experience can be passed reliably enough to enable them all to act as if the experience were common to them.

Moreover, the informational commons does not presuppose a rich repertoire of shared values or a deep sense of common identity among the actors. If the interaction of actors in the global order takes place in conditions of relatively thick material interdependence, and they are sufficiently self-aware and mutually aware, they will be caught in nets of deliberative interdependence, and they will need to master skills of interactive deliberative practical reasoning to achieve their ends regardless of what they are. A sense of common interest, and even common identity, *might* develop as a result, but they need not, and they certainly are not presupposed. Likewise, healthy deliberative normative practices do not presuppose thick communal bonds, deeply shared values, or sense of common identity. Deliberative normative practices are essentially *discursive*, hence they involve training in techniques of linking reasons to conclusions or decisions and using them as reasons for further conclusions and decisions; but none of this *presupposes* shared values or communal bonds. It presupposes, rather, a significant degree of overlapping experience and shared attempts to articulate its public significance, all in the context of asserting claims and counter-claims on resources and behavior. There is a practice only in such a commons, but this is communal in only a very thin, low-temperature sense. Thus, it is possible for customs to develop when sentiment-based (or creed-based) communal bonds are lacking.

Of course, basic "training" in discursive techniques does not take place at the global level. Actors in the global environment are institutions (or complex, structured sets of institutions), which are many normative/institutional layers distant from flesh-and-blood human individuals and the "basic" normative practices in which their practical agency is rooted. Nevertheless, rational action of institutional collectivities is possible just because such institutional actors are constructed out of roles, positions, and statuses occupied by individuals rooted and trained up in basic normative practices (or of other institutionally organized collectivities so constructed). These institutional actors in turn develop the capacities for participation in deliberative normative practices by extending the capacities of their functionaries, and by drawing on the resources of common experience that are available to them. We can accept, of course, that the ability of a collection of rational actors actually to form and govern themselves by custom varies widely as the breadth of their common experience varies and their attempts to form customary bonds succeed or fail. Success tends to expand the commons and provide resources which in turn increase the ability to form such customs, while failure can set back the enterprise. What can be achieved, or hoped for, might be very limited at one time and extensive at another, as a function of past successes and failures. So, we must conclude that the extent to which customs are likely to form in the global environment at any point in time is not settled by the nature of the actors or the environment statically considered, but rather tends to be influenced by the history of their interactions. The normative practice account is not ruled out by these considerations and may provide resources for better understanding the dynamics of this process of custom-formation.

Custom and the limits of interest

Thus, we may reasonably conclude that the global environment can sustain customary norms. However, a more deeply rooted skepticism, familiar in the literature of international law, threatens to undermine the account. It comes in moderate and radical forms. Consider first its moderate form.

Simma and Alston agree broadly with my characterization of the social environment of custom in international law, but they argue that it severely limits the kind of norms that can arise. "[U]controversial instances" of custom in the global order arise only "from constant interaction, from claims and tolerances as to what sovereign States can do to *each other*."[32] Thus, they insist, the rights and obligations generated by such customs can only be bilateral – correlative rights and duties strictly *inter se* – "running between" individual sovereign states. This strictly bilateral interaction "is intrinsic to, and essential to, the kind of State practice leading to the formation of customary international law ... [T]he processes of customary international law can only be triggered, and continue working, in situations in which States interact."[33] This argument challenges any attempts to ground human rights and other humanitarian principles in norms of customary international law. If they are right, there is no way to mount an argument for customary obligations *erga omnes*.

This is an intriguing argument, but it is not clear what sustains it. Nothing in the notion of convention-custom, or the special social environment in which convention-customs arise, limits parties to bilateral relations or prevents them from embracing common values or articulating conditions for the practice of norms of general obligation (obligations *erga omnes*) along the lines I sketched above. Simma and Alston say that no "uncontroversial instances" of custom have yet allowed for legal obligations outside the pale of bilateralism, but at most this shows that *as yet* no claims of obligations *erga omnes* are universally and automatically accepted, not that they *cannot be* or that there is something about the nature of the parties or their custom-generating relations that prevents them from acknowledging them. It does not even show that there are not at present international customs underwriting *erga omnes* obligations, but only that claims of such obligations sometimes meet resistance in the international community. That is not enough to show they do not now exist, let alone that they are not possible. Customs, I have argued, arise from *discursive* normative

[32] B. Simma and P. Alston, "The Sources of Human Rights Law: Custom, Jus Cogens, and General Principles," *Australian Yearbook of International Law*, 12 (1988–9), 199 (original emphasis).

[33] Simma and Alston, "The Sources of Human Rights Law," 199; see also B. Simma, "From Bilateralism to Community Interest in International Law," *Recueil des cours*, Académie de droit international, vol. 250 (The Hague: Martinus Nijhoff, 1997), 230–1.

practices, practices in which *word* (the articulation of claim and counter-claim) is as important as *deed* and indispensable for determining the normative significance of deeds. Discursive normative-practices provide the resources for assessing controversial cases as well. If the only customs to be admitted were those that were uncontroversial, custom would soon shrivel into irrelevance. Yet, customary regimes are remarkably resilient and self-transforming. Customs, embedded in discursive, eminently practical, normative practices, are constantly in motion, adjusting not only to new material circumstances, but also to changing understandings of the moral and practical demands of the social environment in which parties to them live and interact.

However, the source of the problem may lie not in the notion of custom or in custom arising from interaction in conditions of thick interdependence, but rather in the nature of the *parties* engaged in that interaction. It might be argued that *states* by their nature are capable only of bilateral normative relations. This more radical challenge rests on a very narrow view of what we can expect from states. It is sometimes said that states are discrete, independent, sovereign entities in a global order that is a "society of juxtaposition," in which members are moved solely by "sanctified egoism." Within such limits we can hope at most for fragile peace and limited cooperation.[34] The limits on the normative relations possible in the international order are a function of the limits of the nature of its parties.

Weil argues for this claim about the nature of states on essentially normative grounds, resting his case on the moral equality and absolute sovereignty of states. But this argument, and the vision of rational but amoral states on which it rests, fails on moral and on logical grounds. It fails on logical grounds because amoral states are said to be morally bound to recognize the autonomy (equality and sovereignty) of other states. It fails on moral grounds because a system of such amoral and entirely unaccountable yet rational agents is morally unacceptable. The moral costs of according states such absolute sovereignty are simply too high. Much of the structure and practice of humanitarian law, human rights law, and law of war is testimony to a deep unwillingness to accept this bleak picture. It is compelling only if it turns out that states *cannot* intelligibly be treated as accountable moral agents.

[34] P. Weil, "Towards Relative Normativity in International Law?" *American Journal of International Law*, 77 (1983), 418–20.

This is what certain recent rational-choice accounts of custom argue.[35] They do not seek to explain the nature and rational force of custom in international law, they explain it away. They argue that customary norms *do not* and *cannot* function in the international domain. This radical challenge depends in part on the empirical accuracy of the picture of the global order as a "society of juxtaposition" and, more fundamentally, on the claim that states *cannot* behave otherwise, in particular they never act on norms or rules, but can only act to realize their self-interest. I cannot here give this thesis the full attention it deserves. Instead, I will mention two reasons for skepticism about this skeptical theory. First, it could command serious attention if a compelling case could be made for the empirical claim that customary norms never guide the deliberations, decisions, and actions of states. Rational-choice theorists purport to offer such an argument, but in fact the conclusion is built into the methodology on which their argument is based. Using a device calibrated to detect only interest-driven actions and decisions, what they find is that only interest drives actions and decisions. Given their assumptions, this conclusion is not surprising, or illuminating.

However, the problem with this thesis is deeper. The truth of the thesis undermines its intelligibility. On this view, rules and norms can have at most only strategic significance for states – that is, states can recognize the advantage of appearing to follow them and they can be compelled by external sanctions to act in accord with them, but nothing more is possible. This claim cannot be true. States are *institutions* (usually very complex, hierarchically ordered, institutionally structured sets of institutions) and, necessarily, institutions are norm-defined, norm-governed collectivities. Of course, some collectivities although unstructured by norms are capable of behavior of remarkable regularity. Schools of fish can make their way to and from spawning grounds all without the guidance of norms. But human institutions exist and are capable of acting intelligibly – indeed, are capable of having interests such that we can intelligibly speak of them acting from self-interest – only insofar as they and others recognize them as defined and governed by norms, capable of grasping and following norms *as norms* (rather than merely strategic markers of the parameters of their anomic choices).

[35] For example, J. L. Goldsmith and E. A. Posner, "A Theory of Customary International Law," *University of Chicago Law Review*, 66 (1999), 1113–77; and J. L. Goldsmith and E. A. Posner, *The Limits of International Law* (Oxford: Oxford University Press, 2005).

Likewise, in order to act from self-interest, in order to *have* coherent interests they can pursue, states must be capable of, and frequently indulge in, norm-guided behavior. But then, to deny the possibility of states recognizing and following norms is to deny them the capacity to act as collective entities in their self-interest. The thesis self-destructs.

Although there is much more to say on this topic, it is fair to conclude, I think, that there is nothing unique to the international domain – neither the nature of the actors involved, nor the nature of their typical relations, nor the absence of communal bonds – to stand in the way of taking the above normative practice account of custom to illuminate the nature and typical mode of operation of customary international law. Despite obvious disanalogies, international actors, like individual human agents, can and do engage in discursive, practically concrete normative practices which, in a social environment of material and deliberative interdependence, yield, nurture, and sustain customary norms. Many such customary norms have a central place in the law governing the interactions among states and other actors in the international domain.

13

Customary international law and the quest for global justice

JOHN TASIOULAS*

Hope without fear?

Customary international law (CIL) excites both hope and fear among international lawyers. It excites hope among partisans of the idea that international law is an important means for advancing the cause of global justice; indeed, they would go further and insist that international law's legitimacy – the very justifiability of its claim to set normative standards for its subjects – turns on whether it gives adequate expression to the demands of global justice. I use the label 'global justice' in a broad sense, to encompass moral values and principles, including but not limited to the minimalist values of peaceful co-existence and co-operation, that should be respected by all states whether in their internal affairs (transnational justice) or in their relations with other states (international justice). The requirements of global justice include norms establishing human rights, authorizing humanitarian intervention and assistance, enjoining environmental protection, and so on. But how can morally attractive standards of this sort, which are regularly flouted throughout the world today, acquire the status of international laws that are opposable against all states?

Reliance upon treaties is prey to well-known difficulties: not all states have signed up or are likely to sign up to norms of the relevant type. Moreover, many states that have formally agreed to such norms have done so subject to eviscerating reservations. Alternatively, one might characterize certain principles of global justice either as peremptory

* I am grateful to the editors of this volume for their comments. My thanks are also owed to Philip Allott, James Crawford, Andrew Altman and Tim Sellers who commented on an earlier version of this paper at conferences held at the University of Cambridge and the University of North Carolina, Greensboro.

norms of *jus cogens*,[1] understood as moral principles accessible to natural reason, or as 'general principles recognized by all civilized nations'.[2] But the first manoeuvre is not easily distinguishable from a barefaced appeal to supposed universal moral truths, a putative source of legal norms that outruns anything licensed by recognizably *legal* reasoning. After all, it is unrealistic to suppose that public international law has *always* incorporated prohibitions against human rights violations or crimes against humanity, simply because these norms embody demands that natural law makes on any minimally just system of international law. As to the second ploy, apart from relying on a poorly regarded and seldom-invoked source of law, it also displays a high degree of wishful thinking. This is because there is little reason to suppose that norms prohibiting torture or sex discrimination, for example, are 'recognized by all civilized nations'. At any rate, there is little reason to suppose this in the absence of a benchmark of 'civilization' that is so morally freighted that the problems confronting the *jus cogens* strategy simply reappear in a different guise.

By invoking the idea of CIL, one can hope to establish the legal status of certain global justice principles (or sufficiently close approximations to them) without encountering the problems that beset reliance on treaties or pure ethical reasoning. This is because a customary norm does not require the consent of all states in order to come into existence; but, when it has come into existence, it is opposable against all states without exception (provided the norm is not a regional custom). However, the existence of a customary norm is not determined purely by ethical reasoning; instead, it must have a requisite grounding in general state practice and *opinio juris*. Still, custom as positivistically conceived (see the next section below) is no panacea for the legal embodiment of norms of global justice. On this view, the formation of a CIL requires general and consistent state practice in conformity with a putative norm, together with *opinio juris* to the effect that the practice accords with international law. These requirements can be very difficult to secure, especially in the case of norms that impinge adversely on the interests of powerful states. Moreover, they are unlikely to be secured expeditiously, with the result that international law will remain defective or mute regarding problems that demand immediate action, such as

[1] L. May, *Crimes against Humanity* (Cambridge University Press, 2005).

[2] B. Simma and P. Alston, 'The Sources of Human Rights Law: Custom, Jus Cogens, and General Principles', *Australian Year Book of International Law* 12 (1992): 82.

environmental and humanitarian crises. The problem of delay is aggravated if states are restricted to engaging only in lawful acts when seeking to reform CIL. Such a strategy will demand the lapse of any existing custom found to be defective (through the falling away of the state practice and *opinio juris* that sustains the norm) followed by the gradual accumulation of both these elements in favour of the superior norm.

These perceived imperfections in the system of international law formation have led some leading proponents of global justice to advocate the reform of international law through *illegal* state action, subject of course to certain carefully specified guidelines. Acts that violate existing laws that are thought to be seriously defective – for example, the norm prohibiting armed intervention against another state without Security Council authorization, even in order to prevent genocide – hasten both the demise of the offending law and the creation of a new, improved customary norm or treaty regime.[3] But this avenue also suffers from disadvantages: in many cases, it will be highly unlikely that the requisite state practice and *opinio juris* will accumulate within an acceptable time-frame, while in the meantime the costs of contravening existing law are incurred. Perhaps it will be said that both disadvantages are unavoidable, given the welcome absence of a global legislature that can instantly enact the relevant principles into law, and also that the second set of costs are typically insignificant in light of the prospective benefits. But such a response is too hasty. The costs of creating law in this way may often be worth bearing, but they are by no means always insignificant. After all, what is at issue here is the value of the rule of law in international relations. Crudely stated, this is the requirement that the deployment of coercive power by states should conform to pre-existing legal norms that are clear, stable, accessible, non-conflicting etc. – something in which weaker states typically have a deep interest. And the suggested means of law-creation is especially problematic in those areas of law, such as armed intervention and criminal law, where rule of law values assume especially great importance.[4]

[3] See, for example, A. Buchanan, 'From Nuremburg to Kosovo: The Morality of Illegal International Legal Reform', *Ethics* 111 (2001): 673–705; and R. E. Goodin, 'Toward an International Rule of Law: Distinguishing International Law-Breakers from Would-Be Law-Makers', *Journal of Ethics* 9 (2005): 225–46.

[4] Cf. the proposals that the law of armed humanitarian intervention and international criminal law need to be reformed by, respectively, states engaging in interventions unauthorized by existing law and trying and punishing people for acts that were not international crimes at the time they perpetrated them: see Buchanan, 'From Nuremburg

Of course, I do not mean to suggest that rule of law considerations always trump the case for illegal law reform; nonetheless, they are important costs associated with the latter strategy. And their existence should lead us to question the assumption that incurring these costs, together with those of delay, are unavoidable if international law is better to secure the demands of global justice. In particular, we should not accept that, in the absence of a global legislature, reforming violations of existing law are the only, or the dominant, realistic means for enhancing the moral quality of international law. This is because the positivist interpretation of customary law presupposed by the advocates of illegal law reform is itself highly questionable. It is here that the hope excited by customary law that I spoke of at the beginning comes into its own. It is sustained by the thought that certain key norms of global justice can be found *already* to have the status of customary norms, or else that they can come to acquire that status without the need for general and consistent state practice in conformity with them (including practice that is illegal according to existing law). And the reason for this is that, on an alternative, interpretative understanding of custom (see the third section of this essay), the ethical appeal of a candidate norm figures among the criteria for determining whether it is a valid norm of CIL in such a way that a customary norm may exist even in the absence of widespread state practice, or even overwhelming state consent, in its favour.

If this interpretative understanding of custom can be vindicated, this would enhance the prospects of showing that certain important moral obligations are opposable against all states. This would be so irrespective of whether any particular state has consented to the norms and, in the case of *jus cogens* norms – assuming they are now construed as peremptory customary norms rather than natural law principles – irrespective also of any state's manifest and persistent objections to the legalization of the norm. Moreover, a subsidiary benefit would be to improve the prospects of reforming CIL in a way that brings it into greater alignment with basic requirements of global justice. This is because a relevant factor in determining whether any such change has occurred will be the ethical attractiveness of the putative newly emergent norm.

But that others should be alarmed by, rather than find cause for hope in, what has been called 'the cult of custom' is also readily

to Kosovo'; and A. Altman and C. H. Wellman, 'A Defence of International Criminal Law', *Ethics* 115 (2004): 35–67.

understandable.[5] For why should we accept that the ethical soundness of a norm has any bearing on its status as customary law? The danger in accepting this idea is that custom becomes, not a source of legal norms the existence and content of which is robustly independent of anyone's viewpoint on contestable ethical and political issues, but either a political battlefield in which indeterminacy is rampant or else the puppet of some arbitrarily privileged ideological standpoint. Now, some of the hopeful might suspect that what unites many of the fearful is a resistance to the global justice agenda, a resistance they seek to hide behind the fig-leaf of concern about legality in international affairs. Whether or not there is any truth in this diagnosis, disquiet about the invocation of ethical judgments in determining the existence of CIL is clearly not confined to those who are hostile to the agenda of securing global justice through international law.

Allen Buchanan, for example, has elaborated a demanding human rights-based normative theory of international law. But he also insists that the legal implementation of main elements of the theory is best achieved through illegal law reform that is motivated at a deeper level by a genuine commitment to the rule of law. He regards as multiply problematic the strategy of claiming that some of his favoured principles – such as a norm licensing humanitarian intervention outside the UN framework – already enjoy legal status:

> When faced with the prospect that significant reform seems to require violating existing law, some international legal scholars yield to the temptation to evade the issue of whether illegal acts of reform can be morally justifiable. They do this by stretching the concept of legality – arguing that the needed reform is not really illegal. Such evasion ought to be vigorously resisted, both because it leads to an overly malleable conception of the law and to a confusion between claims about what the law is and what it ought to be, and because it concedes too much to the Legal Absolutist, by proceeding as if it is necessary to show that an act directed toward reform is legally permissible in order to establish that it is justifiable.[6]

Buchanan's scepticism is well motivated. It is certainly important to retain a conception of CIL that is not merely epiphenomenal with

[5] W. M. Reisman, 'The Cult of Custom in the Late 20th Century', *California Western International Law Journal* 17 (1987): 133.

[6] A. Buchanan, *Justice, Legitimacy, and Self-Determination: Moral Foundations for International Law* (OUP, 2004), p. 468.

respect to one's views about global justice, that does not erase the distinction between *lex lata* and *lex ferenda*, and that does not succumb to the absolutist myth that it is never morally justified to break the law. But, even with all that granted, Buchanan veers too far in the opposite direction, seriously underestimating the extent to which custom can be a vehicle for achieving a global justice agenda without succumbing to his three objections.[7] He is right to insist that we should not evade the question of whether illegal law reform is ever justified, and I believe he is also right to argue that it is *sometimes* justified. But he is wrong to evade the question of when a norm is a norm of CIL by simply taking for granted a supposed positivist orthodoxy on norm-formation.[8]

Tackling the latter question may reveal greater scope for pursuing global justice *within* the existing international legal system than the positivist conception appeared to allow, and this in turn directly bears on the responsible pursuit of the illegal reform strategy. This is for at least two reasons. First, we need a reliable assessment of how unjust existing international law is before deciding whether illegal reform is justified to bring about its improvement. This demands that we have some means of determining the existence of valid customary norms, which in turn requires that we defend our understanding of the nature of CIL, not simply presuppose it. Secondly, the justifiability of the illegal reform strategy in any given case is partly determined by its likelihood of success in bringing about a desirable change in the law. This in turn is influenced by whether we employ an interpretative or a positivist conception of custom. *Ceteris paribus*, the former is more likely to lead to success (and to do so more rapidly) than the latter, since only the former makes the moral attractiveness of a putative norm a relevant consideration in judging its legal validity. Moreover, there is a serious problem under this heading facing most advocates of illegal law reform. A definitive component of the positivist doctrine of custom to which they appeal is the 'persistent objector rule', according to which a state can exempt itself from the scope of a norm by clearly and consistently voicing its opposition to it during the period of its formation. This threatens to render many attempts at illegal law reform largely nugatory,

[7] Cf. also Philip Allott, who asserts that customary international law 'as at present conceived' offers no genuine prospect of giving effect to a whole range of morally compelling norms. P. Allott, *Eunomia: New Order for a New World* (OUP, 1990), p. 336.

[8] For this explicit evasion in his argument, see Buchanan, 'From Kosovo to Nuremberg', p. 680.

since powerful states will be able to evade subjection to the superior customary norms by repudiating them in word and deed. On an interpretative conception of custom, by contrast, the persistent objector rule does not apply to peremptory norms of *ius cogens*, understood now as norms of CIL, since their content is so morally compelling that no exemption from their scope can be permitted. Therefore, in defending an interpretative account of custom, I not only offer an *alternative* method to illegal reform for improving international law, I also address an important issue *integral* to the effective implementation of that very strategy.

Positivism and the idolatry of the state

Positivism, as a normative account of the formation of CIL, can be characterized as a conjunction of four theses: (i) the existence of widespread and consistent state practice in conformity with a given rule is a *sine qua non* of its being a CIL norm; (ii) *opinio juris* is not a potentially 'independent variable' making an autonomous contribution to the generation of custom, but must either be inferred from a state's practice or else be derived from statements made by the state explaining or justifying its practice; (iii) the process whereby state practice and *opinio juris* combine to generate a norm of CIL should not turn on any assessment of the ethical attractiveness of the norm in question; and (iv) a state can avoid being bound by any norm of CIL by persistently objecting to it during the process of its formation. Regarding (iii), it is perhaps worth noting that the embargo on ethical judgment is focused on the *content* of the putative norm; for it is arguable that even the most uncompromising positivist must admit some element of evaluative judgment in the process of customary norm-formation, at least when it comes to deciding how general and consistent state practice must be in order to issue (together with *opinio juris*) in a customary norm.

Positivism and legitimacy

In order to assess the positivist conception of custom, one must evaluate the political morality that underlies it. Perhaps the consideration most often invoked by positivists is that of consent as the basis of the legitimacy of the international legal order and its constituent norms. Now, even die-hard positivists tend not to adhere to an especially demanding version of this thesis, at least not insofar as they presuppose the legitimacy of substantial tracts of existing international law. To begin with, there is the anaemic notion of consent that is normally operative in international law, whereby the acquiescence of a state in a norm because of its subjection to economic or other pressure by a more powerful state would normally be regarded as consensual. Moreover, even positivists subscribe to the idea that states that have come into existence after the crystallization of a customary norm are bound by it despite not having had the opportunity to consent to it. But there are deeper problems with consent theory. The first is that the consent in question is that of a sovereign state, as presently understood in international law. But a state can be sovereign even if the government that controls it represses its people, with the result that its consent to international norms is granted or withheld in accordance with the perceived self-interest of a tyrannical ruling clique. Why should the consent of such a state be determinative of the legitimacy of international legal norms?

One might respond to this last argument by suggesting that it is only those states that are at least minimally legitimate that enjoy sovereignty. This is already a drastic revision of the traditional view, but tremendous difficulties still remain. Why should even legitimate states enjoy a veto over the opposability against them of any norms to which they have not consented (or which they have consistently opposed), irrespective of the content of those norms or the support they enjoy among other states? The real mistake here is to assume that consent is the ultimate source of all our moral obligations, including the moral obligations that exist in virtue of the law (such as customary norms). But consent cannot possess this status; at most, it can be a subsidiary source of moral obligations, giving rise to *some* obligations under fairly constrained circumstances. What reason is there to believe that all international legal obligations, including all obligations of CIL, should fall within this category? More strongly still, what reason is there to suppose that international legal norms are ethically justified (quite apart from whether they impose a moral obligation to obey them) only if they have received the consent of all (legitimate) states?

Well, a traditionalist might respond by defending consent on instrumental grounds. This is a strategy adopted by Prosper Weil: by not rigorously grounding customary international legal norms in the consent of each and every state subject to them, one risks both rampant indeterminacy in the identification of customary norms and, partly as a result, the danger that powerful states or a majority of states exploit this indeterminacy to foist their values, under the guise of universal legal obligations, on other states that do not share them. The overall result will be severe damage to the capacity of international law to secure the fundamental objectives of peaceful coexistence between, and cooperation among, sovereign and equal states. I responded at length to Weil's argument in an earlier article, showing that the best non-positivist reading of CIL does not have these consequences and that, on the contrary, it is better fitted to securing the objectives of coexistence and cooperation.[9] This line of argument goes through *a fortiori*, I think, if we acknowledge – as we should – that public international law has legitimate ends, such as the protection of human rights and the natural environment, that go well beyond the minimalist objectives recognized by Weil.[10]

Instead of re-enacting old battles, we can move on by noticing an assumption that I share with the traditional positivist view represented by Weil, namely, that the account of custom we should favour is that which is best justified by a political morality that offers the most attractive specification of the values served by international law. One of the more remarkable developments in recent years has been the emergence of writers who defend the positivist position but deny that their defence is mounted from the standpoint of morality. According to them, the fact that the positivist view lacks the ethical appeal of the interpretative view ignores the existence of another level – the level of the political, taken as an autonomous realm – at which the positivist conception can be vindicated. Those of a post-modern cast of mind will explain the interminable struggle between positivist and non-positivist conceptions of international law as indicative of a manifestation of the irreconcilable claims of morality and politics.

The 'autonomy' of politics

Now, the idea that the 'political' is an autonomous realm is open to radically different interpretations. According to a rather weak interpretation, it simply indicates that the political is a fairly distinct subject-matter for

[9] See P. Weil, 'Towards Relative Normativity in International Law?', *American Journal of International Law* 77 (1983): 413; and J. Tasioulas, 'In Defence of Relative Normativity: Communitarian Values and the *Nicaragua* Case', *Oxford Journal of Legal Studies* 16 (1996): 85.

[10] See also Buchanan's valuable criticism of the idea that state consent is either a sufficient or a necessary condition of system legitimacy, in *Justice, Legitimacy, and Self-Determination*, pp. 301–14.

ethical deliberation. It is the subject-matter defined by the coming together of individuals, for their common good, in large-scale communities governed by institutions that claim a monopoly on the legitimate deployment of coercion within a given territory in order to further that common good. In this sense, politics and ethics are not radically discontinuous; instead, the former is a specific field of application for the latter. Within that field certain ethical values and principles – such as democratic decision-making, the rule of law, individual liberty, etc. – assume a centrality that they do not have in other contexts, such as family life, thus giving political morality its own distinctive moral character. This weak interpretation of the autonomy of the political offers no comfort to the positivist; on the contrary, it is precisely the interpretation that demarcates the terrain on which the debate with the traditional positivist takes place.

Another conception of the political is that adumbrated by John Rawls in *Political Liberalism*.[11] Here the contrast is not with morality but rather with comprehensive doctrines, e.g. religious creeds and philosophical theories, since it is conceptions of justice (a central moral value) that are described as 'political'. Employing this notion of the 'political', Rawls has elaborated a Law of Peoples that includes a core doctrine of human rights and a duty of assistance borne by well-ordered societies in relation to burdened societies.[12] His claim is that a just international law would give effect to the Law of Peoples and that well-ordered societies would comply with it for the right (moral) reasons. Although he does not address anything so technical as sources doctrine, it is clear that for Rawls the applicability of the Law of Peoples to political communities is not hostage to their actual consent (as opposed to the hypothetical consent of well-ordered peoples – liberal and decent – behind a veil of ignorance). This interpretation of the 'political' also offers little support to the positivist, at least if the litmus test of positivism is the persistent objector doctrine.

[11] J. Rawls, *Political Liberalism* (Columbia University Press, 1993). According to Rawls, 'political' conceptions of justice bear the following three hallmarks: (a) they are limited in their subject-matter, being primarily concerned with the basic structure of society, or the relations between different societies; (b) they can be presented independently of any particular philosophical or religious worldview ('comprehensive doctrine') that claims to be true; and (c) they appeal to moral values – in particular, the idea of citizens as free and equal who cooperate for mutual benefit – that are latent in the public culture of a liberal democracy.

[12] J. Rawls, *The Law of Peoples* (Harvard University Press, 1999). For criticism, see J. Tasioulas, 'From Utopia to Kazanistan: John Rawls and the Law of Peoples', *Oxford Journal of Legal Studies* 22 (2002): 367.

However, there is a third, and far more radical interpretation of the autonomy of the political. In contrast to the previous two interpretations, on this view politics is a radically autonomous realm that is completely distinct from morality. Thus, according to Paul Kahn, the political 'is a complete system of meaning that is its own source and end', a system that determines from whom sacrifice may be demanded ('friends') and against whom force may be deployed ('enemies'):

> This autonomy makes the state an ultimate value from the perspective of the citizen. It is a normative order closed in upon itself in the same way that a religious order does not rest on yet some higher end or justification. Not even the well-being of individuals serves as such a higher end. Instrumental justifications of the political that rely on well-being will always fail at the moment of conscription. Yet, without the potential of a demand for sacrifice, we are not speaking of modern politics at all. What modern politics demanded of us has always been too much and too terrible to find its reason elsewhere.[13]

It is this understanding of the political that, Kahn believes, underwrites the positivist account of CIL. If the nation-state is an 'ultimate', 'infinite', 'unlimited' value that is to be 'defended at any cost',[14] and if its value is not explicable in terms of sustaining the common good of its members or preserving the natural environment, then there are no standards independent of those the state freely chooses to recognize to which (from a political viewpoint) it may be subjected.[15] Now, one might challenge the inference from the irreducible and ultimate value of the nation-state to the positivist conception of international law. It is hardly obvious, for example, that norms of *jus cogens* threaten the existence of any state. On the contrary, voluntary undertakings – e.g. agreements to host the military bases of a 'friendly' super-power – are perhaps more likely to have this effect. Nor is it clear why, from the perspective that accords ultimate value to the nation-state, any particular moral norm will be recognized, including the moral norm of being bound by one's previously granted consent.

[13] P. W. Kahn, *Putting Liberalism in its Place* (Princeton University Press, 2005), p. 280.

[14] *Ibid.*, pp. 281–3.

[15] 'To the classic international lawyer, who believed that state consent is the sole ground of all international legal norms, the idea of jus cogens makes little sense, just because it suggests a ground of law beyond the consenting agent. That a state would agree to conditions of international law that would threaten its own survival was a possibility ruled out in advance.' *Ibid.*, p. 284.

But let us assume the validity of the inference, for it is certainly true that many who adopt the positivist approach ultimately do so on the basis of something like a statist ideology. In that case, we have a fine illustration of the logician's quip that one man's *modus ponens* is another's *modus tollens*. If a deeply unattractive political theology is the most cogent basis for defending the positivist conception of CIL, this very fact amounts to a *reductio ad absurdum* of that conception. How can that man-made entity, the nation-state, plausibly claim to have value that is both totally unrelated to anything outside itself (human well-being, the natural order etc.) *and* infinitely surpasses any such other values? One can begin to imagine how such value might be accorded to the love of a divine being, the all-powerful, all-good, all-knowing creator of the universe. But the nation-state is nothing like a divine being, despite Kahn's startling claim that in the modern era the nation has displaced God as the perceived source of ultimate value.

The tenuousness of the religious analogy is compounded by the extremism of Kahn's thesis, which goes beyond even what many proponents of the idea of transcendent, religious values are prepared to affirm. For the majority of theists the divine being is characterized partly in terms of its moral perfection. Similarly, the ordinary concept of a state embodies a moral norm, in that one cannot understand what the state is without reference to the idea that its purpose in monopolizing legitimate coercion within a defined territory is that of furthering the common good of the inhabitants of that territory. But for Kahn the concept of a sovereign state does not incorporate any ethical aspirations at all. Moreover, even if religions typically assert a source of value beyond human existence, it is usually thought of as intimately tied up with the values of human existence, sustaining them and bringing them to completion. But Kahn's understanding of autonomy of the political rejects any *inherent* connection between the value of the nation-state and the furtherance of human interests – that any particular state should wed itself to the rule of law, human rights, democracy etc. is a further, contingent matter about how the political community's will is exercised. That the nation-state, so understood, should be accorded value, let alone 'ultimate' and 'infinite' value, is not just mysterious but perverse.

To let matters rest on that uncompromising note is hardly satisfactory. Some diagnosis is needed to explain how Kahn might have arrived at such conclusions. First, perhaps some vicious political ideologies – for instance, fascism and various forms of ultra-nationalism – embody the kind of idolatry of the nation-state that he describes.[16] Indeed, Kahn's discussion is obviously influenced by the Nazi jurisprudent Carl Schmitt's theory that politics has a peculiar logic based on the 'friend–enemy' distinction. But, from the fact that such extremist ideologies exist, and have been influential, it does not follow that they identify a set of genuine, let alone absolute, values as opposed to pathological misconceptions.[17] Secondly, Kahn seems to be misled by the fact that the state may call upon its citizens to make the 'ultimate sacrifice', to lay down their lives to ensure its continued existence. For the situations in which this demand is justifiable are plausibly understood in terms of values independent of the state structure itself, i.e. the values that the preservation of this particular state will serve, as well as the moral obligations one has incurred as a citizen of such a state. Kahn appears to assume that if, in sacrificing one's life in this way, one is not serving one's self-interest (either directly, or by following rules that are for the mutual benefit of all members of the state), then one must be acting to preserve the 'infinite' value of the nation-state itself. But these two alternatives ignore a vastly proliferating middle ground of *ethical* values and principles that might justify self-sacrifice. I may have good and sufficient reason to risk my life in light of moral reasons to protect the interests of others, reasons that are best complied with by sacrificing my life to maintain in being the kind of nation-state that can best further those interests. There is no need to postulate anything so radical as a domain of autonomous political meanings in order to make sense of any legitimate call for self-sacrifice.

There is one final diagnostic observation worth registering. Kahn rightly rejects political rationalism, the idea that political decision-making can and should always be exclusively determined by the workings of reason; instead, reason requires supplementation by (individual and collective) will. For example, the practical options that reason presents are often diverse and incommensurable in value, so that in order to select one rather than another, as reason itself often demands that I do, an exercise of will is needed that is not itself fully determined

[16] Kahn, *Putting Liberalism in its Place*, pp. 19–20, 234–5.

[17] On one reading, Kahn is not describing genuine values, but rather certain widespread tendencies in history, e.g. 'Personally, I have little taste for the politics of faith and sacrifice that I believe to be constitutive of an American culture of popular sovereignty': *ibid.*, p. 19 n. 24; see also *ibid.*, p. 229. On the other hand, he also argues that liberal aspirations presuppose, as a condition of their intelligibility, the substratum formed by independent, political meanings: this is what 'putting liberalism in its place' involves.

by reason. Moreover, the making of such choices often itself has value, giving expression to one's individuality and providing a basis for the development of character and for certain values related to its assessment, such as integrity or spontaneity. Parallel observations might be made about the role of reason in guiding collective or political deliberation. Indeed, one of the functions of positive law generally is to provide guidance in cases where it is needed, but pure ethical reasoning 'runs out'. But all this presupposes that the will operates within a framework established by reason. Indeed, for an act of will even to be intelligible, its object must be the sort of thing we can make sense of under the aspect of the good. Kahn, however, misconstrues the significance of the will in practical deliberation, inverting its relation to reason. In the political case, he thinks that the will has priority because it establishes a set of distinctive political meanings, generating a sense of identity, the bearers of which may or may not then go on to embrace sound ethical values. This gets matters precisely back to front and a symptom of this is that the operations of the will are thereby condemned to unintelligibility. We can certainly create a meaningful life for ourselves through various forms of commitment and identification, both individual and collective. However, we do not do so *ex nihilo*, but only against the background of what we can intelligibly regard as valuable. I conclude that a compelling case for a positivist understanding of custom, based on the thesis of the radical autonomy of the political, remains to be made.

The interpretative account of custom

With doubt cast on the positivist conception of custom, space has now been created to consider the merits of a non-positivist alternative that remains within the broadly traditional understanding of that source, i.e. that according to which it involves the elements of *usus* and *opinio juris*.

A disjunctive account of opinio juris

Before embarking on this task, it is necessary to respond to a seemingly devastating objection to any attempt to rehabilitate a broadly traditional conception of CIL. This is the familiar claim that the notion of *opinio juris* deployed by that conception is 'paradoxical'.[18] First, it is necessary

[18] For a recent claim to this effect, see J. L. Goldsmith and E. A. Posner, *The Limits of International Law* (OUP, 2005), p. 24. The authors take this objection, along with three

to clarify the nature of the problem. The problem, as I understand it, is this. On the traditional understanding of *opinio juris*, the emergence (or revision) of CIL depends upon states *mistakenly* believing, or successfully pretending mistakenly to believe, that the pattern of behaviour to which they are referring is *already* lawful. This is not a literal contradiction in the traditional conception of custom itself. There is nothing contradictory in affirming that, for a norm to *become* legally valid, states must (successfully pretend to) mistakenly believe that it is *already* legally valid. So the traditional conception is not strictly 'paradoxical'. But the problem identified is nonetheless a serious flaw in that conception because a plausible requirement on any adequate source of law is that it fulfil a requirement of transparency. In other words, its successful operation in generating new law or revising existing law must not depend on mistaken beliefs (or pretended such beliefs) on the part of the agents that create or revise the law as to what it is that they are doing.

The transparency requirement itself expresses a general constraint on the legitimate deployment of power. Political legitimacy demands that exercises of political power be publicly assessable in terms of standards that appropriately constrain political decision-making. A corollary of their being assessable in this way is a transparency requirement, according to which exercises of political power must be sincerely and accurately presented and defended by their agents as the acts that they are. Legislators, for example, must have both an understanding, and make an honest avowal, of what it is that they are doing when they make laws. This is a prelude both to their providing a justification for their legislative acts and to the public evaluation of those acts and justifications. But the traditional conception of the genesis of custom involves an in-built transgression of this transparency requirement, since it is a condition of the creation of custom that those engaged in creating it mistakenly believe (or successfully present themselves as mistakenly believing) that the norm in question is already law.

So, if the objection stands, it is not only the concentration of power in the hands of unaccountable governmental and bureaucratic elites controlling organizations such as the WTO or the World Bank that poses a significant threat to international legitimacy in the contemporary world. The process of customary norm creation does so as well, and of its very nature. If the problem can receive no cogent response, we may have to

less significant ones, to warrant the jettisoning of the traditional understanding of CIL as involving *usus* and *opinio*.

turn our backs on custom as a source of international law, especially if we are looking to it as a means of legalizing norms of global justice. For it would be no small irony to pursue a global justice agenda through a mechanism that is *inherently* flawed in point of legitimacy. In any case, I hope enough has been said to justify resisting the studied, but unconvincing, insouciance that some international lawyers adopt in response to the question of custom's genesis.[19] Such an attitude inevitably provokes a sceptical backlash that seeks to debunk customary international law as traditionally conceived; this is especially so when customary norms are being increasingly invoked against states that have not consented to them. A better approach is to tackle the question head-on.

Fortunately, a relatively straightforward solution to the problem is available. This involves adopting a *disjunctive* conception of the content of *opinio juris*, one that distinguishes two broad types of cases: (1) cases where *opinio juris* concerns the *creation* or *revision* of customary international law; and (2) cases where *opinio juris* concerns the *persistence* across time of a norm that has already come into existence at some earlier stage. For the problem that has been identified does not implicate category (2) cases. There is nothing obviously perplexing about the claim that, once a norm of CIL has come into existence, its persistence depends upon continued state practice and *opinio juris*, and that the content of the *opinio juris* should include as a component the belief that the relevant pattern of behaviour is *already* lawful. Thus, the content of *opinio juris* has to be understood in disjunctive terms, as relating either to situations of creation/revision or to those of continued existence, or (in cases where the legal status of the norm is uncertain) to both. The flaw, therefore, in the traditional rendering of *opinio juris* was to assume that, variation in the content of the norm being accepted aside, it is a unitary attitude, i.e. one whose content does not vary as between situations of creating a legal rule and those of following or endorsing a legal rule that is taken already to exist.

So, to take category (1) cases, *opinio juris* can be characterized as broadly involving the following content:

[19] For a characteristic dismissal of the problem of *communis error facit jus*, with the bland reassurance that '[t]he process by which customary rules change and develop presents theoretical difficulties; but it is a process which does occur', see H. Thirlway, 'The Sources of International Law as a Consensual Bond', in Malcolm Evans (ed.), *International Law* (OUP, 2003), p. 128.

> [**OJ1**] The creation of an international legal rule according to which the specified pattern of behaviour would be lawful is ethically justified, and such a legal rule should be created by means of a process that involves general state practice consistent with it and an ethical endorsement by states of its establishment as a legal rule.

Alternatively, in category (2) cases, where a state purports to act in accordance with (or purports to invoke) a rule that is already part of the corpus of customary international law, the content of its *opinio juris* would be as follows:

> [**OJ2**] The specified pattern of behaviour is in accordance with an international legal rule that has been appropriately created through general state practice and *opinio juris* (i.e. OJ1), and that rule is ethically justified.

Both OJ1 and OJ2 presuppose a broader, systemic ethical commitment on the part of a state whose *opinio juris* is in question, i.e.:

> [**SC**] The process of creating international legal rules through general state practice and *opinio* juris is an ethically legitimate one, i.e. it provides a *pro tanto* reason for the exercise of power within the international system.

This disjunctive interpretation of *opinio juris* defuses the problem of transparency without implausibly attributing overly complicated attitudes to states. And it does so in a way that makes good sense of familiar statements, such as the ICJ's assertion, in the *North Sea Continential Shelf Cases*, that, for *opinio juris* to exist, '[t]he States concerned must . . . feel that they are conforming to what amounts to a legal obligation'.[20] Statements such as this can be accepted as true (insofar as they refer to OJ2, at least in those cases where the relevant legal norm is obligation-imposing), but incomplete (insofar as they neglect OJ1). A further advantage of that account is that it can readily accommodate situations in which a state is uncertain of the legal standing of the relevant rule on the basis of which it acts or which it endorses. Here an *opinio juris* that is itself disjunctive in content (i.e. the proposition 'OJ2 or, if the norm is not already law, OJ2' is affirmed) may be ascribed to the state. Finally, this account leaves open the possibility that a state's mistaken belief, or pretended mistaken belief, that *X* is a norm of CIL can contribute to the

[20] Para. 177. It is, of course, a mistake to suppose that *opinio juris* always involves the claim that the relevant pattern of behaviour is obligatory, as opposed to some other possible deontic modality, e.g. rights, permissions, etc.

process whereby *X becomes* a legally valid norm. But this is not a *necessary* feature of the account of the genesis of custom that is made possible by the disjunctive interpretation, which is precisely the problem that confronted the 'traditional' understanding of *opinio juris*.

A critic might take issue with the liberal use of the adjective 'ethical' in characterizing the beliefs and commitments schematically represented by OJ1, OJ2 and SC.[21] Why should it be thought that an 'ethical' matter is at stake, requiring an 'ethical' justification, in the case of each individual customary law or even in endorsing the general process whereby customary laws are generated? The answer lies in the capaciousness of my understanding of ethical. The domain of the ethical is the domain of reasons that bear on an agent that derive from a proper regard for human interests, both his own and, especially, those of others. The other assumption I make is about the implicit standing that OJ1, OJ2 and SC accord to ethical justification, i.e. that it is broadly objectivist in character. The objectivist aspiration of ethical thought I take to be an essential component of that mode of thought's self-understanding. It is the claim that it is possible to assess ethical beliefs and commitments as true or false, justified or unjustified, by reference to standards that are not arbitrary or simply given, but which can instead be rationally vindicated against competing standards. Whether that aspiration can be fulfilled is another matter, but I take the aspiration to be inherent in our ordinary ethical self-understanding, differentiating it in one important way from expressions of personal taste.[22]

An interpretative account

The interpretative account of custom can be seen as providing a justification for the ICJ's derivation, in the *Nicaragua* case, of customary norms of non-use of force and non-intervention despite the apparent existence of substantial contrary state practice.[23] This is because *how*

[21] For another interpretation of *opinio juris* that emphasizes its 'ethical', or at least 'practical' rather than strictly legal, character but overlooks the need for a disjunctive account, see the sophisticated discussion in J. Finnis, *Natural Law and Natural Rights* (OUP, 1980), pp. 238–45.

[22] See J. Tasioulas, 'The Legal Relevance of Ethical Objectivity', *American Journal of Jurisprudence* 47 (2002): 211–54.

[23] In this and the next four paragraphs I draw on the discussion in J. Tasioulas, 'In Defence of Relative Normativity: Communitarian Values and the *Nicaragua* Case', *Oxford Journal of Legal Studies* 16 (1996): 85–128, at 109–15.

much state practice and *opinio juris* is needed to establish a customary norm, and in what proportion, depends in crucial part on an evaluation of the content of the putative norm. The basic idea is nicely captured by Frederic L. Kirgis' suggestion that the *Nicaragua* Court adopted a view of CIL according to which 'the elements of custom [are] not [regarded] as fixed and mutually exclusive, but as interchangeable along a sliding scale'.[24] So, very frequent and consistent state practice may establish a restrictive customary norm without much independent showing of *opinio juris*. As frequency and consistency diminish, more in the way of *opinio juris* may be required. Conversely, a clearly demonstrated *opinio juris* may establish a norm despite a lack of general state practice consistent with the putative norm. The exact nature of the 'trade off' between state practice and *opinio juris* will depend on a judgment about the efficacy of the putative norm in achieving the goals of international law (peace, human rights, environmental protection and so on) in a legitimate manner.[25]

Kirgis' schematization of the *Nicaragua* method can be elaborated by reference to Dworkin's account of law as an interpretative concept, where (constructive) interpretation is understood as 'a matter of imposing purpose on an object or practice in order to make of it the best possible example of the form or genre to which it is taken to belong'.[26] The 'raw data', or 'text', to be interpreted is state practice and *opinio juris*. The interpretation aims to derive a norm that presents the data in its best light, given the genre to which it belongs. That genre is international law, and the assessment of what counts as showing something within that genre in its best light depends upon the values that international law must be understood as aiming to secure. To use some Dworkinian jargon, interpretations of customary law must pass tests of fit and substance in making sense of the raw data. The dimension of fit imposes a rough threshold requirement that a viable interpretation of a part of CIL must be adequately supported by the raw data picked out by general practice and *opinio juris*. The dimension of substance stipulates, broadly, that, where more than one interpretation satisfies the threshold test imposed by the dimension of fit, that interpretation is to be selected as best which makes the practice appear in its best light. In the case of legal practice, this is the interpretation which possesses the greatest

24 F. L. Kirgis, 'Custom on a Sliding Scale', *American Journal of International Law* 81 (1987): 146.

25 *Ibid.*, p. 149. 26 R. M. Dworkin, *Law's Empire* (Fontana Press, 1986), p. 52.

ethical appeal. With respect to custom, 'ethical appeal' is determined by reference to the ethical values it is intended to secure. I have already suggested that these values include peaceful coexistence, human rights and environmental values, among others. It is international law's efficacy in furthering these values in the right way, rather than any presumed grounding in the consent of states, that is the chief test of its legitimacy.

Now, the crucial point here is that the two dimensions are not regulated by a lexical ordering of fit over substance; instead, they must be balanced against each other in order to identify the best interpretation. Such 'balancing' is possible precisely because the dimension of fit, like that of substance, is responsive to and expressive of value judgments.[27] Dworkin specifies the values secured by 'fit' in terms of integrity; but this is a point at which one need not buy into Dworkin's broader theoretical commitments. One may speak instead (or in addition) of those values secured by the rule of law, such as predictability, respect for liberty and human dignity, as well as the value of allowing states to make international political decisions, for example self-determination and political participation. The fact that the dimension of fit itself reflects such value commitments has various implications. One is that an interpretation meeting the threshold of fit may have its remaining infelicities of fit compensated for by its substantive appeal. It also means, more radically, that the 'minimum level' of fit is not an 'external', invariant standard unconditioned by substantive considerations.

A decision-maker who accepts an interpretative approach to norm-formation must develop a working conception of interpretation which will include, *inter alia*, more specific beliefs about the relationship between fit and substance. All of these beliefs are ultimately responsive to an account of the values that govern international law. Once we recognize that fit must be balanced against substance, we can treat Kirgis' sliding scale conception of custom as a sketch of that part of a working theory of the interpretation of customary law that elaborates the relationship between fit and substance. The sliding-scale conception permits the adoption of an interpretation as best even though it fares relatively poorly on the dimension of fit (e.g. because, despite considerable support in normative words (*opinio juris*), little state practice supports the putative norm and considerable practice conflicts with it) provided the putative norm possesses very strong appeal on the

[27] *Ibid*., p. 257.

substantive dimension (i.e. it expresses an essential part of the good which the institution of CIL is supposed to achieve, such as peaceful coexistence).

So understood, the *Nicaragua* judgment reveals the potential complexity of the interplay between fit and substance. Almost invariably, there will be a variety of classes of raw data which an interpretation must fit. The two major types of raw data which an interpretation of custom must fit are general state practice and *opinio juris*. Part of the reason why we can tolerate the poor fit of the norms prohibiting the use of force and intervention with general state practice is that the responsiveness of the dimension of fit to background substantive ethical considerations extends to our theory of the categories of data an interpretation must fit, the relationship between them and their relative weight in determining satisfactoriness of fit. In this regard, *Nicaragua* makes four main assumptions about *opinio juris*: (a) that it is an independent ingredient in the formation of custom and not merely a normative attitude to be inferred, inductively, from general state practice; (b) that it may be derived from norms enshrined in widely accepted treaties or resolutions of international organizations; (c) that it can, in appropriate cases, provide a sufficient basis for the derivation of a norm despite the absence of much in the way of widespread and consistent state practice; and (d) that the scope of the resultant customary norm may be universal and therefore binding on states that have not expressed the requisite *opinio juris* or, indeed (in the case of *jus* cogens norms) that have persistently opposed it.

Why should we adopt the loose-limbed account of the relationship between *opinio juris* and state practice, as opposed to a positivistic insistence that *opinio juris* is inferred from, or 'attached to', state practice? The fundamental reason is that this understanding is better equipped to generate customary norms that are likely to be legitimate, i.e. norms that are more effective in furthering the goals of international law in the right way. Kirgis himself indicates the key way in which this is so: according centrality to state practice will lead to legal silences – some 'ominous' and others enormously inconvenient – with respect to areas where there is much contrary state practice (e.g. human rights norms and the laws of war) or where state practice has not had the opportunity to develop (e.g. the law of outer space). Enabling *opinio juris* to play the more prominent role contemplated by the *Nicaragua* approach ameliorates this problem, thereby enhancing international law's legitimacy. It does not eradicate the problem, of course, and the need for the progressive development of customary law – sometimes, through illegal action intended to bring about reform – will sometimes remain. But it represents a significant advance on the positivistic conception of custom.

One further way in which the interpretative account enhances the legitimacy of international law is worth stressing. By detaching *opinio juris* from any *necessary* connection with state practice, the interpretative account of custom enables us to deny that it is only the *opinio juris* of states that counts in the process of customary norm formation. Instead, we can accommodate within the formal structures of international law creation a role for various non-state actors, such as international organizations (e.g. the UN General Assembly, the ICJ, the WTO etc.), peoples (understood as collectivities conceptually distinct from states), non-governmental organizations (e.g. the International Committee of the Red Cross, Human Rights Watch, Amnesty International, etc.), and so on. The importance of non-state *opinio juris* in the formation of customary law is evident in the significance accorded to General Assembly resolutions in the *Nicaragua* case. Not limiting inquiries into *opinio juris* to the attitudes of states quite properly reflects the declining importance of the sovereign state in an increasingly 'inclusive' international legal system. States are no longer the exclusive subjects of international legal norms, even though they remain the primary bearers of international rights and duties. Moreover, non-state entities are playing an increasing role in the creation, development and enforcement of international law. By taking account of non-state *opinio juris*, while acknowledging the primacy of states in the process of norm-formation, international law can be more responsive to ideas and norms elaborated within both international governmental institutions and global civil society. This promises to strengthen the legitimacy of international law not only by enhancing its capacity to achieve the ends of global justice, but also by doing so through a procedure that introduces an element of global democratic participation.

Indeed, having decoupled *opinio juris* from state practice, we should go on to question whether the practice that is relevant to the formation of customary norms is exclusively that of *states*. It would seem rather peculiar to maintain this restriction in cases where the norms in question have as their subjects actors other than states, for example organs of the United Nations or peoples. But, even in cases where the norms primarily apply to states (e.g. the norms of non-use of force and non-intervention), it is entirely plausible to take the practice of non-state bodies, for example the UN Security Council, into consideration in determining the international practice bearing on the existence and content of a putative norm.[28] Of course, resort to the attitudes and activities of non-state actors in customary norm formation is not without its problems, not least because those actors are manifestly susceptible to many of the maladies of chauvinism, corruption, inefficiency and unresponsiveness that also afflict states. But what is being offered here is not a panacea, but rather an improvement on the blinkered statist perspective that is imported by positivistic readings of custom.

Objections and replies

Consider now four objections to the interpretative conception of custom. According to the first, the account is rendered problematic by its reliance on a disputable general theory of law, namely, Dworkin's theory of 'law as integrity'. We have already seen why this objection is not as strong as it might seem: there is no necessity to regard the value of 'integrity' – understood as a certain kind of equality – respecting consistency in principle that generates an obligation to obey the law – as the driving ideal behind the interpretative account. On the contrary, that account expresses a view of international law's legitimacy as dependent on its furtherance of certain values, e.g. human rights, peaceful co-existence, environmental protection, etc. as tempered by the requirements of the rule of law (predictability, liberty, etc.) and the values of political participation (including the political self-determination of states). Two further points are worth registering in this connection. First, the thesis that the formation of custom is determined by an interpretative process does not automatically embroil us in Dworkin's not-always-edifying controversy with legal positivists (where positivism is understood not in the way we have so far, as a normative theory about how law should be made or identified, but rather as a conceptual thesis about the nature of law). Indeed, even a Hartian could in principle

[28] As Robert McCorquodale has put it: 'In an international legal system where non-state actors are participants, the practice of these actors, their role in the creation, development, and enforcement of law, and their actions within their national communities (which can become part of 'state practice'), can, and should, form a part of customary international law.' R. McCorquodale, 'An Inclusive International Legal System', *Leiden Journal of International Law* 17 (2004): 477–504, at 498. The entire article is a helpful discussion of the contemporary international legal system as not *exclusively* a state-based system.

accept that one prong of the international legal system's rule of recognition – that relating to CIL – imposes an interpretative test for determining the validity of legal norms. Whether it does so will be primarily a matter, for him, of whether this is the rule of recognition that is accepted by the officials of the system. Secondly, one can disconnect the interpretative conception of custom from any strong claim of determinacy as to its deliverances, for example to the effect that the outcome of correct interpretation will be the identification of the 'single right answer' regarding the content of CIL. If we accept (as I think we should) that interpretations of customary law are responsive to a diversity of potentially conflicting and incommensurable values, then it may be the case that more than one interpretation of state practice and *opinio juris* counts as admissible according to the theory.

A second objection is that the interpretative conception breaks with the traditional, two-element view of CIL because it countenances the possibility of 'one-legged' custom, i.e. customary norms founded exclusively on the basis of *opinio juris* without any support in state practice (or *vice versa*). It is not clear why this should be an objection, but we can take it as targeting the interpretative account's claim to be working within the traditional understanding of custom.[29] We should begin by challenging the assumption that the interpretative account endorses the idea that either state practice, or *opinio juris*, taken by themselves can suffice for the creation of a customary norm. This is incorrect because no amount of raw data, on its own, suffices for this purpose. Instead, the whole point of the interpretative account is that whether a customary norm exists depends on a process that involves presenting the raw data in its best light, and this will inevitably engage the interpreter's substantive convictions: it will never be enough simply to point to the presence of state practice or *opinio juris*. But perhaps the objection is that the interpretative account admits the possibility that a customary

[29] This criticism is advanced in A. E. Roberts, 'Traditional and Modern Approaches to Customary International Law: A Reconciliation', *American Journal of International Law* 95 (2001): 757, at 773. Her objection seems to be that custom grounded exclusively in state practice is *apologetic* while custom grounded exclusively in *opinio juris* is utopian. Unfortunately, no satisfactory account is given of these two pejorative adjectives. At times Roberts appears to suggest that any account of custom that issues in customary norms that deviate from existing practice is unacceptably 'utopian' (p. 769). But this is mistaken: laws are normative standards, not descriptions of what has happened nor predictions of what will happen. Again, she sometimes uses the notion of 'apology' to rule out the possibility that bad or defective laws might exist (p. 773). But this flies in the face of the fact that unjust laws can be laws (although laws lacking in moral legitimacy).

norm can be found where the only raw data in its favour is state practice or, alternatively, *opinio juris*. The first possibility is one I find difficult to comprehend. Mere behavioural regularities cannot generate customary norms. Rather, the thought advanced by Kirgis and myself is that, in some cases, a customary norm may be found on the basis of widespread state practice and no *independent* showing of *opinio juris*. In other words, the *opinio juris* needed to establish the norm can be inferred from the state practice itself. What about the second possibility, that of a norm established on the basis of *opinio juris* and not state practice? Although the interpretative conception does not live or die on the basis of this claim, I find it hard to see why it should be dismissed out of hand. If unanimity of *opinio juris* develops concerning some aspects of the regulation of travel in outer space, years before such travel is possible on any significant scale, why should this prevent the emergence of customary norms on this topic?

A third objection focuses on the interpretative account's reliance on 'objective' moral values. Anthea Roberts, for example, has sought to 'build on' previous work by Kirgis and myself by jettisoning this objectivist commitment.[30] She embraces a moral conventionalism, according to which morality consists in the 'commonly held subjective views about actions that are right and wrong, which a representative majority of states has recognized in treaties and declarations'.[31] This feeds directly into the account of custom she advances in opposition to the interpretative approach. According to the latter, both state practice and *opinio juris* are raw data that have to be taken into account in the process of norm-formation, but they do not dictate whether a norm is morally attractive or not. Instead, the determination of how morally attractive a norm is will be a matter for the interpreter's independent ethical judgment. Roberts, however, eliminates a role for any such judgment because she makes the attractiveness of a putative norm a function of the level and representativeness of state support, especially in the form of state *opinio juris*, that is in its favour.[32]

But why should anyone think that the moral standing of norms against torture, sexual discrimination or genocide are a function of what 'a representative majority of states has recognized in treaties and declarations'? Does the moral force of the human right not to be tortured really depend on whether most states – many of which are oppressive and unrepresentative of their own members – recognize that

[30] *Ibid.*, p. 760. [31] *Ibid.*, p. 762. [32] *Ibid.*, p. 778.

norm in treaties and declarations? Would the spread of various forms of religious fundamentalism throughout the world, with the result that it was not a 'commonly held subjective view' that religious minorities and gays have a right to be free from persecution or that women have a right to higher education, entail that such norms were no longer morally justified? Now, Roberts has a familiar-sounding defence to this line of thought, one that focuses on the need to avoid what she calls 'normative chauvinism', especially in the form of 'Western ideological bias':

> Focusing on commonly held, or intersubjective, values avoids the need to consider whether moral values can be objectively determined and it explains why these values can change over time. It also denotes an agreed set of values rather than requiring interpreters to determine what they believe the substantive aims of international law should be. It builds the concept of procedural normativity into the dimension of substance because these values have been accepted by a majority of states, which helps prevent accusations of Western ideological bias.[33]

Leave aside the red herring about change in values.[34] I say this response is familiar, because it amounts to an oft-committed, and oft-refuted, error.[35] If the status of morality is allowed to be subjective, so too must be both the anxiety about 'Western ideological bias' and the suggestion that such bias is best overcome through compliance with a representative-majoritarian moral principle. States that reject standard Western moral views will also likely reject many of the views that are supported by a 'representative majority of states'. If foisting the former on them is chauvinist, why is it any less so to foist the latter? The principle of majoritarianism, being a moral principle, must on a non-objectivist account share the same status as the 'Western' values favouring non-discrimination against religious minorities, gays and women.

[33] *Ibid.*, p. 789.

[34] Objectivists can allow for all sorts of benign 'change' in 'values', e.g. (a) people's moral beliefs might improve over time, (b) the demands that correct values make will differ as circumstances change (e.g. the advent of certain technological capacities may justify new moral duties, such as a duty to help couples procreate by providing IVF treatment), and (c) pluralist objectivists can allow for a society moving from one acceptable value system to another such system.

[35] 'This is *relativism*, the anthropologist's heresy, possibly the most absurd view to have been advanced even in moral philosophy . . . Whatever its results, the view is clearly inconsistent, since it makes a claim [about the need to avoid chauvinism], about what is right and wrong in one's dealings with other societies, which uses a *nonrelative* sense of "right" not allowed for [by the theory that values are "subjective"].' B. Williams, *Morality: An Introduction to Ethics* (CUP, 1972).

Strangely, in light of the foregoing, Roberts suggests that friends of global justice should adopt her view of custom in preference to the interpretative account, because it encompasses more demanding requirements, such as human rights norms.[36] One error here, of course, arises from a misreading of my original article: from the fact that I focused on coexistence and cooperation for dialectical purposes related to my critique of Weil, it is wrongly inferred that the interpretative account is limited to those values. Instead, I explicitly contemplated the extension of that account to human rights norms (not least because of the interdependence of coexistence and justice).[37] In any case, we have already identified the debilitating flaw in Roberts' view. Whereas Kahn set up the state as a source of 'supreme value' independent of morality, she commits the even graver error of making morality a creature of collective state will, thereby depriving us of a standpoint from which the consensus of states can be subjected to cogent moral criticism.

The fourth objection is that the interpretative account of custom, whatever its merits in principle, is now a dead-letter in practice; in particular, the objection goes, the ICJ's seeming flirtation with that conception was decisively terminated in the *Nuclear Weapons* case.[38] In the latter case, the ICJ referred to 'the continuing tensions between the nascent *opinio juris* on the one hand, and the still strong adherence to the practice of deterrence on the other' (para. 73). This is just the sort of dissonance between state practice and *opinio juris* encountered by the Court in *Nicaragua* ten years earlier, and the framing of the issue in these terms ties in with my claim that *opinio juris* can be an independent variable, so that it need not be simply inferred from, or 'attached to', state practice in any given case. But, whereas in *Nicaragua* the Court affirmed the customary standing of the non-use of force and non-intervention norms, in *Nuclear Weapons* the majority of the Court famously held that it 'cannot conclude definitively whether the threat or use of nuclear weapons would be lawful or unlawful in an extreme circumstance of self-defence, in which the very survival of a State would

[36] E.g. 'Tasioulas limits his discussion of substantive aims to the coexistence and cooperation of states, which does not account for many modern aims of international law such as human rights': Roberts, 'Traditional and Modern Approaches', p. 778.

[37] Tasioulas, 'In Defence of Relative Normativity', pp. 122–3.

[38] For the claim that the *Nuclear Weapons* case constitutes a manifest departure from the interpretative method I discerned in *Nicaragua*, see H. Charlesworth and C. Chinkin, *The Boundaries of International Law: A Feminist Analysis* (Manchester University Press, 2000), p. 95 n. 210.

be at stake' (para. 105(2)(E)). It therefore refused to endorse the existence of a norm completely prohibiting the threat or use of nuclear weapons.[39]

It is, of course, no part of the ambitions of the interpretative conception of custom that it should predict the outcome of all ICJ decisions nor justify them *ex post*. On the contrary, it is intended as a template for guiding judicial decision-making and assessing its correctness. Nevertheless, it is an important practical question whether that conception has been repudiated by the ICJ in the *Nuclear Weapons* case. Moreover, assuming one is inclined to believe, as I am, that the Court in that case arrived at a reasonable decision – a perfectly acceptable reading of the existing law (albeit not the only possible such reading)[40] – the question arises how it can be differentiated from the *Nicaragua* case in a way that makes sense within the interpretative account. Here, I think, a proponent of that approach can point to two distinguishing features in order to show that *Nuclear Weapons* does not repudiate the interpretative method adopted in *Nicaragua*.

The first concerns the dimension of fit. In *Nicaragua*, the Court was confronted with significant levels of inconsistent state practice, on the one hand, and overwhelming levels of supporting *opinio juris* on the other. In *Nuclear Weapons*, by contrast, highly imperfect state practice was coupled with distinctly patchy *opinio juris* regarding the advisability, or existence, of a legal norm prohibiting the threat or use of nuclear weapons. The second feature relates to the dimension of substance. The moral case for legal norms prohibiting the use of force and intervention (subject to exceptions for self-defence, collective measures and, perhaps, humanitarian intervention outside the Charter in some extreme situations) is extremely compelling. These norms form the cornerstone of the international legal system, establishing a basis on which further values might be secured. Indeed, they were rightly characterized by the Court as principles of *jus cogens*, so that derogation from them is impermissible irrespective of whether a state has persistently objected to them during their formation. By contrast, the moral case for a legal norm prohibiting

[39] However, the Court was unanimous in holding that there already exists a legal obligation to 'bring to a conclusion negotiations leading to nuclear disarmament' (para. 105(2)(F)).

[40] Here I agree with the insightful analysis of the Court's decision in R. A. Falk, 'Nuclear Weapons, International Law and the World Court: A Historic Encounter', *American Journal of International Law* 91 (1997): 64–75.

the threat or use of nuclear weapons is far less clear-cut. Two points bear this out.

First, it is not obvious that an undefeated moral case exists for establishing a legal prohibition, at least in anything like the short to medium term. Much here will turn on an assessment of the morality of nuclear deterrence. Moreover, even if one thinks that nuclear deterrence is a gravely immoral way of securing peace and stability, the ethical question of how the international community best extricates itself from the existing situation is itself enormously complex. A norm requiring unilateral nuclear disarmament, for example, is not obviously vindicated within non-ideal theory. The lack of a decisive moral case for prohibition was a point registered by Judge Rosalyn Higgins: 'It is not clear to me that either a pronouncement of illegality in all circumstances of the use of nuclear weapons or the answers formulated by the Court in paragraph 2E best serve to protect mankind against the unimaginable suffering that we all fear' (Dissenting Opinion, para. 41). Admittedly, Judge Higgins was a member of the dissenting minority, but her observation is one that, on the interpretative conception, also supports the majority's decision not to affirm a legal prohibition of nuclear weapons.

Secondly, even if one believes that, *ceteris paribus*, there is a compelling moral case for a legal ban on the threat or use of nuclear weapons, moral significance attaches to the fact that many states reasonably (if mistakenly) adopt a contrary view. The fact of that reasonable disagreement counts against the legalization of the norm, at least for the time being. Such a norm will be compromised both in its efficacy and in the respect it shows those who reasonably disagree. Their inconsistent *opinio juris* deserves the kind of respect that, for example, inconsistent *opinio juris* regarding the use of force norm or the prohibition of genocide does not. Both points here reflect the fact that the interpretative account does not naively operate with an 'ideal' set of moral principles which it aims to convert into legal norms without further ado.[41] Instead, the moral considerations taken into account in the interpretative process include those concerned with non-ideal circumstances that generate problems of transition from a defective moral situation and problems of likely non-compliance and (reasonable) disagreement.

[41] Hence we should reject as an unhelpful caricature the description of proponents of the interpretative account as 'anti-formalist critics who wanted to realize the good society *now* and had no doubt that they knew how to go about this' in M. Koskenniemi, 'What Is International Law For', in M. Evans (ed.), *International Law* (OUP, 2003), p. 101.

INDEX OF NAMES

Made in United States
Cleveland, OH
12 February 2025

14308196R10206